Ius Gentium: Comparative Perspectives on Law and Justice

Volume 64

More information about this series at http://www.springer.com/series/7888

Pierre Auriel · Olivier Beaud
Carl Wellman
Editors

The Rule of Crisis

Terrorism, Emergency Legislation and the Rule of Law

Springer

Editors
Pierre Auriel
Université Paris-II Panthéon-Assas
Paris
France

Olivier Beaud
Université Paris-II Panthéon-Assas
Paris
France

Carl Wellman
Department of Philosophy
Washington University in St. Louis
St. Louis, MO
USA

ISSN 1534-6781 ISSN 2214-9902 (electronic)
Ius Gentium: Comparative Perspectives on Law and Justice
ISBN 978-3-030-09000-5 ISBN 978-3-319-74473-5 (eBook)
https://doi.org/10.1007/978-3-319-74473-5

Printed on acid-free paper

This Springer imprint is published by the registered company Springer International Publishing AG part of Springer Nature
The registered company address is: Gewerbestrasse 11, 6330 Cham, Switzerland

Contents

Contributors

Pierre Auriel Centre de droit Européen, Institut Michel Villey pour la culture juridique et la philosophie du droit, University Paris-II Panthéon-Assas, Paris, France

Olivier Beaud Institut Michel Villey pour la culture juridique et la philosophie du droit, University Paris-II Panthéon-Assas, Paris, France

Helen M. Fenwick University of Durham, Durham, UK

Cécile Guérin-Bargues Institut Michel Villey pour la culture juridique et la philosophie du droit, University Paris Nanterre, Paris, France

Alon Harel Hebrew University of Jerusalem, Jerusalem, Israel

Matthias Jestaedt University of Freiburg, Institut für Staatswissenschaft und Rechtsphilosophie, Freiburg im Breisgau, Germany

Tomasz Tadeusz Koncewicz Department of European and Comparative Law, Faculty of Law and Administration, University of Gdańsk, Gdańsk, Poland; LAPA Crane Fellow, Program in Law and Public Affairs, Princeton University, Princeton, USA

Suzie Navot The Striks School of Law, College of Management Academic Studies, Rishon Lezion, Israel

Kent Roach Prichard Wilson Chair in Law and Public Policy, Faculty of Law, University of Toronto, Toronto, Canada

François Saint-Bonnet University Paris-II Panthéon-Assas, Institut Michel Villey pour la culture juridique et la philosophie du droit, Paris, France

Assaf Sharon Tel Aviv University, Tel Aviv-Yafo, Israel

Tom Sorell University of Warwick, Coventry, UK

Carl Wellman Washington University, St. Louis, USA

Jerzy Zajadło Department of Theory and Philosophy of State and Law, Faculty of Law and Administration, University of Gdańsk, Gdańsk, Poland

Introduction

Pierre Auriel

Abstract In the aftermath of the November 2015 Paris Terrorist Attacks, the Maison française d'Oxford organised a conference on emergency legislation from a comparative point of view. This conference forms the basis of this book. Having described this project and its methodological framework, this introduction presents two central arguments of this book. First, the diversity of emergency or anti-terrorism legislation precludes the possibility of a universal category for all of them should be regarded as a preliminary for any research on this topic. Second, the protection against arbitrary power rests ultimately on a common legal and political culture shared by a society and, especially, its political actors.

1 Background Remarks

In the aftermath of the November 2015 Paris Terrorist Attacks, the French legal and political discussion focused on the state of emergency declared by François Hollande. As a French Research Center specialised in humanities, the Maison française d'Oxford and its members were directly concerned by these exchanges. Its specific situation as a part of a foreign university gave us the opportunity to think about these questions from a different point of view. France was not the only country experiencing terrorist attacks and, as a consequence, implementing emergency legislation. It appeared that a comprehensive comparative point of view might be the key of an engaging discussion on these topics. Our project was to bring together several highly qualified academics from different countries in order to think on this common experience.

Could we build a common conceptual framework? Were the risks and adverse consequences common to each country? Were foreign experiences relevant to our

P. Auriel (✉)
Centre de droit Européen, Institut Michel Villey pour la culture juridique et la philosophie du droit, University Paris-II Panthéon-Assas, Paris, France
e-mail: p.auriel@gmail.com

P. Auriel et al. (eds.), *The Rule of Crisis*, Ius Gentium: Comparative Perspectives on Law and Justice 64, https://doi.org/10.1007/978-3-319-74473-5_1

situation? Or was each occurrence of emergency legislation completely different with distinct issues?

On 29 April, the Maison Française d'Oxford, with the support of the Institute of European and Comparative Law (University of Oxford), the Institut Michel Villey (University Paris-II Panthéon-Assas) and the Oxford Jurisprudence Discussion Group, hosted a conference on emergency legislation adopted to counter terrorism[1] which forms the basis of this book. Most of the participants accepted the idea[2] animated by the lack of comprehensive work on this topic.

As the number of terrorist attacks has increased in Europe and North America, emergency legislation is becoming one of the major issues in public law. Countless books and articles have been written on the "war on terror", how it has changed the law, but despite their importance and their qualities, two elements are lacking.

They do not precisely focus on emergency legislation but on other aspects of the war on terror. Indeed, war on terror justifies the creation of mass surveillance programme, targeted killings or the enactment of new criminal legislation against terrorists or foreign combatants. This legislation abolished some of the basic safeguards secured by human rights and should, therefore, be considered a relevant legal issue. Moreover, emergency legislation raises particular issues important in its own rights.

Furthermore, none of these books and articles offers a comparative analysis of this kind of legislation. By bringing together French, English, Israeli, Polish, German, Canadian and American academics, this book aims to fill this gap.

We do not claim to have fully achieved this goal as such a project is always limited, both by its area of research and by the perspective it chooses to adopt. However, our goal was not to create an encyclopaedia about emergency legislation. The very mechanism of scientific research rests on the fact that no one can achieve perfection. Carl Wellman pointed out during the conference that a good scientific collective work does not give all the answers but raises new questions and proposes new approaches. We, therefore, sought to produce a useful examination on meaningful emergency legal systems in order to provide a starting point to further inquiries. This process has meant exploring several methodological points of view and accepting the possible contradictions between them. We hope that by thoroughly formulating the issues posed by emergency legislation, this book will stimulate research, fill absences and offer possibilities for reconcile contradictions.

---

[1]For the co-organisation of this conference, I am deeply indebted to members of the Maison française d'Oxford—Anne Simonin, Claire Stevenson, Nathalie Malliot and Fabien Girard—and of the Institute of European and Comparative Law—John Cartwright and Jenny Dix. On a personal note, I wish to thank Eduardo Rios Ludena, Elodie Djordjevic, Camille Moisan, Bertrand Thery, Karyn Anderson and Audrey Ghazi for their support and their help.

[2]Only John Gardner (University of Oxford) and David Anderson QC (former Independent Reviewer of Terrorism Legislation) are missing. Their respective schedule does not allow them to participate in this book but their intervention was inspiring.

2 Methodological Remarks

An initial observation has to be made. Emergency legislation, state of crisis or anti-terrorist laws are often considered as belonging to a common category. In particular, an important intellectual tradition has used the concept of state of exception as the main concept to describe all contemporary legislation designed to fight against terrorism.[3] According to this tradition, events threatening the very existence of the state or individual liberties justify suspending the rule of law and fundamental rights. In these situations, states may adopt any decision necessary to safeguard its existence as *Nécessité fait loi.* Despite the cultural and political importance of such an approach, the editors of this book are highly sceptical of viewing contemporary emergency legislation as falling under this rubric.[4] This approach has two fundamental flaws. The first one is due to its own logic. For this intellectual tradition, a state of exception rests on the state's ability to fully abolish the rule of law. The decisions made under this regime are, therefore, genuinely *hors-la-loi.* Legal aspects of the state of exception can be read as only a masquerade used to legitimize these sovereign decisions. But as we shall see, especially in the second part of this book, positive and contemporary emergency situations are not lawless. On the contrary, they are precise legal mechanisms limiting our fundamental rights in order to control exceptional situations. The very goal of this book is to understand these legal mechanisms. To put it in another way, in this book, the legal dimension of these phenomena will be considered in its own right and not only as a masquerade.

The second flaw, shared by several contemporary analyses of emergency legislation or anti-terrorist laws, consists of viewing this legislation as a singular category. Academics are thinking a global "Age of Crisis" whose hallmark is a "permanent state of emergency" identical in each country.[5] But this approach is groundless. Even excluding specific uses of emergency legislation (the Hungarian state of emergency decreed to massive immigration, Erdogan's answer to a Coup d'Etat or the Venezuelan economic state of emergency) and focusing on reactions to the contemporary wave of terrorism, one should notice that all of this legislation is bound to historical and cultural particularism. These particular legal systems cannot be melted into a singular model. Each of them has a specific form, creates specific issues or has a different impact on society. At a certain point, a comparison is vain.

In these circumstances, a specialist in comparative law is presented with a dilemma. On the one hand, he or she can try to create a singular model rejecting all the particularities of this legislation. Comparative law exists but it is pointless for

[3]The epitome of this way of thinking is Agamben's book on the State of exception. See Agamben (2005).

[4]For a vigorously effective and articulate analysis, see Troper (2011). Also, see François Saint-Bonnet's chapter in this volume.

[5]See, for instance Greene (2018).

explaining reality as it based on legislation which does not exist. On the other hand, he or she can embrace this particularity but any generalisation would be doomed. In this case, a comparative lawyer studies existing legislation but he or she can only reach the empirical observation of the impossibility of any kind of comparison. Therefore, comparative law does not exist.

Between Charybdis and Scylla, this book tries to find the right way. In the first part, we provide several conceptual frameworks useful to analyse this legislation. None of them can be generalised, but they are valuable starting point to an inquiry on each particular legislation. The second part of this book provides a presentation of several anti-terrorist legislation. Except by delivering trivial statements on each country, the format of this book prevented a systematic overview. Each chapter was to draw attention at consequential situations and as such we tried to pick exemplary emergency legislation out: the French state of emergency, the permanent Israeli state of emergency or American exceptionalism[6] are, for example, three typical situations used as paradigms from which scholars examine the concept of emergency legislation. Addressing these ideal-type models should be useful for any future investigations. Historical situations may also be the source of fruitful reasoning as long-term consequences of emergency legislation may only appear in a posteriori inquiry. Germany, France and Poland are quite useful examples in that regard.

Some of our choices may be questionable. The scope of these studies could have embraced states of emergency in South Africa in the 1960s and 1980s, the use of emergency powers in Ireland or the actual states of emergency in Turkey or Venezuela, but the contemporary wave of terrorist attacks has specific features, methods and targets, as well as its own indirect goals, temporality and ideology that yield a totally different set of outcomes.[7]

From a methodological point of view, we had to add one last remark. The usefulness of this book depends on how the most useful perspective is selected. Despite their importance, we decided to exclude sociological or historical inquiries as the aim of this book was to provide a juridical description of emergency legislation and a clarification of basic concepts and of the fundamental interrogations they rise.

That being said, we could not avoid including a moral, legal, political or sociological evaluation of emergency legislation. And if the book focuses on the legal aspects, historical occurrences of emergency legislation are used to put them in context.

There are several ways to discuss a legal concept, and the different approaches adopted in this book are an efficient demonstration of that. While Carl Wellman makes an analytical inquiry on emergency legislation, Alon Harel, Hassaf Sharon, François Saint-Bonnet and Tom Sorell discuss the legal conceptual framework used to understand this legislation. Chapters on France, Israel, Poland or Germany explore the historical dimension of emergency legislation; Cecile Guérin-Bargues', Kent Roach's or Helen Fenwick's chapters are focused on contemporary case law.

[6]I purposely used Kent Roach's expression. See his chapter in this volume.

[7]On this topic, see François Saint-Bonnet's chapter in this volume.

3 Structure of This Book

The starting point of any scientific discussion should be the clarification of basic concepts. It is precisely what Carl Wellman's preliminary chapter aims to do. The nature of this clarification should be well understood. As an analytical philosopher, Carl Wellman is not looking to simply describe positive law, neither is he providing a normative statement on what should be the legal measures to counter terrorism. His goal is to produce "an analysis of several concepts relevant to legal measures designed to combat terrorism"[8] that can be used as a tool for the drafting and evaluation of emergency legislation. He rigorously redefines the common framework used to understand emergency legislation.

After defining terrorism as "the attempt to coerce an indirect target by means of terror produced by the use or threat of violence against a direct target",[9] he explains that the kind of emergency relevant to emergency legislation is "an unusual situation severely threatening the public welfare that cannot be dealt with adequately by the exercise of executive powers authorised by the normally applicable law"[10] and asks how terrorism might constitute such an emergency.

This preliminary contribution is the most rigorous formulation of our ordinary conception of emergency legislation which he describes as a partial abolition of the rule of law. Using references to Locke, Carl Wellman points out that the state obligation to guarantee core human rights justifies a partial abolition of the rule of law.[11]

Carl Wellman accurately describes these emergency legislation as a partial abolition of the rule of law. The core of fundamental rights is guaranteed, jurisdictions still work, legal and political rules still contain the executive despite the obvious increase of its powers and rules organise the relation between emergency and normal situations. How such a partial abolition is set in place? How rules operate in emergency legislation?

This less radical approach allows us to see phenomena unseen from the traditional point of view about the state of exception, for instance, the impact of legal constraints on executive powers and the reason why some states do not use emergency powers.[12] Taking these legal constraints into account is important as it asks the question: how might they be overruled? Also, giving up the Manichean and oversimplifying view of the relation between exception laws and emergencies allows a more accurate and useful description of legal structure and dynamic of emergency legislation.

---

[8]See in this volume Carl Wellman, "Conceptual Analysis and Emergency Legislation", section 3.

[9]See in this volume Carl Wellman, "Conceptual Analysis and Emergency Legislation", section 1

[10]See Footnote 9.

[11]See in this volume Carl Wellman, "Conceptual Analysis and Emergency Legislation", section 2.

[12]See in this volume Cécile Guérin-Bargues, The French Case or the Hidden Dangers of a Long Term State of Emergency; and Matthias Jestaedt, The German Reticence vis-à-vis the State of Emergency.

As this first analysis is made, one has to keep in mind that Carl Wellman's purpose is not to provide a definitive answer. In fact, the first part of this book will frontally discuss such model. Should we accept it? Is it universal? What is its moral effect? Is it adequate to counter contemporary terrorism?

In the first part of this book, two points of view are confronted. Briefly summarised, Tom Sorell, Alon Harel and Assaf Sharon present the conceptual framework used to understand emergency legislation, in particular, the partial abolition of the rule of law. François Saint-Bonnet and Kent Roach, however, examine the phenomenon using concrete experiences. These different approaches allow a full review of emergency legislation while avoiding an oversimplification of the conceptual framework. On the contrary, they invite the reader to further investigation.

Indeed, Tom Sorell proposed a philosophical construction whose epistemological statute of this theory must be well understood. Unlike Carl Wellman's, Tom Sorell's model provides normative foundations to emergency legislation which may be used to evaluate current emergency legislation.

His theory is focused on two main issues: which events justify the use of emergency powers? And by what means these emergency powers can be limited? Using the Hobbesian framework and its necessity to protect security as a cornerstone for his theory, Tom Sorell submitted a "toned down theory".[13] But, while Hobbesianism is based on individual self-love, Tom Sorell's reasoning is based on "fundamentalist attachments to a point of view or a way of life, a person or a place".[14] Sober Hobbesianism, however, from which the idea of a partial abolition of the rule of law is drawn, "criminalizes certain expressions of fundamentalist attachments, and limits pretext both for violence and for departures from a normal legal order that simulates some of the features of a liberal order".[15]

Kent Roach's text warns us against an oversimplification of our understanding of emergency legislation by using a universal model and explores what he calls "the American exceptionalism". His extremely rich overview of the case law on this topic reveals that unlike other countries like France, Canada or the UK, the United States' answer to this threat uses two specific means. First, "the US has made frequent use of criminal prosecutions as a means to apprehend terrorist suspects at home".[16] Second, "the use of fairly unrestrained powers by the American executive and the army so long as they are directed abroad and target people who are not American citizens".[17]

Considering the distinction between American and non-American citizens, the use of the "business as usual" approach to terrorism and also the non-adoption of

[13]See in this volume Tom Sorell, "Emergencies in Sober Hobbesianism", section 1.

[14]See Footnote 13.

[15]See Footnote 13.

[16]See in this volume Kent Roach, "The Continued Exceptionalism of the American Response to Daesh", section 1.

[17]See in this volume Kent Roach, "The Continued Exceptionalism of the American Response to Daesh", section 1.

state of emergency by the congress, the American model is different from the common framework of emergency legislation. To be more specific, there is a partial abolition of the rule of law but only non-American citizens are concerned. The role of the jurisdictions is obviously far from their role in a state of emergency as in France or in Israel.[18] Following Kent Roach, this American exceptionalism provides a higher guarantee of rights.

From a different point of view, François Saint-Bonnet also shows the limits of this common model. He points out that since 9/11, every country is permanently affected by the threat of terrorist attacks and that if it is not constant (the attacks do not happen every day), it is nevertheless permanent (an attack can happen at any time). In response, state of exception involves spatial and temporal limits as exceptional law can only be applied for a certain time in some certain areas. It is obvious then that this kind of measure is largely inefficient to fight against terrorism and we have to think about a new paradigm from which we will find appropriate answers.

Alon Harel and Assah Sharon's chapter adopts a very different position. They analyse the category of exceptions cases, the prevention of which requires normally prohibited measures. From a moral point of view, their core argument is that "moral rules, even deontological rules, are not inviolable. Under extreme conditions, violations may be warranted, indeed required. Nevertheless, justified violations retain the moral significance underlying the general prohibition".[19] Such argument is a strong moral critic against a legal answer to emergencies, and one could even understand it as a validation of the state of exception approach. But its importance challenges us to take it into account.

The conclusion of these four chapters is clear: emergency legislation is not a Manichean phenomenon, and it should appear clearly that academic and political reflections should go deeper into these complex issues which are still to be resolved. Tom Sorell's idea of a partial abolition of the rule of law highlights the limits of this abolition; Kent Roach reveals the diversity of legislation adopted to counter terrorist attacks; François Saint-Bonnet questions their efficiency; Alon Harel and Assaf Sharon show the moral hazard of rule-governed answers to emergency situations like terrorist attacks.

In order to provide answers to these issues, one should also know the practical and historical effects of emergency legislation. This is the object of the second part of this book.

Two main issues arise: how emergency powers can be controlled? And what are the long-term effects of this kind of legislation? A scheme will appear through these different demonstrations. In time of emergency, the ultimate guarantee of fundamental rights does not rest in the constitutional text or in jurisdictional safeguards.

---

[18]See in this volume Cécile Guérin-Bargues, "The French Case or the Hidden Dangers of a Long Term State of Emergency" and Suzie Navot, "Emergency as a state of mind—the case of Israel".

[19]See in this volume Alon Harel and Assaf Sharon, "Dignity, Emergency and Exception", section 5.

What is protecting our democracy against the authoritarian features of the state of emergency is our political and legal culture. By explaining this central element through an analysis of several occurrences of emergency legislation, these chapters bring a major contribution to our understanding of the nature of our democracy.

UK—like other European States—is facing a new problem with the current wave of terrorist attacks as "nationals who have travelled abroad to fight and train with ISIS, and then returned to the UK".[20] Helen M. Fenwick studies the legal answers available, especially the executive, non-trial-based, counter-terror measures based on a citizenship deprivation.[21] One of the major issues derived from these kinds of solutions is the conformity of such measures with ECHR. Helen M. Fenwick describes how national and European jurisdictions dealt with these issues and the dynamic put in place. The relationship between jurisdictions, Parliament and Government sets a cycle: "Human rights-based court and parliamentary decisions 'improve' the measure and normalise it, but at the same time arguably diminish its efficacy, meaning that it slowly falls into disuse".[22] As these measures as less efficient, Government have to implement new sets of measures and a new control by Parliaments and courts will "improve" these measures.

This cycle is a two-sided phenomenon. On the one hand, it may be seen as a sign of an efficient democratic system as all the institutions participate in the improvement of the legislation. On the other hand, it may be considered as proof of the failure to protect human rights. The Government always ends up introducing more repressive iterations of this measure in order to guarantee security. Avoiding a Manichean and statist vision of emergency powers, Helen Fenwick's analysis highlights the complexity of the institutional control of this mechanism.

Tomasz Tadeusz Koncewicz and Jerzy Zajadło's chapter deals with an interesting issue for any states considering enacting emergency legislation. Shortly before its fall, the authoritarian regime of Jaruzelski adopted martial law. The two highest Polish Courts—the Supreme Court and the Constitutional Tribunal—had to deal with legal problems raised by this law. In a very detailed way, Tomasz Tadeusz Koncewicz and Jerzy Zajadło give a complete narration of the conflict between these two jurisdictions and thus show "the shortcomings of the positivistic line of thinking so predominant in Polish courts when faced with the question of principles that call for judicial imagination, courage and constitutional fidelity to more than just a legal text".[23] Indeed, this conflict reveals the limits of a positivist legal

[20]See in this volume Helen Fenwick, "Reconciling international human rights law with executive non-trial-based counter-terror measures: the case of UK temporary exclusion orders", section 1.

[21]One should keep in mind that other countries used similar measure. For instance, there is a particularly virulent political debate in France, on *déchéance de la nationalité* measure.

[22]See in this volume Helen Fenwick, "Reconciling international human rights law with executive non-trial-based counter-terror measures: the case of UK temporary exclusion orders", section 1.

[23]See in this volume Jerzy Zajadło and Tomasz Tadeusz Koncewicz, "Polish Martial Law on the docket—Judging the Past and the Clash of Judicial Narratives", section 1 and Helen M. Fenwick, "Reconciling international human rights law with executive non-trial-based counter-terror measures: the case of UK temporary exclusion orders", section 1.

philosophy in controlling this kind of legislation. Its analysis shows how the reality of such review depends on the political culture and courage of these jurisdictions. The guarantee of rights and the control of emergency legislation ultimately depend on the liberal tradition of a state.

The long-term effects of this legislation should also be taken into account. Suzie Navot and Cécile Guérin-Bargue point out a modification of our political organisation due to the state of emergency. Israel is the paradigmatic example that allows the study of this question. After an outstanding summary of the Israeli permanent state of emergency and its constitutional background, Suzie Navot considers the role of the Supreme Court and its "significant contribution to the protection of human rights, even in times of emergency".[24] Indeed, "since the very early stages of the State of Israel, the Supreme Court has defended human rights and created what was to be known as the Bill of Judicial Rights".[25] As an echo to Tadeusz Koncewicz and Jerzy Zajadło's contribution, Suzie Navot's demonstration shows how the Supreme Court refused the silence of the law in time of emergency.

One should not be naïve. Despite the political courage of the Supreme Court, major issues remain. As emergency is permanent, "emergency powers are part of the legal and political system, a perpetual aspect of normal political life".[26] A striking effect of this situation is "the migration of emergency mechanisms" as Israel's Government uses "emergency powers even for administrating routine economic policies".[27] The consequence is that the balance between political institutions and, more deeply, the political culture of Israel has been modified.

Similar long-term effect of state of emergency appears in Cécile Guérin-Bargues's text. Her demonstration is based on a comprehensive analysis of the contemporary French legal framework and case law on this topic. Beyond this primal interest, this analysis confirms that a long-term state of emergency "encourages the public authorities to emancipate themselves from the balance of power",[28] emphasises the role of executive powers and shows that the increase of executive powers happens "without any real prior judicial control".[29] The recent evolution of French anti-terrorist legislation confirmed her point. The state of emergency ended in 1 November 2017. But, a controversial anti-terrorism law was adopted the 18 October 2017. This law makes permanent several measures of the previous state of emergency.

This endangers the guarantee of rights beyond the scope of emergency measures. Following Cécile Guérin-Bargues's reasoning, the risk of this long-term state of

[24]See in this volume Suzie Navot, "Emergency as a state of mind—the case of Israel", section 3.3.

[25]See Footnote 24.

[26]See in this volume Suzie Navot, "Emergency as a state of mind—the case of Israel", section 4.

[27]See Footnote 26.

[28]See in this volume Cécile Guérin-Bargues, "The French Case or the Hidden Dangers of a Long Term State of Emergency", section 2.3.

[29]See in this volume Cécile Guérin-Bargues, "The French Case or the Hidden Dangers of a Long Term State of Emergency", section 3.

emergency is "an inflexion of the normal functioning of public institutions"[30] which is similar to Suzie Navot's idea of a migration of emergency mechanisms in ordinary law.

Olivier Beaud completes these works on the French example and put them in context by focusing on past uses of state of emergency. He ends up with a similar conclusion, but, according to him, it is the political culture of the Conseil d'État and the Conseil constitutionnel—two of the highest French jurisdictions—which allowed them to tolerate an authoritarian legislation.

The exact opposite appears in Germany. Matthias Jestaedt provides a complete overview of German debate on emergency legislation and studies several historical moments. Since the adoption of the Basic Law, "Germany has always demonstrated a clear reserve towards the recognition of the state of emergency as a legal regime considering it as an inferior type of the rule of law".[31] This reserve is "a reaction to the 'Weimar circumstances' on the one hand and to the political, moral, legal, cultural and social catastrophe of National Socialism on the other".[32] Olivier Beaud and Matthias Jestaedt's analysis is the mirror image of this major difference between the French and German political culture about state of emergency. Again, the statute of the political background appears as a key of the understanding of emergency legislation.

4 Concluding Remarks

This introduction has not exhausted all the topics broached in this book. Emergency legislation has become a major feature of our legal and political world and a lot of questions remain. These texts reveal the extraordinary complexity as well as the pernicious effects of these phenomena. As an academic object and a political issue, we shall continue to question the concept of emergency legislation and we hope that this book will work as an invitation to continue this inquiry.

Above all, we hope that a reader of this book will accept two arguments as undeniable at least. First, the diversity of emergency or anti-terrorism legislation precludes the possibility of a universal category for all of them should be regarded as a preliminary for any research on this topic. Second, the protection against arbitrary power rests ultimately on a common legal and political culture shared by a society and, especially, its political actors. This idea is not a new one. In the Council Room in the Palazzo Publicco in Siena, Italy, Ambrogio Lorenzetti painted three fresco panels commonly called "The Allegory of Good and Bad

[30] See in this volume Cécile Guérin-Bargues, "The French Case or the Hidden Dangers of a Long Term State of Emergency", section 3.2.

[31] See in this volume Matthias Jestaedt, "The German Reticence vis-à-vis the State of Emergency", section 6.

[32] See in this volume Matthias Jestaedt, "The German Reticence vis-à-vis the State of Emergency", section 2.

Government". These panels have a function: to remind the Council—the executive organ of Siena's Government—of the moral codes it should respect. The permanent and pictorial presence of this moral code was supposed to be an effective limit to the rule of arbitrary power.

But in another Italian city, Machiavelli started the great revolution of our political modernity, resulting in constitutional laws replacing moral codes. Lorenzetti's panels would come to lose its practical meaning as the very idea of a common moral code became problematic. Painted between 1338 and 1339, Lorenzetti's panels were based on a Thomism moral shared by every member of the *polis.*[33] In our post-modern society, such a unity of our moral obligations would be considered impossible. Furthermore, moral obligations have also come to appear useless. Especially, after World War II, positive law and fundamental rights have come to be regarded as to be the only barrier against the barbarism of an unjust power.

Nevertheless, all the specific case studies in this book reveal one trend: constitutional laws are a crucial protection of our fundamental rights today but they are pointless without a shared conviction of the necessity of such protection. In other words, the question raised by these studies is the old question of the *virtù* of a political community and its leader. A comprehensive understanding of this subject implies that we have the courage to address this question seriously.

Reference

Agamben G (2005) State of exception (trans: Kevin A). The University of Chicago Press, Chicago

Boucheron P (2015) Conjurer la peur : Essai sur la force politique des images, Sienne, 1338 (Points 2015)

Greene A (2018) Permanent states of emergency and the rule of law constitutions in an age of crisis. Hart Publishing, UK

Skinner Q (1987) "Ambrogio Lorenzetti: The Artist as Political Philosopher",*Proceed of the British Academy* (1987)

Troper M (2011) "L'état d'exception n'a rien d'exceptionnel", Le Droit et la Nécessité (PUF 2011)

[33]On this point, see Quentin Skinner (1987); See also Boucheron (2015).

Conceptual Analysis and Emergency Legislation

Carl Wellman

Abstract This essay will demonstrate by an analysis of the concepts of terrorism, an emergency, and the rule of law how conceptual analysis can be useful for the drafting and evaluation of emergency legislation to counter the threat of terrorism. It suggests that terrorism is best defined as "the attempt to coerce an indirect target by means of terror produced by the use or threat of violence against a direct target." An advantage of this definition is that it excludes violent attacks such as the recent mass shootings in US schools that are a very different kind of public threat requiring a very different solution. It explains that the sort of emergency relevant to emergency legislation is an unusual situation severely threatening the public welfare that cannot be dealt with adequately by the exercise of executive powers authorized by the normally applicable law. This provides a potential justification for emergency legislation as a means to protect the well-being of the citizens. It argues that a thick conception of the rule of law requiring protection of individual rights is most appropriate for the evaluation of emergency legislation and analyzes rights as complexes of Hohfeldian positions with a core defining position plus associated positions that together confer freedom and control over the defining core upon the right-holder in face of one or more second parties. This conception of the rule of law imposes limits upon morally justifiable emergency legislation.

1 Terrorism, Emergency and Rule of Law

Can conceptual analysis provide a useful tool for the drafting and evaluation of emergency legislation? This essay will show how this is possible by an analysis of several concepts relevant to legal measures designed to combat terrorism. The obvious place to begin is with the concept of terrorism itself. The Oxford English Dictionary reports that in contemporary usage the word "terrorism" is ambiguous. In a general sense, it refers to "The unofficial or unauthorized use of violence and

C. Wellman (✉)
Washington University, St. Louis, USA
e-mail: wellman@wustl.edu

P. Auriel et al. (eds.), *The Rule of Crisis*, Ius Gentium: Comparative Perspectives on Law and Justice 64, https://doi.org/10.1007/978-3-319-74473-5_2

intimidation in the pursuit of political aims [...]." In an extended or weakened sense, it refers to "the instilling of fear or terror; intimidation, coercion, bullying." It is clearly the former that is more relevant to the subject of our conference.

This concept applies to many, probably most, of the paradigm instances of terrorism such as the repeated bombings of the IRA in the UK, the September 11 bombing of the twin towers in New York, and the November 13 attacks in Paris. However, I would not limit the concept of terrorism to the use of violence in the pursuit of political aims. The Charlie Hebdo attack that killed 11 people and the violence of the Mexican drug cartels against each other and against government personnel are essentially similar and might well equally call for emergency legislation. But the former was in pursuit of religious aims, not political, and the latter had an economic motive. For our purposes, what we need is a relevant but broader concept.

Elsewhere I have defined terrorism as "the attempt to coerce an indirect target by means of terror produced by the use or threat of violence against a direct target."[1] In the September 11 bombings, for example, the direct targets of the violence were the twin towers and the people working in them, while the indirect targets were the US government and the American public supporting what Al Qaeda insisted were unjust policies. And in the November 13 attacks, the direct targets were the people in the Bataclan Theater and other places struck by suicide bombers and the indirect target was the French government that the Islamic State and the Levant intended to coerce into discontinuing its airstrikes in Syria and Iraq.

However, one must interpret the word "violence" in this definition in terms of its general and primary sense, not its more suggestive secondary sense. The Oxford English Dictionary defines "violence" as "1a. The deliberate exercise of physical force against a person, property, etc.; physically violent behavior or treatment." Although examples of terrorism that come first to mind, such as the bombing of the twin towers in New York or the suicide bombings in Paris, were physically violent, terrorists could exercise physical force gently to disrupt a strategic communication network or disable a power grid serving a large area in the target country.

One advantage of this conceptual analysis is that it excludes violent attacks such as the recent mass shootings in US schools. Although these doubtless demand legislative reform of some sort, they are a very different kind of public threat because they did not have any indirect target. For example, they were not intended to coerce teachers into acting differently or school boards to change their policies. Hence, they require a different response from that needed to combat terrorism.

Another advantage is that it reveals the purposive nature of terrorism. It is essentially an attempt to coerce an indirect target. The IRA terrorists were attempting to coerce the British government into giving up control of Ireland and those who bombed the twin towers regarded their terrorism as one part of a campaign to force the USA to abandon its intervention in the Middle East. This suggests that repression is not always the best response to terrorism. Sometimes

[1]Wellman (2013), 8.

cooperation with the terrorists is more useful. Given ideal circumstances, a government might attempt to eliminate or at least reduce an injustice that motivates the terrorists or, accepting political realism, it might pay the ransom demanded to free citizens captured by them.

A third advantage of this analysis is that it makes explicit two essential features of terrorism, violence, and coercion, which make it morally objectionable. These might well explain, at least in part, why emergency legislation to counter terrorism is justified. Violence, in the sense presupposed here, is treatment tending to harm persons or their property. Violence inflicted upon the primary targets of terrorism is morally objectionable because it violates the moral rights to personal security and property, even life, of its primary targets. In most legal systems, it would also violate their analogous legal rights. Moreover, the prevention of terrorism ought to be a central concern of any government because its legitimacy depends upon it protecting the fundamental moral rights of its subjects. Because governing a population requires a coercive legal system and coercion is prima facie wrong, the right to govern demands justification. Presumably what justifies governmental coercion is that the government protects its subjects from much greater harms, especially the violation of their basic moral rights.

My definition of "terrorism" was intended to reveal the morally important features of terrorism. For legal purposes, a somewhat different definition might well be required. An illuminating example is the definition of "terrorism" in Section 1 of the United Kingdom Terrorism Act 2000. Here "terrorism" is defined as:

(1) the use or threat of action where—(a) the action falls within subsection (2), (b) the use or threat is designed to influence the government or to intimidate the public or a section of the public, and (c) the use or threat is made for the purpose of advancing a political, religious, or ideological cause.
(2) Action falls within this subsection if it—(a) involves serious violence against a person, (b) involves serious damage to property, (c) endangers a person's life, other than the person committing the action, (d) creates serious risk to the health or safety of the public or a section of the public, or (e) is designed seriously to interfere with or seriously disrupt an electronic system.
(3) The use or threat of action falling within subsection (2) which involves the use of firearms or explosives is terrorism whether or not subsection (1)(b) is satisfied.

Two merits of this definition are that it reveals features of terrorism that might justify emergency legislation and that it makes explicit the purposive nature of terrorism. Unfortunately, subsection (3) extends the definition of terrorism to actions that are not similarly purposive and thereby fails to distinguish very different threats to public security.

The Oxford English Dictionary informs us that historically the word "emergency" had been used with a variety of meanings, but that in modern use it means simply "A juncture that arises or 'turns up'; esp. a state of things unexpectedly arising and urgently demanding immediate action." However, this use is context dependent because there are very different kinds of emergencies. For example, a heart attack constitutes a medical emergency while losing one's employment usually results in a financial emergency. What kind of an emergency is relevant to our present purposes? Presumably, the sort reported as 3d in the Oxford English Dictionary: "spec.; as a political term, to describe a condition approximating to that of war…; also **state of emergency**, wherein the normal constitution is suspended." What calls for conceptual analysis is precisely how terrorism might constitute a condition approximating to that of war and that might demand emergency legislation.

Harold C. Relyea, in a Congressional Research Service report on national emergency powers, finds the historical background for emergency powers in John Locke's Second Treatise of Government, specifically the following passage.

> Many things there are, which the Law can by no means provide for. And these must necessarily be left to the discretion of him, that has the Executive Power in his hands, to be ordered by him, as the public good and advantage may require: nay, 'tis fit that the Laws themselves should in some Cases give way to the Executive Power, or rather to this Fundamental Law of Nature and Government, viz. That as much as may be, *all* the Members of the society are to be *preserved.*[2]

Relyea describes the emergency concept as follows:

> There are at least four aspects of an emergency condition. The first is its temporal character: an emergency is sudden, unforeseen and of unknown duration. The second is its potential gravity: an emergency is dangerous and threatening to life and well-being. The third, in terms of governmental role and authority, is the matter of perception: who discerns this phenomenon? Fourth, there is the element of response: by definition an emergency requires immediate action, but is, as well, unanticipated and, therefore, as Corwin notes, cannot always be "dealt with according to rule."[3]

In addition to the distinguished jurist Edward S. Corwin, he cites a decision of the United States Supreme Court that recognized emergency powers when urgent public need demanded relief.[4]

However, I would follow Locke more closely and not describe the governmental role and authority in terms of perception. Instead, it arises from the fact that the emergency is dangerous and threatening to the preservation of the public good. Perhaps, then, the sort of emergency relevant to emergency legislation is an unusual situation severely threatening the public welfare that cannot be dealt with adequately by the exercise of executive powers authorized by the normally applicable law.

How long can an emergency justifying emergency legislation be considered unusual? In its General Comment 29, States of Emergency (Article 4) the Human Rights Committee asserted that:

---

[2]Locke (1960).

[3]Relyea (2001), 4 and Corwin (1957), 147–148.

[4]*Home Building and Loan Association v. Blaisdell*, 290 U.S. 398 (1934) at 440.

> Measures derogating from provisions of the Covenant must be of an exceptional and temporary nature. Before a State moves to invoke article 4, two fundamental conditions must be met: the situation must amount to a public emergency which threatens the life of the nation, and the State party must have officially proclaimed a state of emergency. The latter requirement is essential for the maintenance of the principles of legality and the rule of law at times when they are most needed.

However, in the case of *A. and Others v. the United Kingdom,* the European Court of Human Rights reported that:

> While the United Nations Human Rights Committee has observed that measures derogating from the provisions of the ICCPR must be of "an exceptional and temporary nature" (see paragraph 109 above), the Court's case-law has never, to date, explicitly incorporated the requirement that the emergency be temporary, although the question of the proportionality of the response may be linked to the duration of the emergency. Indeed, the cases cited above, relating to the security situation in Northern Ireland, demonstrate that it is possible for a "public emergency" within the meaning of Article 15 to continue for many years.[5]

Under such circumstances, the distinction between emergency powers and the powers conferred by the normally applicable law becomes tenuous.

Should one also agree with Locke that there are many things "which the Law can by no means provide for" and with Corwin that public emergencies cannot always be dealt with "according to rule"? This implies that emergency legislation is either inadequate to deal with the most serious emergencies or that it is sometimes inconsistent with the rule of law. No doubt existing emergency legislation is sometimes inadequate. That is why contemporary terrorism seems to call for changes in the law of our nations. But would legal reforms that expand emergency powers to render them adequate to counter the threat of terrorism violate the rule of law?

This depends in large measure on how one conceives of the rule of law. The Oxford English Dictionary defines "rule of law" in the relevant sense as:

> The authority and influence of law in society, esp. as when viewed as a constraint on individual and institutional behavior; (hence) the principle whereby all members of a society (including those in government) are considered equally subject to publicly disclosed legal codes and processes.

This definition clearly indicates the concept we need at this point in our investigation. Any uncertainty about the relevant meaning of this expression does not arise from its ambiguity or doubt about how it is applicable to emergency legislation. It derives from the fact that its use is theory-laden. Unlike the words "terrorism" and "emergency" that arose in the everyday language of ordinary speakers and writers and must be made more clear and precise for theoretical purposes, the expression "the rule of law" was born in diverse political and legal theories. Kenneth Henley reports that:

> In Plato's Laws, Aristotle's Politics, Thomas Aquinas's "Treatise on Law" in Summa Theologica, and John Locke's Second Treatise of Government, the rule of law developed as

---

[5] *A. and Others v. The United Kingdom*, § 178.

> a regulative ideal opposed to unconstrained political power. It is central to all forms of modern liberalism, including the German tradition of the *Rechtsstaat* stemming from Immanuel Kant.[6]

Hence, there are a variety of conceptions of the rule of law that have what Ludwig Wittgenstein called a family resemblance. What we must do is either to identify the family member most useful for our understanding of emergency legislation or give a clear analysis of a new member of this conceptual family.

Wikipedia informs us that one finds at least two principal conceptions of the rule of law, a "thin" formalist conception and a "thick" substantive conception. It explains:

> Most legal theorists believe that the rule of law has purely formal characteristics, meaning that the law must be publicly declared, with prospective application, and possess the characteristics of generality, equality, and certainty, but there are no requirements with regard to the content of the law. Others, including a few legal theorists, believe that the rule of law necessarily entails protection of individual rights.

I believe that the latter is more appropriate for any assessment of emergency legislation. This is because the primary purpose of establishing and maintaining the rule of law in any legal system is to prevent the abuse of governmental power and any governmental response to terrorism that violates individual rights would presumably be an abuse of emergency powers.

Let me be a little more explicit. The rule of law obviously requires that the government respect the constitutional and statutory rights of its subjects. But I would add that the rule of law fully prevents the abuse of governmental power only if it also respects human rights, not only those human rights recognized in its national legal system or established in international law, but also those fundamental moral rights one possesses as a human being. And as a legal realist who believes that real law consists, not merely of rules and principles in a constitutional document or in published statutes, but of how these authoritative sources are applied in practice, I insist that the rule of law also requires that the exercise of governmental power must be subject to judicial review in courts that observe due process.

2 A Conflict of Rights

However, the application of individual rights by public officials or the courts is not automatic and infallible. The legal texts that confer rights upon those subject to the legal system are typically imprecise and often contain controversial terminology. Here, then, is another place where conceptual analysis is required. Because governments often respond to terrorism by subjecting suspected terrorists to arrest or detention in special facilities, let us focus on the human right to liberty. What will call for conceptual analysis here are at least three basic human rights texts. Article 5

---

[6]Henley (1999), 766.

of the Universal Declaration of Human Rights of 1948 asserts briefly: "Everyone has the right to life, liberty, and security of person." More helpful is Article 5 of the European Convention on Human Rights of 1950 that begins: "Everyone has the right to liberty and security of person. No one shall be deprived of his liberty save in the following cases and in accordance with a procedure prescribed by law." Article 9.1 of the International Covenant on Civil and Political Rights of 1966 asserts similarly that: "Everyone has the right to liberty and security of person. No one shall be subjected to arbitrary arrest or detention. No one shall be deprived of his liberty except on such grounds and in accordance with such procedures as are established by law." Presumably, these texts firmly establish a human right to liberty in international law. What remains unclear is the precise nature of this human right.

The European Convention on Human Rights distinguishes between human rights and fundamental freedoms. Its preface announces: "Considering that the aim of the Council of Europe is the achievement of greater unity between its Members and that one of the methods by which the aim is to be pursued is the maintenance and further realization of Human Rights and Fundamental Freedoms […]." It then asserts that fundamental freedoms depend upon human rights. However, in the body of the Convention, it affirms "the right to freedom of thought, conscience, and religion" and the "right to freedom of expression." Why, then, distinguish between human rights and fundamental freedoms?

I believe that the answer to this question is suggested by Wesley Newcomb Hohfeld in his Fundamental Legal Conceptions. After a survey of the literature of jurisprudence and the texts of judicial decisions, he concludes that the expression "a right" is ambiguous. It refers indiscriminately to what are now called liberties, claims, powers, and immunities.[7] However, he insists that in the strict sense, only claims are rights. This is because only legal claims have correlative legal duties.[8] Thus, the creditor's right to be repaid is the logical correlative of the debtor's duty to repay the debt owed to the creditor. But the logical correlative of one's liberty of walking on the public pavement is simply the absence of any duty not to do so. My guess is that the authors of the European Convention on Human Rights distinguished between human rights and fundamental freedoms because they also presupposed the logical correlativity of rights and duties and equated freedoms with liberties.

In my own theory of rights, I have adopted Hohfeld's conceptual distinctions between liberties, claims, powers, and immunities. The theoretical value of recognizing four very different positions of one subject to a legal system is that it makes clear how a right really functions in legal practice. For example, a legal liberty makes it permissible for the right-holder to act in some specified manner while a legal claim imposes upon some second party a duty owed to the right-holder.

---

[7]Hohfeld (1917), 36.

[8]Hohfeld (1917), 38.

However, I do not agree with Hohfeld that in the strict sense a legal right is simply a legal claim. If the creditor's right to be repaid were merely a legal claim, it would not hold firm and thus advantage the right-holder against a defiant debtor. It could constitute a real right only in conjunction with a power to sue in the event that the debtor refuses to repay the debt and an immunity against cancellation of the debt by the debtor announcing "I hereby cancel my duty of repayment." To my mind, a real right consists of a complex of Hohfeldian positions, a defining core position plus associated positions that together confer freedom and control over the defining core upon the right-holder in face of one or more second parties.[9] For example, the US constitutional right to freedom of speech consists at least of the core legal liberty of expressing one's opinions and feelings as one wishes together with an immunity from any legislation that would prohibit such expressions and a power to take legal action in the event that some public official attempts to limit one's liberty of speaking freely. The constitutional right to just compensation is a core legal claim of a property-owner against the government to just compensation for any property taken for public use, together with the power to sue for such compensation, a liberty to exercise this power, and an immunity against having this claim abolished by any federal or state legislation. The constitutional right to vote consists of a core legal power to vote together with a legal liberty of exercising this power, and an immunity against having one's power to vote taken away by federal or state legislation. The constitutional right against double jeopardy consists of a core legal immunity against any conviction for a criminal act after having been declared innocent of this crime in a previous trial together with a power to appeal any court decision convicting one after having been declared innocent, a liberty to exercise this power, and an immunity against having any of these Hohfeldian legal positions extinguished by legislation. Thus, there are at least four species of rights: liberty-rights, claim-rights, power-rights, and immunity-rights.

What kind of a right is the human right to liberty? The European Convention on Human Rights defines the right to liberty in terms of a correlative duty: "No one shall be deprived of his liberty save in the following cases and in accordance with a procedure prescribed by law." Hence, it is a negative claim-right, a right that imposes upon the State and others a duty not to deprive one of his or her liberty. And the International Covenant on Civil and Political Rights also defines it, somewhat more fully, in terms of a correlative duty: "No one shall be subjected to arbitrary arrest or detention. No one shall be deprived of his liberty except on such grounds and in accordance with such procedures as are established by law."

Although one might have expected the human right to liberty to be a liberty-right, in fact, it is a claim-right. This illustrates the way in which an Hohfeldian analysis of rights can eliminate misconceptions concerning important rights.

Article 5 of the European Convention and Article 9 of the International Covenant begin with exactly the same assertion: "Everyone has the right to liberty

[9]Wellman (1985), 81–119.

and security of person." If taken literally, this affirms one right, "the right," with a content that includes two components, "liberty and security of person." This is especially puzzling because terrorism is often thought to require a choice between liberty and security. Any emergency legislation must choose between ensuring greater security of the citizens at the expense of individual liberty or preserving individual liberties at the expense of the personal security of the public. How should one interpret this puzzling language?

The Council of Europe/Court of Human Rights Guide on Article 5 of the Convention: Right to Liberty and Security discusses deprivations of liberty in great detail but almost ignores personal security. The Human Rights Committee General Comment No. 35: Article 9 (Liberty and Personal Security) asserts that "Article 9 recognizes and protects both liberty of person and security of person." In paragraphs 5 through 8, it provides a detailed explanation of liberty in terms of deprivations of liberty. In paragraph 8, it gives a detailed explanation of security of person in very different terms. With considerable hesitation, I suggest that we interpret the European Convention and the International Covenant to refer to two distinct rights, the right to liberty, and the right to security of person. Primarily, they assert a human right to liberty, but with the insistence that any permissible deprivation of liberty must not violate the right to security of person.

What is the content of the human right to liberty? We have seen that it is a negative claim-right. Thus, its defining core is a claim under international law not to be deprived of one's liberty. Against whom does this claim hold? Who is the second party with the logically correlative duty? Paragraphs 10 through 16 of the *G*uide on Article 5 of the Convention refer to governmental actions that might deprive a person of liberty, and paragraphs 17 through 19 refer explicitly to obligations of "the State." Similarly, paragraphs 5 and 6 of the General Comment No. 35 of the Human Rights Committee give examples of deprivations of liberty by a government and paragraph 7 refers explicitly to "States parties." This is what one would expect. Because in international law, the human right to liberty is conferred by treaties such as the European Convention and the International Covenant, it imposes obligations primarily upon those nation states that have ratified these treaties. Therefore, one's human right to liberty is a claim-right holding primarily against the state to which one is subject, provided that this state is a party to the relevant human rights treaty.

What is the scope of the liberty protected by this human right? The Guide on Article 5 describes the scope of application in terms of "liberty of movement" and "restrictions on movement." Hence, presumably the liberty protected by this human right is the liberty of an individual to move about from place to place within the territory of a nation state. This is confirmed by paragraph 3 of the General Comment no. 35 that explains: "liberty of person concerns freedom from confinement of the body, not a general freedom of action." Thus, the human right to liberty protects only a very limited, but immensely important, kind of liberty.

The human right to liberty is a right not to be deprived of one's liberty. What constitutes a deprivation of liberty? Paragraph 7 of the Guide on Article 5 explains that: "The notion of deprivation of liberty within the meaning of Article 5 § 1 contains both an objective element of a person's confinement in a particular restricted space for a not negligible length of time, and an additional subjective element in that the person has not validly consented to the confinement in question." The General Comment No. 35 similarly explains a deprivation of liberty in terms of "severe restriction of motion [...] without free consent." And in paragraph, 5 it also helps to clarify the concept of deprivation by explaining that:

> Examples of deprivation of liberty include police custody, arraign, remand detention, imprisonment after conviction, house arrest, administrative detention, involuntary hospitalization, institutional custody of children and confinement in a restricted area of an airport, as well as being involuntarily transported. They also include certain further restriction on a person who is already detained, for example, solitary confinement or the use of physical restraining devices.

Notice that most of these are instances of governmental action.

What factors determine whether some instance of confinement, such as the examples above, constitute a deprivation of liberty? The European Court of Human Rights considered this matter in the *Guzzardi case*. Mr. Guzzardi was convicted of conspiracy and being an accomplice in a kidnapping. After serving for a period in a Milan goal, he was taken to the Island of Asinara where his movements were confined to an area of about 2.5 km^2. He appealed to the European Commission on Human Rights and subsequently to the European Court of Human Rights that noted:

> The Commission was of the view that on Asinara the applicant suffered a deprivation of liberty within the meaning of the Article; it attached particular significance to the extremely small size of the area where he was confined, the almost permanent supervision to which he was subject, the all but complete impossibility for him to make social contacts and the length of his enforced stay at Cala Reale.[10]

Thus, a number of factors in addition to the size of the area to which one is confined are relevant to whether one is being deprived of one's liberty.

The government disputed this analysis and argued that there were a number of differences between Guzzardi's confinement on the island and conditions in a prison.

> The applicant was able to leave and return to his dwelling as he wished between the hours of 7 a.m. and 10 p.m. His wife and son lived with him for fourteen of the some sixteen months he spent on Asinara; the inviolability of his home and of the intimacy of his family life, two rights that the Convention guaranteed solely to free people, were respected. Even as regards his social relations, he was treated much more favourably than someone in penal detention; he was at liberty to meet, within the boundaries of Cala Reale, the members of the small community of free people – about two hundred individuals – living on the island, notably at Cala d'Oliva; to go to Sardinia or the mainland if so authorized; to correspond by letter or telegram without any control; to use the telephone, subject to notifying the carabinieri of the name and number of his correspondent.[11]

---

[10] *Guzzardi v. Italy*, § 90.

[11] *Guzzardi v. Italy*, § 91.

The Court granted that the government's reasoning was not without weight. Nevertheless, the Court held that Mr. Guzzardi had been deprived of his liberty for a number of reasons, no one of which was conclusive.

> While the area around which the applicant could move far exceeded the dimensions of a cell and was not bounded by any physical barrier, it covered no more than a tiny fraction of an island to which access was difficult and about nine-tenths of which was occupied by a prison. Mr. Guzzardi was housed in part of the hamlet of Caka Reale which consisted mainly of the buildings of a former medical establishment which were in a state of disrepair or even dilapidation, a carabinieri station, a school and a chapel. He lived there principally in the company of other persons subjected to the same measures and of policemen. The permanent population of Asinara resided almost entirely in Cala d'Oliva, which Mr. Guzzardi could not visit, and would appear to have made hardly any use of its right to go to Casa Reale. Consequently, there were few opportunities for social contacts available to the applicant other than with his near family, his fellow "residents" and the supervisory staff. Supervision was carried out strictly and on an almost constant basis. Thus, Mr. Guzzardi was not able to leave his dwelling between 10 p.m. and 7 a.m. without giving prior notification to the authorities in due time. He had to report to the authorities twice a day and inform them of the name and number of his correspondent whenever he wished to use his telephone. He needed the consent of the authorities for each of his trips to Sardinia or the mainland, trips which were rare and, understandably, made under the supervision of the carabinieri, He was liable to punishment by "arrest" if he failed to comply with any of his obligations.[12]

Clearly, then, the concept of a deprivation of liberty involved a variety of considerations made explicit by the European Court of Human Rights.

However, not all deprivations of liberty are violations of the human right to liberty. Article 5 of the European Convention lists six cases, such as the lawful detention of a person after conviction by a competent court or the lawful detention of persons for the prevention of the spreading of infectious diseases, in which the deprivation of liberty is permissible. And the International Covenant specifies that: "No one shall be deprived of his liberty except on such grounds and in accordance with such procedure as is established by law."

It would be misleading to conceive of the human right to liberty as simply the right not to be deprived of one's liberty by some action of a state party because this suggests that this right imposes only negative duties upon states. But paragraphs 2 through 5 of Article 5 of the European Convention and of Article 9 the International Covenant impose positive obligations to provide procedural protections for the liberty of the right-holder. These include being informed of the reasons for one's arrest or to compensation for wrongful arrest or detention. Moreover, a state party has an obligation to protect the liberty of the right-holder from deprivation by private individuals or organizations. Paragraph 17 of the Guide on Article 5 of the Convention reads:

---

[12]*Guzzardi v. Italy*, § 95.

> Article 5 § 1, first sentence, lays down a positive obligation on the State not only to refrain from active infringement of the rights in question, but also to take appropriate steps to provide protection against an unlawful interference with those rights to everyone within its jurisdiction.

And Paragraph 7 of the General Comment No. 35 reads in part:

> State Parties have the duty to take appropriate measures to protect the right to liberty of persons against deprivation by third parties. States parties must protect individuals against abduction or detention by individual criminals or irregular groups, including armed or terrorist groups, operating within their territory.

Paradoxically, a negative claim-right can impose positive as well as negative duties upon second parties. My conception of a right as a cluster of Hohfeldian positions can explain this because these positive obligations are associated positions that function to protect the defining negative obligation not to deprive anyone of his or her liberty.

There is an additional complication in the human right to liberty that calls for conceptual analysis. Both Article 15 of the European Convention on Human Rights and Article 4 of the International Covenant on Civil and Political Rights provide that

> "In time of war or other public emergency threatening the life of the nation" a state party "may take measures derogating from its obligations [...]."

But what is it to derogate from an obligation? The Oxford English Dictionary defines "derogation" in the relevant sense as "the partial abrogation or repeal of a law, contract, treaty, legal right, etc." Presumably, emergency legislation does not repeal the human right to liberty or any treaty establishing it in international law. At most, it can partially abrogate or abolish one or more obligations imposed by the ratification of one or more human rights treaties establishing this right in international law. Any such abrogation can, however, be only partial. This is because both the relevant treaties require that derogation may continue only as long as the emergency lasts and also because no derogation is permitted regarding some obligations, for example, obligations imposed by the right to the fundamental requirements of fair trial.

Derogation from an obligation imposed by the human right to liberty is permissible only in time of war or other public emergency "threatening the life of the nation." But what is it for an emergency situation to threaten the life of the nation? If taken literally, these words would seem to require that, like an armed conflict with a very powerful nation state, the emergency threatens the very existence of the nation as an independent state. If so, terrorism would seldom if ever justify emergency legislation derogating from any of the obligations imposed by the human right to liberty. The European Court of Human Rights confronted this issue in the case of *Lawless v. Ireland.* Lawless, a member of the Irish Republican Army, contended that the emergency situation declared under the Irish Offenses Against the State Act did not constitute an emergency threatening the life of the nation. The European Court of Human Rights argued that:

> In the general context of Article 15 of the Convention, the natural and customary meaning of the words 'other public emergency threatening the life of the nation' is sufficiently clear; they refer to an exceptional situation of crisis or emergency which affects the whole population and constitutes a threat to the organized life of the community of which the State is composed.[13]

Accordingly, it ruled that the terrorist threat of the IRA did constitute an emergency threatening the life of the nation.

Another human right that ought to be respected by the rule of law is the right to life. This would seem to be relevant to terrorism in three ways. First, because terrorists often deliberately kill innocent persons, it would seem that they often violate the right to life of their victims. If so, this might well justify emergency legislation to counter terrorism. Second, presumably the human right to life imposes positive obligations upon the state to protect the right to life of all those subject to its jurisdiction. If so, then the state may well be required to enact counter-terrorism legislation. Third, the right to life might limit the permissible use of lethal force in any justified emergency powers.

The human right to life is asserted in a considerable number of international documents, most notably the Universal Declaration of Human Rights, The European Convention on Human Rights, and the International Covenant on Civil and Political Rights. Of these, the European Convention is most helpful for the conceptual analysis of this right because of the cases in which the European Court of Human Rights has considered controversial interpretations of its language. Let us, therefore, focus our attention on this document, with occasional glances at the International Covenant.

Article 2.1 of the European Convention reads: "Everyone's right to life shall be protected by law. No one shall be deprived of his life intentionally save in the execution of a sentence of a court following his conviction of a crime for which this penalty is provided by law." The first sentence imposes a positive duty upon the state to enact and enforce measures to protect the right to life of all persons subject to its jurisdiction. The second imposes a negative duty not to deprive any person of his life intentionally except for legally prescribed capital punishment.

Article 6.1 of the International Covenant on Civil and Political Rights reads: "Every human being has the inherent right to life. This right shall be protected by law. No one shall be arbitrarily deprived of his life." Here, it is the second sentence that imposes a positive obligation to enact and enforce measures to protect the right to life of all persons subject to the jurisdiction of the state, and the third sentence imposes a negative obligation not to arbitrarily deprive any person of his life.

How should one interpret the meaning of the word "life" in these and other human rights documents? Let us begin with the earlier Universal Declaration of Human Rights of 1948. Article 3 reads simply: "Everyone has the right to life, liberty, and security of person." No further explanation of the right to life occurs in this document. However, some interpreters point out that the Preamble begins with

---

[13]*Lawless v. Ireland* (1961) 1 E.H.R.R. 15 at 31.

the words: "Whereas recognition of the inherent dignity and of the equal and inalienable rights of all members of the human family is the foundation of freedom, justice, and peace in the world," and Article 1 asserts that: "All human beings are born free and equal in dignity and rights. They are endowed with reason and conscience and should act toward one another in a spirit of brotherhood." These passages suggest that the right to life should be taken to be not merely a right to continued biological existence, but the right to a life with dignity. However, it is hard to find additional evidence to confirm this interpretation.

The European Convention on Human Rights confers the right to life in Article 2. The relevant passage reads: "Everyone's right to life shall be protected by law. No one shall be deprived of his life intentionally save in the execution of a sentence of a court following his conviction of a crime for which this penalty is provided by law." The Council of Europe's Human Rights Handbook, No. 8.—The Right to Life—reports that:

> Article 2 protects "everyone's" right to "life". "Life" here means human life: neither the right to life of animals, nor the right to existence of "legal persons" is covered by the concept. Animals are not "persons" and hence are not included in the concept of "everyone" (toute personne) and are therefore not protected by the Convention at all. [...] The Convention does not otherwise clarify what "life" is, or when it – and therewith the protection of Article 2 of the Convention – begins or ends.

Although the Convention does preface its articles with a reference to the Universal Declaration of Human Rights, it does not mention human dignity at all. However, the European Court of Human Rights in paragraph 65 of the case of *Pretty v. The United Kingdom* asserts that: "The very essence of the Convention is respect for human dignity and human freedom. Without in any way negating the principle of sanctity of life protected under the Convention, the Court considers that it is under Article 8 that notions of the quality of life take on significance." Accordingly in paragraph 39, the Court asserts that: "Article 2 of the Convention [...] is unconcerned with issues to do with the quality of living or what a person chooses to do with his life." How these limits on the concept of life are consistent with respect for human dignity, the very essence of the Convention, is unexplained. In any event, one cannot find any authoritative legal sources that do very much to clarify the meaning of "life" in Article 2 of the European Convention on Human Rights.

Article 6.1 of the International Covenant on Civil and Political Rights asserts: "Every human being has the inherent right to life. This right shall be protected by law. No one shall be arbitrarily deprived of his life." Because there is no international court of human rights, one cannot appeal to judicial decisions to clarify the meaning of "life" in this document. However, there is one passage in the General Comment No. 6: Article 6 (Right to Life) that promises to be helpful. Paragraph 5 reads:

> Moreover, the Committee has noted that the right to life has been too often narrowly interpreted. The expression "inherent right to life" cannot properly be understood in a restrictive manner, and the protection of this right requires that States adopt positive

> measures. In this connection, the Committee considers that it would be desirable for States parties to take all possible measures to reduce infant mortality and to increase life expectancy, especially in adopting measures to eliminate malnutrition and epidemics.

On close reading, one recognizes that here the Committee is insisting on a broader range of protective measures, not a broader conception of life. Hence, the meaning of "life" in the International Covenant remains unexplained.

A more recent regional human rights document explains the right to life more fully. Article 3.2 of the Asian Human Rights Charter of 1998 reads in part:

> Foremost among rights is the right to life, from which flow other rights and freedoms. The right to life is not confined to mere physical or animal existence but includes the right to every limb or faculty through which life is enjoyed. It signifies the right to live with basic human dignity, the right to livelihood, the right to a habitat or home, the right to education and the right to a clean and healthy environment for without these there can be no real and effective exercise or enjoyment of the right to life.

Here, the word "life" in the expression "the right to life" is clearly a life of human dignity, although what constitutes human dignity remains unexplained. One could argue that this document simply makes explicit what has been implicit in all the previous human rights documents intended to protect human rights as conceived by the Universal Declaration of Human Rights that grounded them on human dignity. But this would violate the usual criteria for the interpretation of legal sources.

What, then, is the conception of life presupposed by the moral right to life? I find a suggestion by Justice Stevens in *Cruzan v. Director, Mo. Health Dept.* convincing. At issue in this case before, the United States Supreme Court is whether discontinuing medical treatment for a patient in an irreversible coma would violate her right to life. Justice Stevens argued that it would not because:

> Nancy Cruzan is obviously "*alive*" in a physiological sense. But for patients like Nancy Cruzan, who have no consciousness and no chance of recovery, there is a serious question as to whether the mere persistence of their bodies is "life" as that word is commonly understood, or as it is used in both the Constitution and the Declaration of Independence. […] Life, particularly human life, is not commonly thought of as a merely physiological condition or function. Its sanctity is often thought to derive from the impossibility of any such reduction. When people speak of life, they often mean to describe the experiences that comprise a person's history, as when it is said that somebody "led a good life."[14]

Accordingly, I would conceive of "life," in the sense relevant to the moral right to life, as the ongoing experiences that make a human life go well or badly. One advantage of this conceptual analysis is that it ties the right to life to the human values that ground it.

Terrorists often kill human beings, sometimes large numbers of them. Do terrorists thereby violate the right to life of their victims? The European Convention and the International Covenant are treaties that establish the human right to life in international law. Thus, they impose obligations only upon those nation states that

[14]*Cruzan v. Director, Mo. Health Dept.*, 497 U.S. 261 (1990) at 345–346.

have ratified these treaties. Therefore, presumably the legal human right to life does not hold against individual terrorists or terrorist organizations.

How, then, should one interpret the Commission on Human Rights Resolution 1998/47, Human Rights and Terrorism that asserts in part: "Taking into account that acts of terrorism in all their forms and manifestations aimed at the destruction of human rights have continued despite national and international efforts. Bearing in mind that the most essential and basic human right is the right to life."?

Notice that the first sentence of Article 2.1 of the European Convention, "Everyone's right to life shall be protected by law." suggests that the legal right to life serves to protect a preexisting moral right to life. This suggestion is confirmed by the first two sentences of Article 6.1 of the International Covenant: "Every human being has the inherent right to life. This right shall be protected by law." This language clearly distinguishes between the inherent moral right to life and the protecting legal right to life. Perhaps, the Commission is asserting that terrorism violates the moral rather than the legal human right to life.

What, then, is the content of the moral right to life? Elsewhere I have explained that what we call the moral right to life is really a rights-package, a cluster of moral rights concerning the life of the right-holder. The first and most important of these rights is:

> A moral claim-right not to be killed by another. If there really is any human right to life, it surely contains this component. This claim-right holds against all second parties – states, private organizations and individual persons. One's right to life is equally violated when one is arbitrarily executed by some government, rubbed out by the Mafia or fatally shot by a bank robber. No doubt the scope of this claim-right is limited by exceptions such as self-defense, just warfare or capital punishment. Exactly where to draw the line is hard to know. Therefore, I propose that we content ourselves for the time being with a somewhat vague definition and render it more precise when the need arises.[15]

If my interpretation of the moral human right to life is correct, then terrorists do often violate this right.

Such violations might well constitute a moral, but not legal, justification for emergency legislation.

Second, does the human right to life impose a duty upon nation states to enact emergency legislation? The right to life in international law might often do so, for both the European Convention and the International Covenant explicitly provide that the right to life "shall be protected by law."

This obligation is analyzed at some length by the European Court of Human Rights in the case of *Osman v. The United Kingdom.*

> The Court notes that the first sentence of Article 2 § 1 enjoins the State not only to refrain from the intentional and unlawful taking of life, but also to take appropriate steps to safeguard the lives of those within its jurisdiction. [...] It is common ground that the State's obligation in this respect extends beyond its primary duty to secure the right to life by putting in place effective criminal-law provisions to deter the commission of offences against the person backed up by law-enforcement machinery for the prevention,

[15]Wellman (1997), 245–246.

> suppression and sanctioning of breaches of such provisions. It is thus accepted by those appearing before the Court that Article 2 of the Convention may also imply in certain well-defined circumstances a positive obligation on the authorities to take preventive operational measures to protect an individual whose life is at risk from the acts of another individual.[16]

However, emergency legislation would be required only if the normally applicable law is inadequate to protect the right to life reasonably well and new legislation would significantly reduce violations of the right to life.

Does the moral right to life impose a comparable duty to enact emergency legislation to counter terrorism? If my analysis of the moral right to life is correct, it might well do so. Conceiving of the moral right to life as a rights-package suggests that one component would be: "A moral claim-right to be rescued from danger of death. Unlike the negative claim-rights not to be killed and not to have one's life endangered, this positive right does not hold against all second parties. It holds only against those who are in a position to rescue one without excessive sacrifice."[17] Moreover, I have explained that:

> There are at least two moral reasons that ground the duty not to kill a human being. One is that the act of killing a human normally results in grievous harm, the loss of a life and thereby the loss of every other value that constitutes a person's well-being. No doubt others are harmed as well, if only by the threat to public security created by any killing, but it is the harm des to the person killed that is central to one's right not to be killed. Another duty-imposing reason is that the act of killing is highly invasive; it intrudes into one's life in a disruptive manner and thereby invades the most private zones of the self.[18]

These reasons seem equally relevant to the moral duty to rescue another human being from the danger of death. Sometimes one's government would be in a position to at least reduce the danger of death from terrorism by enacting emergency legislation. Under such circumstances, it would have a moral obligation to do so.

Third, does the human right to life limit the emergency powers that may permissibly be conferred by legislation? Although Article 2.2 of the European Convention allows for the use of lethal force in combatting terrorism, it provides for only three conditions under which it is permissible.

The deprivation of life shall not be regarded as inflicted in contravention of this article when it results from the use of force which is no more than absolutely necessary (a) in defense of any person from unlawful violence, (b) in order to effect a lawful arrest or to prevent escape of a person lawfully detained, (c) in action lawfully taken for the purpose of quelling a riot or insurrection.

Although the *I*nternational Covenant contains no similar provisions, paragraph 3 of the General Comment 6 of the Human Rights Committee specifies that:

---

[16] *Osman v. The United Kingdom*, § 115.

[17] Wellman (1997), 247.

[18] Wellman (1997), 252.

> The protection against arbitrary deprivation of life which is explicitly required by the third sentence of article6 (1) is of paramount importance. The committee considers that States parties should take measures not only to prevent and punish deprivation of life by criminal acts, but also to prevent arbitrary killings by their own security forces. The deprivation of life by the authorities of the State is a matter of the utmost gravity.

Accordingly, the legal human right to life unquestionably does limit the emergency powers that may be permissibly conferred by legislation.

One matter of both theoretical and practical importance that calls for conceptual analysis is how strictly the words "absolutely necessary" in Article 2.2 of the European Convention should be taken. The European Court of Human Rights considered this issue in *McCann and Others v. United Kingdom.*

> It must also be borne in mind that, as a provision (art. 2) which not only safeguards the right to life but sets out the circumstances when the deprivation of life may be justified, Article 2 (art. 2) ranks as one of the most fundamental provisions in the Convention – indeed one which, in peacetime, admits of no derogation under Article 15 (art. 15) of the Convention, it also enshrines one of the basic values of the democratic societies making up the Council of Europe.[19]
>
> In this respect the use of the term "absolutely necessary" in Article 2 para. 2 (art. 2-2) indicates that a stricter and more compelling test of necessity must be employed than that normally applicable when determining whether State action is"necessary in a democratic society" under paragraph 2 of Articles 8 to 11 [...] of the Convention. In particular, the force must be strictly proportionate to the achievement of the aims set out in sub-paragraphs 2 (a), (b) and (c) of Article 2 (art. 2-2-a-b-c).[20]

Clearly, this is a very strict limitation on the use of lethal force to combat terrorism.

Two more recent cases clarify the meaning of "absolutely necessary" in the European Convention on Human Rights. *Wasilewska and Kalucka v. Poland* concerns an attempt by officers of the Lodz and Tomaszow Mazowiecki Police Forces and from a special anti-terrorist group to arrest three men they mistakenly believed to be armed and dangerous. Paragraph 11 reads: "The whole operation lasted 15 s during which about 40 bullets were fired at the car as it was driving off, according to an expert at no more than 20 kph. In spite of the claims by the police officers that they had been aiming at the tyres, none of the tyres had been damaged."[21] The applicants claimed that in this operation Mr. Kalucki had been killed in breach of Article 2 of the European Convention. The Court explained that:

> The text of Article 2, read as a whole, demonstrates that it covers not only intentional killing but also situations where it is permitted to "use force" which may result, as an unintended outcome, in the deprivation if life. The deliberate or intended use of force is only one factor, however, to be taken into account in assessing its necessity. Any use of force must be no more than "absolutely necessary" for the achievement of one or more of

[19] *McCann and Others v. United Kingdom*, § 147.

[20] *McCann and Others v. United Kingdom*, § 149.

[21] *Wasilewska and Kalucka v. Poland*, § 11.

> the purposes set out in sub-paragraphs (a) to (c) of the second paragraph of Article 2. […] In particular, the force used must be proportionate to the achievement of the permitted aims (see *McCann and Others*, cited above, §§ 148–149).[22]

Given the facts of the case, the Court held that there had been a violation of Article 2 in the death of Mr. Kalucki.

The case of *Finogenov and Others v. Russia* concerns the attempt by the Russian security forces to rescue a large number of hostages held by heavily armed terrorists. The Court describes the situation as follows:

> On the evening of 23 October 2002 a group of terrorists belonging to the Chechen separastist movement (over 40 people), led by Mr B., armed with machine guns and explosives, took hostages in the "Dubrovka" theater in Moscow (also known as the "Nord-Ost" theater, from the name of a musical comedy which was formerly performed there). For three days more than nine hundred people were held at gunpoint in the theater's auditorium. In addition, the theater building was booby-trapped and eighteen suicide bombers were positioned in the hall among the hostages. Another group of terrorists occupied the theater's administrative premises.[23]

Believing that large numbers of hostages would be killed were they to attempt to take the theater sheer force of arms, the Russian security forces pumped narcotic gas through the building's ventilation system. After the terrorists lost consciousness, the special squad stormed the building. Most of the suicide bombers were shot while unconscious and others were killed in the ensuing gunfire. As a result of the operation, the majority of the hostages were released but 129 hostages died. The Court concluded in paragraph 236 that "the use of gas during the storming was not in the circumstances a disproportionate measure, and as such, did not breach Article 2 of the Convention." These two cases make explicit a principle of proportionality implicit in the words "absolutely necessary" in the language defining the right to life in international law. Thus, the legal human right confers a very stringent claim-right not to be killed upon the state.

Almost certainly, the first component in the moral package-right to life, the moral claim-right not to be killed by another, also limits the permissible use of lethal force. Although there are surely exceptions to this right, their precise nature remains controversial. Moreover, a second component of the moral right to life probably limits the permissible use of lethal force by the authorities. I have argued for this component as follows:

> A moral claim-right that others not endanger one's life. That the right to life contains some such component is suggested, although not proven, by William Blackstone's treatment of the common law right to life as one part of the right to personal security (Blackstone, vol. 1, pp. 129–130). Moreover, it is plausible to suppose that the grounds of one's right not to be killed would ground, although perhaps less strongly, a right not to have one's life endangered by others.[24]

---

[22]*Wasilewska and Kalucka v. Poland*, § 42.

[23]*Finogenov and Others v. Russia*, § 8.

[24]Wellman (1997), 246.

Thus, the permissible use of lethal force to combat terrorism is limited by both the legal and the moral right to life.

The time has come to draw a few conclusions. What is conceptual analysis? Although it may require consulting a dictionary, it is not lexicography. It is not a description of the meaning of some troublesome language in its ordinary use, but an interpretation of this language to make it more useful for the understanding or evaluation of some special subject matter. A good example is the interpretation of the words "other public emergency threatening the life of the nation" as meaning "an exceptional situation of crisis or emergency which affects the whole population and constitutes a threat to the organized life of the community of which the State is composed" by the European Court of Human Rights in *Lawless v. Ireland.* It may resolve the ambiguity of some linguistic expression, as Wesley Newcomb Hohfeld showed that in the legal literature "a right" can refer to a liberty or a claim or a power or an immunity. Again, my conception of a right s a complex of Hohfeldian positions that, if respected, confers dominion on the right-holder in face of one or more second parties is not a definition of "a right." It is a model or pattern for the analysis of any right to make its content more clear and precise. In judicial decisions, conceptual analysis typically makes explicit what is merely implicit in the authoritative legal source being applied to the facts of the case. Thus, in *Wasilewska and Others v. Poland,* the European Court of Human Rights found a principle of proportionality implicit in the requirement of "absolute necessity" for the use of lethal force. Whatever form it may take, the usefulness of conceptual analysis relative to the conceptual puzzles in some this limited context that it is intended to solve.

3 Concluding Remarks

How might conceptual analysis be useful in the drafting of emergency legislation to counter terrorism? The analysis of terrorism as the attempt to coerce an indirect target by means of terror produced by the use of violence against a direct target points to the kind of threat that this legislation must meet. Some such description of the threat needs to be included in those provisions specifying when emergency powers may be exercised. Also included should be a definition of "an emergency" along the lines of the analysis proposed previously in this essay. Conceiving of the rule of law as substantive rather than merely formal shows that limitations should be written into emergency legislation to at least provide for judicial review and to respect constitutional and human rights. Presumably this will be aided by conceiving of a right as a complex of Hohfeldian positions that confers freedom and control upon the right-holder in face of one or more second parties. For example, the human right to liberty is a negative claim-right with a defining core consisting of a claim against a state party not to deprive one of the liberty of moving about and several associated Hohfeldian positions that protect this core claim. Finally, the conceptual analysis of derogation explains that emergency legislation may abolish only some of the limitations imposed by human rights and even then only temporarily.

How might conceptual analysis be useful in the evaluation of emergency legislation? Because emergency powers authorize the government to impose restrictions upon the citizens, their exercise is justified only if they eliminate, or at least reduce, some threat to the public welfare. The conceptual analysis of terrorism indicates the relevant threat. It also specifies two features of terrorism, coercion, and violence, two morally relevant properties that might well justify restrictions imposed upon the citizens. And the detailed analysis of human rights in terms of Hohfeldian positions points to the various ways in which they impose legal, and often moral, limitations upon justified emergency legislation. But whether the emergency powers authorized by the legislation would in practice eliminate or reduce the threat to the public welfare depends upon empirical information not provided by conceptual analysis. And the moral relevance of coercion and violence, as well as their importance in relation to other morally relevant facts, can be known only by moral theory. Hence, my conclusion is that conceptual analysis has a genuine but limited usefulness in the drafting and evaluation of emergency legislation.

References

Corwin ES (1957) The president: office and powers, 1787–1957, 4th edn. New-York University Press, 147–148

Henley K (1999) Rule of law. In: Gray CB (ed) The philosophy of law: an encyclopedia. Garland Publications, 766

Hohfeld WN (1917) Fundamental legal conceptions as applied in judicial reasoning. 26 Yale Law J 710

Locke J (1960) Second treatise of government. In: Laslett P (ed) Two treatises of government. Cambridge University Press, 374–375

Relyea HC (2001) National emergency powers. Congressional Research Service, Library of the Congress, p 4

Wellman C (1985) A theory of rights. Rowman & Allanheld

——— (1997) An approach to rights: studies in the philosophy of law and morals. Kluwer Academic Publishers

——— (2013) Terrorism and counterterrorism: a moral assessment. Springer

Part I
Concepts and Justification of Emergency Legislations

Emergencies in Sober Hobbesianism

Tom Sorell

Abstract Although there are problems with applying the unexpurgated Hobbes to the demands of modern terrorism and civil war, a toned-down but recognizable version of the theory does lend itself to these kinds of violent challenges to state power. Sober Hobbesianism is my term for the toned-down theory. According to me, this form of Hobbesianism gives security great weight while at the same time limiting the legal repression that is sometimes proposed in the name of security during emergencies. Instead of tracing war to simple difference of opinion, and common or garden self-love, sober Hobbesianism traces war to disagreements in which there are fundamentalist attachments to a point of view or way of life or a person or place. A fundamentalist attachment is an attachment to something one would rather die or kill for than not have. Sober Hobbesianism criminalizes certain expressions of fundamentalist attachments and limits pretexts both for violence and for departures from a normal legal order that simulates some of the features of a liberal order.

1 From Unreconstructed Hobbes to Sober Hobbesianism

Thomas Hobbes might seem an unlikely source for a theory of emergency powers applicable to liberal democracies in our own day. He advocated the concentration of political, judicial, economic and military authority and was in favour of great latitude for a monarch or assembly in the choice of means to security. His theory demands absolute submission to law on the part of citizens, with no constitutional limitations on what laws can require.[1] The same theory demands preventive

---

[1]There are natural law limitations which a sovereign power can ignore if abiding by them would endanger public security.

T. Sorell (✉)
University of Warwick, Coventry, UK
e-mail: T.Sorell@warwick.ac.uk

P. Auriel et al. (eds.), *The Rule of Crisis*, Ius Gentium: Comparative Perspectives on Law and Justice 64, https://doi.org/10.1007/978-3-319-74473-5_3

measures against sedition and has a very expansive conception of seditious behaviour. What is more, the concentration of power with wide discretion is supposed to be politics as usual.

What ties these elements together is the idea that social life for human beings is always potentially incendiary. The default condition of human beings living ungoverned in groups is war—cold or hot—and the primary purpose of government is to act against the causes of war in human behaviour and human circumstances. For Hobbes, communal human life is the permanent possibility of emergency, and the duties and powers of government are fundamentally to do with the pre-emption of emergency. They are not to do with the distribution of goods that permit each of us to pursue respect worthy life-plans or choices. They are not to do with equipping people for the local pursuit of human flourishing. They are not to do with the fulfilment of human rights. They are for keeping people safe from one another and from conquest.

Although there are problems with applying the unexpurgated Hobbes to the demands of modern terrorism and civil war, a toned-down but recognizable version of the theory does lend itself to these kinds of violent challenges to state power. '*Sober Hobbesianism*' is my term for the toned-down theory. According to me, this form of Hobbesianism gives security great weight while at the same time limiting the legal repression that is sometimes proposed in the name of security during emergencies. Instead of tracing war to simple difference of opinion, and common or garden self-love, sober Hobbesianism traces war to disagreements in which there are *fundamentalist* attachments to a point of view or way of life or a person or place. A fundamentalist attachment is an attachment to something one would rather kill or be killed for than lose. Sober Hobbesianism criminalizes certain expressions of fundamentalist attachments and limits pretexts both for violence and for departures from a normal legal order, simulating some of the features of a liberal order.

I have previously explained how to get from unreconstructed Hobbes to sober Hobbesianism.[2] The main working parts of unreconstructed Hobbesianism are (1) a theory of how human beings naturally and pre-scientifically arrive at the valuations of things they pursue or avoid; (2) the postulation of a so-called 'right of nature'; (3) an argument about how (1) and (2) combine to produce general violent conflict when people pursue a thing they cannot both have; and (4) a theory of how violent conflict and its bad by-products can be avoided in the long term. I now briefly enlarge on (1–4).

(1) According to Hobbes, people naturally tend to regard as good what produces immediate pleasure, and to count as bad what produces pain or displeasure. Different people are differently constituted and have different accumulated sensory experiences, and these, as well as rhetoric, account for differences in valuations. People who are able to reflect on pursuing the immediately pleasurable and avoiding the immediately painful can sometimes get enough

[2]Sorell (2013), chs. 2 and 3.

detachment from their appetites and aversions to judge that even painful things are good on balance, e.g. because of their long-term good consequences. This sort of detachment is the beginning of a science of good and evil—that is, a theory that distinguishes between *prima facie* goods and goods all-things-considered. Although people can learn from experience to distinguish between apparent and real goods, they can also learn from scientific demonstrations of the good and bad effects of different corporeal things on humans and the good and bad effects of different courses of action. But many people never get even to the stage of reflecting on their own scheme of apparent goods and are at the mercy of their habits of pursuit or avoidance. They may also be swayed by the preferences of those who are powerful or admired—sometimes through persuasive speech—or refine their patterns of pursuit or avoidance by a more or less uncritical imitation. Either way, they are likely to end up in the competitive and even violent pursuit of whatever appeals to them.

(2) There is no objective criterion for what to pursue and how to pursue it if the good itself is no more than a matter of what individuals have an appetite for. Until people agree on, or submit to, imposed common standards, they are naturally entitled to be their own uncritical judges of what to pursue or avoid. Or, in other words, they have the right to be their own judges of ends and means, especially where others are apt to pursue their own ends ruthlessly. This is what Hobbes calls the 'right of nature'.

(3) The right of nature permits violent people to pursue things violently. But it also gives peaceful and accommodating people a reason to pre-empt the violence of violent people by violence of their own. In fact, the right of nature gives everyone—of whatever temperament—the right to lie, kill and maim if they are not to become the victims of deception, physical injury or murder themselves. In other words, the right of nature permits and, on some natural additional assumptions, even requires people to interact violently. The additional assumptions are that some people pursue their own ends violently and that these may be hard to tell apart from the reasonable and accommodating until it is too late—until one has learnt the hard way that they will stop at nothing. In other words, so long as each retains the right of nature and is guided by their own appetites and aversions, each is at war with every other person living locally.

(4) Hobbes's answer to war of all against all is a simultaneous mass transfer by each of the right of nature to a third party, who is to decide for them all what courses of action they must each follow. This third party becomes sovereign on accepting the transfer and understands that the purpose of the transfer is to deliver all from war. The reason the mass transfer of the right of nature can in principle make sense to otherwise distrustful parties is that everyone has an aversion to death, and war hastens death. What is more, since war results from a plurality of wills spurred by a plurality of apparent goods, the reduction of wills to one is already a peace-promoting measure. Again, since people may revoke the transfer if the sovereign's will reignites war or threatens lives in other ways, it is not absolutely binding.

The mass simultaneous transfer of right is accomplished by a speech act. Each of the many promises not to be his own judge of ends and means if, for the sake of peace, others promise the same. The person to whom the right of judging ends and means is passed is some third party external to the mutual promising. It could be an individual (corresponding to the case of monarchy) or a council. This person accepts to be the judge, and his or her choice of ends and means are embodied in a system of public precepts and prohibitions intelligible as the *legislation* of a sovereign power. For subjects, abiding by the mutual promise is a matter of abstaining from practical judgement on matters pronounced upon by law. Or, as Hobbes puts it, abiding by the mutual promise is a matter of absolute submission to the sovereign. The only just ground of release from submission is an actual threat to one's life–either from the sovereign or from non-cooperating subjects.

The sovereign's free hand as legislator is likely to repel liberals. If the sovereign declares a curfew at sunset, or makes it compulsory for each householder to put bars on windows, then, so far as Hobbes's political philosophy is concerned, the sovereign is entirely within his rights to do so. The sovereign accepts the transfer of the right of nature so as to legislate for peace, and a law establishing a curfew or requiring bars on windows is intelligible as a peacekeeping measure. Suppose that the sovereign declares alcohol consumption illegal, on the ground that people who get drunk are a mortal danger to one another? That, too, is a legislative option for the sovereign. So also, to name measures on the English legislative agenda in the 1620s, is a tax that raises money for building a naval fleet, or a law requiring citizens to billet soldiers.

Peace-keeping, in short, can involve far-reaching and burdensome measures, the only restriction on them being their intelligibility to a sovereign as means of domestic security or security from conquest. If the sovereign sincerely but irrationally believes that his realm is under threat of invasion by creatures from another planet, and that emitting radio signals of a certain frequency is a countermeasure, then lavish spending on radio transmitters, too, is entirely legitimate, according to Hobbes. Of course the more bizarre the measure the less effective it is likely to be, and the more short-lived the sovereign's authority when his security measures fail in practice. Still, the fact that so much depends on the sovereign's fallible human judgment, and that it may sometimes please the sovereign to be gratuitously repressive, means that sovereignty can easily be misused.

One safeguard against that misuse is recourse by the sovereign to a science of rulership, such as Hobbes provided in his three treatises on sovereignty. Another is a deep psychological identification of the sovereign with the interests of his subjects, exactly what Hobbes calls for in *Leviathan* chapter 30. But since there is no challenging the sovereign's judgment from within a commonwealth–that would be for a subject or subjects to take back the right of nature—and since even the science or counsel that the sovereign consults may be incorrectly disregarded, the scope for uselessly extreme restrictions on people's liberty is great.

The problem is made worse by three kinds of exaggeration in Hobbes's theories of war and the antidote to war: (a) he sets the threshold for war-provoking disagreement far too low. In his earliest political treatise, where sovereignty is connected with reducing many wills to one, he writes as if whenever practical judgment is distributed, it is plagued by indecision and perhaps even faction leading to war. This is behind his unofficial favouritism of monarchy over other constitutional forms. Relatedly, the unreconstructed Hobbes saw the seeds of all-out conflict in ordinary disagreement, academic disputation, and the speeches or publications of powerful people whose self-love made them feel underrated. Laws against even small-scale public disputes or self-aggrandizing personal publicity would have been for him quite natural measures for the sovereign to implement.

(b) The second exaggeration is to do with the *permanent latency* of all-out war in human nature, and the supposition that it is just below the surface in the behaviour of even a law-abiding citizenry. Hobbes often writes as if government is a permanent effort at stifling dispositions to engage in violence that are never eradicated. For example, he often implies that widespread public challenges to the sovereign power would *immediately* reinstate the war of all against all, with all its dangers, as if practices of civility and non-aggression developed in the possibly very long intervals *between* periods of civil war would instantly crumble. In other words, he seems to underrate the force of *customs* of peace and civility.

To uncover the third exaggeration, it is necessary to point out that Hobbes gives no eligibility conditions for the role of the third party who accepts to be sovereign in the state of nature: presumably it could be anyone; yet it is essential for good sovereignty that the person who takes on that role identify with a whole people who submit to him. It is essential, that is, that the third party subordinates the interests of the individual he is to the interests of the many. But this generates a dilemma. Either detachment from one's own interests is possible for any individual naturally, in which case detachment, rather than submission, may be the peace-making measure par excellence; or else detachment is not naturally possible, in which case there is a big gap in Hobbes's picture of the recipient of the mass transfer of the right of nature. Hobbes wants to say that the normal inability of people to behave reflectively and to see their interests as only some among many is a cause of war, but (c) —and here we come to the third exaggeration–he overstates the difficulty of achieving detachment and so implies that there *are* after all eligibility conditions for being the receiving third party in the mass transfer of the right of nature.

I think the only way out of this dilemma is for Hobbes to concede that detachment is achievable but difficult for individual human beings. But this opens the possibility of a *democracy* composed of those who are capable of detachment, a democracy with *no* need to transfer the right of nature. It also opens the possibility for each individual of telling real from apparent goods, and of counting as real goods more than peace, including the good of unaggressively leading one's own life.

Sober Hobbesianism is unreconstructed Hobbes minus the exaggerations. It is in the permissiveness of the legal regime of the unreconstructed Hobbes and in the low threshold that human behaviour has to reach to count as aggressive that we encounter the main sources of overstatement. These are the elements which sober Hobbesianism addresses. In relation to exaggeration (a), sober Hobbesianism implies that collective practical judgment is *not* sufficient for indecision, particularly when people exercise detachment from their own interests, or relatively narrow collective interests. Sober Hobbesianism undoes Hobbes's obsession with unitary sovereign judgment. The requirements of communal security can be judged by a plurality of agents, so long as their procedures for overseeing security are adequate to reaching impartial decisions speedily.

More generally, and again contrary to unreconstructed Hobbesianism, only *some* disagreements are precursors of all-out war. Foremost among these are disagreements arising from what I have previously called *fundamentalist* attachments.[3] These are non-negotiable attachments to purposes or people or objects, attachments that people would rather be killed or kill for than lose. Even these have to become very contagious in order credibly to provoke a war of all against all, but there are conceivable countercultural fundamentalist attachments that might attract such a backlash.

How does sober Hobbesianism deal with exaggeration (b)? It implies that the longer-lived a stable government is, the less likely it is that subjects refrain from violence merely because they are forced to, and the less likely it is, consequently, that they will immediately revert to violence in a general emergency. Sober Hobbesianism gives weight to the transmission of practices of civility and is open to the establishment of institutions that inculcate these practices.

Again, and now coming to exaggeration (c), sober Hobbesianism implies that people *can* reflect on and maybe revalue downwards things that they habitually pursue. It implies that people can reflect and revalue downwards the value something has in virtue of satisfying *their* interests. Crediting people with the ability to gain detachment even about personal interests, sober Hobbesianism makes room for personal autonomy consistent with communal security.

1.1 The Liberalism in Sober Hobbesianism

Sober Hobbesianism is a variety of liberalism. It promotes the autonomy of self-critical pursuers of a variety of goods, so long as these goods do not endanger life. It assumes that citizens have reflective capacities and that they are not at the mercy of their strongest desires and aversions. It assumes that people can be moved by what is in anyone's interest, and not only by what is good for themselves. But it also gives great weight to the protection of life and freedom from injury, and it calls for institutions designed to secure these things. In other words, it values security. Sober Hobbesianism recalls the unreconstructed Hobbes not in making security the *organizing* value of communal life, but in making security of life the *overarching constraint* on the organizing value, namely the exercise by anyone of autonomy.

[3]Sorell (2013), 40 ff.

In my earlier working out of the theory,[4] I looked to Raz for the elements of the kind of liberalism I was looking for. His *Morality and Freedom* outlines a liberalism geared to autonomy and associates that with a kind of practical reasoning that is reflective. Raz's theory further recommended itself in view of (1) its connecting individual reasons for action with reasons for the existence of institutions; (2) its theory of a right grounded in an interest in aspects of well-being; (3) its recognition that the autonomous pursuit of well-being depends on stable, non-violent social forms, some independent of state institutions; (4) its recognition of the right to life as a fundamental right; and (5) its claim that conditions of autonomy involve internal critical and reasoning capacities that both individuals and the state have duties not to reduce and even to enhance.[5] These capacities are of the kind needed in autonomous agents to counteract unreasoned fundamentalisms, and indeed all fundamentalisms.[6]

The three most important requirements of practical rationality from a sober Hobbesian point of view are (1) the ability to detach oneself from one's appetites and ask whether there are reasons for satisfying them independently of the force of appetite or aversion itself; (2) the ability to see one's own appetites and aversions as only some among others distributed among all of the people one lives with or near; and (3) the ability to see that the satisfaction of appetites now or soon is not necessarily better than their satisfaction later. These abilities enable one to criticize and even weaken the associated appetites, and therefore to make decisions without being at the mercy of appetites. They can also make it possible to weaken the effect of appetite that conflicts with being law-abiding, and aversion to doing what the law asks. In short, critical abilities in each person can make it possible for people to think about law in the more impartial way that Hobbes associates with sovereignty. Not just law but public policy allows for this approach. Instead of thinking for others without their appetites and identifying with their interests in survival and prosperity—as a sovereign is supposed to—one thinks for oneself, but without being carried away by the fact that some of the appetites calling for satisfaction are one's own. Instead, some common denominator reachable by detachment comes to put different appetites and aversions on a level.

Points (1–3) do not have counterparts in every form of liberalism. Different varieties of liberalism carry with them differing conceptions of practical rationality, and not all versions of liberalism seem to give the same value to the capacity for detachment from and critical reflection on appetite and passionately felt loyalties. In the same way, not all versions of liberalism give weight to institutions or policies that encourage critical reflection. Since the passionately felt loyalties counteracted by personal critical reflection can include those that generate fundamentalism, not

[4]Sorell (2013), 4.

[5]Here I adapt a little the formulation in Sorell (2013), 60.

[6]The following five paragraphs are drawn from Sorell (2013), 71–74.

all versions of liberalism pre-empt or counteract fundamentalism. Not all versions of liberalism, for that matter, make much of other capacities for self-restraint, such as the capacity to forgo fattening food, or to forgo purchases until one has saved the money needed to pay for them.[7] Although liberalism implies that life within the state should to the greatest degree possible be determined by private choice, liberals disagree over whether private choices are to be respected regardless of how they are arrived at, or whether they ought to be informed, self-critical, objectively in the interest of the chooser, or all three.

Liberals also disagree over whether, and, if so, when, the state has a role in improving the outcomes of private choice by restricting liberties or excluding certain choices by force. The difference between Hobbes's own position and liberal positions is partly to do with whether coercion by the state is a first or last resort in the response to peace-disturbing free expression or free association. But the difference is also connected with the character of the threats regarded by each position as the most urgent to prevent. Hobbes tended to worry most about sedition—exercises of freedom intended to, or with the potential to, destabilize government. Neo-Hobbesianism emphasizes the danger from projects or attachments on which people are willing to stake their lives.[8] These attachments can lead to violence without the violence leading to the overthrow of government.

Mill and other liberals concerned with tolerance sometimes worry about officious intervention and its limits. Should I prevent someone walking on a bridge that is about to collapse? Yes, Mill says, if he is unaware of the condition of the bridge: the high risk of harm makes the intervention justifiable. Other cases are less easy to decide. Should I do or say something if two people in a bus I am riding on have a loud conversation in which they express strongly racialist sentiments? Differently, should I do or say anything if two people on a crowded public beach at midday decide to have sex? For the most part I set aside questions about personal interventions in non-life-threatening situations and concentrate on interventions by the state. Many jurisdictions have laws against having sex in public places, and some punish expressions of racial hatred without necessarily criminalizing one-off outbursts on buses.

Since my argument against the unreconstructed Hobbes is to the effect that practical rationality in each of the many and not just the sovereign can tell against violence and the ruthless pursuit of self-interest, against sedition and against other sources of harm, including public harm, I am interested in versions of liberalism that concede that personal choice is sometimes defective. I am interested in versions that also insist that personal choice can and should be improved, if possible by agents themselves, but, failing that, with the help of state institutions. This is a modestly perfectionist position.

---

[7]For a theory that does, see Galston (1991).

[8]Neo-Hobbesianism is a position intermediate between unreconstructed and sober Hobbesianism. See Sorell (2013), 60 ff. It postulates the possibility of widely distributed capacities for self-critical practical reason, but retains security as the organizing goal of the state.

The perfectionism in liberalism with Hobbesian sobriety implies that the answer to the possibility of large-scale violent conflict is not the delegation of all powers of control to a sovereign but the cultivation of personal powers of detachment as a basis for restraint, tolerance and cooperation, and, where these give out or fail to be formed, the introduction by democratic means of coercive laws that prevent the violent pursuit of particular goals. A modestly perfectionist liberalism with Hobbesian sobriety differs from neo-Hobbesianism by making the use of public coercion conditional on the failure of self-imposed norms of conflict prevention. By making coercion a last resort, it breaks from Hobbesianism—neo- or unreconstructed.

Can Raz's form of liberalism, which is in tune with unreconstructed Hobbesianism up to a point, which is in tune up to a point also with the perfectionist version of neo-Hobbesianism, also address problems raised by fundamentalist attachments? If liberalism came with scepticism about the very category of non-negotiable goods, and if it developed institutions for calling into question claims that particular values were worth fighting or dying for within a liberal state, then its anti-fundamentalism might be beyond question. But liberalism itself sometimes seems to contain a category of non-negotiable goods—usually implicit in the idea of inalienable rights, and liberals of some kinds claim that a failure to respect those rights can justify (violent) rebellion even against a state that claims to be liberal.[9] A Razian theory that incorporates Hobbesian insights can address this problem. It can address this problem if it adopts the sober Hobbesian diagnosis of fundamentalism as a source of harm, and if it retains the idea that rights can exist and yet be limited or overridden. The Razian theory can then say both that there is a right to free speech *and* that it can be limited if expressing fundamentalist attachments to certain audiences is likely to produce violence.

The doctrine in *Morality and Freedom* needs to be revised to meet these requirements. As it is, its endorsement of strong personal attachments and its rejection of choices detached from social forms are sometimes in tension with one another or else are overfriendly to fundamentalisms.[10] Specifically, its commitment to 'internal critical and reasoning capacities' is in tension with its tendency to deny that we can detach ourselves from social forms: sober Hobbesianism holds that social forms can be objects of critical scrutiny and rejection, e.g. when judged by the criterion of whether they cause physical injury or shorten biological life. Social forms might also be judged defective on account of being over conventional or quasi-ritualized. Raz is wary of adopting points of view on life that are geared to biology and that in general have pretensions to getting outside social forms.

[9]See the Preamble to the Universal Declaration of Human Rights.

[10]Sorell (2013), 74 ff.

1.2 The Anti-fundamentalism of Sober Hobbesianism

Sober Hobbesianism permits a form of liberal democracy, but its liberalism is relatively thin. The right to life is fundamental, and securing it can limit other rights usually associated with liberalism, including freedoms of speech and association. Although the principal purpose of the state is to facilitate the exercise of autonomy by individuals, it is to be facilitated only if people pursue their life-plans non-violently. Non-negotiable attachments to things one is willing to kill for are *not* elements of preferred life-plans in liberalism. Either the attachments have to admit of negotiation, or, if they cannot, the use of violent means to maintain those attachments has to be outlawed. For example, attachments to children are often non-negotiable, perhaps blamelessly so: that does not mean that court orders prohibiting access can blamelessly be fought to the death, or flouted by means of an abduction. Sober Hobbesianism is likely to recommend both institutions and social forms that discourage non-negotiable attachments, even when they involve children. Sober Hobbesianism is likely, for example, to endorse the existence of family courts. In the form they are known in Western liberal democracies, these courts acknowledge the brute strength of attachments to children, while also not treating the strength of those attachments as overriding in decisions about custody or rights of access.

The case of attachments to children does not set the pattern for how non-negotiable attachments in general are treated by sober Hobbesianism. For one thing, non-negotiable attachments to children are frequently not contested, and so are not asserted violently. They may coexist perfectly well with public order because they underlie normal, privately displayed, parental behaviour.[11] Hobbes treated *religious* commitments as if they did not have to be displayed to everyone else, either. He claimed that attachment to the tenets of the Christian faith was a matter of inner belief or disposition not necessarily visible or offensive to others, and going through the motions of an approved public worship at variance with one's beliefs could not offend a God who could read inner beliefs. According to Hobbes, there was no need for people to advertise their faith to one another, not for the purposes of redemption and reception into a sought after afterlife.

Keeping faith separate from professions of faith and out of the public eye is hard where freedom of expression is a right, even if an overridable right, as in a sober Hobbesian state. This brings us to the problem of expressing non-negotiable attachment to a religion that is claimed to be the one true faith. To address the problem, the sober Hobbesian state will have to propose institutions and practices of education that defuse fundamentalism by making second nature the *criticism* of non-negotiable attachments. These practices will stigmatize dogmatism and

[11]This possibility of coexistence is not due to the existence of a non-political private order constituted by the family. Hobbes was in fact perfectly clear that parents do have power over children that is at least analogous to political power. The chapter in *Leviathan* which addresses this matter is called 'Of Dominion Paternall and Despotical'.

institutionalize the legitimacy of requests for justification. Appeals to authority, and justification by quotation from unchallengeable texts, be they the Koran or Mao's Little Red Book, will be discouraged. Perhaps the methods of secular Anglo-American philosophy are adaptable for the purpose of cultivating the appropriate critical reflexes. If so, then, contrary to unreconstructed Hobbesianism, philosophical disputation about the truth may come to have a use in staving *off* war, not inviting it.

But education is only part of the story. Sober Hobbesian government must formulate in legislation and policy documents criteria under which fundamentalist attachments are unacceptably extreme. Unacceptably extreme attachments may include attachments to war or violence itself, or to war or violence as non-optional means of pursuing something else. Unacceptable expressions of attachments may include not only violent assertions of these attachments, but projects of recruitment to groups that assert attachments violently. Again, the sober Hobbesian state can criminalize action by someone or some group who presumes to be their own judge of the reasonableness of their attachments and what can be done to maintain them.

In other words, the state can limit very severely the things that can justify violence or taking life even in the name of things that many people are willing to die for. Staying close to its roots, sober Hobbesianism can say that the only thing that justifies violence is individual or collective self-defence against the threat of death. The threat of death does not mean the threat of death to one's way of life[12]: it is biological life that must be threatened. Here sober Hobbesianism is at its most Hobbesian. For it is a hallmark of unreconstructed Hobbesianism that only the sovereign decides what is worth fighting for, and that the primary thing that is outlawed with the threat of force is violence, life-threatening violence before all other forms.

Recall that my category of fundamentalist attachments was devised to improve on Hobbes's idea that communal human life itself is an emergency waiting to happen. It is not plausible to claim, as Hobbes does, that appetites in local competitors for things that cannot be shared are by themselves a war in the making. After all, the appetites could be mild or short-lived or present in unaggressive people. For the same and further reasons, it is implausible to claim that factual or theoretical disagreements will make people come to blows. It is much more plausible to associate war in the making with the existence of widely held, loudly proclaimed, countercultural or procultural fundamentalism.

Countercultural fundamentalism is non-negotiable attachment to values that are overwhelmingly ignored or rejected locally, say allegiance to country Y expressed in country X, or a commitment to religion X expressed in a place where people are overwhelmingly committed to religion Y. To express countercultural fundamentalism is to send a provocative message to those who participate in what the fundamentalists conceive as the majority culture. The message is that the majority

---

[12]See Sorell (2013), ch 5.

are attached to the wrong things, and that being attached to those things is offensive to those going against the culture, who are not about to defer to that culture, and are willing to kill rather than do so. Of course, the message may overstate the intentions of the fundamentalists. Or it may fail to outrage more than a few of the majority. Nevertheless, one can see that the message might be *meant* to outrage the majority and start a general conflict. In the meantime, the outrage of the few against the fundamentalists can lead to killings that in turn engender *pro*cultural fundamentalist attachments in the majority culture. Or again, procultural fundamentalism may grow up unprovoked by countercultural fundamentalism—it may develop in pockets of local racist sentiment, for example—and again threaten violence against up to then peaceful minorities.

If that makes sense, legislation against fundamentalism and its expression might be foremost in a body of law with a Hobbesian inspiration, that is, a body of law meant primarily to keep the peace. It would not be an afterthought prompted by the growth of fundamentalist groups. The sober Hobbesian state would recognize that public commitments to die for or kill other than in self-defence directly engage with the purpose of the state.[13] This is so even when the purpose of the state is not to establish security pure and simple but instead to facilitate the non-violent and non-lethal exercise of autonomy. Of course, legislation against other, non-fundamentalist but potentially lethal crime is also in order from a Hobbesian perspective, but not because that crime conveys or is meant to convey an aggressively offensive message to a majority population, a message that could incite a civil war. It deserves criminalization because of the right to life of the individuals who might be the one-off victims of lethal crime in an otherwise stable political order.

Criminalization is the means by which, in unreconstructed Hobbesianism, government staves off *both* common or garden crime *and* civil war. Law in general is security law, because the guiding purpose of an unreconstructed Hobbesian state is to protect people's lives and a modest well-being against the ingredients of war in communal life. There are no distinctively sweeping and temporarily invoked emergency powers that the sovereign has to put on the statute books: the whole body of law is supposed to pre-empt emergency. Sober Hobbesianism, by contrast, though it does not maintain that the whole body of law is supposed to pre-empt emergency, does hold that the body of law is pervaded by security considerations.

Citizens are to be permitted to lead their own lives, but non-violently. This means that they can adopt any of a wide variety of life-plans so long as they abjure violence, and so long as their non-violent behaviour does not put others at risk of injury or death. For example, consider a city dweller who likes to stroll at night studying the different types who come out at night in cities. This is a non-violent practice that a certain kind of literary-minded citizen might go in for. Yet in a public health emergency, non-violent carriers of a virus might be forcibly quarantined by a

[13]This is so even, or may be particularly, when fundamentalism is expressed from behind bars by people who are behind bars for encouraging people to commit terrorist offences. The UK government has only recently begun to consider the separation of unrepentant prisoners who have histories of radicalizing others. This measure is strongly supported by sober Hobbesianism.

sober Hobbesian government. This would certainly constrain the life of a dedicated but infected *flaneur*. Yet the constraint, which is anyway temporary and non-arbitrary, is justifiable because of the possibly life-threatening harm of the practice in those circumstances. Other liberalisms would baulk at quarantining the infectious, but incorrectly, because of the status of the right to life as fundamental.

1.3 'Good Law' and Emergency Powers Under Sober Hobbesianism

How in general is a sober Hobbesian government to decide when to constrain autonomous activity for the sake of security? Here it pays to begin by asking the same question of unreconstructed Hobbesianism. Its primary answer is 'Through law'[14] but where the sovereign's framing of law is informed by Hobbes's concept of a *good* law (see *Leviathan*, chapter 30). For a law to be good, it has to be necessary for security, not simply a recognizable security measure.

A law taxing people in order to raise money for military weapons would not be necessary if it predictably left them so poor that they had to steal or kill to get enough to eat. Far from being necessary, the measure would be self-defeating. Similarly, an all-night curfew might keep malefactors and their possible victims at a safe distance from one another, but if the curfew also interfered with movements of food supplies or caused people to feel imprisoned in their own homes and receptive to demagoguery intended to make them rise up against this confinement, then, again, it would be an invitation to violence rather than a safeguard against it. In a different way, a law enabling precautionary personal searches might be unnecessary if it were introduced without any evidence that, in the places the searches were carried out, people were often hiding dangerous materials or weapons.

Hobbes's concept of the good law suggests that a balance needs to be struck. On the one hand, the legal regime should recognize sources of harmless well-being—a reasonably full stomach, family life, unencumbered movement for those minding their own business—and allow the many to get on with the enjoyment of these things. The many must also have the freedom to work and create the wealth to pay for an unavoidable defensive war and routine internal policing. On the other hand, the legal regime should snuff out violence as far as possible and restrict whatever liberties encourage violence.

Good law calls for two forms of self-restraint on the part of the sovereign. The first is the by now familiar restraint of the appetites of the natural person the sovereign is, if the sovereign is a monarch, or the natural appetites of the few who are members of an assembly, if sovereign is an assembly. The demands of the appetites of the self or selves must be subordinated to the security needs of the

[14]Hobbes also recommends institutions of sovereign-worship and certain educational measures.

many.[15] Second, the sovereign must not think that his opinion alone counts. Though it is worse to be dependent on too much advice than to use one's own head as sovereign, best of all is to listen to the advice of good counsellors—those who, when asked, give dispassionate advice for the sake of public safety.[16] In particular, a sovereign ought to make use of civil science—that is, read *Leviathan* or *De cive*, which Hobbes perhaps intended as counsel of a particularly superior, conclusive and kind.[17]

What ties together these two forms of self-restraint is the way both act against personal bias and personal passions and make detached judgement the basis of law. On the one hand, in framing laws or policies, the sovereign tries to take the point of view of the many he personifies rather than his own personal point of view; on the other, he is supposed to form a judgement based on the views of those whose experience makes them expert, or on the basis of rigorous reasoning. He is not supposed to be guided by mere personal hunches, or by the badly skewed advice of a horde of sycophants.

Apart from the sovereign's self-restraint, what is required in good law is that it be effective (actually reduce injury, death and the likelihood of either) and that it be impartially applied. A law must be necessary in order to be good, and it cannot be necessary if it serves no purpose, or is not fit for its assigned purpose. Furthermore, a law or general precept addressed to everyone cannot be a good law if in practice it can be violated with impunity by some of its addressees while others always suffer its advertised penalties. To put it in Hobbes's way, a good law must not only be necessary but be in keeping with the natural law of equity.

Although many laws that Hobbes counted good are illiberal, there is no inconsistency between liberalism and effective and consistently applied law.[18] Which brings us to the question of emergency powers taken by liberal governments. When sober Hobbesianism is supplemented with Hobbes's conception of a good law, it is able to pronounce critically on many emergency measures adopted ad hoc. Leaving aside emergency measures prompted by natural disasters, including public health emergencies, we can concentrate on those that have been introduced internationally since the attacks on New York and Washington on 11 September 2001. Sober Hobbesianism does not, as might be thought, offer carte blanche to counterterrorist measures of all kinds. Although its criticisms of these measures are only *thinly* liberal ones, the targets of sober Hobbesianism and the targets of more full-blooded liberalism are often the same.

---

[15]For elaboration, see Sorell (2015).

[16]See Leviathan, ch. 25, p. 182. 4. See Sorell (1986), 135.

[17]See ibid.

[18]Good law is consistent with liberalism without being inspired by liberal values. See my 'Law and Equity in Hobbes'.

2 Post 9/11 Security

The background to both the introduction and criticism of emergency powers is the thought that in the post 9/11 world, a 'new normal' is emerging, that is, a legal regime even in liberal democracies appropriate to a prolonged period of emergency. It is a regime typified by legislating ad hoc for emergency—within an emergency. Appropriating Hobbes's concept of good law, I shall argue that even when a new normal[19] is motivated by a concern with security, it is not necessarily acceptable from a Hobbesian point of view: for one thing, the new regime may be predictably ineffective; for another, the threat it is directed against may not be big enough or imminent enough to count as an emergency.[20]

Surveys of post 9/11 legislation and government action internationally seem to reveal at least four trends: (1) an increase in public and covert surveillance in liberal democratic states[21]; (2) ad hoc revision of the law in certain liberal democratic states to limit protections for suspects in counterterrorism investigations[22]; (3) exploitation by liberal democratic state security services of investigatory practices and detention in illiberal states[23]; and (4) opportunistic uses by illiberal states of counterterrorism as a pretext for illiberal measures directed at ordinary citizens of those states. I shall focus first on (2). It is exemplified by legal measures introduced in the USA and the UK to provide for prolonged and even indefinite periods of detention without charge for suspects in counterterrorism cases. It is also exemplified by the creation ad hoc of special tribunals to try such suspects, tribunals operating under unusual rules, and by attempts to deport foreign counterterrorist suspects to human rights-abusing, and in particular jus cogens-violating, jurisdictions. Sometimes such measures involve derogations from human rights treaties, as in the UK government derogation from the European Convention of Human Rights (ECHR), Article 5, in November 2001.

Can (2) be justified? Clearly a liberal justification is difficult or impossible to mount, particularly when human rights protections, such as those codified by the ECHR, and the UK counterpart of that Convention, the Human Rights Act (1998), have something like the force of constitutional provisions. Is it any easier to mount a sober Hobbesian defence? That depends on how Hobbesianism bears on ad hoc revisions of the law in general, on whether, in the circumstances in which ad hoc revisions are being introduced by the UK and the USA, they are genuine emergency

---

[19]The phrase 'new normal' is inspired by US Vice-president Dick Cheney's claim that the steps being taken against counterterrorism in the US after a supposed period of emergency.

[20]The following sixteen paragraphs are adapted from Sorell, *Emergencies and Politics* (2013), 153–161.

[21]See www.privacyinternational.org/survey/phr2003/threats.htm#Increased%20Communications%20Surveillance%20and%20Search%20and%20Seizure%20Powers.

[22]Hicks (2005), 216–217.

[23]See Mayer (2005); Hicks (2005), 215. For a perspective other than an Anglo-American one, see Sadurski (2006).

measures, and on whether, even if they are regarded as emergency measures, they are necessary or sufficient for preventing a significant loss of life. When these different considerations are weighed, I shall suggest, a sober Hobbesian approach is no more likely to vindicate (2) than a more mainstream liberalism.

It is true that in unreconstructed Hobbesianism, the sovereign is above the law and able to impose it or repeal it at will.[24] Even in that version of Hobbesianism, however, the sovereign is subject to the moral law of equity. As the ultimate judge of right and wrong, the sovereign falls under what *Leviathan* counts as the eleventh law of nature: "if a man be trusted to be judge between man and man, it is a precept of the law of nature, that he deal equally between them. For without that, the Controversies of men cannot be determined but by Warre."[25] Not that this is a precept that the sovereign is obliged to follow in practice, if he sincerely thinks that his, i.e. the public's, safety is imperilled by doing so. The laws of nature only oblige in the sense of having to be given weight in foro interno, i.e. in deliberation before it issues in action. They may be overridden if, e.g., the agent's life might be lost by abiding by them. The question is whether a breach of the law of equity can typically be sincerely thought to be overridden by considerations of public safety.

2.1 Detention

Many of the revised rules of detention and trial in counterterrorism that we are considering deal unequally between offenders involved in terrorist action and people thought to be involved in highly organized violent crime or successful long-term serial murder. But it is unclear that the danger to the public posed by these sorts of criminals need be greater than the danger posed by terrorism, and so it is unclear whether different methods of detention are necessary either. Admittedly, certain considerations do distinguish the cases, e.g. the greater legal difficulty in some terrorist cases of assembling evidence, of exposing the identities of witnesses, or of introducing evidence that might allow terrorists to draw inferences about the sources of evidence; but these are not considerations that trump a law of nature in unreconstructed Hobbesianism.

When it comes to sober Hobbesianism, there is no presumption that the sovereign is above the law, and no presumption that equity in Hobbes's sense fails to apply. On the contrary, the presumption that everyone counts for one and no more than one is written into the exercise of democratic detached judgement that is at the heart of sober Hobbesianism. From the angle of sober Hobbesianism, it matters that suspects held for having harmed or murdered or for planning to harm or murder are

[24]Hobbes (1996), 184.
[25]Ibid 108.

treated similarly. Departures from equity might in principle be justified if an imminent threat to life on a significant scale could be counteracted as a result—in short, if the context for the departure were an emergency situation. It is not entirely clear that this is the context for changes to detention rules that we are considering. The fact that wars are emergencies and that ad hoc counterterrorism procedures are routinely represented as belonging to an ongoing 'War on Terror' no more establishes that the threshold for emergency has been met than a 'declaration of war' against gang crime would justify comparable changes to the detention and interrogation regime for gangs with a record of murder and assault.

Again, the UK government's counterterrorism strategy[26] contemplates a long-term effort of challenging the claims of Islamic extremists among the UK Islamic community so as to undercut terrorist recruitment and radicalization more generally; if this is an emergency measure, it is a necessarily slow-working one, and one that is conducted by persuasion rather than by legislative change.[27] Could persuasion over the long term and anti-radicalization by media techniques really be represented as measures being adopted in an emergency? Being slow working, they cannot possibly be effective against an imminent threat to life. Operating as they do to change minds, they must be assumed to be pitched to people who are not so consumed by fear or distrust that they cannot be receptive to the relevant messages. In other words, the context for this part of the counterterrorism strategy is not being assumed even by the UK government to be a state of emergency. Rather, it is a state of heightened public attention and willingness to express views in a speech setting subject to familiar liberal rules. Admittedly, the heightened public attention may belong to the aftermath of an emergency situation, namely the 7/7 attacks in London in 2005, but that emergency situation was not part of a longer emergency that started in New York in September 2001; it was a short-lived, local emergency situation from which the people affected—perhaps inhabitants of Central London at most—subsequently returned to normal, or something close to normal.

In claiming that the context for UK counterterrorism strategy is not an emergency context, I am not in the least implying that there is no terrorist threat to worry about, or that it does not call for some extraordinary measures. I am claiming rather that it is not an emergency context in the sense of the UK being permanently on the verge of attack. Even the UK authorities concede variations in threat levels, not all of which indicate the high probability of, e.g. another 7/7 bombing. I am also claiming that the introduction of extraordinary measures needs justification. When extraordinary measures are proposed and ordinary measures might be effective, the onus is on a government to show that those extraordinary measures are necessary for the sake of preventing loss of life or other significant harm. I take this to be in the spirit of Hobbes on 'good' law. Not only must the new measures be necessary—in the sense that they act on a threat that the ordinary measures do not act on; they

---

[26]See http://security.homeoffice.gov.uk/counter-terrorism-strategy.

[27]'Preventing Extremism Together' Report of Working Groups (August 2005) www.communities.gov.uk/documents/communities/pdf/152164.pdf.

must indicate a route from the extraordinary back to the normal or indicate a connection between the institutions for the normal administration of justice—which command a wide consensus—and the abnormal.

Extraordinary measures can meet these conditions by being time-limited and by needing authorization when they are used from those who are familiar with legal norms for normal times and capable of judging the relative claims of security and liberty in particular cases. Extraordinary measures can also meet these conditions by passing through a legislative process in normal times in which the opinions of security experts and human rights defenders are given a fair hearing. These requirements are met more fully by UK detention and deportation regulations than by, e.g. ad hoc provisions in the USA for the detention and trial of those once imprisoned at Guantanamo. In the case of Guantanamo, inmates were taken by the US government to have the status of military irregulars and a tribunal regime was invented for them mostly under the direction of the Executive branch,[28] as opposed to the legislature.[29] The Judiciary, what is more, made a series of objections to the departures of this invented regime from constitutional protections, ruling in June, 2008 that Guantanamo detainees could challenge their imprisonment in US courts.[30]

When it comes to the justification of the ad hoc detention measures we have been considering, then, we find that there is a fall at the first hurdle: that of demonstrating their necessity. Where there is clear evidence that some of those detained without charge are dangerous, that can usually be made material for a criminal prosecution and so for the customary detention with charges, in which case detention without charges is unnecessary; where there is no such evidence, on the other hand, and so no material for prosecution, it is hard to see what evidence for the need for detention there is, either. Proponents of indefinite or long detention without charge might have a more intelligible position if there were great restrictions on legally admissible evidence of the danger posed by particular terrorist suspects, or great legal restrictions on methods for acquiring such evidence. Then indefinite detention might be claimed to be necessary for eliciting, through confession, say, evidence that could not be obtained in any other way. Even so, the case for departures in counterterrorism from the normal standards of admitting evidence, and normal methods of evidence gathering, seems much stronger than the case for departures from normal standards of detention. For one thing, violations of privacy are intuitively less serious than loss of liberty; for another, so long as surveillance is

---

[28]For a complete survey of counterterrorism legislation in the US as well as several Executive Orders dealing with Guantanamo detainees, see the heading 'Domestic Security' at www.counterterrorismtraining.gov/leg/index.html.

[29]The passage of the Detainee Treatment Act (2005) introduced protections for detainees. It contains several loopholes, however. See www.law.harvard.edu/students/orgs/hrj/iss19/suleman.shtml#Heading23.

[30]For a general discussion of the role judges should have in challenging the ad hoc legislation of governments in alleged emergencies, see Dyzenhaus (2009). For a diagnosis of some of the sources of occasional judicial timidity in this area, see Dyzenhaus (2007).

not indiscriminate and omnipresent, and so long as there are safeguards when a prima facie case for its use has been made, surveillance, including secret surveillance, seems eminently justifiable. For one thing, violations of privacy are intuitively less serious than loss of liberty; for another, so long as surveillance is not indiscriminate and omnipresent, and so long as there are safeguards when a prima facie case for its use has been made, surveillance, including secret surveillance, seems eminently justifiable. Again, so long as the surveillance comes from sources that someone versed in normal standards of admissible evidence could regard as reliable, the dangers of the evidence being manufactured might be mitigated.

2.2 *Surveillance*

In the UK, surveillance is of data and persons.[31] Communications data, ranging from names and addresses of registered holders of landlines and mobile telephones to logs of calls made, to IP addresses and registered users of email accounts, are available to the police if a 'necessity' test is passed. This means persuading 'senior officers of a public authority' that the surveillance is required. National security is one ground for communications data surveillance, which in many cases is personally authorized by the member of Cabinet in charge of the Home Office.

There is a wide range of further grounds for targeted surveillance, ranging from 'public safety' to tax evasion to an individual's mental or physical health. Surveillance of persons can be 'directed' or 'intrusive'. Directed surveillance occurs when suspects are followed and observed in public places by police or intelligence officers. Intrusive surveillance is where observation occurs in private places: homes, hotel rooms and cars, or where communications are intercepted, usually electronically. Directed surveillance requires warrants from senior police officers. These warrants are time-limited. Intrusive surveillance is considered necessary only where those observed are suspected of serious crimes and the seniority of the officers whose authorization is required is higher than for directed surveillance. Authorizations of this kind are in turn reviewed by the Office of Surveillance Commissioners. Soon a new unified office of communications data oversight is likely to be introduced, providing a check on Home Office authorizations, as well as bringing together a plurality of existing oversight bodies.

Not all surveillance evidence is legally admissible. Evidence from intercepted communications is not. The UK government has sometimes sought to avoid disclosing this evidence by introducing forms of detention and restricted movement that can be approved by law officers working under unusual rules. To the extent that

[31]See www.homeoffice.gov.uk/security/surveillance/types-of-surveillance.

the inadmissibility of this evidence is cited as a justification for recourse to these new procedures, such as those associated with 'control orders' under the Prevention of Terrorism Act (2005), the inadmissibility rule seems unjustified. Perhaps it deserves to be abolished anyway.[32] Though admitting evidence from intercepted communications seems to erode the sphere in which anyone at all can speak his mind without fear of the consequences, the hurdle that has to be crossed for the interception to be authorized in the first place is not low. Where the benefit of intruding on unguarded conversation is the prevention of a serious crime, and where not being able to admit such evidence contributes to an arbitrary extension of powers of arrest, the badness of intrusion seems heavily outweighed.[33]

Not that privacy is of no importance. If that were so, then no hurdle at all would appropriately be put in the way of applying electronic intercepts, and there would indeed be an invitation to nosy officials to investigate the tax or medical records of people they had grudges against or were simply curious about. Nothing that has emerged so far justifies the warrantless wiretapping that has sometimes gone on in the USA since 9/11.[34] But it is hard to explain or define the value of privacy entirely satisfactorily in legal terms,[35] and the right to privacy sometimes claimed by citizens against the state is hard to reconcile with their undeniable appetite for journalistic intrusions on the lives of celebrities, or voyeuristic reality television. It may also be inconsistent with the exhibitionism and self-advertisement associated with social networking Internet sites.

The value of privacy rises in proportion to the need to live in public and to make public professions of belief or loyalty. Thus, in the China of the Cultural Revolution or in East Germany when the Stasi was at its strongest, the value of a sphere in

[32]A private member's bill to make evidence based on intercepts admissible was introduced in the House of Lords in the 2006–7 Session of Parliament. For the text, see www.parliament.the-stationery-office.co.uk/pa/pabills/200607/ interception of communications admissibility of evidence.html. The admissibility of intercept evidence may also be addressed in upcoming reforms of communications data legislation.

[33]See Sorell (2016).

[34]Risen and Lichtblau (2005).

[35]See Galison and Wilson (2005). It is important not to be misled by analogies in this area. The fact that it seems very undesirable to be viewable naked by others whenever they want to is not a proof that surveillance is highly undesirable, since (i) having one's data accessed does not necessarily expose one very much; (ii) it is never supposed to be undertaken on someone else's whim, but for the sake of some important benefit. The nakedness analogy is used by Lustgarten and Leigh in (1994), 39–40. B. Goold argues on the strength of the analogy and on the unpleasantness of having information about one collected without one's consent that 'there is a clear relationship between privacy and the construction of personal identity'. See Goold (2007), 63. This line of thought suffers from the obscurity of the associated concept of personal identity. The fact that information collected about me can be false and unflattering and therefore harmful to me is certainly a reason for safeguards, but this doesn't change who I am. Nor does the cultivation by a person of a self-deceiving self-image determine who he is. Still less does the piercing of this self-image by unwanted home truths necessarily count as humiliation. The idea that each person should be able to project the self-image he likes best sounds like a spin-doctor's charter, and not the basis for an argument, as in Goold, that privacy is a human right.

which the unorthodox or irreverent could be spoken, or in which relationships independent of politics could be cultivated, would have been of the first importance.[36] Where public standards of life penetrate even the fine detail of what one wears, whether one shaves, and what one reads or listens to, the value of privacy stands out very clearly. But where practically anything can be done publicly without anyone feeling embarrassed or disgusted, matters are not so straightforward. Wanting to do things in private can look and feel like prudery or evasiveness or snobbery; privacy can be seen as a cost.

In between these extremes, a generally valued sphere of privacy still does exist. Virtually everyone thinks that privacy is a requirement of romantic and family relationships, and such relationships seem to be highly valued universally. So if for no other reason than to protect these relationships, there should be a presumption against the violation of privacy. That said, it is hard to deny that the value of privacy can be outweighed. A terrorist who reveals his secret plans to his lover may do so in the context of pursuing a private or family life to which international law recognizes that he has a right. But if an electronic bug in his bedroom picks up the conversation in which the plans are revealed and the security services decide that the terrorist should then and there be arrested, so as to disrupt the terrorist operation and prevent loss of life, that seems perfectly justifiable notwithstanding the need in general not to penetrate the sphere of intimate relationships. The value of life hugely outweighs the value of privacy when they conflict. For one thing, life is a condition of privacy of all kinds.

Surveys of public opinion—important at least for emergency measures in force in democracies—seem to show that where terrorism is concerned, even fairly indiscriminate covert access to communications and personal data is acceptable to citizens, at any rate in some regions of the world. A Eurobarometer study of 27.000 EU inhabitants published in February 2008 showed that 82% of those questioned had no objection to monitoring of personal details connected to taking a flight, and 75% were content to have all their Internet usage monitored.[37] It is possible that people who worry about violations of privacy and security make it hard for surveyors to contact them, which skews the results in favour of surveillance.[38] But it is also possible that, in the popular mind, security trumps privacy where the two are perceived to conflict, so that laws permitting intrusion in counterterrorism are legitimate.

I have been concentrating on the UK. In the USA, the USA/Patriot Act, introduced shortly after the 9/11 attacks, made it much easier for the government or the security services to access large data bases of, e.g. Internet providers in criminal investigations. Not only could data legally be monitored covertly, but there was no requirement to show that those whom the data concerned had committed or would

---

[36]Chang (1991); see also the film by Florian Henckel von Donnersmarck, *The Lives of Other* (2006).

[37]http://ec.europa.eu/publicopinion/flash/fl225sumen.pdf.

[38]Haggerty and Gazso (2002).

commit a crime. Provisions so sweeping are very hard to show to be necessary, and so they fail even the unreconstructed Hobbesian test of 'good law'. Similarly for the Foreign Intelligence Surveillance Act (1978) under which warrantless surveillance went on in the US. The Foreign Intelligence Surveillance Act as amended in 2008 introduced obstacles similar to those for intrusive surveillance in the UK when it comes to approval for electronic surveillance of those outside the US communicating with Americans: the electronic monitoring had to be of people suspected of involvement in terrorism. But this seems to be an afterthought, and it comes late in mitigating the effects of a law that is bad even by Hobbesian standards.

In 2013, Edward Snowden revealed that in the USA and the UK, there has been large-scale secret bulk collection of communications data, including personal communications data. In the USA, the bulk collection is intended to identify the associates of individuals against which there are definite intelligence-based suspicions of terrorist activity. But it is known that there has also been collection of communications data produced by governments allied to the USA, including the personal communications data of the Chancellor of Germany, Angela Merkel. Spying on allies raises issues of its own, but let us concentrate on bulk collection by government of communications data from its own citizens. Is it, as some journalists have claimed, intrusion befitting the Stasi State? If it is that the conclusion bears not only on USA but British practice, since GCHQ also engages in bulk collection on a large scale.

In a sequence of other papers,[39] I have claimed that bulk collection is actually less intrusive than more conventional surveillance technologies. This is because, being big data analytics, it often looks for patterns of communication at a very high level of generality. It starts from terrorist suspects about whom there is definite human intelligence and then uses machine algorithms to identify telephone numbers linked to the suspect's telephone number, sometimes at several removes. Bulk collection can also reveal connections people and organizations by credit card transactions. Where algorithms or human analysts identify some of the links as worthy of further investigation, conventional investigation techniques including human surveillance, or targeted surveillance assisted by bugs or wiretaps, are used with authorizations to investigate individuals further. It is at that stage that, according to me, significant intrusion begins.

Although the NSA measures are grossly disproportionate as a means of pursuing terrorists, they are not necessarily intrusive in the sense of bringing human attention to bear on details that people would rather not have disclosed or known. The measures consist of 'collecting everything'—collecting vast amounts of citizens' communication data—and then mining it, sifting through it with search terms—*not* listening or looking at everything. Since the point of mining is to get to a residue of the information collected that *can* be examined because it has met certain algorithmic tests of relevance, its effect is to *exclude* much of what is collected from any investigation or attention at all. 'Collecting everything' does not mean looking into

[39]Sorell (2013), Sorell and Guelke (2016).

everything—except in as much as the subsequent mining engages everything in order to exclude a lot.

Again, the purpose of the mining is not to identify the politically heterodox as in Stasiland, but to head off terrorist attacks. The means may be out of proportion to the end, but the end—preventing terrorism—is not human-rights-violating. It is true that if the search terms used by the mining express some sort of discriminatory bias, that is a count against the mining, but this is a different ground for objection from privacy violation—which is what surveillance usually elicits. Again, it is true that the NSA has sometimes operated outside the law and without informed oversight by even security-cleared American politicians. That is a way of associating bulk collection with a democratic deficit, but not necessarily with intrusion, still less intrusion comparable to Stasi intrusion. Sober Hobbesianism is able to engage with the objection from lack of democratic oversight. It could also engage with the relative ineffectiveness of NSA bulk collection in finding needles in haystacks.

3 Conclusion

Sober Hobbesianism removes some of the excesses of unreconstructed Hobbesianism. It is less obsessed than unreconstructed Hobbesianism with highly unitary government. It is less paranoid about sharp public disagreement, refusing to see it as war in the offing. It is friendly to democracy. It promotes not autonomy *tout court*, but only non-violently exercised autonomy. It is intolerant of fundamentalist attachment s and projects, because of they are potential causes of violence. Sober Hobbesianism appropriates from Hobbes himself the concept of good law and often reaches the conclusion that legislation made ad hoc to cope with emergencies, especially terrorist emergencies, is *not* good law. Although it is less tolerant of fundamentalist free speech than ordinary liberalism, it does not seem to me wrong to be.

References

Chang J (1991) Wild swans. Harper Collins, London

Dyzenhaus D (2007) Deference, security, and human rights. In: Goold BJ, Lazarus L (eds). Hart Publishing, UK

Dyzenhaus D (2009) The constitution of law. Legality in a time of emergency. Cambridge University Press, Cambridge

Galison P, Wilson M (2005) Our privacy, ourselves in an age of technological intrusions. In: Wilson RA (ed) Human rights in the 'war on terror'. Cambridge University Press, Cambridge

Galston WA (1991) Liberal purposes: goods, virtues, and diversity in the liberal state. Cambridge University Press, Cambridge

Goold BJ (2007) Privacy, identity and security. In: Goold BJ, Lazarus L (eds) Security and human rights. Hart Publishing, UK

Haggerty KD, Gazso A (2002) The public politics of opinion research on surveillance and privacy. Surveill Soc 3:173
Hicks N (2005) The impact of counter terror on the promotion and protection of human rights: a global perspective. In: Wilson RA (ed) Human rights in the 'war on terror'. Cambridge University Press, Cambridge
Hobbes T (1996) Leviathan. In: Tuck R (ed). Cambridge University Press, Cambridge
Lustgarten L, Leigh I (1994). In: From the cold: national security and parliamentary democracy. Oxford University Press, Oxford
Mayer J (2005) Outsourcing torture. The secret history of America's "extraordinary Rendition" program New-Yorker (14 Feb 2005)
Risen J, Lichtblau E (2005) Bush lets U.S. Spy on callers without courts New-York Times (16 Dec 2005). www.nytimes.com/2005/12/16/politics/16program.html
Sadurski W (ed) (2006) Political rights under stress in 21st century Europe. Oxford University Press, Oxford
Sorell T (1986) Hobbes. Routledge & Kegan Paul, London
Sorell T (2013a) Power and surveillance. The Philosophers' Magazine
Sorell T (2013b) Emergencies and politics: a sober Hobbesian approach. Cambridge University Press, Cambridge
Sorell T (2015) The burdensome freedom of sovereigns. In: Foisneau L, Sorell T (eds) Leviathan after 350 years. Oxford University Press, Oxford
Sorell T (2016) The scope of serious crime and preventive justice. Crim Justice Ethics 35:163
Sorell T, Guelke J (2016) Liberal democratic regulation and technological advance. In: Brownsword R, Scotford E, Yeung K (eds) The Oxford handbook of law, regulation, and technology, Oxford University Press, Oxford

The State of Exception and the Terrorist Threat—An Obsolete Combination

François Saint-Bonnet

Abstract It has stood to reason since time immemorial: extraordinary threats call for extraordinary measures. Yet whereas external and domestic threats caused the state of exception to be conceived in terms of time and space, combatting jihadist terrorists calls for an entirely different approach to which the state of exception is hardly suited.

1 Premodern Conceptions of the State of Exception

Some city-states in ancient Greece had *aesymnetai*, magistrates appointed for "as long as they were needed"[1] (Denys d'Halicarnasse), "for a term of years or until certain duties had been performed"[2] (Aristotle). They generally served to handle situations of "internal" unrest such as insurrection, rebellion and social crisis. An extraordinary magistrate was unnecessary in situations of external threat where citizen-soldiers were sent to fight, as those who went to defend their freedom had no lack of bravery or valour.

In Rome, the dictatorship was a cornerstone of the political and constitutional system, especially in the fourth and third centuries BCE.[3] It consisted of assigning powers over the heads of the two consuls to a single leader—the dictator—whose special mission was to avert the peril endowed with all the means to do so. This organisation was seen as a way of guaranteeing freedom on both fronts: the freedom

[1]*Antiquités Romaines*, V, 73, 3.
[2]*Politics*, III, XIV. See Aristotle (1999) 73.
[3]The last dictatorship of the classical republican era dates back to 202 BCE.

F. Saint-Bonnet (✉)
University Paris-II Panthéon-Assas, Institut Michel Villey pour la culture juridique et la philosophie du droit, Paris, France
e-mail: francois.saint-bonnet@club-internet.fr

P. Auriel et al. (eds.), *The Rule of Crisis*, Ius Gentium: Comparative Perspectives on Law and Justice 64, https://doi.org/10.1007/978-3-319-74473-5_4

of the city itself, able then to rally effectively against the external enemy or risk of social breakdown, and the freedom of the citizens who—brought up with the memory of the ruthless Tarquins—only had to endure "monarchic" power temporarily and at most for six months.[4] Despite misuse of the measure in the first century BCE with the "unconstitutional" exploits of Sulla and Caesar, the dictatorship was constantly upheld as a pillar of political wisdom, constitutional agility and model civicism.

Lessons can be drawn from these two ancient experiences of the state of exception. A specially appointed judge took extraordinary measures in a delimited space for a limited period of time. The measures applied to relatively small areas, as small as the city-states themselves including Rome in the fourth century BCE. In the event of a conflict with another city-state, the battle would be fought on a line of opposing phalanxes of hoplites. Despite the growing complexity of military methods as of the fifth century—mobile units of "peltasts"[5] armed with javelins and mounted troops—and the proportional increase in the generals' role, combat was waged by two fronts seeking to gain ground by breaking through the enemy line. Winning this kind of confrontation took discipline and selflessness. The period also saw the progression of entrenchment behind strong fortified walls and the art of siege (poliorcetics). Military "campaigns" were confined to a few months—the summer period—while "decisive" battles were sometimes fought in a single day. In the case of internal conflicts, hostilities between the "elite" and the "common people" could drag on and it could take years to restore harmony, but the crucial period—the civil war itself (*stasis*)—albeit costly in human lives, was relatively short (from a few days to a few weeks at most).[6]

Ancient constitutional regimes put in place special powers in the event of acute crisis: these arrangements specific to this ancient form of state of exception had to be temporary to prevent them from turning into tyranny or monarchy. The ancients kept the length of such special powers short—from days, as in the famous case of Cincinnatus, to months, and six months maximum for dictators in Rome—for more than just constitutional reasons. They were short because no one really felt the need for them for any longer period of time. Military campaigns were not usually conducted beyond the summer period, and the highly intense phase of civil war never dragged on when it was so suicidal for the city.

Restriction in time and space was a decisive mark of the state of exception in this period but, as we shall see, it remains a decisive element in the modern era. The next step is to analyse the characteristics of the terrorist threat—a threat that is limited neither in time nor space—to show that combatting this scourge calls for an entirely different approach.

---

[4]On this point, see our book, Saint-Bonnet (2001), 43–80.

[5]Named after their shield, the *pelte*.

[6]Gehrke (1987).

2 French Revolution and the Real State of Siege

The terms and conditions of defence in the Middle Ages differed from those found in ancient times. Excepting the monasteries—havens of peace within which no one was allowed to carry weapons—special rules were laid down in the event of threats to castles and fortified towns, especially the extraordinary requisitioning of men and goods. Castles and towns alike faced essentially external threats (rival princes) to fortifications surrounded by walls, while the surrounding territories were not secured.

Yet from a strictly legal point of view, such situations were neither exceptions nor states of exception. In the essentially finalistic (Thomistic) view of the law, the authority has to provide for the common good in all circumstances. In the event of a threat to the very existence of the community (feudal or communal), there is a clear, incontrovertible need for tougher measures. The rights and responsibilities provided for in periods of peace become in a way "illegal", because they are inapt to save the group from peril and cannot provide for the "common good". Here, there is a sort of legal continuum between periods of peace and peril: there is no place for exception here, and consequently no place for a state of exception.

The demarcation lines drawn by castle and fortified town walls gave way to a single militarised border around the entire kingdom in the seventeenth century. This "iron belt" (Vauban) comprised a series of fortifications forming a strip a few kilometres wide all the way around France. Subjects within the kingdom were protected from threats provided they renounced violence. Those outside the kingdom found themselves abroad without the slightest guarantee bar perhaps "safe-conduct". The level of security within the strip itself varied depending on the situation.

Under the french Ancien Régime,[7] the level of security was dictated by the extent of measures taken to preserve and defend each stronghold. The stronghold's governor received his orders in writing from the war minister or, as was often the custom, took the initiative of acting with respect to the civilian population, without any particular consideration for their property. As in the Middle Ages, there could be no real break between a "normal" state and a state "of exception", any more than between a "state of peace" and a "state of war", as protection from danger, an *ever-present* need, could be ensured in different ways depending on the situation.

The clear break came with the French Revolution. As nomophiles and positivists, the period's players were intent on strictly regulating the different legal situations in the border "areas" based on threat level. The Law of 8–10 July 1791 on the strongholds specified the circumstances in which the military authority was authorised to intervene in the area of jurisdiction reserved, in principle, for the civil

[7]The matter was the subject of the beginnings of codification with the ordinances of 1 August 1733 on stronghold command and service, 25 June 1750 on the governors and lieutenants general of the provinces, stronghold governors and staff and service therein, and 1 March 1768 on settling service at the strongholds and in the quarters. On these points, see the excellent thesis by Le Gal 2011).

authorities. Supplemented in 1811, this law differentiated between the state of *peace* ("normal" distribution of powers between civil and military authorities), the state of *war* when the country is in conflict, but the stronghold is not under fire (expansion of military power), and the state of *siege* when communication is cut off between the stronghold under fire and the exterior (total transfer). This is what is called a *real* or *military* state of siege.

Thus, for the first time since the emergence of the modern state as a fortress[8] whose towers and walls would ring the entire kingdom, a real legislation of *exception* was adopted. Rather than the military being left to take action based on their own assessment of the situation, they had to comply strictly with provisions whose content differed depending on the threat's distance and extent of potential harm. The introduction of exception into the mechanism somewhat changed its meaning: whereas the real exception (*ex capere* = elusive) is totally indeterminate, it turns into a dispensation (alternative legal solution) when it becomes part of the law.

Nevertheless, this new state of exception retained its old characteristics. It was a limited expansion of the authorities' powers in time[9] and space[10] combined with a proportional contraction of the rights and liberties of the civilians placed under military command. It also tied in fundamentally with the frontier notion, the idea of geographic area.

Yet as in antiquity, the state of exception did not just change the distribution of powers and level of liberties in order to oppose a foreign enemy in a situation of combat between states. It did so also when the institutions and their leaders were confronted with insurrectionaries, rebels, insurgents and civil warmongers.

3 1791–1849: Keeping the State-of-Siege Technique

Right from the early days of the French Revolution, those who had come to power through rebellion and insurrection were confronted with armed groups intent on emulating them in the belief that they had failed or betrayed the ideals they defended. Against these compatriots—described as "enemies of the people" or "enemies of the nation"—the revolutionaries were quick to enforce the state of siege of the law of 1791 in the parts of the country where they were holed up. The "siege" was in a way "inversed". First, the army surrounded a rebel area (a district

[8]Bossuet wrote that, "By the hand of such a great king [Louis XIV], the whole of France no longer forms, as it were, merely a single fortress displaying a formidable front. With complete coverage, it is capable of keeping peace securely within; but also of going to war wherever necessary, and striking near and far with equal force". (Bossuet 1683), 598.

[9]Article 12 of the law stipulates that the state of siege shall end, "Once an end has been put to the investment and, in the event of the attacks having commenced, only after the besiegers' structures have been destroyed and the breaches repaired or readied for defence".

[10]The area under a state of siege extended over up to 1800 toises (approximately 3500 m), or large cannon range.

or an entire town, and sometimes an entire department) to prevent the insurgents from fleeing. The army then entered the area to flush them out, seize their weapons, destroy their means of propaganda, etc. This was called a "fictive" or "political" state of siege. Use of the law of 1791 consisted of no more and no less an interpretation of the *contra legem* mechanism, a fact that did not fail to shock the orthodox, legalistic revolutionaries. Consequently, the Directoirean assemblies passed the law of 10 Fructidor, V (27 August 1797) to be able to legally activate the state-of-siege measure in communes within the national borders. Under the Directoirean, placement under this measure was decided on by the assemblies. Under the consulate and the empire (Constitution of the VIII), these powers—extended until the suspension of the constitution—were still the assemblies' in principle, but passed to the government in their absence.[11] The Charte constitutionnelle of 1814 gave the king the possibility to issue ordinances "for the security of the state" (Article 14) without consulting the assemblies. It was Charles X's misuse of this article that was to precipitate his downfall in 1830.[12]

This state-of-siege measure was widely used and extensively interpreted to combat the "constitutional enemies" that the different nineteenth-century regimes had to face: Monarchists under the Republic, Republicans under the Empire and the Restoration, and Republicans, Legitimists and Bonapartists under the July Monarchy.

The regimes used this law to brand their staunchest political opponents—those prepared to take up arms—as enemies. This enabled them to bring in the army. In principle, the domestic forces of order (police and paramilitary police) pursue criminals and offenders while the army fights foreign enemies on the borders, or within if the country has been invaded. With the use of the state of siege, the insurgent compatriot was transformed into a bellicose alien deprived, as such, of the legal protection normally extended to lawbreakers by criminal law. These "constitutional enemies" sought initially to capture or take control of a territory—a rebel town or department—in the hope that the movement would gain other towns, that the army would rally, and that the people would rise up to drive out the ruling power. They, like hostile armies, sought to conquer lands. It was consequently vital that the "legitimate" authorities dislodge them from the "insurrectionary hotspots" they were controlling.

As long as the insurgency remained small scale, the state-of-siege technique could "clean" an area by emptying it of its subversive elements. The approach remained space bound, as the insurrectionary hotspot could be easily contained, and consequently time bound as the "insurgents" could be driven out in a few days or weeks. The state of exception could therefore be bounded provided the authorities

[11]Article 92: "In the event of armed rebellion or unrest threatening the security of the state, the law may suspend in the places and for the time which it shall determine, the authority of the constitution. This suspension may be declared temporarily, in the same event, by a government order when the legislative body is in recess, provided this body is convened at the earliest convenience by an article of the same order".

[12]On this point, see our book, (2001), 316–334.

did not abuse the extraordinary powers extended by the law. However, the use of a state of siege designed for military combat for "political" ends did not provide all the ideal legal assurances. It fell to the men of the Second Republic to pass the important law of 9 August 1849 on the state of siege; a law that is still in force today.

4 The Compelled Creation of the State-of-Exception Technique During the Decolonisation Time

The legislative junction between military and political states of siege came in 1849, driven by a major debate that, unusually for the issue, was held free of any immediate threat to the country, a factor that made for high-quality in-depth discussions. The law of 1849 considered that a state of siege could be declared in the event of "imminent danger to internal or external security". The law passed in 1878 then carefully specified that the imminent danger had to come from "a foreign war or an armed insurrection". This stipulation was an important one, as it underscored the need for the state of siege to be geographically grounded: it could only be declared in areas actually exposed to fire, whether from a regular army or insurgents. Article 5 stipulated that, "In fortified towns and military posts, a state of siege may be declared by the military commander in the cases provided for by the law of 10 July 1791 and the decree of 24 December 1811". Elsewhere, the political authority was responsible for declaring the change in an area from a normal state to a state of exception, entailing the transfer to the military authority of "powers vested in the civil authority to maintain order and police". However, "the civil authority continues [...] to exercise those of these powers of which it has not been relieved by the military authority" (Article 7). In practice, this meant that the military tribunals had jurisdiction over, "Crimes against the Republic's safety, against the Constitution, and against public peace and order", even if their perpetrators were civilians, as they were classed as enemy combatants (Article 8). The other powers concerned "control of the area": the power to conduct searches, day and night; remove known criminals; order the surrender of weapons and munitions, even those legally held; and prohibit publications and meetings of a nature to sustain disorder (Article 9). Aside from these prerogatives, "The citizens continue, notwithstanding the state of siege, to exercise all those rights guaranteed by the Constitution whose enjoyment is not suspended" (Article 11). Once the danger had passed and the areas concerned had been cleaned up, the state of siege could and had to be lifted promptly.

However, the First World War brought a serious challenge to the restriction of the state of siege in time and space.[13] The period's judicial doctrine regarded the

[13]Delsol, rapporteur to the French Senate on the law of 1878, had tried to be reassuring in a climate of distrust of the executive shortly after the crisis of 16 May 1877: "The state of siege authorised by the commission's bill is a state of siege located in those parts of the land where imminent

law of 5 August 1914,[14] placing the entire country under a state of siege "throughout the entire duration of the war", as a clear illegality albeit justified by the gravity of the situation.[15] This justification would give rise to the legal precedent known as "exceptional circumstances" under administrative law. Extension of the spatial bounds—the areas beyond the front line were not in "imminent danger"—and the time restriction—the end of hostilities—was seen as a misuse of the law of 1849, even though this had to be accepted precisely for reasons of need.

Notwithstanding the urgent need to transcend the framework set by the law of 1849, the 1914–1918 experience led to a two-way extension of the concept of the state of exception. The geographic extension can be explained by the fact that this was *total* war, requiring all the country's forces, including economic, to work towards the military objective. The temporal extension—and despite occasional attenuation of the effects of the state of siege[16]—was justified by the nature of the war, i.e. the huge stability of the positions encouraged by the digging of trenches. Nevertheless, this two-way extension did nothing to challenge the idea of a clear-cut, legible break between a "normal" period and a state "of exception".

The clarity of the line between periods of calm and times of danger was blurred by the appearance of a new form of hostility driven by a determination to overturn the established order, but also by an ambition to change the status quo in the name of an ideology. In the twentieth century, this hostility took the form of revolutionary parties determined to overthrow not only the ruling constitutional regime, but also the modern, liberal, "bourgeois" form of government, and this—in their stated intentions at least—worldwide. This form of subversion also took the shape of liberation movements in the colonised territories, in particular following the Second World War. This "ideological enemy", similar to the "partisan" figure theorised by the controversial Carl Schmitt[17] in the 1960s, readily used violence: un-uniformed combatants fought in the ranks of armed political parties committed to liberating an "enslaved nation" or "subjugated people" from the yoke of the grasping "capitalist

---

danger is found. It will therefore always be a very limited state of siege from the point of view of perimeter, and will not be able to operate outside the perimeter within which it is established. It is my firm hope that we will never again see a political situation that makes a state of siege necessary in 42 departments". (French Senate, 16 March 1878, *Journal Officiel*, p. 2900. The 42 departments refer to the war of 1870).

[14]*Bull. des Lois*, No. 135, p. 2268.

[15]Especially Joseph Barthélémy in his articles in the *Revue du Droit Public*. See our article, Saint-Bonnet (2016), 87.

[16]A circular from Interior Minister Malvy dated 1 September 1915 provided for, "As of 5 September [of that same year], prefects and mayors, on the national territory outside of the area of the armies, to freely [exercise], as in times of peace, all the attributions assigned them in policing and keeping order. The military authority shall henceforth [exercise] only those extraordinary powers pursuant to Article 9 of the law of 1849, and which the civil authority does not exercise under normal circumstances".

[17]The criteria elected were "irregularity" (i.e. an un-uniformed, non-state enemy), "increased mobility of the active combat" and a "heightened intensity of political commitment" (Schmitt 2004) 13.

bourgeoisie" or "colonial exploiters". These movements set out to destabilise governments using both arms and propaganda with the aim of establishing a new peaceful, radiant, utopian society built on strong dogmatic certitudes. The "partisans" used guerrilla warfare and terrorism in their struggle, shattering the classic distinctions between criminal and combatant, between police repression and military conflict, and between civil unrest and foreign war. Guerrilla warfare was the logical tactical choice for those who had neither the technology nor the logistics of regular armies, but the moral fibre of heroes, the discipline of patriots and the self-sacrifice of martyrs. Numerous countries had to live in a state of latent war for long periods, neither in a state of exception nor a normal state.

For reasons associated with decolonisation, France passed the law of 3 April 1955 on the state of emergency based largely on the law of 1849 on the state of siege, save that the extraordinary powers are not transferred to the military authority, but remain in civil hands. However, this law does nothing to change the time and space frame specific to the state of exception. Prior to 2015, it had never been enforced over a vast territory for a long period of time. As soon as it was passed, it was applied at once to Algeria: in the Constantine's region in April, throughout the East in May, and in all the "French departments of Algeria" in August and through to December. It was then declared for two weeks to quell the OAS in May 1958, and then again after the Generals' putsch of April 1961, when the state of emergency remained in effect for over two years.[18] More recently, a state of emergency was declared in certain insurgent parts of New Caledonia in 1985 and in rioting suburbs in 2005.

5 The Mismatch Between the State-of-Exception Technique and the Fight Against Contemporary Waves of Terrorism

France used the state of emergency in response to the terrorist threat for the first time in 2015. It was still in effect at the time of writing—April 2017—placing the country in a sort of permanent false state of exception: "false" because very few measures (searches and house arrests) have been used since January 2016, and "permanent" because those who call for it to be lifted are seen as irresponsible idealists. We now need to see why the state of emergency is unsuited to a terrorist threat that is bound by neither space (being global) nor time (the ultimate aim being the conversion of all humanity to radical Islam), and why intelligence is the better option.

[18]The extensions were not passed by parliament, but adopted by the President of the French Republic on 24 April pursuant to the Head of State's special powers under Article 16 of the French Constitution and then under the referendum law of 13 April 1962.

2015 was not the first time France was hit by a wave of terrorism. From 1892 to 1894, anarchist proponents of "propaganda by the deed" assassinated judges and even a president of the republic, shot or stabbed to death. They bombed cafés and the Chamber of Deputies, attacking not only "bourgeois" symbols and the state (oppressor by definition), but also nonentities such as a 19-year-old shoemaker. These anarchists looked death in the eye, like Ravachol who, having refused to sign his plea for pardon, went to the guillotine with a smile on his face. Their often-revenge-based actions triggered mass hysteria.

The government hit back with a battery of laws to stop the manufacture and possession of explosives, make associations «de malfaiteurs» an offence and ban anarchist newspapers. These provisions, which some called "villainous",[19] restricted a number of rights and liberties. The law of 28 July 1894 went so far as to raise "anarchist propaganda" to the rank of a crime of opinion. The repression of opinions was therefore deemed a choice route to combat this "ideological enemy". The libertarian movement abandoned terrorism at the start of the twentieth century, although historians have never established whether the repressive arsenal played any direct role in this decision.

Throughout this episode of late nineteenth-century terror, no one thought to declare a state of siege as the enemy had no spatial footing and no one knew how long this ideological and police struggle would last. The same held true in January 2015 when the attacks were perpetrated against Charlie Hebdo's editorial offices and the Hypercacher supermarket. What had crossed no one's mind in January became self-evident in November? Yet the terrorists' thinking, motives and means of action were barely any different. They remained partisans of radical Islam, faithful to ISIS. They sought to kill a maximum number of people and die as "martyrs" in the process, but they in no way sought to conquer or control part of the territory. They used weapons of war (AK47), explosive belts and, later, vehicles driven into the crowd. They were still networked globally with a command of the IT tools they needed to cross distances. From 14 November 2015 to 8 January 2016, only one of the more than 3000 raids under the state of emergency gave rise to a charge of terrorism.

If the French authorities are to be believed, the intelligence services foiled some 15–20 attacks from November 2015 to January 2017. In the face of a religious enemy who knows no global bounds, impermeable borders are powerless to guarantee security. Surveillance is therefore stepping in. Criminal law is extending farther beyond the strict field of law enforcement, taking an inquisitorial approach to intentions and "dangerous profiles". The intelligence services cooperate with their allies to infiltrate, where believed necessary, individuals' private lives to collect information to prevent attacks; watching, tapping and combing mobile phone memories. Yet many of these members of the public have already paraded

---

[19]Francis de Pressensé, Léon Blum and Émile Pouget had a pamphlet published in 1899 entitled *Les Lois Scélérates de 1893–1894* (de Pressensé et al. 1899): this adjective was to remain attached to these laws otherwise largely approved in their time.

entire swaths of their private lives on digital networks run by globalised firms that, like Google and Facebook, use the information for commercial ends. The government no longer restricts itself to managing public order objectively perceived as "material" (peace, health and security[20]). It uses persuasion, "preaching" by its cohorts of new "clerics", educators-preachers of good: re-education for de-radicalisation, anti-jihadist propaganda videos and civic education courses.[21]

This fight against terrorism can only be effective if it is global and permanent; if it is a new norm, a new "normality", the exact opposite of the state of exception.

References

Aristotle (1999) *Politics*, Benjamin Jowett tr, Batoche Books

Bossuet J-B (1683) Oraison Funèbre Pour Marie-Thérèse d'Autriche à Saint-Denis pe 1er Septembre, *Oeuvres complètes*, vol 4 (Méquignon & Gaume 1846)

de Pressensé F, Blum L, Pouget E (1899) *Les Lois Scélérates de 1893–1894* (Editions de la Revue Blanche)

Gehrke H-J (1987) *Stasis: Untersuchungen Zu Den Inneren Kriegen in Den Griechischen Staaten Des 5. Und 4. Jahrhunderts v. Chr* (Beck 1985)

Le Gal S (2011) Origines de l'Etat de Siège En France Ancien Régime-Révolution, Université de Lyon III

Saint-Bonnet F (2001) *L' Etat d'exception* (Presses Universitaires de France—PUF)

Saint-Bonnet F (2016) 'L'abnégation Des Hommes, Le Sacrifice de La Légalité. La Grande Guerre et L'impossible Naissance D'un Droit Administratif D'exception' VIII Jus Politicum 87

Schmitt C (2004) The theory of the partisan. Michingan State University Press, Michingan

[20]Legal experts define these three elements as forming the components of "material" public order as opposed to the very vague "immaterial" public order comprising, for example, the "minimal requirements of life in society" put forward to ban face covering in public, i.e. wearing a full-face veil.

[21]Courses can, for example, be ordered for individuals sentenced for wearing a full-face veil despite the ban of the law of 2010.

The Continued Exceptionalism of the American Response to Daesh

Kent Roach

Abstract This paper will discuss the American response to Daesh in relation to those of a number of other countries including France and Canada as well as supranational institutions including the UN Security Council and the Council of Europe. It will be suggested that American First Amendment Culture and legislative gridlock have helped prevent the enactment of new emergency type laws enacted in other democracies. Moreover, it will be suggested that such a response may have some virtues compared to European approaches based on emergency powers, less restrained alternatives to the criminal sanction and the regulation of expression.

1 Introduction

The exceptionalism of the American response to 9/11 and al-Qaeda has been the frequent subject of fierce and often justified criticism. The Guantanamo Bay experiment of creating a third regime that combined the laws of war and crime has been a failure, one acknowledged by President Obama, but not by President Trump who has promised to make increased use of the military prison. The dangers of the Patriot Act enacted quickly and without any significant dissent after 9/11 have been underlined by the Snowden revelations about mass surveillance. American courts have refused to hold American officials responsible for the torture of high value detainees including in CIA black sites, leaving such work to the European Court of Human Rights and other non-American courts. The debacle of the war, occupation and subsequent destabilization of Iraq, is also widely accepted, most recently by the Chilcot Inquiry in the UK.

The thesis of this chapter is that the American response to the new wave of terrorism inspired by Daesh [sometimes called the Islamic State in Syria and Iraq

K. Roach (✉)
Prichard Wilson Chair in Law and Public Policy, Faculty of Law,
University of Toronto, Toronto, Canada
e-mail: kent.roach@utoronto.ca

P. Auriel et al. (eds.), *The Rule of Crisis*, Ius Gentium: Comparative Perspectives on Law and Justice 64, https://doi.org/10.1007/978-3-319-74473-5_5

(ISIS) or in the Levant (ISIL)] has remained exceptional compared to the approach taken by other democracies.

Although the future under Trump is difficult to predict, American responses so far do not neatly fit into models of emergency powers, accommodation of emergencies in ordinary law, the use extra-legal measures or the business as usual used in other democracies.[1] In particular, the USA has not employed emergencies powers as France has in response to Daesh-inspired terrorism acts. Although US officials acted extra-legally especially with respect to renditions and detentions and torture at black sites, no single official has been held criminally or civilly responsible in the USA for such illegalities,[2] thus removing the alleging political and legal restraints and deterrence that are part of the extra-legal measures model.[3] Finally and notwithstanding the 2001 Patriot Act, the USA has also not yet significantly ramped up its domestic laws to accommodate the threat of Daesh and other foreign terrorist fighters as have Canada, Australia and many European states.

To be sure, there are elements of both the business as usual and extra-legalism in the American response. Much of the initial US response to 9/11 was extra-legal. At home, authorities made pre-textual use of immigration law and material witness warrants to engage in preventive detention of many Muslim men. Abroad, the conduct was even more dramatic and involved kidnapping and renditions of terrorist suspects to countries such as Egypt and Syria that routinely used torture as well as detention and torture by CIA officials at black sites. The Trump Presidency may see a revival of such practices and possibly worst.

Illegal American executive actions have gone beyond the extra-legal measures model to constitute a more systemic form of extra-legalism. By extra-legalism, I mean that the American legal system has systemically refused to subject extra-legal conduct to judicial review by virtue of the US's exceptionally broad state secrets doctrine and by its use of narrow standing rules and broad concepts of qualified immunity for officials who are sued and non-justiciable political questions. Another dimension of American extra-legalism is its frequent reliance on coordinate construction or departmentalism that posits that the executive is a legitimate interpreter of constitutional norms.[4] This helps explain why the infamous torture memos written by John Yoo and approved by Jay Bybee were treated by American officials as a form of law,[5] even though they never were authorized by the legislature or approved by the judiciary. As I have argued in detail elsewhere, the American legal

---

[1]For an overview of these models, see Gross and Aoláin (2006).

[2]Pfander (2017). US officials have, however, been charged criminally by several European states, notably Italy, and European states have been held accountable in the European Court of Human Rights for their complicity in US-led renditions and black sites.

[3]Gross (2003), 1011.

[4]Tushnet (1999) and Kramer (2006).

[5]Goldsmith (2009).

system has transformed the extra-legal conduct of American security officials into a more systemic and pernicious form of extra-legalism that facilitates rather than restrains extra-legal conduct.[6]

The elements of the business as usual approach to terrorism in the USA are found in the relatively restrained American domestic approach to terrorism. The USA has made frequent use of criminal prosecutions as a means to apprehend terrorist suspects at home. It has not experimented with less restrained alternatives to the criminal sanction at home such as preventive arrests, control orders and residence assignment orders that have been controversial in many other democracies including UK, France and Canada. The US reliance on business as usual under its criminal justice system, however, incorporates elements of the exceptional: the USA routinely imprisons much greater proportions of its population than any other democracy. There is also an element of business as usual in the US reliance on military force to respond to terrorism. The USA has a history of using its exceptional military power as a means of retaliation to terrorist incidents including the 1998 al-Qaeda bombings of two US embassies in Africa. In short, the American approach to terrorism is complex and in comparative perspective has remained exceptional. It does not fit neatly into established models of emergencies.

The exceptionalism of the American response to Daesh provides an opportunity to explore the precise features of American exceptionalism and to contribute to our understanding of the different ways that democracies respond to real or perceived emergencies. In particular, comparing the response of the USA and other democracies to Daesh reveals how the American domestic state is comparatively restrained by a libertarian domestic constitutional culture. For example, the First Amendment has prevented the enactment of new offences based on speech associated with terrorism that have been enacted in Australia, Canada and some European states. The American Bill of Rights has also prevented the USA from enacting a particularly popular Daesh era counter-terrorism measure: attempts to strip citizenship from recently naturalized citizens who have engaged in terrorism. Instead, the American domestic response to Daesh terrorism has remained rooted in a criminal justice model that relies on material support of terrorism prosecutions. American criminal justice itself is exceptionally punitive among democracies. It produces harsh sentences, high levels of imprisonment and the use of the death penalty not found in most other democracies. The exceptional libertarianism of American constitutional culture and its willingness to rely on existing criminal laws and prosecutions to respond to Daesh may actually be an asset in combatting Daesh-inspired terrorism if one doubts the efficacy or propriety of speech-based and citizenship stripping counter-terrorism measures and if one believes that a criminal justice response is an appropriate response to punish but also hopefully deglorify terrorism.

The restraints on the American domestic state are only half the story. A second dimension of American exceptionalism is the use of fairly unrestrained powers by

---

[6]Roach (2011) 163–9, 235-7-8 and Roach (2012), 1724–28.

the American executive and military so long as they are directed abroad and target people who are not American citizens. As Antoine Garapon observed in 2006, "the American authorities still remain strongly attached to these fundamental distinctions between internal and international, and nationals and foreigners, despite its being rendered partially obsolete by terrorism."[7] The Obama administration continued to use foreign focused powers used by the Bush administration to invade Afghanistan and Iraq to engage in increased targeted killing of suspected terrorists and to wage war against Daesh in Iraq and Syria, all without explicit Congressional authorization or effective judicial supervision. The Trump administration will also likely continue to use and increase such powers in an attempt to defeat Daesh militarily even at the cost of bolstering repressive regimes in Syria and elsewhere. The efficacy of such approaches may depend on the degree to which one accepts that Daesh can be defeated militarily. The Trump administration has already attempted to extend powers used against non-Americans by enacting restrictions against immigration despite claims and some judicial rulings that they are discriminatory against Muslims and will punish many innocent people.

It is not possible fully to appreciate the American response to emergencies by exclusively focusing on either the restrained domestic response or the much less restrained external response. Both must be considered. Indeed, their inter-relation must be explored. There is a danger that observers, perhaps especially those from outside the USA, will focus only on the unrestrained external response as symbolized by Guantanamo Bay and miss the comparatively restrained American domestic response to terrorism. This danger is especially magnified if the American domestic response has some advantages over the more aggressive approach taken as many other democracies enact multiple new laws aimed at foreign terrorist fighters or declare emergencies that threaten to become permanent given the nature of the threat.

The first part of this chapter will discuss how the USA has been affected by the threat of Daesh-inspired terrorism. There may be an understandable tendency in Europe, especially in France which has suffered so much, to discount the extent to which the USA, seemingly sheltered by an ocean, has suffered from Daesh-inspired terrorism. The June 2016 Orlando shootings that resulted in 49 deaths commanded global attention, but many prior episodes of domestic terrorism in the USA are surprisingly much less well known. One factor may be the exceptional prevalence of all sorts of gun violence in the USA. Another factor may be the routine use of criminal prosecutions rather than exceptional measures against suspected and surviving terrorists.

The second part of this chapter will examine American domestic responses to Daesh-inspired violence and attempts by Americans to join Daesh. The USA has largely relied on criminal prosecutions under existing offences, generally offences that have long criminalized material support of terrorism and have been interpreted

[7] Garapon (2006), 2061. For similar arguments that the USA has traditionally defined terrorism as an external threat, see Cole (2009).

by the courts very broadly. The American criminalization response has been assisted by high rates of guilty pleas and conviction rates. It has also resulted in the death penalty being imposed in the case of the surviving Boston Marathon bomber and Major Hasan who fatally shot 13 people at Fort Hood in 2009. It is also facilitated by wholesale rejections of entrapment defences by juries even in the face of evidence that some terrorist suspects have been exploited by elaborate undercover operations or strings.

The American reliance on criminal prosecutions also helps explain why there has not been interest in using alternatives to the criminal sanction such as control orders, peace bonds or residence assignment orders as used in the UK, Canada and France. There has also been little attempt to prosecute Daesh sympathizers under speech-based offences based on advocacy or apologie of terrorism or in attempting to strip dual nationals convicted of terrorism of American citizenship. The USA has been more respectful of freedom of expression and freedom of religion than the UK or France. To be sure, the American domestic response of relying on criminal prosecutions has its harsh side,[8] but it may also hold some advantages in depriving Daesh of publicity and glory that may help attract new recruits.

The third part of this chapter will focus on the dog that did not bark in the form of the lack of American legislative response to Daesh-inspired acts of terrorism including the 2013 Boston Marathon bombing, the 2015 San Bernardino shootings and the 2016 attack on the Pulse nightclub in Orlando. It is difficult to imagine that a terrorist attack that produced 49 deaths such as the Orlando attack would not have resulted in the enactment of new terrorism laws in most democracies. For example, in Canada, the killing of two persons in Daesh-inspired terrorism in October 2014 led to a massive overhaul of its terrorism laws.[9]

The polarized nature of American politics, especially around gun control, and the checks and balances of its Congressional system of government meant that Congress was unable to restore previous restrictions on ownership of automatic assault rifles or enact new laws to prevent those on terrorist no fly watch lists from possessing such weapons even after the Orlando massacre. In addition, no new powers were given to the police or intelligence agencies. Some may criticize this type of legislative inertia. In many ways, it makes the USA a less regulated and more dangerous country than most other western democracies. It may also encourage extra-legal conduct by American security officials and even private illegal conduct such as hate crimes and vigilante violence. Nevertheless, it may also be advantage if one is concerned that the enactment of panicked emergency legislation may actually cause more harm than good to democracies.

The fourth part of this chapter will briefly examine American military efforts to defeat Daesh and other suspected terrorists. It will be suggested that there is a continuity between the US's initial post 9/11 response which relied on military force, military detention and military trials to a degree that was exceptional among

[8]Said (2015).

[9]For a fuller account of the Canadian response, see Forcese and Roach (2015).

democracies except perhaps Israel and the US approach during the Obama administration. Indeed, this continuity is underlined by the fact that the US war against Daesh is still authorized by the same Congressional authorization of military force that was issued against al-Qaeda immediately after 9/11. American reliance on military force and its continued reliance on the bare bones but open-ended Congressional authorization of the use of military force enacted immediately after 9/11 can be seen as a flip side of a domestic state that is constrained by a Bill of Rights that includes First Amendment protections of speech and Second Amendment protections of arms and has been interpreted as precluding citizenship stripping.

It is too soon to know whether American military efforts against Daesh will be more successful than its efforts against al-Qaeda. The American-led Operation Inherent Resolve has had some success against Daesh in Iraq and Syria and degrading its claims to form a caliphate. The Obama administration has also claimed success in killing about 2500 suspected terrorists outside of Afghanistan and Iraq, but with disputed claims about how many innocent civilians were also killed. To be sure, there are dangers that the military effort may have counter-productive effects especially with regard to the impact of returned or thwarted Daesh fighters in other countries and the creation of conditions such as humanitarian disasters and failed and brutal states in the region that may be conducive to terrorism. My primary point, however, is to illustrate the continuity between the US's exceptional reliance on military means to defeat al-Qaeda and Daesh.

The conclusion of this paper will summarize the descriptive and normative claims made in the paper. Descriptively the USA has so far avoided enacting many new foreign terrorist fighter measures that many democracies have. The USA has been less active in this regard than Canada even though the USA has on a per capita basis suffered many more Daesh-related domestic terrorism casualties. At the same time, the USA has continued to focus enormous resources in its attempt to defeat terrorists on the battlefield.

The Trump Presidency will test these aspects of American exceptionalism. If the past is an indication of the future, however, it can be predicted that Trump will encounter more difficulty implementing an emergency or authoritarian regime at home than abroad. Indeed, initial judicial restraints of Trump's initial "Muslim ban" on immigration from seven countries and the acceptance of Syrian refugees provide some grounds for optimism about the restraining effects of American domestic constitutionalism.

Past precedents, including the expansion of the US global war against terrorism under both Presidents Bush and Obama, suggests that President Trump may not need Congressional authorization for the most controversial measures he employs and the American "extra-legalism" system will fail to hold his officials to account for illegal actions taken to defeat terrorism. Trump would not be the first President to act in an extra-legal manner. President Lincoln suspended habeas corpus during the Civil War without Congressional approval, President Franklin Roosevelt executed German spies during World War II before the Supreme Court had ruled on the legality of their military trials and President George W Bush authorized a range of extra-legal conduct in the wake of 9/11.

At least up to the Trump Presidency, American exceptionalism may have had some advantages in countering Daesh that were not present in its response to al-Qaeda. In particular, its domestic criminal justice response may help to repress and deglorify terrorism in a more effective manner than speech prosecutions, control orders and citizenship stripping measures used in other democracies. In addition, and even more tentatively, it will be suggested that America's military response may be more effective in defeating Daesh and its claims to form an Islamic State than it was in combatting al-Qaeda. That said, the Trump Presidency will likely produce setbacks both with respect to its proposed discriminatory and overinclusive use of immigration law as anti-terrorism law and by other measures that could feed a "clash of civilizations"[10] narrative that could bolster Daesh. Trump's initial "Muslim ban" on immigration including the acceptance of Syrian refugees fits into this pattern as do reports that he may rebrand nascent efforts to counter violent extremism, including a rise in hate crimes against Muslims, into efforts only to counter "radical Islamic extremism".[11]

2 The USA and Daesh-Inspired Terrorism

European observers could be forgiven for believing that the USA has escaped much of the immediate burden of Daesh-inspired terrorism and that this might help explain comparative American restraint in responding to this new terrorist threat. Although the Orlando attacks that killed 49 in June 2016 came close, there has fortunately been nothing equivalent in the USA to the two Paris attacks and the subsequent attack in Nice in terms of symbolic impact and death tolls. Moreover, the horrendous 9/11 attacks, as well as frequent gun violence in the USA, also serve as a type of a catastrophic benchmark that minimize some of the impact of the ISIS-inspired terrorism that the USA has experienced.

Although the threat level is different, any idea of Fortress America which is immune from terrorism is a myth. A helpful data set compiled by the New America Foundation indicates that 94 people have been killed in the USA as a result of "violent jihadist violence" since 9/11. It also reveals a much longer list of terrorist plots that fortunately did not result in deaths.[12] Taken together, this data suggests that the USA has experienced a real threat of Daesh-inspired terrorism even if the threat is not as great as that faced in Europe. Even only considering the 63 victims

---

[10]Huntington (1996).

[11]"Trump to focus counter-extremism program solely on Islam- sources" Reuters Feb. 2, 2017 at http://www.reuters.com/article/us-usa-trump-extremists-program-exclusiv-idUSKBN15G5VO.

[12]"Deadly attacks since 9/11" at http://securitydata.newamerica.net/extremists/deadly-attacks.html. The data also contains a much larger group of terror plots. See http://securitydata.newamerica.net/extremists/terror-plots.html.

of the December 2015 San Bernardino and June 2016 Orlando attacks, the American death toll per capita is greater than that in Canada which has suffered two Daesh-related terrorist deaths[13] and Australia which has suffered three Daesh-related terrorist deaths.[14]

One of the first attacks inspired by the more populist Daesh ideology involved an Army psychiatrist Nidal Hasan who used a high-capacity handgun to kill 13 and wound 30 people in 2009 on the Fort Hood army base a few weeks before he was scheduled to be deployed to Afghanistan. Hasan was wounded but survived the attack. In a significant pattern, he was convicted not of terrorism but of murder. He was sentenced to death after a court martial. He was subject to a military trial because he committed the murders as a member of the American military. After his apprehension and charge, Hasan renounced his American citizenship on the basis that it would require him "to support/defend man-made constitution (like the Constitution of the United States) over the commandments mandated by Islam."[15] He also subsequently wrote to the Daesh leader Abu Bakr al-Baghdadi with a request that he be made a citizen of the Islamic State.[16] Although it has received considerable publicity, the Hasan case for better or worse did not generate the political attention or legislative change that it might have in other democracies. One factor may simply be the Americans have become inured to mass shootings. Indeed, five years later, there was another mass shooting at Fort Hood. The killer even was able to purchase a similar semi-automatic gun from the same "Guns Galore" store where Hasan purchased his weapon.[17]

Hasan communicated multiple times with Anwar al-Awlaki, an American born propagandist and terrorist who played an inspirational role in many other cases of terrorism including the Boston Marathon bombing, the 2009 underwear bomber plot involving Umar Farouk Adbulmutallab and the Charlie Hebdo killings. The American approach to Awlaki reflects some of the exceptional nature of American counter-terrorism. Awlaki would likely have been prosecuted for advocacy or

[13]These incidents occurred in October 2014 and killed two members of the Canadian Forces as well as the two lone perpetrators. Even in 2014, this death toll was eclipsed by the killing of three police officers by a right wing extremist Justin Bourque. See Canadian Network for Research on Terrorism, Security and Society Canadian Incident Database at http://extremism.ca/results.aspx?Pivot=Year. Since that time, six worshippers in a Quebec City mosque were killed by a lone gun man in January 2017 in what many have characterized as an act of anti-Muslim terrorism.

[14]Two hostages were killed in a Daesh-related incident in the Lindt Café in Sydney in December 2014, and a civilian police employee was killed in Sydney in November 2015. See Global Terrorism Database at http://www.start.umd.edu/gtd/search/IncidentSummary.aspx?gtdid=201510020040.

[15]Bergen (2016), 83.

[16]"Fort Hood shooter writes to ISIS leader, asks to become 'citizen' of Islamic State" CNN News 29 August 2014 at http://www.cnn.com/2014/08/28/us/isis-fort-hood-shooter/index.html?hpt=hp_t2.

[17]Manny Fernandez, Serge F Kovaleski and Eric Schmitt, "Soldier's Attack at Base Echoed 2009 Rampage" *New York Times* (4 March 2014) https://www.nytimes.com/2014/04/04/us/fort-hood-security-problems.html.

apologie of terrorism in the UK or France. In the USA, such charges were not constitutionally possible because of the First Amendment. Indeed, the USA responded to the UN's call in Security Council Resolution 1624 on states to enact laws against the incitement of terrorism by stating that the First Amendment does not allow for the prohibition of speech unless it incites or produces imminent lawless action and that this means that "the majority of terrorist propaganda" cannot be criminalized in the USA.[18] Awlaki was first investigated by the FBI for a possible "Al Capone" charge involving interstate transportation in the Washington DC area for purposes of prostitution. He was subsequently killed by a drone strike in Yemen that killed another American citizen Samir Khan who helped him produce Inspire, a magazine operated by al-Qaeda in the Arabian Peninsula but which shared with Daesh a similar populist origin geared to recruiting terrorists.[19]

2.1 Low Profile Acts of Terrorism and Gun Violence

In 2009, a Muslim convert Carlos Bledsoe killed one soldier and wounded another in Little Rock, Arkansas, after several failed attempts to commit violence against the homes of Jewish rabbis and a Jewish community centre in Nashville. Bledsoe, who had changed his name to Abdulhakim Mujahid Muhammad, had spent time and been imprisoned in Yemen. He was interviewed by the FBI both in Yemen and after he was deported to the USA. He was not charged with terrorism or under federal law in relation to the killing with the local prosecutor commenting that the case was "an awful killing, its just like a lot of other killings we have."[20] This may have been an attempt to downplay the fact that the FBI had contact with Bledsoe. In any event, Bledsoe faced the death sentence under state law, but pled guilty and was sentenced to twelve life sentences plus an additional 180 years in prison. At his sentencing Bledsoe stated: "I wasn't insane or post-traumatic nor was I was forced to do this act. Which I believe is justified according to Islamic Laws and the Islamic Religion Jihad to fight those who wage war on Islam and Muslims."[21]

A similar approach of conducting a murder prosecution under state law was taken in another case involving Alton Nolen, an African American who converted to Islam while in prison. Nolen displayed photographs associated with the Islamic State on his Facebook page. He beheaded a female victim at his place of work and injured two others. Like other terrorists attracted to Daesh, Nolen had a previous criminal record, in his case for theft and assaulting police officers. Prosecutors charged Nolen with first degree murder and sought the death penalty. Nolen agreed

---

[18]US Country Report S/2006/397 See also Roach (2011), 227–229.

[19]Shane (2016) ch 6.

[20]James Dao, "A Muslim Son, a Murder and Many Questions" *New York Times* (16 February 2010).

[21]Bergen (2016) 66.

to plea guilty and accept the death penalty stating that he was being held captive "by disbelievers in Allah, the one and only God [...] its part of my religion that when death faces you, you do not back down."[22] The judge, however, refused to accept the plea ruling Nolen not to be mentally competent. The case has surprisingly received little attention in the USA despite the sensational nature of the beheading and despite some attempts by state legislators to use the case to introduce legislation making a symbolic statement against Sharia law.[23]

The use of the ordinary criminal law to prosecute terrorists may help normalize acts of terrorism and respond to difficulties in proving more complex intents or motives that may be necessary to obtain a terrorism conviction. It may also help dampen media interest that may both harm community relations and inadvertently encourage others to engage in terrorism. For example, gruesome acts in France such as a June 2015 beheading outside of Lyon, June 2016 stabbings of a police officer and a July 2016 killing of a Priest received much more publicity than the acts of Bledsoe and Nolen.

American police officers have been targeted in several incidents by people claiming allegiance to Daesh, but none of these incidents have received as much attention as the killing of five police officers in Dallas Texas and another three police officers in Baton Rouge in July, 2016, as part of the controversy over police shootings of African Americans. In January 2016, Edward Archer shot a Philadelphia police officer with a stolen semi-automatic hand gun. Archer subsequently pledged allegiance to the Islamic State, but the police stressed that the crime had nothing to do with Islam.[24] In June 2015, Boston police shot and killed Ussamah Rahim when he attempted to use a knife against them. Rahim was being investigated for terrorism at the time. In October, 2014, Zale Thompson attacked two New York City police officers with a hatchet before being killed by police. He was reported to have radicalized through Daesh websites, but also to have been angered by police shootings of African Americans and to have supported the new Black Panther party.[25] If one accepts that terrorists gain from publicity, the lack of publicity given to these police killings may be a virtue rather than a vice. The comparative lack of attention to these acts of terrorism may also be related to the

---

[22]'Man Accused of Beheading a Female Coworker after Being Suspended from His Job Begs Judge to Let Him Plead Guilty and Die by Lethal Injection' *Daily Mail* (20 May 2016) http://www.dailymail.co.uk/news/article-3600849/Man-accused-Oklahoma-beheading-scheduled-plea-hearing.html.

[23]Abby Ohlheiser, "What We Know about Alton Nolen, Who Has Been Charged with Murder in the Oklahoma Beheading Case" *The Washington Post* (30 September 2014) https://www.washingtonpost.com/news/post-nation/wp/2014/09/30/what-we-know-about-alton-nolen-who-has-been-charged-with-murder-in-the-oklahoma-beheading-case/.

[24]Jon Hurdle and Richard Pérez-Pena, "Gunman Said He Shot Philadelphia Policeman for ISIS, Police Say" *The New York Times* (1 August 2016) https://www.nytimes.com/2016/01/09/us/philadelphia-police-officer-wounded-in-ambush-on-his-patrol-car.html.

[25]Michael Schwirtz and William K. Rashibaum, "Attacker With Hatchet Is Said to Have Grown Radical on His Own" *The New York Times* (24 October 2014) https://www.nytimes.com/2014/10/25/nyregion/man-who-attacked-police-with-hatchet-ranted-about-us-officials-say.html.

high rate of violence directed at the police in the USA. In 2016, 64 police officers were killed by firearms in the US; in 2015 41 were killed and in 2011 73 police officers were killed by firearms.[26] It may also reflect American preoccupations with race. All three incidents, as well as the Nolen and Bledsoe cases examined above, involved African American suspects and may have been viewed by the media and the public primarily through the prism of race rather than religion.

In July 2015, Mohammod Abdulazeez killed five people and injured two others with an assault rifle at a Tennessee military recruiting centre before being killed by police. There was evidence that he was influenced by al Awalki and had expressed grievances against American military policy and his desire for martyrdom.[27] At the same time, the FBI and the press stressed that he had mental health and substance abuse issues. The relative lack of attention to such an act of terrorism that resulted in five deaths may be related to the exceptional level of gun violence in the USA. Treating terrorism as routine crime may help make acts of terrorism less effective and disruptive. It may also help democracies accept that the threat of Daesh-inspired terrorism cannot be eliminated for the foreseeable future.

In a chilling precursor to the targeting of gay people in Orlando, Ali Muhammad Brown used a gay dating site to lure two gay men to a gay bar in Seattle where he killed both of them with a hand gun. Like many Daesh-inspired terrorists, he was also involved with other crimes and is also charged with murder and terrorism under New Jersey law for an alleged carjacking and murder. Brown is reported to have defended the killing as "just kills" based on retaliation for US foreign policy.[28] Again perhaps because of a decision to prosecute under state as opposed to federal law, this case has also received minimal media coverage. In 2015, Brown received a 36 year sentence for an armed robbery even before he faced trial on the murder charges under Washington law and terrorism and murder charges under New Jersey law.[29] The US's exceptionally punitive criminal justice system based on long

---

[26]Camila Domonoske, "Number Of Police Officers Killed By Firearms Rose In 2016, Study Finds" *National Public Radio* (30 December 2016) http://www.npr.org/sections/thetwo-way/2016/12/30/507536360/number-of-police-officers-killed-by-firearms-rose-in-2016-study-finds.

[27]Manny Fernandez and others, "In Chattanooga, a Young Man in a Downward Spiral" *The New York Times* (20 July 2015) https://www.nytimes.com/2015/07/21/us/chattanooga-gunman-wrote-of-suicide-and-martyrdom-official-says.html.

[28]James Queally, "Seattle Man Says He Killed 4 in Wash., N.J. to Gain Revenge against U.S." *Los Angeles Times* (20 August 2014) http://www.latimes.com/nation/nationnow/la-na-nn-seattle-shootings-confessions-20140820-story.html accessed 15 April 2017; "LGBT Americans Have Always Lived under the Threat of Violence. Will Orlando Force Straight People to Acknowledge It?" *Los Angeles Times* (15 June 2016) http://www.latimes.com/opinion/opinion-la/la-ol-violence-pulse-lgbt-queer-orlando-attack-massacre-20160614-snap-story.html, accessed 15 April 2017.

[29]Billy Wichert, "Accused Brendan Tevlin Killer Gets Lengthy Prison Term in Armed Robbery" *NJ.com* (20 January 2016) http://www.nj.com/essex/index.ssf/2016/01/accused_brendan_tevlin_killer_gets_lengthy_prison.html.

sentences may make it less important than in other democracies to obtain terrorism specific convictions or to develop post-release controls for those convicted of terrorism.

In January, 2017, 26 year old, Esteban Santiago, who had previously served for the USA in Iraq, killed five people in Fort Lauderdale airport with a handgun he had legally transported in his luggage. The man who had mental health issues and said his mind was controlled by the CIA has been reported to have told police he was motivated by Daesh videos, but he was not charged with terrorism.[30] Later that month, 37 year old Joshua Cummings, an Islam convert and former member of the Army, killed a Denver security guard in a little publicized incident. He later told reporters he supported Daesh.[31]

2.2 Higher Profile Acts of Terrorism: Boston, San Bernardino and Orlando

A much higher profile case was the Boston Marathon bombing carried out in April 2013 by Tamerlan and Dzhokhar Tsarnaev. It killed 4 people and injured 400 others. The surviving brother Dzhokhar Tsarnaev was convicted of 30 charges in April 2015 including murder and the use of weapons of mass destruction. He was sentenced to death upon the recommendation of a Boston jury. At 21 years of age, he is the youngest person on death row in the USA where he is now held in a super maximum security prison. He may appeal his conviction on the basis that the trial should not have been held in Boston and that his defence had inadequate time to prepare. Both this case and the Hasan case illustrate that the USA will not hesitate to employ the death penalty against surviving terrorists, a penalty that would not be available in Europe or in many other democracies. The use of the death penalty may make a criminal justice response more acceptable for those who want revenge and retribution for deadly acts of terrorism. At the same time, the death penalty is unlikely to deter terrorists prepared to die for their cause, and it may even have a perverse effect of rewarding terrorists as martyrs. In the case of Tsarnaev, it has led to threats by al-Qaeda of retaliation against the USA if he ever is executed.

Two more high profile incident of Daesh-related terrorism in the USA involve two men who were killed by the police in Garland, Texas in 2016 when they

[30]'Suspect in Fort Lauderdale Shootings Pleads Not Guilty' *The New York Times* (30 January 2017) https://www.nytimes.com/2017/01/30/arts/esteban-santiago-fort-lauderdale-airport-shooting.html.

[31]"Denver slaying suspect says he supports the Islamic State" *New York Times* (17 February 2017).

attacked a showing of cartoons of the prophet Mohammed.[32] In November 2016, Ohio State student Abdul Razak Ali Artan injured 13 persons before being killed by campus police. The case received more publicity after President elect Trump visited the victims and the police officer who killed Artan. Artan had come to the USA from Somalia in 2014, and Trump cited the case as additional support for his proposal to adopt restrictive immigration policies targeting largely Muslim-based countries that have experienced terrorism.[33]

The two highest profile acts of ISIS terrorism in the USA so far have been the San Bernardino shootings in December 2015 by Syed Rizwan Farook and his wife Tashfeen Malik that left 14 dead and the June 2016 Orlando shootings by Omar Mateen that left 49 people dead. Both Farook and Mateen were American citizens, and the latter demonstrated signs of extremism and was removed from his job providing court room security. Farook was successfully employed and had a young child. Farook's wife was born in Pakistan and spent much of her life in Saudi Arabia. All three perpetrators were killed by the police, but one other person, a convert to Islam, has been charged with material support of terrorism for his alleged role in providing guns and explosive materials to Farook and Malik. An exceptional feature of the American response to both these incidents is that no federal legislation including gun control legislation was enacted in response to either high profile and deadly incidents.

Minus, the Orlando attack, the death toll from right wing extremism in the USA would have been very similar to the death toll from Islamic terrorism.[34] Acts of terrorism are different from other acts of violence often because of their political or religious motive and the high media coverage that they generally receive. That said, it is likely that background rates of violent death have some relevance to how terrorist deaths are judged in a democracy. A 2016 study confirms American exceptionalism in terms of violent death rates and in particular deaths from guns as compared to other developed democracies. It found based on 2010 data that the USA had 7 times the homicide rate compared to other OECD countries and 25 times the rate of deaths by firearms.[35] An acceptance of high rates of firearm deaths may help to explain why the USA has not enacted new terrorism laws in response to the significant amount of Daesh-related terrorism that it has suffered domestically.

---

[32]Department of Justice News Release at https://www.justice.gov/opa/pr/phoenix-man-convicted-conspiracy-support-isil-and-other-terrorism-related-offenses.

[33]Kevin Stankiewicz and T Rees Shapiro, "Trump Visits Ohio State Victims, Officer Who Killed Attacker" *The Washington Post* (12 August 2016) https://www.washingtonpost.com/news/grade-point/wp/2016/12/08/trump-to-visit-victims-of-ohio-state-university-attack/?utm_term=.f972a2464775.

[34]"Deadly Attacks Since 9/11" at http://securitydata.newamerica.net/extremists/deadly-attacks.html.

[35]Grinshteyn and Hemenway (2016), 271 Table 4.

3 The American Domestic Response to Daesh-Inspired Terrorism

The primary American response to Daesh-inspired terrorism has not been the enactment of new and controversial laws, but rather criminal terrorism prosecutions that have become almost routine.

A report released by the Centre on National Security has detailed 101 Daesh-related prosecutions between 31 March 2014 and 30 June 2016. The vast majority (80%) involved material support of terrorism charges in the Federal courts with almost 70 of the charges alleging the provision of material support to a foreign terrorist group or attempting or conspiring to do so. This offence was amended in 2015 to increase the maximum sentence from 15 to 20 years.[36] The average age of those prosecuted is 26 years old, 80% are American citizens, one third are converts to Islam, and more than 10% have been treated for mental illness.

Of the 101 cases, 46 have already resulted in convictions. The vast majority of these convictions, 39 of 46, are the result of guilty pleas which are routine in the American criminal justice system. There have been no recorded acquittals in these Daesh-related case producing an astounding 100% conviction rate that is closer to those in non-democracies such as China. Only 14 persons have been sentenced, and the average sentence has been 9.2 years.[37] The prosecutions also demonstrate the ability of the criminal law to respond before actual harm with over 30 cases involving either conspiracy to travel or thwarted travel and only 10 cases involving those who had actually departed from the USA. Only three cases involved a live bomb, and in all of these cases, an undercover agent was involved. As will be seen, informers and undercover agents play a critical role in Daesh-related American terrorism prosecutions.

3.1 The Use of Informers and the Illusory Entrapment Defence

The Centre on National Security reports that 59% of the 101 cases since March, 2014 have involved an informant or undercover agent. This number increases to 71% of all domestic terrorism cases.[38] These figures confirm the extensive use of the criminal sanction against Daesh supporters in the USA and the frequent use of undercover operatives.

---

[36] 18 USC 2239 B. The 2015 amendment is contained in Pub L 114-23.

[37] Center on National Security, "Case by Case ISIS Prosecutions in the United States March 1, 2014-June 30, 2016" (2016).

[38] Ibid 18.

Unlike in many European states, undercover operations in the USA do not require prior judicial authorization.[39] They are only lightly regulated after the fact by the entrapment defence. American federal law takes a subjective approach to the entrapment defence. This means that the defence will not apply if the accused was predisposed to commit the crime even though he or she was induced by state agents to commit the crime in a manner that might have led many to commit the crime. American courts have stressed that predisposition can be found even if the accused only had "a rather generalized idea" or "state of mind intent to inflict harm on the United States, be willing to die like a martyr, be receptive to a recruiter's presentation, whether over the course of a week or several months, of the specifics of an operational plan, and welcome an invitation to participate."[40]

In the USA, the jury decides whether there has been entrapment. American juries have never accepted an entrapment defence in terrorism cases. They have probably been influenced by the fact that a successful entrapment defence allows the accused to go free and that much of the evidence of the accused's predisposition in terrorism cases relates to extreme religious and political views. American juries reject entrapment defences despite significant evidence that undercover operatives have engaged in misconduct and often exploited terrorist suspects. For example, Emmanuel Latchman, a mentally ill panhandler, was driven to a Walmart and given $40 to buy a machete and other supplies for a planned terrorist attack before being arrested and charged with material support of terrorism. A former FBI undercover agent who now researches national security law has argued that the FBI "is manufacturing terrorism cases…these people are five steps away from being a danger to the United States."[41]

The illusory nature of the entrapment defence in American terrorism cases reveals that part of the appeal of a criminal justice response to terrorism may be the ease in which it is applied. As will be seen in the next section, in Canada, there has been more interest in less restrained alternatives to the criminal sanction such as peace bonds or control orders. One factor may be that Canada has an entrapment defence that is more protective than the American test. The Canadian test unlike the American federal test is triggered by objectionable disreputable state conduct even if the accused is subjectively predisposed to commit a crime. Moreover, judges in Canada and not the jury decide whether the accused has an entrapment defence and independent and professional judges may be less amenable to being prejudiced by evidence of the accused's unpopular religious or political views. Although rejected in a number of previous Canadian cases, a Canadian judge recently accepted the entrapment defence in a case where over 250 police officers were involved in a sting targeting an addicted and mentally vulnerable couple who had converted to Islam. As a result of the successful entrapment defence, the criminal convictions of the

---

[39]See general Roach (2010).

[40]US v. Cromitie 727 F.3d 192, 207-08 (2d Cir, 2013).

[41]Eric Lichtblau, "F.B.I. Steps Up Use of Stings in ISIS Cases" *The New York Times* (7 June 2016) https://www.nytimes.com/2016/06/08/us/fbi-isis-terrorism-stings.html, accessed 15 April 2017.

couple for targeting a Canada Day celebration at the British Columbia legislature with pressure cooker bombs were reversed.[42] Once their convictions were overturned, however, the police sought to place the couple under a peace bond or a control order.[43] Such alternatives to the criminal sanction are not used in the USA though they are used in other democracies including Australia, France and the UK.

4 Why Has the American Domestic Response Been Comparatively Restrained?

As discussed above, the USA may use terrorism prosecutions in cases where other democracies would use less restrained alternatives to the criminal sanction such as control orders. The USA may also use intensive stings leading to terrorism prosecutions as a substitute for charging those who have expressed sympathy for Daesh or al-Qaeda with speech-based crimes such as advocating or apologie of terrorism. In this way, the USA can still respect First Amendment values by not punishing speech directly while it can label and often severely punish terrorist sympathizers with actual crimes of terrorism.

The United States Supreme Court has rejected a First Amendment challenge to the broad material support of terrorism offence routinely used in the USA. The Court ruled that the law did not infringe the First Amendment because it only criminalized material support of a terrorist group and not simple advocacy of its cause. At the same time, the Court interpreted material support very broadly and as not requiring that the accused intend that violence be committed.[44] Following this case, persons have been convicted of material support of terrorism for translating and posting material sympathetic to al-Qaeda.[45] In Europe, such a person might be charged and convicted of speech-based offence which is generally punished less severely than terrorism offences. In Australia and Canada, they might be charged under controversial new crimes of advocating terrorism that were recently enacted in response to Daesh-inspired acts of terrorism. In the USA, however, they would more likely be charged (and convicted or even plea guilty) of material support of terrorism.

The breadth of the American material support of terrorism offence, as well as the illusory nature of the entrapment defence, helps to explain why the USA has so far remained comfortable with terrorism prosecutions and has not attempted to enact

[42]R. v. Nuttall 2016 BCSC 1404.

[43]Betsy Trumpener, "Crown Seeks 'Terrorism Peace Bond' for Couple Convicted Then Freed in B.C. Legislature Bomb Plot" *CBC News* (29 July 2016) http://www.cbc.ca/news/canada/british-columbia/crown-seeks-peace-bond-for-john-nuttall-and-amanda-korody-under-fear-of-terrorism-criminal-code-section-1.3701536.

[44]Holder v. Humanitarian Law Project 561 U.S. 1 (2010).

[45]Said (2015) 70.

novel counter-terrorism measures such as peace bonds (Canada), control orders (UK and Australia) or residence assignment orders (France). The breadth of the material support offence, in addition to First Amendment traditions that are hostile to attempts to regulate the content of speech, also help explain why the USA has not enacted new offences targeting advocacy or apologie of terrorism.

4.1 USA Freedom Act *and Legislative Restrictions on Torture*

The exceptionalism of the USA in not enacting new domestic counter-terrorism measures to respond to Daesh is underlined by some of the laws that the USA has recently enacted. These laws have placed some restraints on state counter-terrorism activities at a time when many democracies were enacting or planning new laws to facilitate increased counter-terrorism activities. For example, the 2015 USA Freedom Act amended section 215 of the Patriot Act to prohibit the National Security Agenda from collecting meta data.[46] At the same time, however, the law imposed data retention requirements and allowed the state to obtain access to such material on the basis of a warrant issued under the Foreign Intelligence Surveillance Act (FISA), albeit subject to new provisions allowing for the government's case for a warrant to be subject to adversarial challenge. Although some privacy and civil liberties groups opposed the law as too weak, the law at a symbolic level sought to limit state surveillance. In this sense, it continued the trend to American exceptionalism based on a domestic constitutional culture that is more libertarian than that found in many European states and even in countries such as Australia and Canada that in many respects seem quite similar to the USA.

Another piece of federal legislation that addressed terrorism was article 1045 of the National Defence Authorization Act of 2016[47] that prohibited any US official from using methods of interrogation not authorized in the Army Field Manuel. This was belated legislative support for President Obama's executive action to repudiate the use of torture of terrorist suspects during the Bush administration. It will be interesting to see if this provision or the Army Field Manuel is amended by the Trump administration to allow harsher interrogation techniques to be used against terrorist suspects.

One hypothesis is that the US will remain reluctant explicitly to authorize harsh interrogations even while it may employ them under Trump. This approach would resemble the extra-legal approach to counter-terrorism defended by Oren Gross. The extra-legal approach has the virtue of allowing the official law to be untainted by torture or other explicit violations of human rights. At the same time, the extra-legal approach may not have the restraining effects on officials predicted by

---

[46]Public Law 114-23.

[47]2016 HR 1735.

Professor Gross if officials can confidently predict that they will not be prosecuted or successfully sued as a result of their illegal actions. Given that no official was held criminally accountable for abuses by the Bush administration even during the Obama administration, officials in the Trump administration may reasonably be confident that they can act illegally and in violation of human rights with impunity. The same is true with respect to civil liability. The US approach to constitutional torts is generally to allow civil suits only against officials in their individual capacity and not against the US state. The American courts have, however, effectively shut down the possibility of such civil suits because of concerns that even the threat of civil liability for abuses will deter vigorous national security decision-making.[48] The criminal and civil impunity for illegal counter-terrorism activity is disturbing for those committed to the rule of law and compensation for those who suffered abuse. It is exceptional compared to European actions that have imposed criminal and civil liability on those who have been complicit in American renditions and black sites. At the same time, American condonation of extra-legal conduct by its national security officials may help explain why American law remains comparatively unaffected by terrorist emergencies.

4.2 US Constitutional Restrictions on Citizenship Stripping

Another example of the comparative libertarianism of the US's domestic constitutional culture is its failure to enact or seriously explore provisions that would allow citizenship to be stripped from recently naturalized citizens convicted of terrorism offences or engaged as foreign fighters such as enacted in Canada in 2014, facilitated by 2014 legislative amendments in the UK[49] and enacted in Australia in 2016.[50]

In 1967, the United States Supreme Court held that Congress had no power to strip citizenship from an American citizen in the absence of voluntary renunciation. Justice Black appealed to American exceptionalism in arguing that while "Other nations are governed by their own constitutions [...]. In our country the people are sovereign and the Government cannot sever its relationship to the people by taking away their citizenship."[51] He based this conclusion on liberal principles of limited government verging on natural law. At the same time, he also concluded for the Court that any doubt was removed by the reference in the 14th Amendment passed after the Civil War to "All persons born or naturalized in the United States [...] are citizens of the United States." He reasoned that "There is no indication in these

---

[48] *Ashcroft v. Iqbal* 556 U.S. 662 (2009); *Ashcroft v. al Kidd* 563 U.S. 731 (2011) See generally Pfander (2017) chs. 4 and 5.

[49] *Immigration Act*, 2014 s.66

[50] *Australian Citizenship (Allegiance to Australia)* Act, 2016

[51] *Afroyim v. Rusk* 387 U.S. 253 at 257 (1967)

words of a fleeting citizenship, good at the moment it is acquired but subject to destruction by the Government at any time. […] Once acquired, this Fourteenth Amendment citizenship was not to be shifted, cancelled, or diluted at the will of the Federal Government, the States, or any other governmental unit".[52] If anything, this ruling is even more absolute than First Amendment protections of freedom of speech and religion. This approach deprives American law-makers of the symbolically expressive and popular measure of stripping citizenship of some who engage in terrorism.[53] American exceptionalism with respect to citizenship stripping may, however, be an advantage because it avoids many problems associated with the measure including the singling out of recently naturalized citizens and citizens who have another country of citizenship as second class citizens who are subject to such a controversial sanction. It also avoids the practical problems of administering such a sanction that will can leave terrorists stateless or force their return to countries such as Egypt and Syria that routinely use torture as a counter-terrorism measure.

4.3 The Lack of Response to Gun Violence

From a comparative perspective, the failure of the US Congress to enact any legislation, including gun control legislation, in response to the June 2016 Orlando attack that killed 49 people at the Pulse nightclub may be the most striking and even shocking act of American restraint. For better or worse, it is difficult to imagine any other democracy not responding with new legislation to such a shocking and hateful act of terrorism.

The American lack of response to Orlando is related to its toxic and shocking approach to gun control. The USA has the highest rate of gun ownership in the world. In part because of its Second Amendment guaranteeing the right to bear arms and its polarized politics, Congress was unable to enact laws banning semi assault laws after the 2012 killing of twenty school children in Newtown, Connecticut or the San Bernardino or Orlando shootings in 2015 and 2016 that resulted in 63 deaths. In all three cases, the perpetrator used an automatic assault rifle. The gun was originally designed for the American military and has been

[52]Ibid at 262.

[53]This is not to say that there have not been attempts to implement citizenship stripping in the US. Senator Ted Cruz has long campaigned for citizenship stripping of terrorists, and then, President elect Trump proposed that those who burned the American flag have their citizenship stripped. Most, however, dismiss such proposals as clearly unconstitutional. David A Graham, "The Republican Vogue for Stripping Citizenship" [2016] *The Atlantic*. https://www.theatlantic.com/politics/archive/2016/11/the-republican-vogue-for-stripping-citizenship/508979/, accessed 15 April 2017.

Alan Feuer, "AR-15 Rifles Are Beloved, Reviled and a Common Element in Mass Shootings" *The New York Times* (13 June 2016) https://www.nytimes.com/2016/06/14/nyregion/ar-15-rifles-are-beloved-reviled-and-a-common-element-in-mass-shootings.html, accessed 15 April 2017.

defended as "America's rifle" by the influential National Rifle Association with sales increasing after each mass shooting. No official statistics are kept on ownership of the gun, but some estimate as many of 10–12 million are owned by Americans.

In 2008, the United States Supreme Court clarified in a 5:4 decision that the Second Amendment included the right to gun ownership.[54] Four separate proposals for increased gun control after the Orlando shooting were defeated because partisan splits made it impossible to command a 60 person majority that was necessary to overcome the use of a filibusters to block legislation in the US Senate.[55] A compromise proposal that would have placed some restrictions on the ability of people on the terrorist no fly list to buy guns received some bi-partisan support and 52 votes, but that was not enough for the proposal to be enacted into law.[56] Republican Senator Lindsey Graham supported the proposal on the basis that the "Constitution is a sacred document but its not a suicide pact. This is not hard for me. Due process is important, but at the end of the day we are at war."[57] Despite such bi-partisan support, not even this limited legislation was enacted after Orlando. This lack of response to the use of guns by Daesh-inspired terrorists in the USA is not likely to change under Trump even though a strong case can be made that increased gun control would be a proportionate and sensible means to attempt to limit some of the damage that could be done by terrorists.

4.4 Comparisons to Canada's Less Restrained Domestic Response

The restrained US approach to Daesh can be compared with the much less restrained approach of its northern neighbour Canada which suffered two acts of Daesh-inspired violence in October 2014 which resulted in two deaths. Canada had in 2013 already enacted three new terrorism offences specifically targeting foreign terrorist fighters. The USA has not enacted such new offences in part because of the breadth of the existing material support offences. Another factor may be that the

---

[54]US v. Heller 554 U.S. 570 (2008) The Second Amendment also applies to state and local governments. Macdonald v. City of Chicago 561 U.S. 742 (2010).

[55]Kristina Peterson and Siobhan Hughes, "Senate Rejects Four Gun-Control Proposals" *Wall Street Journal* (21 June 2016) <http://www.wsj.com/articles/congress-latest-gun-law-effort-faces-another-likely-impasse-1466458575>.

[56]David M Herszenhorn and Emmarie Huetteman, "Democrats End Sit-In After 25 h, Drawing Attention to Gun Control" *The New York Times* (23 June 2016) https://www.nytimes.com/2016/06/24/us/politics/senate-gun-control.html.

[57]Carl Hulse, "Gun Control Wall, Bolstered by Republicans, Shows a Crack" *The New York Times* (29 June 2016) https://www.nytimes.com/2016/06/30/us/politics/gun-control-republicans-congress.html.

USA is more resistant to international demands by the UN and other supra national bodies to enact new terrorism offences.

Canada responded to the 2014 attacks with new legislation increasing the powers of its civilian security intelligence agency to take actions to reduce security threats potentially in violation of domestic and foreign laws and its constitutional bill of rights. Such actions were provided for by legislation and would generally have to be authorized by a judicial warrant. This constitutes a legalized and democratic approach to illegality. US officials have also been prepared to violate laws in an attempt to prevent terrorism, but such actions are not authorized in law and often do not require a warrant. In this way, the US approach to terrorist emergencies has been closer to Oren Gross's extra-legal model,[58] but subject to the important exception that even the threat of ex post accountability for illegal conduct has been lacking. The result, however, consistent with Professor Gross's theory has resulted in the USA not attempting to legalize illegality or enact explicit incursions on the rights of domestic citizens in a way that as he predicts can easily become permanent and spread into other areas of the large.

Another feature of Canada's 2015 terrorism legislation was provisions that made it easier to impose peace bonds in an attempt to control terrorist suspects in the community. As discussed above, such peace bonds have been sought after a criminal case collapsed when a Canadian judge ruled that a vulnerable couple of Muslim converts had been entrapped into committing terrorist crimes. One problem with peace bonds or control orders used in Australia and the UK or residence assignment orders used in France is that they constitute a Goldilocks remedy that may be too strong when applied to those who simply express sympathy for terrorism but too weak when applied to determined terrorists. In Canada, one person subject to a terrorist peace bond was nevertheless able to move from being a sympathizer to a person who constructed two bombs before being killed by the police.[59] In France, one of the terrorist killers of an 85 year old Priest in Normandy in 2016 was subject to a assigned residence order including an electronic tracking bracelet.[60] In this regard, the American reliance on actual terrorism prosecutions resulting in long prison terms may be an advantage in combatting Daesh both because such prosecutions appear more legitimate than less restrained alternatives to the criminal sanction and because they result in long-term incapacitation of terrorists.

Although Canada like the USA has a constitutional bill of rights, it has been more willing to impinge on the rights of expression and citizenship than the USA. In 2014, the Harper government enacted the *Strengthening Canadian Citizenship Act*[61] making it easier to deprive naturalized Canadians convicted of terrorism and

---

[58]Gross "Chaos and Rules" supra.

[59]"Aaron Driver, ISIS sympathizer, was planning 'imminent' attack, police say" CBC News August 11, 2016 at http://www.cbc.ca/news/canada/aaron-driver-imminent-attack-1.3716997.

[60]"French ask whether Priest's killer, listed as a terrorist threat, could have been stopped" New York Times July 27, 2016 at http://www.nytimes.com/2016/07/28/world/europe/france-attack-priest-church-syria.html?_r=0.

[61]S.C. 2014 c. 22.

national security offences inside or outside of Canada. Some of these provisions have been repealed by the new Justin Trudeau government. Nevertheless, they would not be possible in the USA even under Trump.

The Harper government also enacted as part of the controversial Anti-Terrorism Act, 2015,[62] a new offence against advocating terrorism offences in general. This constituted Canada's fifteenth terrorism offence, but a fairly minor one, that because it is triggered simply by expression was subject to a maximum penalty of five years imprisonment. The Canadian offence is more similar to European offences targeting indirect advocacy or glorification or apology of terrorism that will be encouraged by new European Union guideline decisions enacted in the wake of the Paris and other Daesh attacks. Such offences could be used to charge terrorist sympathizers, but they will remain controversial because of their criminalization of expression. Even if upheld as a proportionate restriction on freedom of expression, they may not produce long prison sentences and may also feed into a Daesh narrative of the west as hostile to Muslims and their grievances. Nothing similar to such speech-based terrorist offences has been enacted in the USA where an offence targeting the content of even terrorist-related speech would be vulnerable to First Amendment challenge. At the same time and as discussed above, terrorists sympathizers in the USA have at times been subject to intensive stings and successful prosecutions for material support of terrorism.

The exceptional American reliance on criminal prosecutions to deal with a domestic Daesh threat may turn out to be advantage. The criminal prosecutions used in the USA may be accepted as more legitimate than novel counter-terrorism instruments used in other democracies such as speech offences, control orders and citizenship stripping. In the exceptionally punitive and efficient American criminal justice system, they may also provide longer-term and more reliable forms of incapacitation than alternatives to the criminal sanction.

5 The American External Military Response

The comparatively restrained American domestic response to Daesh if viewed in isolation provides a distorted picture of the US's response. There is a long history of American Presidents responding to terrorism with military force. Ronald Reagan used military force against Libya, and Bill Clinton used cruise missiles against Iraq and Afghanistan in response to both terrorist plots and the 1998 African embassy bombings.[63] There is also confidence in the USA that a forceful military and intelligence response to terrorism will not bleed into the domestic arena because of

[62]S.C. 2015 c. 20.

[63]On the military tradition in US counter-terrorism, see Kent Roach "Uneasy Neighbors: Comparative American and Canadian Counter-Terrorism" (2012) George Mitchell Law Review 1701 at 1721-23.

long standing legislative restrictions on either the military or the Central Intelligence Agency being able to act within the domestic USA.

The domestically restrained US response to Daesh has been accompanied by a most vigorous external response both in the form of Operation Inherent Resolve, the US led and dominated military attacks against Daesh strongholds in Iraq and Syria, as well as the Obama administration's large program of targeted drone killings of suspected terrorists. Drones have been used to kill many suspected terrorists, many of whom were attracted to Daesh, in a number of countries beyond the battlefield of either Iraq or Afghanistan.

From the start of bombing in Iraq in August 2014 to December 2016, 17,005 air strikes were conducted as part of Operation Inherent Resolve with just under 11,000 of these strikes in Iraq and just over 6000 strikes in Syria. The vast majority of these strikes, especially in Syria, were conducted by the USA alone. The US bombings were conducted at an average daily cost of $12.6 million.[64] Although the USA has stressed that Operation Inherent Resolve is a multi-national effort, it has also committed the most troops with over 3500 troops in Iraq compared with under 300 troops committed by coalition partners such as the UK and France.[65]

The Obama administration's increased use of targeted killing also fits into the pattern observed throughout this chapter of the US's comparatively restrained domestic response to Daesh being matched by an exceptionally vigorous external response. Although other states such as Israel have engaged in targeted killings of suspected terrorists before, the American program with its use of drone technology is unprecedented and exceptional. In July, 2016, the Obama administration released information that it had killed between 2372 and 2581 combatants deemed to be a continuing and imminent threat to the USA since 2009.

The Obama administration also admitted that between 64 and 116 non-combatants were killed during this time, but these figures were vigorously contested as too low by many groups.[66] Even taking these numbers at face value, however, they dramatically reveal the scale and force of the American external response and a number of false positives or killing of non-combatants that would not be acceptable in a domestic or criminal justice response. This raises the question of whether the less restrained American external response to terrorism may be a form of compensation for its more restrained American domestic response. In any event, the differences in the two types of responses are significant and make the American response to terrorist emergencies more complex and multi-faceted.

It is soon too to evaluate all the consequences of the American-led military effort. There are varying estimates of both Daesh and civilian causalities. A recent report of US Inspectors General concedes that the attacks may have played a role in

---

[64]"Operation Inherent Resolve" at https://www.defense.gov/News/Special-Reports/0814_Inherent-Resolve (last accessed 31 December 2016).

[65]Inspectors General Quarterly Report at 26 at https://oig.state.gov/system/files/oir_quarterly_march2016.pdf.

[66]Scott Shane "Drone strike statistics answer few questions and raise many" *New York Times* (July 3, 2016).

the return of foreign fighters and terrorists attacks throughout the world including in Europe. The attacks, combined with Syrian and Russian responses, are also connected with various humanitarian disasters including the displacement of millions in Iraq and Syria. Nevertheless, the bombing of oil fields seems to have deprived Daesh of resources in a way that is more immediate and more effective than reliance on the more indirect regulation of terrorism financing. American officials have estimated that about 50,000 Daesh fighters have been killed, but UK estimates are half of that figure.[67] Both figures beg the famous question that US Defence Secretary Donald Rumsfeld asked in relation to Iraq in 2005: "Are we creating more terrorists than we are killing?"[68] The US-led forces have enjoyed some military success and Daesh as of December 2016 is estimated to have control over territory containing 6 million people as compared to a peak of 10 million people.[69] The US military approach will likely continue and may escalate under Trump's proposed massive increase in US military budgets. For an example, an initial US attack in Yemen in February 2017 killed 14 suspected members of al-Qaeda but reportedly nine children. The raid also resulted in the death of one US Navy Seal and the loss of one US military aircraft valued at $75 million.[70]

6 Conclusion

Although Daesh's threat to the USA is not as severe as its threat to either European or middle East states, the USA has after the San Bernardino and Orlando attacks suffered more Daesh-related domestic casualties on a per capita basis than suffered by Australia, Canada and the UK. The USA has, however, not responded to these domestic terrorist attacks with severe new domestic anti-terrorism laws as have many other democracies including Australia, Canada, France and UK.

The American approach to emergencies caused by terrorism has diverged from models of accommodation that has seen the quick enactment of permanent and increasingly tough anti-terrorism laws in many states. This divergence is underlined by the fact that the US Congress has not enacted new foreign terrorist fighter laws in response to a significant amount of domestic terrorism inspired by Daesh including the killing of 49 people in 2016 at the Pulse nightclub in Orlando. It is difficult to imagine many other democracies that would have not enacted new and tougher terrorism laws in response to such acts. The US's neighbour, Canada, for example,

[67]"UK puts figure of ISIS fighters killed at half US figure" CNN News Dec 16, 2016 at http://www.cnn.com/2016/12/16/politics/uk-us-number-isis-fighters-killed/.

[68]"Killing terrorists, creating more" New York Times April 16, 2013 at http://www.nytimes.com/2013/04/15/us/letter-killing-terrorists-creating-more.html.

[69]"Islamic State and the Crisis in Iraq and Syria in Maps" at http://www.bbc.com/news/world-middle-east-27838034.

[70]"Trump's Yemen Raid that Killed Nine Children: What Went Wrong" Newsweek Feb 9, 2017 at http://www.newsweek.com/trumps-yemen-raid-killed-nine-children-what-went-wrong-554611.

enacted two broad laws in response to two acts of terrorism in October, 2014, that killed two people even though the year before it had already enacted new offences targeting foreign terrorist fighters such as those affiliated with Daesh. The American response to Daesh is also distinct from the French response that has relied on a declaration and subsequent extensions of the emergency as well as enacting new terrorism laws.

One factor in this comparative lack of an American legislative response to Daesh has been the checks and balances and political polarization in the American Congressional system. The American legislative paralysis has some parallels in the legislative deadlock that prevented France from enhancing citizenship stripping in the wake of the November 2015 Paris terrorist attacks. A normative lesson may be that the checks and balances of political constitutionalism and even political polarization can be more effective in restraining domestic responses to acts of terrorism than the effects of judicial review, civil society opposition and international criticism.

Another factor that helps explain why there has yet to be an expansion of American domestic counter-terrorism laws is the strength of existing laws including broad offences of material support of terrorism. The exceptionally punitive American criminal justice system has produced conviction rates in terrorism cases that are perilously close to 100%. A number of surviving terrorists including a 21 year old convicted of the Boston Marathon bombing have been sentenced to death in a manner that would not occur in other democracies.

The American criminal justice system is exceptionally punitive, and this is part of the explanation of why the USA has relied upon it in formulating its domestic response to Daesh. Another factor is that many of the Daesh-inspired terrorist acts including the Orlando and San Bernardino attacks have much in common with gun killings that are regrettably routine in the USA.

A criminal justice response has a potential to delegitimate and deglorify acts of terrorism and even to normalize them to some extent. Some of the state criminal prosecutions of Daesh-inspired terrorism in the USA have also received surprising little publicity. This has deprived Daesh of publicity victories even with respect to some gruesome acts of violence including beheadings. That said, there are some aspects of the American criminal justice system including the use of entrapment techniques, frequent guilty pleas and the death penalty that may deprive its criminal justice response of some of its legitimacy as a means of stigmatizing and incapaciting terrorists in the same way as other violent criminals.

The American approach of using ordinary criminal and terrorism prosecutions to counter Daesh-inspired terrorism can be contrasted with the approach in other democracies that have placed more emphasis on controversial speech offences or controls short of conviction and imprisonment. Indeed, convictions for apologie of terrorism and other speech crimes and the use of assigned residence orders, peace bonds or other forms of control orders may feed into a Daesh narrative of the west discriminating and being hostile to Islam. Intermediate sanctions in the community may ultimately be too weak to restrain those who are actually determined terrorists. We have seen this in France in the case of one of the Normandy attackers and in

Canada in the case of a person subject to a peace bond in the community who was able to construct and detonate bombs before being killed by the police. At the same time, intermediate sanctions may also be too strong and have a high rate of false positives when imposed on persons who may associate with or have extremist views but are unlikely to engage in or even prepare to commit acts of violence. The US's more or less routine criminalization of Daesh-inspired terrorism may be a better way to responding to the continuing threat than a variety of controversial emergency or other repressive measures that more easily feed into a narrative of the west being imposed to Islam.

The main US domestic law passed during the Daesh era has been the enactment of the USA Freedom Act in response to the Snowden revelations about bulk collection of American meta data. This reflects a comparative libertarian constitutional culture that extends to both the right and left ends of the increasingly polarized American political spectrum. It also explains why Congress could not even agree on increased regulation of automatic weapons after they were used to kill 49 people in Orlando. Several surprisingly little publicized acts of Daesh violence in the USA, especially those targeting the police, have been viewed more through the lens of race than religion.

The comparatively calm domestic response of the USA to Daesh also reflects an American constitutional tradition that has been resistant to both the regulation of speech and the stripping of citizenship: both controversial measures that have featured prominently in the way that many democracies including the UK have responded to terrorism. Such measures are seen as not constitutionally viable in the USA. That said, the USA has been in a state of emergency under its *National Emergencies Act* since 9/11. These emergency powers have mainly been used to make it easier to call up the National Guard to serve in the military abroad and to expand the military.[71]

The comparative weakness of the American domestic state is, however, offset by its abundant and unprecedented military powers. Using the same combination of Presidential powers and Congress's open-ended post 9/11 authorization of the use of the military force, the USA has led a coalition of nations including France and the UK in the bombing of Daesh targets in Iraq and Syria. The Obama administration also embarked on an unprecedented campaign of targeted killings of suspected terrorists. In doing so, the USA has not even enacted a new authorization for the use of military force. The robust US external approach is also supported by a legal system that has dismissed legal challenges to both military efforts against Daesh[72] and targeted killing[73] as non-justiciable political questions and on the basis of restrictive standing decisions that effectively condone extra-legal conduct. I have

[71]Thronson (2013), 771–777.

[72]Smith v. Obama (US Dist Court) decided Nov 21, 2016 at https://www.justsecurity.org/wp-content/uploads/2016/11/Smith-Opinion-dismissing-case.pdf.

[73]*Al-Aulaqi v. Obama*, No. 10-1469, 2010 U.S. Dist. LEXIS 129601 (D.D.C. Dec. 7, 2010).

previously described this legal system as a form of "extra-legalism"[74] that by providing officials with defacto immunity likely erodes the restraining effects of the extra-legal approach.[75] The Trump administration may take full advantage of the impunity that this system offered to officials in the Bush administration.

Although the negative blowback effects of military activities, especially in relation to the destabilization of Libya and the killing of innocent bystanders during targeted killings should not be ignored, the military degradation of Daesh appears to be less problematic than the US's reliance on military force in its 2003 invasion of Iraq and its 2001 invasion of Afghanistan. In other words, American military force may be more fit for purpose in defeating Daesh's attempts to form a caliphate than to bring democracy to Afghanistan or Iraq. One normative lesson and warning, however, is that short-term military success may not necessarily produce long-term gains. Another is that even successful military interventions may as in Iraq especially have unanticipated and negative effects on the terror threat. To borrow Rumsfeld's famous albeit crude remarks, it remains to be seen whether the USA is killing more terrorists than it is creating.

There is considerable continuity between the US's reliance on military force as a means to combat terrorism. The USA responded to terrorism in the 1980s and 1990s with military force, typically cruise missiles. After 9/11, it invaded first Afghanistan and then Iraq. It has bombed Daesh relying on the same Congressional authorization of the use of force as used with respect to al-Qaeda. American reliance on military force to counter-terrorism may be explained by many factors including, of course, its immense military power. An often neglected factor, however, may be the restraints placed on the American state in enacting domestic laws to combat terrorism. To be sure, the *Patriot Act* and some subsequent laws enabled the American state domestically, but not to the extent that its many critics feared. There was no attempt, as in the UK after 9/11 or in France after Paris to derogate from rights, and the most controversial counter-terrorism measures used by the USA both at home (mass and pre-textual immigration detention) and abroad (rendition, torture, secret prisons) were not authorized by the Patriot Act.

The 2015 USA Freedom Act also demonstrates at least at a symbolic level a desire shared by significant aspects of the right and the left in the USA to place restraints on the American state as it operates domestically. Domestic restraint, combined with a polarized political system, may explain why both President Bush with his invasions of Afghanistan and Iraq and renditions and secret prisons and President Obama with his targeted killing program used foreign directed programs as their keystone counter-terrorism measures. It remains to be seen whether President Trump will follow these patterns.

Much of the above analysis, however, begs the question of how the USA will respond to Daesh under President Trump. Trump has already attempted to use executive immigration policy as a form of anti-terrorism law in his initial "Muslim

---

[74]Roach (2011).

[75]Gross (2003).

ban" against the admission of Syrian refugees and visitors from Iran, Iraq, Syria, Somalia, Yemen, Libya and Sudan, seven Muslim majority countries. Such policies will be politically popular in some quarters, but they are overinclusive and discriminatory with respect to the vast majority of law abiding potential immigrants and refugees and underinclusive with respect to American citizens and permanent residents who may be attracted to terrorism.

The lessons of the Bush era suggest that even if the USA enacts a Patriot Act II under Trump and a new Republican Congress, its bark may be worse than its bite. In other words, an important lesson of the first Bush administration is that the most rights invasive aspects of American counter-terrorism policy were not subject to explicit and democratic legislative authorization and that they were generally not directed against American citizens. As with the post 9/11 abuses of rendition, secret prisons, mass surveillance, pre-textual preventive detention and targeted killing, the worst abuses of the Trump executive may be extra-legal. This would fall into a long tradition of American Presidents and their executive actors acting in an extra-legal manner.

The American approach to terrorism emergencies has some of the features of the extra-legal model that allows official laws to remain rather untainted by increased state powers. An important qualification, however, is that the restraining effects of acting extra-legally were not realized for the first Bush administration as no officials were prosecuted for various abuses including torture. This may have the effect of emboldening a Trump administration determined to be tougher than the rest and that may have reasonable expectations of impunity. This is a dangerous and toxic prospect but one that may mean that American laws will appear comparatively restrained even while they are broken. A critical question will be whether leakers and the press will be able, as they were during the Bush administration, to publicize such lawlessness and in doing so create conditions for future legal challenges and legislative readjustments.

The analysis in this chapter suggests that Trump will encounter many more obstacles in imposing an authoritarian agenda domestically than abroad. In my view, it is unlikely that the USA even under Trump will embrace speech offences, control or assigned residence orders, and citizenship stripping that many other democracies are using in their battle against Daesh. Consistent with the complex post 9/11 pattern of American exceptionalism outlined in this chapter, Trump may have more success in changing America's external policies than its internal domestic policies. Non-American citizens will likely bear the brunt of the Trump administration's counter-terrorism excesses in the form of restrictive and discriminatory immigration policies, probably imposed without legislative change. Trump is also likely to expand military detention at Guantanamo and expand bombings and targeted killing of Daesh targets and to be less concerned with avoiding "collateral damage" than the Obama administration when it engaged in many targeted killings. He may also revive the enhanced interrogation techniques and secret prisons of the Bush era. He will also rely on foreign surrogates to implement some of the harshest counter-terrorism measures.

All of this may actually have the effect of driving more Muslims both inside and outside the USA to be more attracted to Daesh and its hateful ideology or at least to be less willing to cooperate with the American state. This may unfortunately increase the number of terrorist attacks. Again, however, I would predict that the USA will continue to respond to such emergencies in an exceptional manner: one that domestically is comparatively restrained and relies upon criminal prosecutions and one that is much less restrained and harsher towards non-American citizens and relies on the blunt and perhaps counter-productive force of military power, extra-legal measures and immigration restrictions.

Acknowledgements I thank the Pierre Trudeau Foundation for funding a fellowship that facilitated this work.

References

Bergen P (2016) United States of Jihad: investigating America's homegrown terrorist*s*, 1st edn. Crown, New York

Cole D (2009) English lessons: a comparative examination of UK and US responses to terrorism. Curr Legal Probl 62:136

Forcese C, Roach K (2015) False security: the radicalization of Canadian anti-terrorism. Irwin Law, Toronto

Garapon A (2006) The Oak and the Reed: counter-terrorism mechanisms in France and the United States of America. Cardozo Law Rev 27:2041

Goldsmith J (2009) The terror presidency: law and judgment inside the Bush Administration. WW Norton & Company, New York

Grinshteyn E, Hemenway D (2016) Violent death rates: the US compared with other high-income OECD countries, 2010. Am J Med 129:266

Gross O (2003) Chaos and rules: should responses to violent crises always be constitutional? Yale Law J 112:1011

Gross O, Aoláin FN (2006) Law in times of crisis: emergency powers in theory and practice. Cambridge University Press, Cambridge

Huntington SP (1996) The clash of civilizations and the remaking of world order. Simon & Schuster, New York

Kramer LD (2006) The people themselves: popular constitutionalism and judicial review. Oxford University Press, Oxford

Pfander JE (2017) Constitutional torts and the war on terror. Oxford University Press, Oxford

Roach K (2011) The 9/11 effect: comparative counter-terrorism. Cambridge University Press, Cambridge

Roach K (2012) Uneasy neighbors: comparative American and Canadian counter-terrorism. William Mitchell Law Rev 38:1701

Roach K (2010) Entrapment and equality in terrorism prosecutions: a comparative examination of North American and European approaches. Mississipi Law J 80:1455

Said WE (2015) Crimes of terror: the legal and political implications of federal terrorism prosecutions. Oxford University Press, Oxford

Shane S (2016) Objective troy: a terrorist, a president, and the rise of the Drone. Tim Duggan Books, Oxford

Thronson P (2013) Toward comprehensive reform of America's emergency law regime. Univ Michigan J Law Reform 46:737

Tushnet MV (1999) Taking the constitution away from the courts. Princeton University Press, Princeton

Dignity, Emergency, Exception

Alon Harel and Assaf Sharon

Abstract This article analyzes the category of extreme cases—cases involving catastrophic consequences the avoiding of which requires severe measures (e.g., torture, shooting a plane in 9/11 situations). Our proposal maintains that what is most pernicious is not the violation of moral rules as such but their principled or rule-governed violation. Maintaining a normative distinction between acts performed under the direction of principles/rules, on the one hand, and unprincipled, context-generated acts, acts performed under the force of circumstances, on the other, allows for accommodating the necessity of infringements in extreme cases within a (non-conventional) deontological framework. Agents who perform acts in extreme cases ought not to be guided by rules or principles. Instead, they ought to make particular judgments not governed by rules.

1 Introduction

Dignity, according to a prominent conception identified with Immanuel Kant, means incommensurable and non-exchangeable value. Thus, violations of dignity cannot be justified by their contribution to the advancement of other values. On this conception, dignity is seen as underwriting strict constraints admitting of no exceptions. Prohibitions against torture and killing of innocents, for example, are regarded as immune to consequentialist considerations. This conception comes under pressure from extreme cases, where upholding a dignity-based prohibition entails catastrophic consequences. The paper presents and criticizes the two main non-consequentialist approaches to the problem of emergencies and proposes a third approach. Emergencies, we argue, should be understood within the framework

A. Harel (✉)
Hebrew University of Jerusalem, Jerusalem, Israel
e-mail: alon.harel@mail.huji.ac.il

A. Sharon
Tel Aviv University, Tel Aviv-Yafo, Israel
e-mail: assafsharon@post.tau.ac.il

P. Auriel et al. (eds.), *The Rule of Crisis*, Ius Gentium: Comparative Perspectives on Law and Justice 64, https://doi.org/10.1007/978-3-319-74473-5_6

of exceptions. A theory of the relation between rules and exceptions can resolve the problem of emergencies while offering an account of the moral significance of dignity that does not consist in absolute prohibitions. Dignity entails prohibitions not grounded in consequentialist reasoning, which nonetheless are not absolute and at times may have to be violated. Although they allow for exceptions, the stringency of the prohibitions is not mitigated because, on the conception sketched here, exceptions—though justified and even required—remain violations. To explicate this notion of *necessary justified violations,* we analyze the concept of exception as a distinct normative category. Exceptional cases, such as emergencies, might require violations of the rules, but these should be performed *as violations*, that is, not as actions performed under the direction of a distinct set of rules or qualifying conditions to regular rules. Thus, dignity does not mean inviolability, but retains the principled resistance toward consequentialist reasoning of the deontological approach.

2 The Elusiveness of Dignity

Dignity is a notoriously elusive concept. Skeptics have disparaged it as "a squishy, subjective notion, hardly up to the heavyweight moral demands assigned to it," or dismissed it altogether, claiming that "dignity is a useless concept."[1] Schopenhauer disdainfully sneers at "that expression, dignity of man," which, he says, "became the shiboleth of all the perplexed and empty-headed moralists who concealed behind that imposing expression their lack of any real basis of morals, or at any rate, of one that had any meaning."[2]

Faced with such elusiveness it is often useful, instead of searching for definitions confronted by counterexamples, to examine a concept through its presumed implications. Dignity has been employed in the service of a wide variety of causes—supporting women's right to abortions, or the criminalization of abortions, for the abolition of slavery, or the continuation of Iran's nuclear program, opposing stem cell research and even the condemnation of licking ice cream. But before rushing to recruit this incoherent mess in support of the skeptics, the central philosophical implications of dignity ought to be investigated.

According to one prominent conception, the attribution of dignity to human beings entails that particularly strict obligations apply with respect to them. Thus, Kant famously wrote in his *Grundlegung*:

> everything has either a price or a dignity. What has a price can be replaced by something else as its equivalent; what on the other hand is raised above all price and therefore admits of no equivalent has a dignity.[3]

---

[1]Pinker (2008).

[2]Schopenhauer (1995), 100.

[3]Kant (1998), 42.

The notion of dignity as incommensurable value is often taken to underwrite the application of inviolable prohibitions. Here is a typical expression of the idea: "any act of torture or other cruel, inhuman or degrading treatment or punishment is an offense to human dignity," states the UN Declaration against Torture from 1975, proceeding to assert that:

> No exceptional circumstances whatsoever, whether a state of war or a threat of war, internal political instability or any other public emergency, may be invoked as a justification of torture.

Moral precepts like the prohibitions against torture or murder are regarded as absolute and non-negotiable, because violating them infringes upon people's dignity. On the basis of this logic, the German Federal Constitutional Court declared in 2006 unconstitutional and void a provision of a new German anti-terrorism law, clearly enacted in light of the attacks of 9/11. The provision authorized the Minister of Defense to order that a passenger airplane be shot down, if it could be assumed that the aircraft was being used against the lives of others and if downing it was the only means of preventing this present danger. The Court ruled that the new law

> ignores the status of the persons affected as subjects endowed with dignity and inalienable rights. By their killing being used as a means to save others, they are treated as objects and at the same time deprived of their rights; with their lives being disposed of unilaterally by the state, the persons on board the aircraft, who, as victims, are themselves in need of protection, are denied the value which is due to a human being for his or her own sake.[4]

This prominent line of thought gives dignity a substantive role, but also gives rise to new doubts, regarding the cogency of such absolute prohibitions. The prohibitions on killing and torture are grounded in the sacredness of life. This sacredness is designed to support the claim that the life of a person ought never to be sacrificed even for the sake of saving the lives of others. This intuition is sometimes grounded in the separateness of individuals and is regarded as a cornerstone of contemporary liberalism.

On the other hand, there is an equally powerful conviction that when the threat is grave, when consequences might be catastrophic, lives may have to be sacrificed and fundamental rights may have to be overridden. This intuitive judgment is often triggered by the invocation of extreme scenarios involving nuclear bombs in urban centers and similar daunting threats. The leading examples consist of situations in which actions that are normally regarded illegal and immoral are necessary means for preventing great harms, usually the death of many people.

It is tedious though necessary to point out the familiar dilemma raised by extreme cases. On the one hand, there are strong deontological intuitions, which

---

[4]BVerfG, 1 BvR 357/05, 59 NJW 2006, 751 [1 BvR 357/05]. For a summary of the case see Lepsius (2006). And see also Harel and Sharon (2011). (Parts of this section build on arguments we developed there).

suggest that we should not torture or kill innocent individuals even if this is necessary for saving lives.[5] The killing of innocent civilians or the torture of any, especially by the state, seems morally and constitutionally intolerable. On the other hand, preventing such disasters is not only the prime task of the state, but also morally mandatory, even though it might involve the violation of what are otherwise deeply entrenched moral prohibitions.[6]

This familiar dilemma has been addressed by two non-consequentialist approaches.[7] The absolutist conception described above holds fast to the idea of inviolability; prohibitions on killing or torture must be upheld irrespective of the consequences.

> we cannot deliberate on whether such measures are justified by the fact that they will avert still greater evils, for as intentional measures they cannot be justified in terms of any consequences whatever.[8]

Others react to this view with horror. Addressing torture, Judge Richard Posner wrote that "no one who doubts that [if the stakes are high enough, it is permissible] should be in a position of responsibility."[9] Michael Walzer reminds us that "we would not want to be governed by men who consistently adopted [the absolutist] position."[10] In light of this obvious concern, the second approach relaxes the stringency of the prohibition without completely resorting to consequentialism. According to this moderate variant of deontology, it is indeed *generally* morally prohibited to murder or torture irrespective of the consequences. Yet, when the consequences are extreme or catastrophic, the prohibitions lose their force and violations are permitted or even obligatory. This view, often called "threshold deontology," maintains that deontological constraints apply so long as the negative consequences remain under a certain threshold. As a matter of principle, it is argued, there must be some ratio of victims to potential victims that would indeed justify extreme and otherwise prohibited measures.[11]

Though the practical implications of threshold deontology align more easily with common-sense judgments, the theoretical shortcomings of this "moderate"

---

[5]On the conflict between absolutist and utilitarian intuitions, see Nagel (1972). The deontological intuition can also be phrased in terms of rights—agents ought not to violate rights even if doing so would lead to more rights being respected. See, e.g., Nozick (2001). See also Harel (2005), 197–201.

[6]As Thomas Nagel put it: "it is certainly right to adhere to absolutist restrictions unless the utilitarian considerations favoring violation are overpoweringly weighty and extremely certain-nevertheless, when that special condition is met, it may become impossible to adhere to an absolutist position." (Nagel 1972, 126)

[7]We ignore here consequentialist approaches which, by denying that the prohibitions are deontological, deny the existence of the dilemma to begin with.

[8]Nagel (1972), 128.

[9]Posner (2004), 295.

[10]Walzer (1973), 162.

[11]For a useful review of the literature, see Zamir and Medina (2008).

deontological position are evident.[12] Threshold deontologists are not faithful to the rationale underlying deontology. After all, deontological theories maintain that people ought never be used "merely as a means." Yet, it seems that according to threshold deontology people are inevitably used as means as long as the ends are weighty enough. Using a person as a means for saving 900 people is strictly prohibited while using a person merely as a means for the sake of saving, say, 1000 people may, according to threshold deontology, be permissible or even mandatory. This means that there is only a conditional or qualified norm prohibiting the use of people merely as a means. This appears to fly in the face of the Kantian rationale of deontology.

The advocate of threshold deontology would presumably protest and deny that threshold deontology ever permits the use of a person merely as a means. Assuming that the threshold is fixed at n innocent lives, the deontologist would maintain that while torturing one person in order to save $n-1$ people (or less) counts as using the person merely as a means (and is thus strictly prohibited), torturing the same person under the same circumstances in order to save n people (or more) is not. The greater number of saved people in the latter case changes the moral characteristics of the act of torture. Instead of being a case of (impermissible) use of a person merely for the sake of promoting the welfare of others (or protecting their lives), it is a (permissible or even obligatory) act in which the tortured person is treated (also) as an end in itself.

Yet the question remains: what transforms the act of killing some for the sake of saving more from an impermissible action (in which a person is used as a means for the sake of saving others) into a permissible one (in which the dead or tortured person is (also) treated as an end in itself). By setting a price above which torture is permissible threshold deontology apparently undermines the Kantian insight that dignity is priceless—incomparable against any other range of goods.[13]

It is told that once at a party, George Bernard Shaw asked a woman if she would go to bed with him for £1000. The woman ummed and ahhed but finally agreed. He then asked if she would go to bed with him for £10. She exclaimed "Do you take me for a whore?" Shaw replied "Madam, we have already established what you are. All we are doing now is arguing about the price." Christopher Kutz employed the same logic to threshold deontology: "Put crudely, once principles have a price all that is left is the bargaining … Threshold deontology does not avoid this embarrassment, but merely pretends it does not exist."[14]

There is nothing incoherent in maintaining that quantitative changes in the number of people saved as a result of an act of torture may change the moral status of the act. Yet, quantitative concerns of the type described by threshold deontology seem to be in tension with its aggregation proscribing rationale. Such quantitative concerns appear on their face to be much more congenial to consequentialist

[12]See Kagan (1998), 78–84; Zamir and Medina (2008).

[13]Kant, *Groundwork of the Metaphysics of Morals* (1998), 435.

[14]Kutz (2007), 256.

reasoning. Thus, while threshold deontology is a coherent position, it is also an unprincipled one—an unprincipled concession to pragmatism and moral intuitions that is hard to square with the deep normative (anti-aggregationist) commitments of deontology.

The deontologist, then, faces a dilemma. Absolutist deontology is faithful to the principled commitments of deontology, namely, the commitment to treating people as ends and the non-aggregative nature of moral demands at the cost of moral fundamentalism. Threshold deontology, on the other hand, avoids moral fundamentalism at the cost of betraying the deep normative promise of deontology—the idea that individuals have dignity and therefore ought never to be used merely as means. It seems right to question whether the real essence of dignity lies in the absoluteness of the moral prohibitions or whether it lies elsewhere.

3 Necessary Violations

The history of moral thought includes a different, though admittedly less prominent, tradition of dealing with extreme cases. This line of thought is a kind of deontological morality insofar as it recognizes moral prohibitions rooted in dignity that transcends consequences, but it subscribes neither to absolutist nor to threshold deontology. Instead, this line of thought focuses on the inherent limitations of rules and the inescapability of exceptions. Introducing a distinction between rule-governed and circumstance-necessitated action, this conception can accommodate necessary violations of moral constraints while preserving their deontological nature. C. A. J. Coady expresses, albeit somewhat crudely, the attitude driving this approach:

> Many contemporary moral philosophers, sympathetic to just-war thinking, are wary of moral absolutes. They would test the prohibition as expressing a very strong moral presumption against terrorism...but allow for exceptions in extreme circumstances.[15]

Our aim in what follows is to give this view a more precise formulation and supply it with some normative foundations. More specifically, we defend the existence of *necessary justified violations* of rules. In the case of such violations, the justifiability of the act hinges on its moral necessity and entails its status as a violation, albeit a justified violation but a violation nonetheless. Such cases are neither rare nor unique. Emergencies, we maintain, are a sub-category of a much broader and less ceremonious category of exceptions.

To illustrate the approach, we begin with a brief discussion of ancient religious jurisprudence. In the Jewish Talmudic tradition, there is a class of acts that are conceived as necessary violations of the law. A notable example relates to the very act of writing of the oral corpus, which was strictly prohibited. In the face of

[15] Coady (2004), 58.

imminent threat that it might be forgotten, writing the oral tradition became an urgent necessity. To justify doing what is strictly prohibited, the Talmud reads a verse from the Psalms as saying: "When it is time to act for the Lord, you violate the law," and concludes "it is preferable that a letter of the law be uprooted than that the whole law should be forgotten."[16]

The Talmudic rendering of the Psalms verse is explicitly non-literal. The verse reads: "Time to act for the Lord, they have broken your law" (*Psalms*, 119: 126). Clearly, this calls upon the faithful to act in the face of violations of God's laws. The Talmud, in a typical hermeneutic maneuver, reverses the logical structure—instead of the violations necessitating action, the necessity of action requires violation. As the great medieval commentator, Shlomo Yitzhaki, had put it "there are times you must violate the words of the law to do for God."[17] This is the Talmud's way of anchoring the notion of necessary violations in scripture.

It is notable that the Talmud characterizes the required act as a violation of the law, albeit a necessary violation. Unlike numerous other instances, where discrepancies between what the law seems to say and what appears to be circumstantially required are explained simply as cases not falling under the jurisdiction of the law or as cases which require an emendation of a law, in the cases where this principle is employed, the actions performed are described as violations. They are contrary to existing norms and are not justified by some competing norm or principle other than the recognition of the necessity of violations under the circumstances. So, the point is that there can be breakings of the law that are necessary to uphold the spirit of the law or its underlying purpose. In such cases, a violation is called for, rather than obedience to the law—a violation which cannot be incorporated into the legal corpus. Such an act, it follows, is—given the circumstances—the "right thing to do"; and yet it is not governed by law, and hence cannot be incorporated into the legal corpus. Furthermore, it is essential that the act be performed *as a violation*. To appreciate this crucial point, let us examine two other sources dealing with necessary exceptions.

In his discussion of law, Aquinas addresses cases in which "the observance of [a] law would be hurtful to the general welfare." When this is the case, Aquinas says, the law "should not be observed." He argues that "the mere necessity brings with it a dispensation, since necessity knows no law."[18]

What does this mean? Aquinas apparently offers two answers. First, he notes the inherent limitations of law:

> It happens often that the observance of some point of law conduces to the common weal in the majority of instances, and yet in some cases is very hurtful. Since, then, the lawgiver cannot have in view every single case, he shapes the law according to what happens more

[16]Babylonian Talmud, Tractate T'murah, 14b.

[17]Babylonian Talmud, Tractate B'rachot 54a.

[18]St. Thomas Aquinas, *Summa Theologiae*, I–II, q. 96, art. 6.

> frequently by directing his attention to the common good. Wherefore, if a case arises wherein the observance of that law would be hurtful to the general welfare, it should not be observed.[19]

This paragraph seems to reiterate the conviction that law is merely a means to an end and when it does not promote the ends that it is designed to promote, it ought not to apply. Given that the law is shaped "according to what happens most frequently", there inevitably will be circumstances in which the law fails to promote the common good. The statistical rarity of the circumstances of necessity and the difficulty or even impossibility of designing laws that take account of these rare circumstances gives rise to the need to deviate from the law in states of necessity.

Aquinas is relying here on what we may call the Aristotelian view of law. In the *Politics,* Aristotle says: "laws speak only in general terms and cannot provide for circumstances" (1286a). Therefore, he concludes, "laws will have no authority when they miss the mark, though in all other cases retaining their authority" (1286a). To "miss the mark" in this context simply means delivering the wrong moral result. Positive laws, devised by human beings, the thought seems to be, are inevitably imperfect. Good laws are designed to address the normal, common situations. They will unavoidably fail with respect to some of the more unusual, irregular instances.

The practical nature of this Aristotelian view, prevalent in the writings of many philosophers and jurists, invites the following question: if the shortcomings of law are rooted in the limitations of human understanding, when an exception *is* known, should not it be incorporated into the law? For instance, suppose we realize that killing of innocents is justified, even required, for the sake of preventing catastrophe, why not amend the law to reflect this qualification? Or, to use Aquinas's own example, if the law forbidding opening the gates after dark should be violated in order to rescue defenders of the city, why not include this as part of the law itself?

David Lyons pressed essentially the same issue against rule utilitarianism.[20] Rule utilitarianism, Lyons argued, ultimately collapses into act utilitarianism. The reason is simple. If moral correctness or value is determined solely by utility, then whenever breaking the rule produces more utility an amendment can be formulated addressing the exception. Since this can be done for any rule and every exception, the final guide for action will be utility. In the same way, laws should strive to guide people's actions, and therefore, when possible, should include qualifications to address unusual circumstances to which the law does not apply.

This takes us to Aquinas's second and more principled idea—"necessity knows no law." Necessity forms according to Aquinas a category of cases which are *as a matter of principle* not legislatable. This seems to be the basis for the claim that violating a law out of necessity is not to "judge of the law."

---

[19]St. Thomas Aquinas, *Summa Theologica*, I–II, q. 96, art. 6. See also II–II, que. 110 art. 1.

[20]Lyons (1965).

> He who in a case of necessity acts besides the letter of the law does not judge of the law but of a particular case in which he sees that the letter of the law is not to be observed.[21]

One way to understand this is that the person who acts in these cases in discordance with the law does not convey in his action a rejection of the law as such in the same way as a person who violates the law under normal circumstances. Aquinas's argument here relies on his reasoning in earlier articles where he stresses that the role of law is not merely to list right and wrong actions, but to direct people toward virtuous action.

> The purpose of human law is to lead men to virtue, not suddenly but gradually. Wherefore it does not lay upon the multitude of imperfect men the burdens of those who are already virtuous, viz., that they should abstain from all evil. Otherwise, these imperfect ones, being unable to bear such precepts, would break into yet greater evils.[22]

This is why Aquinas insists that

> even if a lawgiver were able to take all the cases into consideration, he ought not to mention them all, in order to avoid confusion.[23]

Setting aside Aquinas's dated paternalism, his analysis, like the Talmudic thought before him, suggests a principled distinction between rules and exceptions. Even perfect rules have to be employed by imperfect creatures. Thus, rules made for human consumption will inevitably issue some erroneous judgments. But the law also has expressive and pedagogic functions. At times ordering a person to do the right thing would inevitably fail to educate him or to convey the moral status of the act. In such cases, the law ought to retain its integrity by refusing to incorporate the exception. By retaining the status of an exception, one can maintain the function of the law as an educational tool leading a person to virtue even when the law fails to guide the person to do what she ought to do.

To explain why incorporation of exceptions into the law can corrupt its normative status and consequently its educating function, we must first say a little more about the concept of moral exception.

4 Exceptions

On its face, the concept of exception is paradoxical. If an instance does not fall under the rule, then it is not an exception; it is simply outside the scope of the rule. If on the other hand, it does fall under it, then it is no exception since the rule applies to it. Let us illustrate. If the rule that one must stop at a red light applies to bicycle riders, then they are no exception to the rule. If it does not apply to bicycles,

---

[21] *Summa Theologica* I-II, q. 96 art. 1.

[22] *Summa Theologica* I-II, q. 96 art. 2.

[23] *Summa Theologica* I-II, q. 96 art. 6.

say because the rule is that only motorized vehicles must stop at red lights, then, again, bicycles are not an exception. They are simply outside the scope of the rule. To be a genuine exception, the rule has to apply in some sense, but not in some other sense.

To make sense of the idea of exception, then, one needs a more complex picture of rules. There must be two kinds of relations between the rule and the instances to which it can apply. Think of familiar examples where we show children pictures on a card and ask which one is the exception. Suppose it is pictures of three cars and a motorcycle. The motorcycle differs from the cars, obviously, but it shares with them the property of being one of the images on the card. With this in mind, let us return to our traffic example. If the law is that only motorized vehicles must stop at a red light, then bicycle riders are not an exception. But rushing to a hospital in a car might be. Running a red light when rushing a fatally wounded person to the hospital is a case which falls under the law, but due to the circumstances, may be excepted from its authority.

Thus, one way to think about exceptions to laws is by distinguishing two aspects of rules—the semantic and the normative. Rules apply to instances semantically when, given ordinary linguistic conventions, the instance falls under the description employed in the rule. Thus, since the case in the ticking bomb scenario is one of torture, it falls under the rule "thou shall not torture." However, the normative judgment issued by this rule, namely that one ought not to torture, does not apply to the case. In other words, a particular case can be an instance of a rule in the semantic sense without being an instance in the normative sense.

This raises our earlier question: why maintain a difference between the semantic and the normative aspects of law? Would it not make more sense to amend the law so that its semantic aspect—what it says, will mirror more precisely (or at least as much as possible) its normative import? We have already mentioned pragmatic concerns suggesting that this may not always be possible, that our ability to foresee potential exceptions is ineluctably limited. There are also considerations of simplicity and clarity that may advise against including every qualification explicitly. If the distinction is between the semantic and the normative dimensions of the law, then this is probably about as much as we can say. There is nothing morally pernicious about running a red light in order to save a person's life (while not endangering others, of course). Omitting explicit mention of the example from the letter of the law serves pragmatic interests. But with respect to moral rules and permissible exceptions to them, there seems to be a distinction between two normative dimensions.

Consider another case from the Talmud, concerning the proper way to greet a bride. One school of rabbis says all brides should be praised as "beautiful and graceful." Another school rejects untruthful flattery: "If she was lame or blind, does one say of her: 'Beautiful and graceful bride'? Whereas the Torah said, 'Keep thee far from a false matter.'"[24] Despite this invocation of an explicit verse strongly

[24]Babylonian Talmud, Tractate Kethubot, 17a.

condemning lying, the Talmud endorses the former view arguing that "Always should the disposition of man be empathic with other people." Whether it is empathy or just common decency, the point is familiar: lying, though generally forbidden, might be the right thing to do when people's feelings are on the line, certainly if their lives are hanging in the balance. This does not mean that the case is not a case of lying, or that the prohibition against lying is subordinate to consequences, but rather that there are circumstances which justify (indeed require) making an exception.

This might seem to conflict with deontological thinking, particularly in light of Kant's famous position with respect to lying. In his late polemical article "On the Supposed Right to Lie from Philanthropy",[25] Kant famously defends a particularly strict approach. Disputing Benjamin Constant's claim that lying is sometimes justifiable, Kant apparently claims that the prohibition on lying is absolute; that one ought never lie, even when the life of an innocent person is at stake. This conclusion seems to take deontological reasoning to an unacceptable, some might say ridiculous, extreme.

Perhaps because of its evident absurdity, this essay has become very famous. Less famous however is a seemingly inconsistent view, which Kant defends in his Lectures on Ethics. There too Kant proclaims that "every lie is objectionable and deserving of contempt" (27:448). But then he proceeds to investigate the possibility of necessary violations of the prohibition against lying. Kant recognizes that "if in all cases we were to remain faithful to every detail of the truth, we might often expose ourselves to the wickedness of others, who want to abuse our truthfulness." The possibility of such abuse is the basis for the concept of "necessary lies" which Kant considers "a very critical point to the moral philosopher."

> For seeing that one may steal, kill or cheat from necessity, the case of emergency subverts the whole of morality, since if that is the plea, it rests upon everyone to judge whether he deems it an emergency or not; and since the ground here is not determined, as to where emergency arises, the moral rules are not certain. For example, somebody, who knows that I have money, asks me: Do you have money at home? If I keep silent, the other concludes that I do. If I say yes, he takes it away from me; if I say no, I tell a lie, so what am I to do? So far as I am constrained, by force used against me, to make an admission, and a wrongful use is made of my statement, and I am unable to save myself by silence, the lie is a weapon of defence; the declaration extorted, that is then misused, permits me to defend myself, for whether my admission or my money is extracted, is all the same. Hence there is no case in which a necessary lie is to occur save where the declaration is wrung from me, and I am also convinced that the other means to make wrongful use of it.[26]

[25]Kant (1996a), 8:423–430.

[26]Kant (1997), 27:448.

Lying, then, though strictly, deontologically forbidden, may be permissible when it is "a weapon of defence." Reflecting on this example, it seems that what makes lying "a weapon of defence" under the circumstances is the fact that it is unavoidable since rightful action (telling the truth) will inevitably be abused.

On its face, this position is inconsistent with the one in the article on lying from philanthropy.[27] Without intending to provide an exegesis of Kant's texts, we wish to point out one concern which appears to be driving Kant's argument there, namely the concern that the principle of truthfulness be an "unconditional duty."

Kant's main objective in his essay on lying is to rebuff Constant's claim that right precedes duty and so, according to Constant, the duty of truthfulness applies only to those who have a right to be told the truth. Kant resists this view since

> the duty of truthfulness [...] makes no distinction between persons to whom one has this duty and those to whom one can exempt oneself from it, since it is, instead, an unconditional duty, which holds in all relations. (8:429)

It is important for our purposes to note that Kant stresses

> not the danger of harming (contingently) but of doing wrong generally, as would happen if I make the duty of truthfulness, which is altogether unconditional [...] into a conditional duty subordinate to other considerations.[28]

The problem is "doing wrong generally, which apparently Kant takes to mean acting in a way that fails to affirm the unconditional nature of the principle of truthfulness. *Endorsing a rule* under which lying is sometimes permissible, even if only in extreme circumstances, is turning an unconditional duty into a conditional one. In each and every case in which the agent considers making an assertion, she ought to consider the possibility that the circumstances are such that she ought to lie. In this sense—and this is the crucial point—lying under some directive or principle justifying it "is much worse than committing an injustice to someone or other, since *such a deed does not always presuppose in the subject a principle of doing so*" (ibid, our emphasis).

Kant's emphasis is not on the fact that lying to someone is hurting them or wronging them in some way. Kant recognizes that this need not be the case and, even when it is the case, it may be (morally) unavoidable. Kant's concern, on our reading of these passages, is also not to defend the absoluteness of the prohibition

[27]Our aim here is neither to interpret nor to reconcile these sources. For an attempt to reconcile them, see Wood (2007) ch 14. For helpful references and analysis, see Schapiro (2006), note 3. Let us merely note that most accounts that try to make sense of Kant's position in the article restrict his view there to cases in which the potential victims of one's actions contribute to the threat against one's well-being. This fails to account for an important type of cases in which the potential victims are not part of the threat or when it is not one's own well-being that is threatened but other people's, like the typical ticking-bomb examples.

[28]For Kant a categorical imperative is always "unconditional", see e.g. Kant (1996b), 6:221.

on lying or even the special stringency of the prohibition. It is rather with the idea that lying can be adopted as a principle; that actions which depart from the moral dictate be performed under a principle permitting them.[29] Thus Kant goes on to say that:

> one who asks permission to think about possible exceptions [to the duty not to lie] is already a liar (in potentia); for he shows that he does not recognize truthfulness as a duty in itself but reserves for himself exceptions to a rule that by its essence does not admit of exceptions. (8:430)

By incorporating exceptions to moral laws, one undermines their status as moral laws, i.e., as duties in themselves. Or, in Kant's own words:

> exceptions would nullify the universality on account of which alone they are called principles.[30]

The problem with incorporating exceptions into laws, then, is that it nullifies their moral status by undermining their unconditionality. *Principled* lying, Kant seems to be saying, is never justifiable because if it were, the duty of truthfulness would become a conditional duty.[31] This would entail that lying is not wrong *as such,* but only relative to circumstances, whereas the heart of the deontological conception is that moral wrongs are wrong *in themselves,* irrespective of circumstances. Circumstances can make them permissible and even necessary, but they cannot eliminate their wrongfulness and therefore cannot justify their incorporation as part of the law.

To be sure, Kant does not explicitly (or, for that matter, implicitly) say this. But this is one way of making sense of his distinction between principled and unprincipled, necessitated lying. The distinction opens up the possibility that unprincipled lying—lying that is not based on principle, but is rather dictated by necessity—may be permissible. In any case, the main point is that the fundamental moral wrong is not the act of asserting a known falsehood, but the incorporation of an exception into the duty of truthfulness, even when the exception is not acted upon. By doing so, Kant says, one is in some sense "already a liar." Thus, if, for instance, I incorporate an exception into the rule dictating truthfulness with the knowledge that I will never have to act on it, I am still at fault for not recognizing truthfulness as a duty in itself.

Is not all this mere wordplay? Calling violations principled or unprincipled does not alter the fact that they are violations dictated by circumstances, i.e., by consequences. The issue, indeed, does not turn on how we label these cases. There is, we propose, a genuine moral difference between action performed as a necessary exception and actions to which the law is not taken to apply in the first place. It is

---

[29]For a discussion of the reasons provided by Kant as to why lying is a general wrong: "a wrong inflicted upon humanity generally," see Weinrib (2008).

[30]See Kant (1996b), 6: 221.

[31]In the *Groundwork* Kant contends that a categorical imperative is "limited by no condition" (Kant, *Groundwork of the Metaphysics of Morals* (1998), 4: 416).

the difference between violating a valid moral rule, although with proper justification, and doing a permissible act to which the law does not apply. In other words, if the prohibition against lying is not unconditional, if its validity depends on circumstances, then lying when the circumstances require doing so is fully equivalent to telling the truth in other instances. But this seems wrong, at least with respect to uncontentious moral wrongs like torture or harming innocents.

On this logic, when justified, violations are morally innocuous; there is, so to speak, no moral residue. Incorporating the exception into the law eradicates its status as a genuine exception and puts it on a par with permissible truths. Instances of justified lying are simply outside the scope of the prohibition, just as bicycles are not included in the traffic law mentioned above. But the main point of deontological reasoning is that the moral status of actions is not exhausted by circumstances and consequences. Torturing a person is a pernicious act even if done with the moral justification issuing from the fact that it is necessary in order to avert calamity. The gravity of consequences may make it the case that violation is necessary, and therefore morally justified, but it does not (and should not) eliminate the pernicious nature of the act.

This makes sense of the incommensurability of dignity without reverting to inviolability. To say that something "is raised above all price and therefore admits of no equivalent" means, according to the conception proposed here, not that its value cannot be confronted with other values, but that other values do not outweigh or overcome it. There is no single scale on which both values are assessed such that when one exceeds the other one can speak in terms of net gain or net loss. This is the logic of price, which Kant's conception of dignity rejects. When dignity is at stake, the loss of one value is not compensated for by gains in another.

Due to its dual normative structure, the concept of exception can capture this complexity. When an exception is necessary, morally pernicious action may be justified, while its perniciousness is not denied. Its moral necessity justifies doing the act despite the fact that it falls under a rule forbidding it. It should be performed as a pernicious act which nevertheless one ought to perform. Thus, a necessary act of torture may be justified, but is still an act of torture which remains in principle wrong and prohibited and ought to be done as such, namely as a necessary violation. It is a pernicious, principally forbidden act which must be done in a specific instance.[32]

---

[32]This better captures what both Nagel and Walzer had in mind in the articles mentioned in notes 6 and 11. Nagel writes: "One may find then that one has no choice but to do something terrible. Nevertheless, even in such cases absolutism retains its force in that one cannot claim justification for the violation. It does not become all right." (Nagel 1972, 136–7). Walzer writes: "sometimes it is right to try to succeed, and then it must also be right to get one's hands dirty. But one's hands get dirty from doing what it is wrong to do. And how can it be wrong to do what is right? Or, how can we get our hands dirty by doing what we ought to do?" (Walzer 1973, 164). Instead of Nagel's "absolutism", we would write "deontology" and, more importantly, in contrast to both Nagel and Walzer we believe that justification can be claimed in such cases, otherwise the "terrible" course of action should not be taken. It seems to us incoherent to say that someone must do something but has no justification for doing it. We believe the proposed framework better captures the idea that

This interpretation of the Kantian line of thought is corroborated in Kant's reflections on regicide. Writing about the assassination of Louis XVI and Charles I Kant says that

> the assassination of a monarch is not itself the worst, for we can still think of the people as doing it from fear that if he remained alive he could marshal his forces and inflict on them the punishment they deserve, so that their killing him would not be an enactment of punitive justice but merely a dictate of self-preservation. It is the formal execution of a monarch that strikes horror in the soul filled with the idea of human rights...[33]

There is no doubt that Kant believed that assassinating a monarch, even an unjust one, is a crime. Nevertheless, he draws a clear distinction between an assassination done for "self-preservation" and a "formal execution," done under the guise of a principle (in this case punitive justice). Kant explains the difference:

> The criminal can commit his misdeed either on a maxim he has taken as an objective rule (as holding universally) or only as an exception to the rule (exempting himself from it occasionally). In the latter case he only deviates from the law (though intentionally)... In the first case, however, he rejects the authority of the law itself... and makes it his rule to act contrary to the law.[34]

Deviating from the dictates of the law may be a crime, but adopting a principle or rule that is contrary to the law is far worse, in Kant's view. By adopting a contrary rule, one undermines the law. This of course does not imply that it is ever permitted to deviate from the law. But it does show that Kant has a specific and independent concern with the reasoning behind the act, whether it is an act of necessary violation or one that substitutes a conditional rule for a general one. Whether it is a justified exception or an instance regarded as outside the scope of the prohibition.

This also implies that the exception should not be incorporated into the law as this is tantamount to introducing a new law and rejecting the original, unconditional law. Necessary deviations should never be codified or perceived to be part of the law. Incorporation of exceptions into the law places the exceptions on a par with other legal directives. The law prohibiting the killing of innocents and the law permitting it are on a par, separated merely by variations of circumstance. But, this undermines a crucial difference—only the prohibition on killing innocents is an acceptable principle. Only the forbidding of torture is an acceptable rule, not its sanction. Such actions are, in principle, violations even when they are justified. By legislating norms that legalize the exceptions, legislators undermine their status as exceptional, as cases that exceed the reach of principled, rule-like directives. By acting on an incorporated exception, one not only violates the law but also undermines it. Or, to use Aquinas's terminology, one "judges of the law."

---

the action is "something terrible" without subscribing to the apparent inconsistency which comes out in comments like "We know he is doing right when he makes the deal because he knows he is doing wrong" (ibid 166).

[33]Kant (1996b), 6: 321.

[34]Id.

5 Conclusion: Emergency and Exception

Despite the varieties in the mode of reasoning, the Talmud and Aquinas (both generally favorable toward the use of rules in moral reasoning) can be interpreted to suggest that sometimes a person ought to act in disaccord with rules, even divine rules. Both seem to recognize the unlegislatability of such exceptions—by legislating them they are no longer exceptions but are rather put on a par with the rest of the legal corpus. Kant's contribution to this debate is crucial in that he is explicitly concerned with maintaining the nature of certain rules as unconditional. Kant resists in particular the view that the duty of truthfulness could be made conditional simply because of the dangers to society brought about by truth telling.

Many contemporary jurists also oppose the incorporation of exceptions into legal rules. Often this sentiment is based on the pragmatic concern that by codifying exceptions one provides strong incentives to abuse the codified exception.[35] In other contexts, the opposition to codification is grounded in more principled considerations, often expressed somewhat vaguely or metaphorically. Incorporating exceptions into the law, it is claimed, is against the "genius and spirit of our law"[36]; it is alien to any system of law; it threatens to stretch or deform the law.[37] Jeremy Waldron wrote that in its effort to sanction waterboarding, "The administration does not just take the prisoners to the waterboards; it wants to drag the law—our law—along with them." The Kantian account of unconditionality and its moral significance provides this intuition with theoretical substance—there is a normative distinction between otherwise equivalent acts when performed as morally necessary violations and when done under the guise of a competing norm. We propose that this difference is best captured by the category of exception, in its normative sense.

This idea opens up a new avenue for thinking about emergencies and dignity. We can think of emergencies as cases that give rise to *necessary justified violations*, namely acts that are morally justified but which nevertheless remain violations of moral rules. This has two principal implications, one theoretical and one practical. First, it entails the practical claim that exceptions of this kind should not be incorporated into the law, at least not as standard qualifications of the law. Incorporating them in this way would undermine their status as violations.[38] When it comes to the law, there is an additional element of publicity—the pernicious character of the act should be publicly manifest. Thus, it should not be incorporated into law.

This takes us to the other, theoretical, implication of the view. Moral rules, even deontological rules, are not inviolable. Under extreme conditions, violations may be warranted, indeed required. Nevertheless, justified violations retain the moral significance underlying the general prohibition. Killing innocents or torturing persons

---

[35]See, e.g., Posner (2006), 85–86; Gross (2004), 240.

[36]See, e.g., Waldron (2005), 1719.

[37]Ibid 1741.

[38]We have elaborated on this point in our "Necessity Knows no Law" (Harel 2005).

is an evil act, even when they are justified. Though justified by the circumstances, they are not made innocuous by them. This is what the notion of dignity can be taken to express. To have dignity, as Kant says, is to have a worth that "admits of no equivalent." To respect dignity is to treat it as value not exchangeable for other values. When it is jeopardized—and, as argued above, it may sometimes have to be jeopardized—it is not compensated for by gains in other values. The lives saved by shooting down the plane do not counterbalance those of the passengers on board and the people protected from attack do not offset the moral burden of torture. These are cases in which moral rules ought to be violated. This does not mean, however, that they are invalid or do not apply to these cases; that the moral character of the act, once permissible, is neutral. Necessary violations are, nonetheless, violations. They are morally pernicious acts which, under the circumstances, are morally necessary and hence justified. But it is justified only *as a violation.*

Politically, this suggests that laws grounded in dignity ought to take the form of unconditional rules. When violation is necessary, it is an exception and must be done *as a violation*, dictated by the force of circumstance, not as a legal action, on a par with observation of the law in other circumstances. Maintaining it as an exception, a violation—even if a necessary violation—of the norms, reflects the fact that something of incommensurable value has been sacrificed.

References

Coady CAJ (2004) Terrorism and innocence. J Ethics 8:37

Gross O (2004) The prohibition on torture and the limits of law. In: Levinson S (ed) Torture: a collection. Oxford University Press, UK

Harel A (2005) Theories of rights. In: Golding MP, Edmundson WA (eds) The Blackwell guide to the philosophy of law and legal theory. Blackwell, London

Harel A, Sharon A (2011) Necessity knows no law: on extreme cases and un-codifiable necessities. Univ Tor Law J 61:845

Kagan S (1998) Normative ethics. Westview Press, USA

Kant I (1996a) On a supposed right to lie from philanthropy. In: Practical philosophy (trans: Gregor MJ (ed)) Cambridge University Press, Cambridge, pp 611–615

Kant I (1996b) The metaphysics of morals (trans: Gregor MJ). Cambridge University Press, UK

Kant I (1997) Lectures on ethics (trans: Louis Infield). Cambridge University Press, UK

Kant I (1998) Groundwork of the metaphysics of morals (trans: Gregor MJ). Cambridge University Press, UK

Kutz C (2007) Torture, necessity and existential politics. Calif Law Rev 95:235

Lepsius O (2006) Human dignity and the downing of aircraft: the German Federal Constitutional Court strikes down a prominent anti-terrorism provision in the New Air-Transport Security Act. German Law J 7:761

Lyons D (1965) Forms and limits of utilitarianism. Clarendon Press, UK

Nagel T (1972) War and massacre. Philos Public Aff 1:123

Nozick R (2001) Anarchy, state and Utopia. Wiley-Blackwell, USA

Pinker S (2008) The stupidity of dignity. The new republic. https://newrepublic.com/article/64674/the-stupidity-dignity

Posner RA (2004) Torture, terrorism, and interrogation. In: Levinson S (ed) Torture. Oxford University Press, UK
Posner RA (2006) Not a suicide pact: the constitution in a time of national emergency, 1st edn. Oxford University Press, USA
Schapiro T (2006) Kantian rigorism and mitigating circumstances. Ethics 117:32
Schopenhauer A (1995) On the basis of morality (trans: Payne EFJ). Hackett Publishing, USA
Waldron J (2005) Torture and positive law: jurisprudence for the White House. Columbia Law Rev 105:1681
Walzer M (1973) Political action: the problem of dirty hands. Philos Public Aff 2:160
Weinrib J (2008) The juridical significance of Kant's "supposed right to lie". Kantian Rev 13:141
Wood AW (2007) Kantian ethics. Cambridge University Press, UK
Zamir E, Medina B (2008) Law, morality, and economics: integrating moral constraints with economic analysis of law. Calif Law Rev 96:323

Part II
Risk and Failure of Emergency Legislations

Reconciling International Human Rights Law with Executive Non-trial-Based Counter-Terror Measures: The Case of UK Temporary Exclusion Orders

Helen M. Fenwick

Abstract Non-trial-based measures, in particular executive detention, have at various times been resorted to by democracies as part of their counter-terror strategies. Western democracies are facing an unprecedented rise in 'home-grown' terrorism; the threats they currently face come mainly from their own citizens. Non-trial-based measures—control orders, TPIMs and now temporary exclusion orders—have been designed to test the limits of human rights' law, in particular of the substantive rights to liberty, freedom from torture or inhuman or degrading treatment, and to private life, but to seek to avoid violating them. But in so doing, they have tended to rely on a minimising recalibration of such rights, since the choice has been made not to accompany the measures with derogations, after a derogating measure, detention without trial, for use only against non-citizens, was found to breach aspects of the ECHR in 2004. Post-2005 reliance on more repressive non-trial-based measures that would clearly or possibly have necessitated a derogation has been accepted by Parliament, but not so far actioned. As has been pointed out many times, reliance on such measures, as a recourse running alongside the criminal process, tends to undermine the moral legitimacy of the use of state power as compared to the claims of terrorists and represents a departure from expected and assumed adherence to constitutional values in a democracy. The unease with which democracies approach the use of such measures, especially against their own citizens, is the subject of this paper, which focuses on their use and underuse over the past ten years in the UK. It argues that the desire to maintain constitutionality while protecting security creates compromises which mean that use of such measures satisfies neither objective: a cycle arises within which a more repressive iteration of the measure is introduced unaccompanied by a derogation, necessitating a recalibration of rights to accommodate it, combined with executive self-restraint in deploying it; human rights-based court and Parliamentary decisions

H. M. Fenwick (✉)
University of Durham, Durham, UK
e-mail: h.m.fenwick@durham.ac.uk

P. Auriel et al. (eds.), *The Rule of Crisis*, Ius Gentium: Comparative Perspectives on Law and Justice 64, https://doi.org/10.1007/978-3-319-74473-5_7

then ‘ameliorate’ the measure and normalise it, but at the same time arguably diminish its efficacy and it falls further into dis-use; security concerns then demand the reintroduction of a more repressive iteration of the measure, threatening to restart the cycle.

1 Introduction

This chapter will consider the difficulties faced by the UK and other democracies post-9/11 to maintain adherence to international human rights law while seeking to protect themselves from terrorist attacks. As a pertinent instance, it focuses on the recent attempt in the UK to create such reconciliation in relation to temporary exclusion orders (TEOs). The situation has worsened recently since there has been an unprecedented rise in ‘home-grown’ terrorism; the threats democracies currently face come mainly from their own citizens,[1] who cannot be deported, if they are mono-nationals. The threat at present comes in particular from nationals who have travelled abroad to fight and train with ISIS and then returned to the UK.[2]

Since 9/11, where deportation of suspects was not an option, the UK has turned to certain liberty-invading non-trial-based measures to combat terrorism as well as continuing to use the criminal justice system where suspects can be charged with offences. But non-trial-based measures may tend to fall foul of human rights law and to undermine the moral legitimacy of the use of state power as compared to the claims of terrorists, since they represent a departure from expected and assumed adherence to constitutional values in a democracy.[3]

Therefore, as discussed below, the UK has explored three methods of reconciling such law with the use of those measures. A derogation was used in respect of detention without trial under Part 4 Anti-Terrorism Crime and Security Act (ACTSA) 2001, but it was rejected by the House of Lords in 2004. Recalibrations of rights rather than a derogation were instead relied on in relation to control orders,

[1]E MacAskill and P Johnson The Guardian 1.11.16, interview with Andrew Parker, current Head of MI5: ‘There will be terrorist attacks in Britain… there are about 3000 “violent Islamic extremists in the UK, mostly British”’. “Home-grown” terrorism appears currently to be linked to a change in strategy by ISIS and similar groups, whereby more spectacular, complex operations that can be fairly readily detected by Western intelligence agencies are being abandoned in favour of more minor strikes by small groups against soft targets such as transport hubs, high profile sporting events or shopping centres, where security is weak, as occurred in Paris in November 2015.

[2]See: H Summers *The Guardian* ‘UK faces terror threat from Isis “not seen since IRA bombings”’ 26.2.17: Max Hill QC, the new Independent Reviewer of Terrorism Legislation, ‘expressed fears about the imminent return of hundreds of British jihadis who have been fighting for Isis in Syria’. David Anderson found in December 2016: ‘The Paris attacks of November 2015 and the Brussels bombings of March 2016 demonstrate that former Daesh fighters have formed organised cells, infiltrated Europe and have the capacity—even as Daesh loses territory in its Iraqi and Syrian heartlands—to wreak havoc and destruction [in Europe]’ (The Terrorism Acts in 2015, para 2.7).

[3]See Walker (2010), 1395 and Drumbi (2007), 1165.

introduced in 2005 as the replacement for detention without trial. Such recalibrations of rights seek to reconcile the conflicting aims of preserving security while maintaining the normal level of adherence to human rights, but, as discussed below, mean that the right in question tends to be downgraded—emptied of part of its content.[4] Currently, that reconciliation is sought in relation to TEOs, not via reliance on recalibration, but via the claim that ECHR jurisdictional competence does not apply to the imposition of temporary exclusion orders (TEOs) abroad under the Counter-terrorism and Security Act 2015 part 1 Chapter 2.

Such attempted reconciliations may fail to satisfy either objective—security and rights preservation—fully. This chapter will contend that in respect of executive liberty-invading non-trial-based measures a cycle may therefore arise within which a more repressive iteration of the measure is initially introduced ('heavy touch' control orders in 2005) unaccompanied by a derogation, and necessitating an unacknowledged downgrading recalibration of rights to accommodate it. Such recalibration tends to come to be combined with executive self-restraint in deploying it, partly due to the expense of the subsequent litigation, combined with the strain on the scheme in question it generates, and adverse publicity. Human rights-based court and Parliamentary decisions then 'ameliorate' the measure and normalise it, but at the same time arguably diminish its efficacy, meaning that it falls further into dis-use; security concerns then demand the reintroduction of a more repressive iteration of the measure, threatening to restart the cycle. TEOs (aimed mainly at returning foreign fighters) which have the potential to prevent nationals re-entering the UK for significant periods, may be poised, as will be discussed, at the beginning of that cycle. Or, alternatively, the governmental apprehension that that cycle may arise if TEOs are deployed may be one factor driving their lack of deployment so far.

The cycle described, as discussed below, arose in relation to control orders. Terrorism Prevention and Investigation Measures (TPIMs), their replacement, currently used to curb the activities of terrorist suspects, may be viewed as a softened and more human rights-compliant iteration of a measure on the control orders model. Unlike control orders, TEOs have been designed to attempt to avoid recalibration of ECHR rights on the basis that the UK has no ECHR (or ICCPR) jurisdictional competence in respect of TEO subjects abroad. The potential violations of international human rights law created by TEOs are also more serious.

2 DownGrading Recalibrations of Rights in Post-9/11 UK Non-trial-Based Measures

Minimising human rights via reinterpretation rather than openly departing from them implies that a re-balancing between societal needs and individual rights *should* occur, in effect emptying the right of part of its content via a derogation by

[4]See Fenwick and Philipson (2011).

stealth or by implying new exceptions into it.[5] Under that approach the executive argument tends to be that the *purpose* of counter-terrorism measures should be taken into account in re-determining the ambit of the right in question or the standards demanded under it. Recalibration of rights includes exploiting gaps and ambiguities in domestic and international human rights law in order to rely on attenuated or minimised versions of the rights as necessitated by the nature of the non-trial-based measures in question.

Once the restrictions under such measures are put into practice, the courts are confronted with a situation in which, unless the right is reinterpreted in a minimising fashion, a breach must be found. As is well known, control orders were introduced once detention without trial under part 4 Anti-Terrorism Crime and Security Act 2001 (ACTSA) for non-national terrorist suspects was abandoned, after the House of Lords invalidated the derogation and declared the scheme incompatible with Articles 5 and 14 ECHR.[6] The rise post-9/11 in so-called home-grown terrorism[7] meant that the search for effective executive measures, not including full executive detention as deployed under part 4 ACTSA against foreign nationals, remained a continuing concern. The result of that concern was that a further non-trial-based measure then emerged as a replacement in the form of control orders applicable to suspect nationals and non-nationals under the Prevention of Terrorism Act 2005 (PTA).[8]

Measures on the control orders model rely on targeting terrorist suspects to curtail their liberty without the need for a trial, by imposing specific restrictions on them, related to the particular types of activity it is thought that they might engage in (due to previous behaviour), with the aim of preventing future terrorist activity before it occurs. While reluctance to resort to imprisonment without trial for nationals as well as non-nationals was evident, measures suitable for use against nationals deemed a security risk where prosecution was viewed as problematic,[9] continued to be perceived as warranted. But while control orders were viewed as desirable to preserve security, the repressive nature of the early control orders

---

[5]Fenwick (2011), 153.

[6]*A and Others v Secretary of State for the Home Dept* (2004) UKHL 56.

[7]See note 1 above. See The Home Affairs Committee 'Counter-terrorism' Seventeenth Report, HC 231, 30th April 2014; Secretary of State for the Home Department 'CONTEST The United Kingdom's Strategy for Countering Terrorism Annual Report' Cm 8583, March 2013, p. 8; April 2014, Cm 8848, p. 15. See generally Beutel (2007).

[8]Section 1(1) PTA defined a 'control order' as 'an order against an individual that imposes obligations on him for purposes connected with protecting members of the public from a risk of terrorism'. The orders could be applied to British and non-British suspects alike. Under Section 1 (3), a control order could impose '*any* obligations that the Secretary of State or the court considers necessary for purposes connected with preventing or restricting involvement by that individual in terrorism-related activity'.

[9]Prosecutions are viewed as problematic partly because security material would have to be presented in a criminal trial, which might jeopardise operations, put informers at risk, or breach agreements with other Security Services.

indicated in particular implicit reliance on a downgraded, attenuated version of the right to liberty under Article 5 ECHR, able to accommodate to the needs of the crisis.[10] That might be termed the first stage of the cycle described above. As non-trial-based counter-terror measures, they were designed to approach or possibly overstep the limits of human rights' law, not only of the right to liberty, but also of the rights to fair trial, and to private life, under Articles 6, 8 ECHR. But in so doing, they had to rely on judicial interpretations allowing a minimising recalibration of such rights, since the choice was made *not* to accompany the measures with a derogation. Post-2005 reliance on more repressive non-trial-based measures that would clearly or possibly have necessitated a derogation was accepted by Parliament[11] in the form of derogating control orders but they were never introduced.

In response (the second stage), the courts then relied on the HRA to impose compatibility with the ECHR.[12] Although the courts' response meant that the control orders' scheme had to be modified to achieve greater ECHR compatibility, albeit this time without rejecting it wholesale,[13] the courts partially acquiesced in the notion of finding that the ECHR could accommodate the scheme. The modifications imposed via court action brought it into closer compliance with both Articles 5 and 6 ECHR, meaning that the scheme itself became in various respects, less repressive, but possibly also less effective. In particular, it was found that 18 h house detention a day, combined with other restrictions would breach Article 5 ECHR (the right to liberty), so shorter periods had to be imposed.[14] It was also found under Article 6 (the fair trial right) that in reviewing the imposition of the control order, the gist of the case against the controlee had to be disclosed to him in the proceedings.[15] Since significant interferences with liberty[16] without trial—although not as significant as originally imposed—had been accepted by the courts as compatible with Article 5, such interferences could then be viewed as having received judicial imprimatur.

[10]They imposed a range of restrictions including 18 h house detention a day and forced relocation: see p. 6 below as to early 'heavy touch' control orders. See Fenwick (2011), 153.

[11]The use of derogations from Article 5 ECHR and Article 9 ICCPR was contemplated in relation to derogating control orders introduced under the Prevention of Terrorism Act 2005, but such orders were never introduced.

[12]See *Secretary of State for the Home Department v JJ* [2007] 3 WLR 642.

[13]See in particular *Secretary of State for the Home Department v AP* [2010] 3 WLR 51.

[14]See in particular the decisions in *Secretary of State for the Home Department v JJ* [2007] 3 WLR 642 and *Secretary of State for the Home Department v B and C* [2010] 1 WLR 1542.

[15]See pp. 29–33 below. This was determined in *A v United Kingdom* (2009) 49 EHRR 29 (Grand Chamber) (in relation to Article 5(4)) and applied to domestic law under Article 6 in *Secretary of State for the Home Department v AF (No 3)* [2007] 3 WLR 681.

[16]They included some acceptance of up to 16 h a day house detention: *Secretary of State for the Home Department v JJ* [2007] 3 WLR 642 [105]. That could be combined with forced relocation where no special features particularly 'destructive of family life' arose: *Secretary of State for the Home Department v AP* [2011] 3 WLR 53 [19–24].

The apparent return to 'business as usual' in human rights' terms in which control orders and their review were accepted in modified form in the courts by reference to the ECHR did not preclude the decision under the Coalition government elected in 2010 to abandon them while retaining a version of the control orders *model* in more Article 5-compliant TPIMs under the Terrorism Prevention and Investigation Measures Act 2011.[17] The Coalition government, obviously influenced by the Liberal-Democrats, clearly viewed an executive non-trial-based scheme of this nature as only tolerable if the obligations imposed were confined to very 'light touch' ones (this could be seen as the third stage). Under TPIMA, the obligations that could be imposed (under the original iteration of TPIMs) were much more limited; they are clearly designed to ensure that Article 5 was very unlikely to be breached, taking account of the control orders case-law. The lengthier house detention requirements under control orders were relaxed, becoming only an 'overnight residence requirement',[18] and the relocation provisions were dropped under the original iteration of TPIMs. But the softened version of control orders that TPIMs represented also gave rise to concerns that they were not effective enough in security terms. In particular, the perception that TPIMs might be ineffective to meet an emergency led to the introduction of enhanced TPIMs, replicating 'heavier touch' (possibly derogating) control orders, in the ETPIMs Bill 2012, but the Bill has not yet been enacted.[19]

Control orders were underused[20] and were accused of inefficacy after a small number of controlees absconded;[21] that was also the case in respect of TPIMs but to a greater extent, reaching a point in 2016 at which only one TPIM was in force[22] and leading to the criticism that they were too ineffective to deploy.[23] Their lack of

---

[17]TPIMA Section 1 provided for repeal of the PTA. Following the model of Part 4 ACTSA preventive detention, control orders were imposed by the Home Secretary, but with court review, on the basis of reasonable suspicion; that model was also used for TPIMs except that the standard was that of 'reasonable belief'. See further on court challenges to control orders and TPIMs pp. 25–34 below.

[18]See Sched 1 para 1, TPIMA.

[19]For discussion of ETPIMs see Fenwick (2013), 877.

[20]See David Anderson QC (previous) Independent Reviewer of the Prevention of Terrorism Act (PTA) pursuant to Section 14(6) PTA 'Control Orders in 2011' Seventh Report March 2012 p. 5. By the end of 2011, 9 control orders were in force. 52 persons had been subjected to them between 2005–11 (p. 4).

[21]See BBC online 'Three on control orders abscond' 27.5.07. But David Anderson found in 2012 that no controlees had absconded for the previous 3 years (ibid, p. 5).

[22]Their use was 'Withering on the vine as a counter-terrorism tool of practical utility': JCHR, 'Post-legislative scrutiny: Terrorism Prevention and Investigation Act 2011' Tenth Report of Session 2013–2014, HL 113 HC 1014, January 2014 at p. 5. In March 2016 only 1 TPIM was in force; it appeared to relate to the claimant EB who was to have his Section 9 review of the TPIM, consolidated with his appeal against the TPIM under s16: see *EB v Secretary of State for the Home Department* [2016] EWHC 137 (Admin).

[23]Two TPIM subjects absconded in 2012 and 2013. Yvette Cooper, then Shadow Home Secretary said on this [see Watt (2014)]: 'There are currently no Tpims in use because the experts have warned that the police and the security services do not believe they are effective enough to be worth using…'. The Home Affairs Committee 'Counter-terrorism' Seventeenth Report, HC 231,

use, partly due to their perceived inefficacy, led to the recommendation that they needed strengthening (the fourth stage),[24] which occurred under the Counter-Terrorism and Security Act 2015 (CTSA): in particular, the forced relocation obligation previously available under control orders was reinstated.[25] The recent strengthening of TPIMs appears to have led to a certain revival of their use in 2016,[26] and may have played a part in the renewal of TPIMA, to 2021.[27] Thus, the saga of the use of the control orders model has gone through a number of stages, eventually achieving a degree of reconciliation with human rights law not evident when the PTA was introduced in 2005. As discussed below, TEOs seek to achieve reconciliation with human rights norms by a different method, which is less likely, it will be argued, to lead to a gradual tempering of the scheme, on the lines of the saga just discussed.

3 Reconciling TEOs with Human Rights' Norms

TEOs borrow a number of features from control orders and TPIMs and were also introduced alongside newly strengthened TPIMs in CTSA; they are imposed by the Home Secretary, with court review, on a low standard of proof—reasonable suspicion—but enable individuals to be subjected to significant restrictions on liberty.

30th April 2014 ('Counter-terrorism Seventeenth Report'), para 109 found that TPIMs need to be strengthened to prevent absconding. Yvette Cooper observed: 'We warned from the start that weakening these crucial counter terror powers was a serious error of judgement by the Home Secretary (Press Release 5th November 2013; http://www.politicshome.com/uk/article/87796/sign_up_pro.html. HC Deb Vol. 585, Cols 24–6, 01.09.14).

[24]The Government had previously stated that it intended to carry out a review of TPIMs as part of a broader review of counter-terrorism powers: JCHR 'TPIMA 2011' note 22, para 82. David Cameron's Task-force for Tackling Violent Extremism had also recommended a range of changes in 2013: 'Tackling Extremism in the UK', December 2013; https://www.gov.uk/government/uploads/system/uploads/attachment_data/file/263181/ETF_FINAL.pdf. Reinstatement of relocation had been recommended in 2014 by David Anderson, the previous independent reviewer of terrorism legislation: 'Terrorism Prevention and Investigation Measures in 2013' Second Report March 2014, at p. 57, recommendation 4.

[25]Section 16 CTSA 2015 amended schedule 1 of the Terrorism Prevention and Investigation Measures Act 2011. That was the most significant change in terms of strengthening TPIMs among the other changes made by CTSA to TPIMs.

[26]Between 1.6.16–31.8.16 6 notices came into force, 5 in respect of British citizens: Memorandum to the Home Affairs Committee: Post-Legislative Scrutiny of the Terrorism Prevention and Investigation Measures Act 2011, October 2016, Cm 9348, para 37.

[27]TPIMA has been renewed until 2021: see the Terrorism Prevention and Investigation Act 2011 (Continuation) Order 2016 made under s21 CTSA, which extended the Secretary of State's TPIM powers, due to expire on 14.12.16, for a further five years, until 13.12.21.

Since they rely on excluding citizens from the UK for a temporary period, they represent more dramatic measures than control orders/TPIMs—in the sense of departing further from accepted norms—so they potentially create a stronger conflict with international human rights law.

But reliance on TEOs to exclude nationals from the UK, thereby seeking to suspend their entitlement to rely on the ECHR for a period, takes a step beyond the recalibrations of rights seen in relation to control orders. TEOs were presented to Parliament as reconcilable with human rights' norms *not* through recalibrations of human rights, or due to reliance on a derogation, but via the argument that by preventing TEO subjects from entering the UK they are, for a time, outside the UK's ECHR jurisdictional competence. The extent to which, if at all, that argument is likely to prove successful is explored below, as are the range of potential rights' violations that could arise due to reliance on TEOs.

4 The Introduction of TEOs as Opposed to Deprivation of Citizenship Orders

The designation of the terror threat level was raised from substantial to severe in 2014[28] and in that year, in the wake of atrocities committed by ISIS, and in relation to fears that returnees from fighting with or supporting ISIS would receive training abroad and would seek to mount terror attacks in Britain,[29] or radicalise others, the Prime Minister announced that the Government would bring forward a 'discretionary power to allow us to exclude British nationals from the UK'.[30] Thus the Conservative leadership originally considered including provision in the 2015 Act to strip persons who had gone to fight with or support ISIS of citizenship, even if they were born in Britain and of mono-citizenship.[31] The introduction of TEOs thus represents a compromise: that original proposal from David Cameron as to

[28]On 29 August 2014 (see MI5 Press Release 'Threat level to the UK from international terrorism raised to severe' https://www.mi5.gov.uk/home/news/news-by-category/threat-level-updates/threat-level-to-the-uk-from-international-terrorism-raised-to-severe.html).

[29]Theresa May (second reading, House of Commons 2.12.14 Col 207) 'We face the very serious prospect that British nationals who have fought with terrorist groups in Syria and Iraq will seek to radicalise others, or carry out attacks here. We have already seen the appalling murder of four civilians outside the Jewish Museum in Brussels, and the recent attack on the Canadian Parliament was a shocking reminder that we are all targets for these terrorist organisations and those whom they inspire'.

[30]Hansard 1 Sep 2014: Column 26. *Official Report*, 1 September 2014; Vol. 585, c. 26.

[31]Consideration of the practicality of withdrawal of citizenship was recommended by the Home Affairs Committee 'Counter-terrorism Seventeenth Report', HC 231, 30 April 2014, paras 96–100.

permanent exclusion from the UK eventually evolved into the introduction of temporary exclusion orders in the Counter-Terrorism and Security Act 2015.[32]

So the government accepts at present—as far as this Act is concerned—that it would be hard to persuade Parliament to introduce measures *permanently* excluding UK nationals from returning to the UK because that would amount to a deprivation of their right to return and to live in the country of their nationality, contrary to international law, as discussed below. TEOs are, therefore, mainly aimed at addressing and neutralising the risk posed by a number of returnees from ISIS-held territory; their various elements, discussed below, appear to have varying levels of connection with that aim.

5 TEO Imposition Requirements

TEOs can be imposed on persons who have a right of abode in the UK and are outside the UK,[33] if the Secretary of State reasonably suspects that the individual is, or has been, involved in terrorism-related activity (TRA) outside the UK.[34] He or she must also reasonably consider that it is necessary to impose a TEO for purposes connected with protecting the public in the UK from a risk of terrorism.[35] 'Terrorism' has the meaning given to it in section 1(1) of the Terrorism Act 2000 (TA).[36] Thus the TA and CTSA must be read together.

Imposition of a TEO is initially in executive hands, and court permission is not then needed if the case is urgent, as it normally would be.[37] The model of imposition used is based partly on the wording used in the PTA and TPIMA for

[32]In the Home Affairs Committee 'Counter-terrorism Seventeenth Report,', HC 231, 30th April 2014, para 98 et seq government proposals for removing British citizenship from foreign terror suspects, leaving them stateless (by Clause 18 of the Immigration Bill 2014), were considered; however, the plans were criticised for being reactive policy-making (para 101) and the House of Lords rejected the amendment (HL Deb, Vol. 753, Col 1167, 7th April 2014). The Home Affairs Committee further observed that even if the plans were implemented, it would still be necessary to find a state willing to receive them and that this fact might limit the utility of such a measure (para 101).

[33]Section 2(5), (6) Conditions C and D. The right of abode arises under the Immigration Act 1971, Section 2.

[34]Section 2(3), Condition A for imposing a TEO. TRA is defined in Section 14(4) and in schedule 1.

[35]Section 2(4) Condition B.

[36]Section 14(2) CTSA. The TA Section 1(1) provides that 'terrorism' means the use or threat, 'for the purpose of advancing a political, religious or ideological cause', of action 'designed to influence a government or to intimidate the public or a section of the public', [Section 1(1)(b)] which 'involves serious violence against any person or serious damage to property, endangers the life of any person', or 'creates a serious risk to the health or safety of the public or a section of the public', or 'is designed seriously to interfere with or seriously to disrupt an electronic system'.

[37]Section 2(7). Condition E is that court permission for the TEO has been given, unless the Secretary of State reasonably considers that the case is urgent: see note 116 below.

imposing control orders and TPIMs. The standard of proof required to impose a TEO is that of reasonable suspicion, as for control orders, a lower standard than that of reasonable belief,[38] the standard initially used for imposition of TPIMs, which has now, however, been raised to the civil standard by the 2015 Act.[39] Reasonable suspicion represents the lowest standard of proof used post-9/11 in the UK for non-trial-based measures.

6 Restrictions Imposed: Varying Roles of TEOs

During the period when the TEO is in force, various restrictions can be imposed. The TEO comes into force when the individual is given notice of its imposition,[40] although notice can be deemed to have been given even if it has not in fact been given.[41] At that point, the passport held by the excluded individual is automatically invalidated.[42] A TEO can remain in force after return to the UK,[43] permitting obligations to be imposed after return.

6.1 Temporary Exclusion from the UK

A significant restriction imposed on the individual subject to a TEO under Section 2 (1) CTSA is that he or she cannot enter the UK for a period of time once the TEO comes into force, until a permit to return is issued. The scheme is backed up by criminal sanctions, including the threat of up to five years' imprisonment if the individual returns to the UK in contravention of the restriction on return specified in the order, without reasonable excuse.[44] The individual can be given a permit to

---

[38]*Secretary of State for the Home Department v CC, CF* [2012] EWHC 2837. In finding that reasonable belief imposes a higher threshold than that which previously applied under the PTA—reasonable suspicion—reliance was placed on *A and Others v Secretary of State for the Home Department* [2005] 1 WLR 414 at [229]; *R v Saik* [2006] 2 WLR 993 was also referred to, in which Lord Brown observed that 'to suspect something to be so is by no means to believe it to be so: it is to believe only that it may be so' [120].

[39]Section 20(1) CTSA, amending Section 3(1) TPIMA.

[40]Section 4(3)(a).

[41]The suspect must be given notice of the imposition of the TEO (Section 13) except where S.I. 2015/438 Temporary Exclusion Orders (Notices) Regulations 2015 applies. This provision about notice could cover the situation in which intelligence indicates that the suspect is in ISIS-held territory or may be seeking to return to the UK, but at present the suspect's whereabouts are not known.

[42]Section 4(9). Under Section 4(10) while it is in force, 'the issue of a British passport to the excluded individual while he or she is outside the United Kingdom is not valid'.

[43]Section 9(3)(b).

[44]Section 10(1).

return to Britain under Section 5 *if* he or she complies with the conditions specified in the permit.[45] If an individual fails to accept such a condition, he/she could then remain excluded from the UK for a period of time, which could be up to two years under s4(2)[46] or more on renewal of the TEO.[47] That possibility is, however, subject to the provisions of Section 6(1) below.

The possibility that a person could be excluded from the UK for a period of years due to non-compliance with conditions imposed is subject to the provision of Section 6(1) which covers the situation in which the TEO subject applies for a permit. If so, it *must* be issued within a 'reasonable period' following an application, but *only if* the TEO subject complies with a requirement that can be imposed by the Secretary of State—and is likely to be made a condition of return in most instances—to attend an interview with a police officer or immigration official at a time and a place specified by the Secretary of State.[48]

So the 'temporary exclusion' aspect of TEOs amounts to this: the applicant, unless issued with a permit to return almost immediately after imposition of the TEO, would be excluded from the UK for some weeks or possibly months; that period of exclusion would be likely to apply to most suspects. But if he or she does not apply for a permit or refuses to attend the interview that period could be two years or more. No ultimate time limit is specified in the Act as to the full period of time during which a person can be subjected to a TEO.

The provisions bearing on the period of exclusion from the UK under Section 5 are thus markedly imprecise: they appear to have been passed by Parliament before the scheme had reached a fully developed stage, suggesting that the more draconian scheme Section 5 envisages is unlikely to be deployed in practice.

It is argued that the temporary exclusion aspect of TEOs may appear to have certain advantages. As TEO subjects would be outside the UK, the state takes the stance that it does not have jurisdictional competence for ECHR purposes, as discussed below, meaning that the UK need not take responsibility for the suspect for a period. No provision is made in CTSA as to their detention abroad, leaving the returnee to the responsibility of a host state which might not maintain the same standard of rights' protection as the UK.

Also the threat of being debarred from the UK for a period, which could be substantial, might persuade returnees to attend the interview abroad when otherwise many of them would probably refuse to do so, given their obviously disaffection and adherence to an extreme anti-democratic and anti-Western ideology. However, it is unclear that the threat of exclusion from the UK for long periods is needed to

---

[45]Section 5(2).

[46]Under Section 4(3) the TEO can remain in force for a period of two years, unless it is revoked or otherwise brought to an end earlier.

[47]The TEO can be renewed after it has expired, if the relevant conditions in Section 2(1) apply: Section 4(8).

[48]Section 6(2).

provide an incentive to attend the interview; given that returnees cannot be compelled to make admissions during it, they might view attendance as a small price to pay to return quickly.

In the short term, exclusion would also mean that the returnee would not be able to engage in terrorist activity in person in the UK while detained, which might be for a considerable period of time, and any conspiracies he might have engaged in on return would be disrupted. But, clearly, detention does not provide a satisfactory solution to the problem of the risk returnees pose: they could pose a risk to the state they are in, or to other states, so excluding them from the UK would fail to discharge the UK's general responsibility to combat terrorism, globally, a point that is pursued below. Further, the very existence of the exclusion aspect of TEOs might deter suspects from seeking to return *at all* from fighting with ISIS or similar groups, but again that would not comport readily with that responsibility.

6.2 Management of the Return

Management of the return of the suspect has been put forward as the main aim of TEOs. The permit to return must make specific provision about the time, manner and place of return to the UK,[49] meaning that the suspect's return is monitored and notified to border officials or police. His or her return is disallowed, except as set out in the permit to return. He or she could also be added to 'no fly' lists. The interview abroad could enable an evaluation of the risk posed by the TEO subject to be evaluated. But the other conditions that can be specified are not set out in the Act; instead, details about permitted obligations may be provided for in regulations, subject to the negative resolution procedure (Section 13); so far, however, the regulations have not been introduced. Under Section 5(3), the individual's failure to comply with a specified condition has the effect of invalidating the permit to return.

6.3 "Permitted Obligations" After Return

The intention is not only to enable the authorities to *manage* the return of the suspect to the UK but to seek to ensure that returnees are monitored *before* return so that any security risk they pose can be addressed after return. 'Permitted obligations' can be imposed by notice on the TEO subject under Section 9(1) CTSA when they have returned to the UK.[50] The 'obligations' refer to a range of conditions

---

[49]Section 5(4).

[50]Outlined in Section 9(2). The notice imposing the obligations comes into force when given to the individual and continues in force until the TEO ends [s9(3)].

listed in Section 9 arising under Schedule 1 Terrorism Prevention and Investigation Measures Act (TPIMA) 2011.

The conditions imposed under Section 9(2) could include being required to report to a police station, to notify the police of the place of residence and as to changes of address[51] and attend an appointment, which can now include attending de-radicalisation programmes.[52] These are the less intrusive obligations capable of being imposed under TPIMA, but it is notable that they can be imposed on a lower standard of proof under the 2015 Act than the standard that would be required under TPIMA.

7 International Human Rights Obligations: TEOs and de Facto Statelessness?

Under the Universal Declaration of Human Rights Article 15(1), everyone has the right to a nationality and Article 15(2) provides that 'No one shall be arbitrarily deprived of his nationality'.[53] The UK is also bound by the 1961 Convention on the Reduction of Statelessness, which provides measures to prevent the creation of new cases of statelessness.[54] It has also been recognised as a fundamental principle of the common law,[55] and in the provision against exile in Magna Carta, that an individual should be free to reside in his own land.[56] These measures appear to rule out permanent exclusion of UK citizens from the UK if it is to continue to adhere to its human rights' obligations. France also contemplated but recently ruled out exclusion of French ISIS-supporters on that basis.[57]

TEOs could, however, be said to place persons in limbo for a period of time as far as their nationality is concerned,[58] with no territory to return to for a period,

[51]Section 9(2) CTSA refers to Schedule 1 to the Terrorism Prevention and Investigation Measures Act 2011 para 10.

[52]Paragraph 10A was inserted by Section 19 CTSA.

[53]See for discussion Mirna and Harrington (2008).

[54]See Gibney (2014) spec. 61–62.

[55]In *Pham v Secretary of State for the Home Dept* [2015] UKSC 19 Lord Mance stressed that the status of citizenship is 'as fundamental at common law as it is in European and international law' (para 97) and referred to the right to reside in or return to the UK as 'a constitutional right' of the citizen.

[56]See clause 39 of Magna Carta which states: 'No free man shall be … outlawed or exiled'. See also Dominic Grieve's comments on this issue: 2nd reading HC 2 Dec 2014, Column 228.

[57]The Constitutional Reform Bill came before the Senate in France on 10.2.16 and a clear majority of MPs in the lower House of Parliament approved the measures, which included removing citizenship from French national convicted terrorists, but they were abandoned on 30.3.16 after criticism from the President's own party.

[58]Dominic Grieve has said on this point: 'the proposal could be in breach of our international legal obligations by rendering a person stateless' (Hansard, 2 Dec 2014: Col 228).

except the community of fighters termed ISIS (or a similar group). The group of fighters making up ISIS and living in the 'Caliphate' is not recognised as a state. But given that once suspects attend an interview they must be allowed to return within a reasonable time; the statutory provisions make it clear that the intention is not to revoke citizenship and is to accept them back into the UK after what would probably be quite a brief period. Thus, the impact of TEOs may be said to bear very little resemblance to a rendering a person stateless within the meaning of the 1961 Convention.

8 Reliance on the ECHR—Territoriality and Jurisdictional Competence

The 2015 Act was passed with the assurance from the Home Secretary—via the Section 19 HRA statement of compatibility and the ECHR memo accompanying CTSA part 1 Chapter 2—that the provisions are Convention-compatible.[59] The statement of compatibility rested on a jurisdictional barrier to reliance on the ECHR rights by a TEO subject from abroad, put forward by the government. It was put forward on the basis that since the subjects would be outside the territory, and therefore jurisdiction of the UK for a period of time they would not be able to rely on the ECHR against the UK during that time—Article 1 ECHR.

It appears, therefore, to be assumed under the TEO provisions—although this is only made explicit in the ECHR memorandum[60]—that a detention abroad and any potential violation of the ECHR resulting from the imposition of the TEO would be the responsibility of the host state in question, not of the UK, and would be under that state's laws.

[59]The ECHR memorandum accompanying CTSA stated that under Article 1 ECHR the UK would not have jurisdictional competence in relation to citizens subjected to a TEO abroad: The ECHR memorandum (BILLS (14–15) 059), para 10: 'TEOs may only be imposed on subjects outside the UK. As such, the ECHR is not directly engaged'. See also Counter-Terrorism and Security Bill—Temporary Exclusion Orders', IA No: HO0144, 21 November 2014.

[60]Ibid; at [12] of the ECHR memo: 'That the ECHR does not apply extra-territorially applies *a fortiori* in respect of temporary exclusion as opposed to deprivation. Compared with deprivation, temporary exclusion involves manifestly less significant interference with an individual's ability to request the UK's assistance overseas or to travel to the UK'. The memo points out that in *S1, U1 and V1 v SSHD* (SIAC judgment of 21.12.12) SIAC found that depriving dual nationals of citizenship while they were in Pakistan did not engage the ECHR.

8.1 Exceptions to the Territoriality Principle

In international human rights law in general, the scope of human rights' obligations is essentially determined by territoriality, but there are certain exceptions whereby states may be found to have such obligations beyond their borders to persons not on the state's territory but within the power or effective control of the state.[61] The Strasbourg jurisprudence on the congruence between territoriality and jurisdictional competence has been somewhat erratic, but has moved towards that position. Article 1 ECHR sets limits on the reach of the Convention since it only applies to everyone within the 'jurisdiction' of a contracting party,[62] and that term originally appeared to refer to the legal *territory* of the contracting states.[63] But the concept of territoriality has to an extent given way to a concept of jurisdiction not in all circumstances dependent on the presence of the individual in question within the physical territory of a contracting state, although a state's jurisdictional competence remains primarily territorial.[64] The territorial reach of the ECHR under HRA, as opposed to that of the ECHR as determined at Strasbourg, appears to mirror the concept of 'jurisdiction' as interpreted at Strasbourg, but not to be intended to go further than it does.[65]

Two exceptions to the link between jurisdictional competence and territoriality can be found. First—a state can be found to have jurisdiction when it exercises effective control due to military force over an area outside its national territory. The first exception is unlikely at present to apply in respect of imposing TEOs since at present the UK does not have ground troops controlling relevant territory. If in future that position changed and the UK controlled some areas of territory

[61]See HRC General Comment No. 31 'Nature of the General Legal Obligation imposed on State Parties to the Covenant' 26.5.04 UN Doc CCPR/C/21/Rev.1/Add.13 (2005); the ICJ 'Legal Consequences of the Construction of a Wall in the Occupied Palestinian Territory' Advisory Opinion 9 July 2004, ICJ Report 136, at paras 109 and 111. See for discussion See Duffy (2015).

[62]Article 1 of the ECHR provides '[t]he High Contracting Parties shall secure to everyone within their jurisdiction the rights and freedoms defined in Section I of this Convention'.

[63]That assumption appeared to be made by some contracting states in the first 20 years approx. of the ECHR's existence (*Cyprus v Turkey* (First and Second Applications) Nos 6780/74 and 6950/75 2 DR 125 (1975)); jurisdiction referred to the concept of 'ratione loci'; it operates as a separate ground of admissibility of complaints.

[64]*Bankovic and others v Belgium* ECHR 2001-XII, para 70.

[65]*Regina v. Secretary of State for Foreign and Commonwealth Affairs (Appellant) ex parte Quark Fishing Limited (Respondents) Regina v. Secretary of State for Foreign and Commonwealth Affairs (Respondent) ex parte Quark Fishing Limited (Appellants) (Conjoined Appeals)* [2005] UKHL 57 applied the 'mirror principle' under the HRA to territoriality. Lord Bingham (para 25) emphasised that the HRA's purpose was not to expand Strasbourg remedies: 'The territorial focus of the Act is clearly shown by the definition of "the Convention" in Section 21 to mean the European Convention as it has effect for the time being in relation to the United Kingdom'.

previously controlled by ISIS, then if troops captured prisoners, some of whom might be British fighters,[66] the UK *would* have jurisdictional competence for ECHR purposes. While TEOs could still be imposed on them, the UK would have to accept that any actions taken would be constrained by adherence to the ECHR. However, the current actions in Syria and in Iraq do not suggest that the involvement of UK ground troops in future is likely.

Second, a state can have jurisdictional competence where its agents exercise authority and control over a person on the territory of another state as found in *Al-Skeini and others v UK*.[67] This exception relates to personal control, not territorial control. The Home Office in the ECHR memo appears to have contemplated this exception. It relied on *Khan v UK*[68] which concerned a dual national suspected of TRA, who had been placed in immigration detention, but had then left the UK voluntarily for Pakistan. While there his leave to remain was cancelled. In finding his application inadmissible, the Court found that the exceptions to territoriality, giving the UK jurisdictional competence, did not apply since Khan had departed voluntarily and was not under the control of British officials in Pakistan. Nevertheless, the government's assumption as to jurisdiction is open to doubt; it did not appear to take full account of the extent to which the concepts of territoriality and of jurisdictional competence do not fully cohere.

The situation of the applicant in *Khan* was not entirely analogous to that of TEO subjects abroad. While they have also left the UK voluntarily, the imposition of the TEO by the Home Secretary is likely to lead to detention in the host state. Further, the TEO subject's ties with the UK are stronger than those of a dual national in Khan's position, since there is no basis for stripping the subject of citizenship. In contrast to the position in *Khan,* they are not likely to be able to move around freely in the host state, and British officials may have some involvement in the detention, not least due to the initial imposition of the TEO. Even if officials of the host state impose a detention following imposition of the TEO, that detention would flow from its original imposition. So any detention abroad would be causally linked to the original imposition by the Home Secretary of the TEO, whether the detention

[66]*Banković and Others v. Belgium and Others* [GC] (dec.), no. 52207/99, ECHR 2001-XII. NATO forces had bombed a Radio station building in Belgrade, killing members of the families of the applicants. The Grand Chamber came to the conclusion that there was no jurisdictional link between the persons who were victims of the act complained of and the respondent States. That was on the basis that jurisdiction was mainly territorial subject to special exceptions where one state exercised authority by agreement with another or had occupied an area of another state; but those exceptions did not apply. Further, while an exception existed where a contracting state exercised effective control on the territory of another contracting state that could not apply in Iraq. Thus, the exception was only found to apply within the '*espace juridique*' or the 'legal space of the contracting parties of the ECHR' (para 80).

[67]See the leading decision in *Al-Skeini and others v UK* 7 July 2011 Application no. 55721/07, cf the *Chagos Islanders* case ECtHR 4th Section, 11 December 2012. For discussion see Milanovic (2012).

[68]Application No. 11987/11, decision of 28.1.2014.

abroad was organised by British officials (with agreement with the authorities in the host state, or partly by such officials, together with those of the host state, or entirely by the officials of that state. Determinations in future as to ECHR jurisdiction in respect of TEO imposition may, however, depend on the *way* that TEOs are administered abroad. It could be found that due to an agreement with the host state, British officials were exercising executive public powers in imposing TEOs combined with conditions, on the territory of another non-contracting or contracting state. But if British officials are not directly involved in exercising authority and control on another state's territory, it might be found that UK jurisdictional competence did not arise.

As indicated, the jurisprudence relates to actual control over the applicant—personal control as opposed to territorial control—by state agents operating *physically* on the territory of another state—as in *Occalan v Turkey*[69] 'directly after being handed over to the Turkish officials by the Kenyan officials in Kenya, the applicant was under effective Turkish authority and therefore within the 'jurisdiction' of Turkey. In *Al-Skeini v UK* it was found: 'it is clear that, whenever the State through its agents exercises control and authority over an individual, and thus jurisdiction, the State is under an obligation under Article 1 to secure to that individual the rights and freedoms under Section 1 of the Convention that are relevant to the situation of that individual'.[70]

The situations in these instances differ from those likely to arise in respect of TEO imposition abroad since the intention appears to be that another state's officials would take responsibility for the TEO subjects. All might be found to depend on the closeness of involvement of UK officials in the imposition of the TEO, and in subsequent arrangements such as organising the interview abroad. Such involvement might accord the UK jurisdictional competence. Or a court might accept that such competence arose due to the initial exercise of authority and control inherent in imposing the TEO, even if British officials did not themselves detain the TEO subject abroad.

On that basis, the UK may not be able to divest itself of responsibility for the treatment of TEO subjects on the basis of reliance simply on territoriality. That might be found under the HRA if a TEO-based claim eventually reached a domestic court. If a claim is eventually heard in the Strasbourg Court, the argument might proceed on the basis—which would not be relevant domestically—that since in deploying TEOs the UK is out of line with the rest of Europe, and Western democracies generally, a stricter approach might be taken to the application of Article 1 due to the lack of consensus on the issue.[71]

---

[69] *Öcalan v Turkey* (Grand Chamber) [2005] ECHR 46221/99, 12 May 2005. See also *Andreou v Turkey* Appl No 4653/99 ECtHR (2008); *Ilascu and others v Molodova and the Russian Federation* Appl No 48797/99 ECtHR Judgment of 8 July 2004.

[70] Emphasis added, at paras 136–137.

[71] For discussion see Dzehtsiarou (2015), especially Chap. 2.

8.2 *Routes to Reliance on the ECHR for TEO Subjects Abroad*

So there may be two main routes to reliance on the ECHR for TEO subjects outside the UK. First, it may be found domestically under the HRA,[72] or eventually at Strasbourg, that reliance on the device of a TEO is not enough to defeat a finding that the UK had jurisdictional competence in relation to the citizen in question while outside the UK because potential rights violations abroad that could be expected to follow imposition of the TEO are so closely causally related to its imposition, following *Al-Skeini but* dependent on the degree of authority exercised.

Second, alternatively, if it was accepted that the UK did *not* have control over the TEO subjects, the ECHR rights, including in particular Article 3, could in theory be relied on against the host state in question if it was a Council of Europe state since it would then be deemed to have such competence. But if the TEO took effect in a non-contracting state, and the UK was *not* found to have jurisdiction for ECHR purposes since the host state's officials were exercising direct control over the TEO subjects, the subject would in effect be in a legal 'black hole' for a period of time.

9 TEOs and Violations of Article 8 ECHR?

If a person was detained abroad after a TEO had been imposed, Article 8(1) (providing a right to respect for private or family life) would be likely to be engaged on at least two bases. First, the detention itself would fall within the guarantee of respect for private life under Article 8(1), so argument for a breach by the UK, as opposed to the host state, would have to begin by finding that the UK had jurisdictional competence. Detentions even of quite short duration engage Article 8(1). The Court found a breach of Article 8 in *Gillan v UK*,[73] which concerned the stopping and searching of a protester and a reporter covering the protest, under section 44 of the Terrorism Act 2000 on the basis that due to the degree of unbridled executive discretion available under the stop and search scheme it failed to satisfy the 'in accordance with the law' requirement under Article 8(2). Recently in *Beghal*,[74] in contrast, the Supreme Court found that the Schedule 7 TA Act scheme, which includes imposing short periods of

[72]See *Smith v Ministry of Defence* [2014] AC 52. In *R(Al-Skeini) v Secretary of State for the Home Dept* [2008] 1 AC 153 the House of Lords rejected a submission that the presumption against the extra-territorial application of legislation would result in the non-applicability of the HRA where jurisdictional competence for ECHR purposes at Strasbourg would apply. That finding was followed by the Court of Appeal in *Sedar Mohammed and Others v Secretary of State for Defence* [2015] EWCA Civ 843, at para 103.

[73]*Gillan v United Kingdom* (App. No. 4158/05) 12 January 2010; (2010) 160 NLJ 104.

[74]*Beghal v Director of Public Prosecutions (Secretary of State for the Home Department and others intervening)* [2015] UKSC 49; [2015] 3 WLR 344.

detention, was found to contain a number of procedural safeguards which satisfied that requirement under Article 8(2). *If* it was found that the UK did have jurisdictional competence in respect of detentions abroad, the CTSA scheme would clearly fail to satisfy the 'in accordance with the law' requirement under Article 8(2) in respect of a detention following imposition of a TEO since the statute itself does not provide a range of safeguards as it does not cover possible detentions. This uncertainty as to the practical operation of the implicit detention element of the scheme in human rights terms may result in the kind of protracted and expensive litigation seen in relation to control orders.

Second, where use of the TEO prevented a suspect from re-joining family members in Britain for a period of time the guarantee of respect for both family and private life under Article 8(1) would—as the government accepts—be engaged in respect of the family members in the UK, who could, therefore, rely on the ECHR under the HRA.[75] The TEO subject could also raise such a claim, but if so, the jurisdictional point would first have to be settled. The challenge could be brought under s6 HRA by family members in the UK in respect of the impact on their family life of the barring from the UK of the TEO subject under the 'family life' head of Article 8(1). Article 8(1) would clearly be engaged, and attention would turn to the exceptions under Article 8(2): one of the legitimate aims under Article 8 (2) would be satisfied since TEOs have the aims of preserving national security, preventing crime and protecting the rights of others. If in practice some TEO subjects were detained fairly briefly under a TEO abroad and therefore excluded from the UK for a fairly short period only, then due to the potentially very serious risks that they could pose, the test of necessity would be likely to be satisfied so long as the detention and exclusion was not applied indiscriminately, regardless of the risks different returnees posed.

In terms of proportionality, the length of the period of time during which the person could not re-join his or her family, and the reasons for extending the period, would clearly be relevant, in terms of the degree of impact on family life.[76]

---

[75]That was accepted in the 2015 ECHR Memo (The ECHR memorandum (BILLS (14–15) 059), para 15.

[76]In *AP v Secretary of State for the Home Department* [2011] 3 WLR 51 (a control orders case) it was found that while an interference under Article 8(1) had occurred since the relocation imposed on the controlee had limited family visits Article 8(2) could in principle apply so as to justify the potential breach of Article 8. On the particular facts, however, the impact of relocation on the applicant did not satisfy the requirements of proportionality since it caused a very particular degree of social isolation in the specific circumstances in question. Imposition of a TEO would have a strong impact on family life, from the point of view of family members and of the applicant since the chances of visiting the applicant would be lower than would apply to relocation in the UK, but the period of separation involved would probably be of shorter duration, given that TPIMs can subsist for 2 years. In *Al-Nashiri* (no. 28761/11, Judgment of 24 July 2014; ECtHR) it was found that transfer of the applicant to the secret prison in Poland also amounted to an interference with his right to private and family life under Article 8, but that interference was of longer duration, entirely barred the possibility of family visits, and could not be brought to an end by the applicant's decision.

The ECHR Memorandum argues, referring to the interview arrangements under TEOs, that an individual subject to a TEO will be able bring the interference under Article 8(1) to an end, by complying with specified procedures which are 'not onerous'.[77] But in considering the demands of proportionality under Article 8(2), it would be relevant under a robustly scrutinised *strictu* sensu version of proportionality that the scheme is overbroad, read literally, and also that a less intrusive alternative option is available, that of a 'notification of return' requirement imposed on suspect returnees on pain of criminal penalty if they failed to comply with it.[78] As mentioned above, such orders might have been able to achieve the same objectives as TEOs, while avoiding the necessity of preventing entry to the UK of returnees for a period, so use of TEOs instead, requiring a temporary exclusion from the UK could be found to be disproportionate to the aims pursued. Such a strict standard might be deployed at Strasbourg if a TEO-based claim eventually reached the Court on the basis—which would not have the same relevance domestically—that since in deploying TEOs the UK is out of line with the rest of Europe, and Western democracies generally, a narrow margin of appreciation only, based on consensus analysis,[79] should be conceded, encouraging reliance on a stricter proportionality test.

10 The Right to Liberty Under Article 5 ECHR and Detention Abroad

As mentioned above, the provisions bearing on the period of exclusion from the UK under s5 CTSA are markedly imprecise: they appear to have been passed by Parliament before the scheme had reached a fully developed stage. The work of negotiating agreements with other states to detain suspects had not been completed

---

[77]The ECHR Memorandum, para 15.

[78]The Joint Committee on Human Rights (Legislative Scrutiny: Counter-Terrorism and Security Bill (2015) Report of Session 2014–2015, HL Paper 86, HC 859, para 3.12) proposed that the exclusion element of TEOs should be replaced by an advance notification of return requirement (carrying a criminal penalty if not adhered to) if the aim was merely to manage suspects' re-entry to the UK.

[79]*See e.g. Oliari and others v Italy* App. nos. 18766/11 (http://hudoc.echr.coe.int/eng#%7B%22appno%22:[%2218766/11%22]%7D) and 36030/11 (http://hudoc.echr.coe.int/eng#%7B%22appno%22:[%2236030/11%22]%7D), judgment of 21 July 2015. Simply put, the 'consensus' doctrine of the Strasbourg Court means that if a member state is out of line with the rest in respect of its response to a Convention right, in terms of law/practice, a narrow margin of appreciation only will usually be conceded to it, meaning that scrutiny of its reasons for adopting its particular stance will be more intense. For discussion see Dzehtsiarou (2015), especially Chap. 2.

at that stage, and it is unclear that it has been since.[80] As discussed, the 2015 Act does not make any provision for the situation of individuals in the period between the imposition of a TEO and the eventual granting of a permit; thus, in terms of resultant restrictions on liberty or full detentions, the TEO scheme does not address the question of Article 5 compatibility. If the host state takes responsibility for the TEO subject for a period as part of an agreement with the UK, the question arises as to where and in what conditions those persons would be held. It would appear that in most or all instances, they would be detained in the host state. Clearly, some of them, if not detained, might abscond, posing a threat to other states, including the host state. Detention, as discussed above, might be for a considerable period abroad —possibly two years or more—if the TEO subject is refusing to co-operate with the requirement to attend an interview. More usually, the imposition of a TEO might result in a short detention, partly to determine the matter of time and manner of return, before the interview and before the subject is issued with a permit to return.

Article 5 is only triggered if a 'deprivation of liberty' occurs, and this depends on a particularly serious interference with liberty, as distinct from more minor interferences which are covered by Protocol 4, Article 2 ECHR covering freedom of movement, which Britain has not ratified. The Strasbourg and domestic case-law supports the proposition that in the paradigm cases of deprivation of liberty—imprisonment or police detention—no further enquiry is necessary: Article 5(1) is engaged.[81] It would not be necessary for the TEO subject to be held in a prison to demonstrate that a deprivation had occurred: full 24-h house arrest was found in *Nikolova v Bulgaria (No 2)*[82] to fall within the paradigm cases.[83] It was further found in *Pekov v Bulgaria*[84] that Article 5(1) would be engaged where house arrest was enforced indirectly due to fear of future sanctions rather than by means of direct coercion and physical restraint. Strasbourg has made it clear that the element of coercion is highly relevant; if the interference with liberty falls into the

[80]The Immigration Minister stated in a letter to the House of Commons 10 March 2015 Secondary Legislation Scrutiny Committee, 33rd Report 24 March 2015, Section 6.01 Correspondence on Temporary Exclusion Orders (Notices) Regulations 2015 (SI 2015/438): 'The Government has engaged with a number of international partners on the implementation of this measure...we have prioritised engagement with Turkey, France, and a number of other EU countries... these are the countries which are currently most likely to be transited by people travelling to or from Syria or Iraq'.

[81]*See Secretary of State for the Home Department v JJ* [2007] UKHL 45; *Secretary of State for the Home Department v E* [2007] UKHL 47.

[82]App. no. 40896/98, 30 December 2004, at para 60.

[83]The European Court of Human Rights held, unanimously, that a deprivation of liberty had occurred and there had been a violation of Article 5(4), in that the applicant had not been able to apply to a court to review the lawfulness of her house arrest. See also *Mancini v Italy* (App no 44955/98) 2 August 2001, at para 17; *Vachev v Bulgaria* (App. No. 42987/98, 8 October 2004), at para 64; *NC v Italy* (App. No. 24952/94), 11 January 2001, at para 33. In *Trijonis v Lithuania* (App. No. 2333/02), 17 March 2005 the applicant's complaint in relation to a period of 24-h home arrest was held to be admissible.

[84]App. No. 50358/99, 30 June 2006.

non-paradigm category, but the obligation in question is backed by the sanctions of arrest and imprisonment if not complied with, that may tip the balance towards a finding that the interference has the character of a deprivation of liberty. TEOs are clearly coercive since it is an offence to return to the UK in breach of the permit to return.[85]

Assuming that Article 5(1) is engaged, detentions resulting from or associated with imposition of a TEO could fall within one of the Article 5 exceptions, but it would appear that it could not do so *if* the UK was deemed to have ECHR jurisdictional competence in relation to rights relevant to the TEO subject's situation—of which Article 5 would clearly be one—since no exception covers executive detention on national security grounds.[86] If the detention was found instead to be the responsibility of the host state, the relevant exception would probably be Article 5(1)(f) which covers detention of 'a person against whom action is being taken with a view to deportation or extradition'; it will only cover lengthy detentions, following *Chahal,*[87] if during the detention deportation is actively being sought with due diligence.[88] It would be arguable that if a lengthy detention occurred abroad Article 5(1)(f) would not cover the situation because the delay in allowing the TEO subject to enter the UK is not entirely consonant with the situation in which deportation is being actively sought, usually via negotiations as to assurances regarding treatment on return,[89] or while court proceedings challenging deportation or extradition are ongoing, since in relation to TEOs the factors causing the delay may be within the control of the UK government. If on the other hand the delay is caused by the TEO subject who is refusing to attend an interview abroad, it could still be argued that deportation is being actively sought.[90]

In an Article 5-based claim, the UK government could put forward the argument that exclusion of the suspect from the UK for a period had the objective of *avoiding* a breach of Article 5, while placing pressure on the suspect to attend the interview

---

[85]Under Section 10(1) CTSA 2015.

[86]Following *Foka v Turkey* App. No. 28940/09, judgment of 24 June 2008, if the detention was under the auspices of UK officials but only covered a period in an airport and then on a plane, Article 5 would be engaged due to the element of coercion, but if the applicant was arrested abroad under s41 TA and then detained, the exception under Article 5(1)(c) would appear to apply.

[87]*Chahal v UK* (1996) 23 EHRR 413, at para 113. In order to detain, deportation proceedings should be in being and it should be clear that they are being prosecuted with due diligence.

[88]*See R (on the application of Hardial Singh) v Governor of Durham Prison* [1984] WLR 704; *A and others v UK* Application no. 3455/05, judgment of 19 February 2009, para 164.

[89]*Othman v UK* (2012) 55 EHRR 1.

[90]But the Strasbourg Court is not willing to extend the scope of the exceptions: in *Kurt v Turkey* (1998) 27 EHRR 373, para 122, it referred to 'the fundamental importance of the guarantees contained in Article 5 for securing the right of individuals in a democracy to be free from arbitrary detention at the hands of the authorities', meaning that the exceptions should be narrowly construed. In *A and others v UK* App. no. 3455/05, judgment of 19 February 2009, para 171, the Court stated: 'If detention does not fit within the confines of the paragraphs as interpreted by the Court, it cannot be made to fit by an appeal to the need to balance the interests of the State against those of the detainee'.

and affording an opportunity to determine the place and manner of return. If the suspect was instead returned immediately to the UK but then subjected to executive detention there for a significant period, without being charged with an offence, no exception under Article 5 would apply, even where national security concerns were especially pressing; the only recourse would be to a derogation under Article 15. So the exclusion element of TEOs combined with the probability of detention abroad appears to be designed to avoid relying on a derogation from Article 5. However, that argument would not be likely to be accepted since it would mean in effect implying a new exception into Article 5 on grounds of protecting national security and arbitrarily linked to the physical location of the suspect.

11 Potential Risk of Article 3 ECHR Treatment Abroad During Detention

If the TEO subject is detained abroad, he or she could potentially suffer Article 3 treatment. Article 3 has both a procedural and a substantive aspect.[91] If serious allegations of ill-treatment are made, the investigation must be both prompt and thorough.[92] If due to the situation in which the TEO subject remained detained abroad, an eventual investigation into such allegations was delayed and hampered, meaning that essential evidence therefore could not be obtained, that in itself could constitute a breach of Article 3 (raised under the HRA on return of the TEO subject) in procedural terms,[93] depending on resolution of the jurisdictional issue.

The Immigration Minister has stated that certain states where TEO subjects might be exposed to a risk of Article 3 treatment[94] are not being approached to create agreements in respect of TEOs.[95] Ministers have also stated that if it was apparent that a particular individual faced a threat of torture in a third country, the Secretary of State should not make a TEO.[96] The ECHR memo further stated that the practice of not depriving UK citizens of citizenship when they are not within the

---

[91]See e.g. *Silih v Slovenia* [2009] ECHR 537.

[92]*Al-Skeini v UK* 7 July 2011 App. no. 55721/07 (GC), at 151, 163–4, 171–3; *Al-Nashiri v Poland* App. no. 28761/11, Judgment of 24 July 2014, at para 486.

[93]*Al-Nashiri v Poland* App. no. 28761/11, Judgment of 24 July 2014.

[94]Article 3 provides a guarantee against use of ‘torture or inhuman or degrading treatment or punishment’.

[95]The Minister stated in a letter to the House of Commons (see note 80): ‘the Government..is mindful of the possibility that those subject to TEOs might be exposed to risks in particular countries as a result…in some instances, in order to avoid these risks materialising, the Government would choose not to liaise with certain countries to enforce a TEO’.

[96]HL Deb, 20 Jan 2015, Col 1309.

UK's jurisdiction if so doing would expose them to a real risk of treatment in breach of Articles 3 or 2 ECHR,[97] would also be followed in respect of the imposition of TEOs.[98]

Nevertheless, the risk of Article 3 treatment in detention abroad cannot be ruled out. Turkey was mentioned as a possible host state for persons subject to TEOs. David Cameron has previously stressed the need for closer cooperation with Turkey in relation to the problem posed by returnees from ISIS-held territory who travel through Turkey.[99] The problem is that under a TEO such persons would probably have to be detained in Turkey. As *Liberty* has pointed out, Turkey's record on subjecting persons to Article 3 treatment has been criticised a number of times[100] by the UN Committee Against Torture.[101] Any agreement reached with Turkey as to detaining persons subject to TEOs could include assurances against the possibility of Article 3 treatment, bearing in mind that such assurances, if of sufficient quality, have been accepted by the Strasbourg Court as mitigating the risk of Article 3 treatment in another state.[102] That was accepted in relation to Jordan, whose record on Article 3 treatment has also frequently been criticised and may be worse than Turkey's.[103] However, given that at present the UK does not accept that it has ECHR jurisdictional competence in respect of TEO subjects abroad, it presumably would not seek such assurances. If it is found in future that it does have such jurisdiction, it is possible, if the TEO scheme is still being pursued, that such assurances would be sought, but it is not clear that they would be accepted domestically or at Strasbourg, given that the UK could avoid the risk of Article 3 treatment merely by receiving the subject back into the UK.

---

[97]Article 2 ECHR provides a right to life subject to certain exceptions.

[98]The ECHR Memo, para 13, see note 75.

[99]David Cameron and Ahmet Davutoglu, press conference in Turkey, 9 December 2014, available at https://www.gov.uk/government/speeches/david-cameron-and-ahmet-davutoglu-press-conference-in-turkey.

[100]*See* Liberty's Second Reading briefing on the Counter-Terrorism and Security Bill in the House of Lords January 2015, para 22.

[101]UN Committee Against Torture Report, Forty-fifth session, 1–19 November 2010, para 7.

[102]*See Othman v UK* App. No. 8139/09 [2012] ECHR 56.

[103]*See* Third periodic reports of States parties in 2014: Jordan, 3 July 2014 CAT/C/JOR/3, para 19. It was found that there was 'a total of 392 cases of ill-treatment of civilians by members of the police in 2013: 26 cases were referred to the Police Court, 11 were referred to the unit commander for trial, 101 were dropped and 254 remain pending'.

12 Compliance with Article 6 ECHR: The Quality of Judicial Oversight in the TEO Scheme

12.1 Introduction

The review mechanisms in the TEO scheme represent an improvement on the position as originally conceived of in the Counter-Terrorism and Security Bill,[104] but create a scheme that hedges the review procedures around with restrictions. The review mechanisms relating to TEOs echo those relating to control orders and TPIMs, but potentially reflect, it will be argued, an even more minimised version of Article 6 ECHR[105] than they do as regards the initial review. CTSA envisages two levels of oversight—first, a more minimal one in relation to the Home Secretary's initial decision to impose a TEO, conducted while the applicant would usually be outside the UK, and second, a fuller, subsequent review of the TEO's imposition once the TEO subject has returned. Both review schemes are governed by rules of court in the form of amendments—Civil Procedure Amendments—(referred to below as CPA)[106] to the Civil Procedure Rules (CPR), which have been made under Schedule 3 CTSA.[107] The amendments rely on the scheme for use of closed material proceedings (CMPs) and Special Advocates (SAs), already established in relation to other non-trial-based measures, including control orders[108] and TPIMs. That scheme was already in certain respects in doubtful compliance with Article 6 ECHR, although the courts had modified it under the HRA to create adherence to fair trial standards.[109] But the new amendments create a modified scheme which reflects the borderline adherence to Article 6 previously apparent *and* appears impliedly to presuppose as regards the initial review that non-adherence to Article 6 is possible if the TEO subject is not in the UK.

The government in the ECHR memo considers that if the applicant is outside the UK, Article 6 will not apply 'directly' due to the principle of extra-territoriality.[110] But in apparently contradictory fashion, Schedule 3 provides that the rules governing TEO proceedings undertaken while the applicant is abroad are not intended

---

[104]See Joint Committee on Human Rights 'Counter-terrorism and Security Bill: Legislative Scrutiny' 5th Report of Session 2014–15 HL Paper 86, HC 859, 7.1.15, paras 3.13 and 3.14.

[105]Article 6(1) provides a guarantee of the right to a fair trial applicable in TEO proceedings as a matter of determining civil obligations, rather than a criminal charge. The guarantees of Article 6 (2) and 6(3) relate to criminal proceedings.

[106]The Civil Procedure (Amendment) Rules 2015 No 406 (L.3), which came into force on 27 March 2015.

[107]Sched 3 covers 'TEO proceedings': the permission of the court under s2(7), the reference to the court in relation to urgently imposed TEOs under Sched 2, the s11 review and appeals: Sched 3 para 1.

[108]See Fenwick and Philipson (2011).

[109]See in particular *Secretary of State for the Home Department v AF (No.3)* [2009] UKHL 28; [2009] 3 WLR 74.

[110]ECHR memo on CTSA (note 75), para 10.

to lead to a breach of Article 6.[111] However, that provision in Schedule 3 may rely impliedly on the non-applicability of Article 6 to the initial review under s3 due to lack of jurisdiction, meaning that while a certain level of due process is created,[112] the relevant Article 6 Strasbourg jurisprudence need not be adhered to under s3 HRA, and Article 6 would not be directly applicable under s6 HRA. But the possibility clearly remains open that a court might find that the rules had led to such a breach in respect of the initial review while the subject was abroad, *if* the jurisdictional issue was determined against the UK. Clearly, if so, a court could rely on the intention of Parliament not to approve provisions enabling a breach of Article 6, and on Section 3 HRA to reinterpret the Schedule 3 provisions and the rules, if necessary in order to avoid such a breach, if it is possible to do so via reinterpretation.[113] A court could rely instead on common law-based due process principles, but that could involve making a determination, as mentioned above, that a court is prepared to review actions and decisions of the domestic executive affecting citizens outside UK territory on the basis of a wider common law jurisdictional competence than that applicable under the ECHR applied via the HRA which has not been established.[114]

Leaving the jurisdictional issue aside, it is clear, for the avoidance of doubt, from *Secretary of State for the Home Department v BC and BB*[115] that Article 6 would be engaged by the initial TEO review: the argument put forward in that case was not accepted to the effect that the obligations imposed under 'light touch' control orders —similar to certain of the obligations under a TPIM—do not require Article 6 compliance in review hearings. *A fortiori* that would be the case in respect of TEO reviews: if under a TEO a person was unable to enter the UK for a significant period, the imposition of that obligation would have as much (or more) impact on the suspect as was created by the 'heavier touch' orders.

12.2 *Initial Review*

The Secretary of State must seek permission from the court (under Section 3 CTSA) to impose the TEO, unless he/she considers on reasonable grounds that due

---

[111]Sched 3 para 5(1) CTSA: 'Nothing in paragraphs 2–4, or in rules of court made under any of those paragraphs, is to be read as requiring the relevant court to act in a manner inconsistent with Article 6 ECHR'.

[112]Sched 3 para 2(1) also provides that the rules of court must ensure 'that the decisions that are the subject of the proceedings are properly reviewed'.

[113]If not, a declaration of the incompatibility between the TEO provisions and Article 6 could be made under s4 HRA.

[114]*See Pham v Secretary of State for the Home Dept* [2015] UKSC 19.

[115][2010] 1 WLR 1542. See also *BM v Secretary of State for the Home Department* [2011] EWCA Civ 366; Lord Justice Thomas said: 'on the open evidence, the control order could not be justified as necessary at the time it was made as the evidence was too vague and speculative' (at para 19).

to urgency the TEO should be imposed without the court's permission.[116] If an urgent TEO is imposed without court permission, Schedule 2 applies, providing that immediately after giving notice of its imposition, the Secretary of State must refer the imposition of the order to the court.[117] It is likely that grounds could be found in most instances for putting forward a case that the TEO must be imposed urgently, given that the would-be returnee will often be in transit between territory held by ISIS or a similar group and Europe, possibly in Turkey, and would be likely to seek to leave for the UK or another part of Europe, if possible, if the TEO was not imposed. It is also possible that a suspect might still be in such territory, but intelligence suggests that he or she is about to seek to leave it for Europe. Imposing the TEO urgently at that point could allow for interception of the suspect at a relevant border, although imposition of a TEO would not provide the only means of enabling interception.[118] The court must withhold permission if the decision of the Secretary of State is 'obviously flawed'.[119] But under Section 3(7) if it does not find that the decision is obviously flawed, it *must* give permission for the order. The court is required to apply judicial review principles in considering whether to give the Secretary of State permission,[120] which begs the question, related to the jurisdictional issue, whether so doing can include raising ECHR points. The arrangements for the initial court review—either as a permission review or after a TEO has been imposed urgently—presuppose a court process that need not amount to 'a hearing';[121] the review can be conducted in private,[122] in the absence of the applicant,[123] without notification to the applicant, and without affording him or her the right to make representations at it, via his legal representative.[124] Clearly, the TEO subject would inevitably be absent since he or she at the time would still be barred from entering the UK. These provisions appear to envisage the possibility of a brief application to a judge to consider permission for the TEO on the papers.

The provisions governing the initial review provide some limited possible routes to certain fair trial safeguards which make gestures in the direction of Article

[116]Section 2(7) Condition E is that—(a) the court gives the Secretary of State permission under Section 3, or (b) the Secretary of State reasonably considers that the urgency of the case requires a temporary exclusion order to be imposed without obtaining such permission.

[117]Para 3(1).

[118]For example, if security intelligence was passed to officials at the relevant border, the suspect could be arrested, and then taken into custody by British officials, with a view to charging him or her with a relevant terrorism offence in the UK (eg under Section 5 TA 2006).

[119]Sections 3(2) and (6).

[120]Section 3(5).

[121]Schedule 3 para 2(2)(b); Rule 88.20 provides that only s11 reviews, appeals and Rule 88.28(2) matters require a hearing.

[122]Schedule 3 para 10; Rule 88.21.

[123]Schedule 3 para 2(2) (e) and in relation to urgently imposed TEOs, schedule 2 para 2(e): 'the relevant court [may] conduct proceedings in the absence of any person, including a party to the proceedings (or any legal representative of that party)'; see also Rule 88.21 CPA.

[124]Section 3(3)(4) and schedule 2 para 3(4).

6-compliance but may fall short of it, as discussed below. A TEO subject is clearly likely to face difficulties in relying even on the very limited safeguards for the initial review from outside the UK,[125] especially given the various ways of prolonging the processes that are made available.[126] The necessary 'evidence' for the formation of the suspicion in question may not be subjected to court review for a period; the excluded person is unlikely to be present at the first review and may not see most or any of the evidence against him or her. The question of disclosure of the gist of the material providing the grounds for suspicion to the TEO subject for purposes of the initial review is considered below. The risk that miscarriages of justice may occur is quite high: some persons may be wrongfully excluded, possibly for prolonged periods. Therefore, the need for more intensive judicial scrutiny is especially apparent. The scheme is impliedly deemed either to reach compliance with a highly minimised version of the Article 6 safeguards, or to avoid breaching Article 6 on the basis that it does not apply due to lack of jurisdiction.

12.3 Subsequent Review

Section 11 of the 2015 Act covers subsequent review, subject to the provisions of Schedule 3 and the CPA, making provision for an individual subject to a TEO to be able to apply to the court for a statutory review of the decision to impose a TEO, a decision that one or more of the necessary conditions in Section 2 were met and continue to be met, and the decision to impose obligations under Section 9. Section 11 can *only* apply when the applicant has returned to the UK[127] indicating that in *this* instance the court would not face a possible jurisdictional barrier in seeking to ensure Article 6-compliance. The complex set of provisions providing possible routes to such compliance in relation to subsequent reviews appear to be intended to persuade Parliament and the courts in the context of combating terrorism, that a basic level of compliance with the established recalibrated version of Article 6 has been achieved.

---

[125]See the comments on this point in *R (Razgar) v Secretary of State for the Home Department* [2002] EWHC 2554 (Admin). The Human Rights Joint Committee Fifth Report 'Legislative Scrutiny: Counter-Terrorism and Security Bill', HL Paper 86, HC 859, published 12 January 2015, in paras 3.8–3.15 recommended strengthening the judicial oversight and commented on the difficulty of relying on judicial review while abroad. See also *BA (Nigeria) (FC) (Respondent) v Secretary of State for the Home Department* [2009] QB 686; the Court of Appeal described the pursuit of an appeal from outside the United Kingdom as having 'a degree of unreality about it'.

[126]See Rule 8824(5)(b).

[127]Section 11(1).

12.4 The Standard of Review

Depending on the way they are interpreted, the provisions governing both initial and subsequent reviews clearly create a very thin veneer of judicial oversight. The 'obviously flawed' terminology in Section 3 governing the initial review indicates a standard of scrutiny below that of *Wednesbury* unreasonableness. Section 11(3) provides that in a subsequent review the court must apply the principles applicable on an application for judicial review and the court has the power to quash the TEO.[128] The terminology used in relation to both sets of reviews was originally used in the Prevention of Terrorism Act 2005 in relation to the imposition of control orders[129] and was replicated in TPIMA.[130] Therefore, the case-law arising in relation to both statutes is relevant.

But the legislative provisions themselves may not determine the standard of review in Section 3 or Section 11 reviews. In relation to control orders, the Court of Appeal employed Section 3 HRA to require that they should be interpreted in a manner that enabled the court to carry out a review of the Secretary of State's decision that complied with the requirements of Article 6.[131] Equally, Sect. 3 could be relied on to reverse the dilution of Article 6—in respect of the standard of review —that the CTSA as presented to Parliament has presupposed. However, while Section 3 HRA and Article 6 could be relied on in respect of Section 11 reviews, since no question as to jurisdictional competence arises, that may not be the case in respect of Section 3 permission reviews since Article 6 may be deemed to be inapplicable. As far as Section 11 is concerned, the courts are likely to apply an exacting standard of review, including 'intense scrutiny'[132] of the necessity for imposing a TEO.[133]

12.5 Closed Material Proceedings and Special Advocates in TEO Proceedings: Minimising Due Process?

The extensive literature on CMPs and SAs has criticised the level of due process they maintain via the Civil Procedure Rules Part 76,[134] now largely replicated in the

---

[128] Section 11(4)(a); it can also give directions to the Secretary of State in relation to revoke the order [Section 11(4)(b)].

[129] Under the PTA the court had to give initial permission for the control order [Section 3(2)(b)] unless the decision to make it was 'obviously flawed'. See also Section 3(10) and Section 11(2) PTA.

[130] Section 6(3) TPIMA.

[131] *Secretary of State v MB* [2006] EWHC 1000.

[132] *Secretary of State for the Home Department v MB* [2006] 3 WLR 839 at paras 63–65.

[133] Section 2(2), Condition B.

[134] See: Nanopoulos (2015), 913; Fenwick and Philipson (2011); Walker (2010), 1395.

CPA for TEO proceedings. They will rely on the familiar closed material procedure (CMP) using special advocates, already well established in the context of control orders/TPIMs,[135] and accepted by the courts and Parliament.[136] The scheme as regards CMP largely echoes that established procedure,[137] especially as regards the highly significant matter of providing a summary of the closed material. So under Schedule 3, special advocates can be appointed to represent the applicant in Section 3 and Section 11 proceedings,[138] and the CPA rules relating to disclosure made under Schedule 3 paragraph 4 allow for proceeding on the basis of closed material: the Secretary of State must be given an opportunity to argue that other material relating to the suspicion against the person in question should only be disclosed to the court and the SA.[139] So unless the basis for the suspicion is in the open material, the facts creating the suspicion need not be disclosed (aside from the possibility of disclosure of a summary) to the applicant or his/her legal representative.[140] The rules echo the CPR rules in providing that where the Secretary of State does not receive the permission of the relevant court to withhold material, she

[135]The provisions applying to TPIM proceedings are found in Part 76 CPR. The closed material is considered by the Special Advocate (SA). Provision is made for the exclusion of a relevant person and his legal representative from a hearing to secure that information is not disclosed contrary to the public interest: rule 76.22. The SA may only communicate with the relevant party before closed material is served upon him, save with permission of the court: rules 76.2, 76.28(2). See further Chamberlain (2009), 314.

[136]*Secretary of State for the Home Department v MB* [2007] 1 AC 440; *A v UK* (2009) 49 EHRR 29; Case C-300/11, *ZZ v Secretary of State for the Home Department* [2013] 3 WLR 813. The Justice and Security Act 2013 makes provision for closed material proceedings (CMP) in PT II, which cover TPIM hearings (s6), but since CMP were and are being used in this context in any event, it does not appear that it will bring about significant change; see *Justice and Security Green Paper* Ministry of Justice, Report Cm 8194 (2011).

[137]Schedule 3 paras 3 and 4 detail the provisions that must be made in relation to disclosure.

[138]Under paragraph 10 the rules may provide that the SA may be appointed if the party and his legal representatives are excluded from the proceedings. This is now actioned in Rule 88.22 CPA. 'Advisers' could also be relied on; schedule 3 paras 8 and 9 provide for the use of advisers appointed by the Lord Chancellor in any 'TEO proceedings'. Schedule 3 para 8 provides that advisers may only be used with permission as designated in para 8(2): with the approval of (a) the Lord President of the Court of Session; (b) the Lord Chief Justice of Northern Ireland; (c) the Lord Chief Justice of England and Wales, in any other case'.

[139]Schedule 3 para 4(1): Rules of court relating to TEO proceedings or appeal proceedings must secure—(a) that the Secretary of State has the opportunity to make an application to the relevant court for permission not to disclose material otherwise than to the relevant court and any person appointed as a special advocate; (b) that such an application is always considered in the absence of every party to the proceedings (and every party's legal representative); (c) that the relevant court is required to give permission for material not to be disclosed if it considers that the disclosure of the material would be contrary to the public interest. These provisions are now reflected in Rule 88.27 CAP.

[140]Rule 88.27.

can still elect not to disclose it.[141] If that occurs, the court can direct the Secretary of State not to rely on the closed material.[142]

Thus, creation of a degree of fairness in the proceedings rests on the SA: Schedule 3 and the CPA rules provide that a SA has the function of making submissions to the court where the applicant and his representative are excluded.[143] The SA cannot communicate with the TEO subject after closed material has been served on him/her,[144] although he or she can make a request to the court to communicate with the subject[145] to which the Secretary of State can object[146] and must, if so, serve notice of the objection on the SA,[147] in which case the court can consider the objection.[148] In the initial review, if a TEO subject has not had notification of the imposition of the TEO,[149] then, while an SA may be appointed, his or her capacity to represent the subject is even more circumscribed.

The provisions as to providing a summary of the closed material largely echo the possibilities of non-disclosure provided in the CPR rules applicable to TPIM proceedings, but impliedly may allow for a greater likelihood of complete non-disclosure of closed material in the initial review. Schedule 3 paragraph 4(1)(d) CTSA provides that if permission is given by the relevant court not to disclose material, it must consider requiring the Secretary of State to provide a summary of the material to every party to the proceedings (and every party's legal representative). That provision has been included with a view to creating compliance with the 'gisting' requirement under Article 6(1) ECHR accepted by the House of Lords in *AF no 3*[150] and applied in control order/TPIM proceedings; an irreducible minimum of disclosure to the suspect of the evidence against him/her must occur. But under the CPA rules governing the TEO scheme, the court must ensure that a summary of that material does not contain material the disclosure of which would be contrary to the public interest.[151] Due to the use of the term 'public interest' that is a broader provision than Section 8(1)(c), Justice and Security Act 2013 which provides, once CMP are declared (Section 6(1)), that 'the court is required to give permission for material not to be disclosed if it considers that the disclosure of the material would be damaging to the interests of national security'. Thus, it will be problematic for a

---

[141]Schedule 3 para 4(2)(a) and (b).

[142]Schedule 3 para 4(3), now reflected in Rule 88.27(7) CAP.

[143]Schedule 3 para 2(2)(e) and Rule 88.23. The power to appoint an SA is covered in Schedule 3 para 10; Rule 88.22.

[144]Rule 88.24(2).

[145]Rule 88.24(4).

[146]Rule 88.24(5).

[147]Rule 8824(5)(b).

[148]Rule 88.2.

[149]See *supra* note 124.

[150]*Secretary of State for the Home Department v AF (No.3)* [2009] UKHL 28; [2009] 3 WLR 74; the decision absorbed into domestic law the gisting requirement (via ss2 and 3 HRA) laid down by the Strasbourg Court [although under Art 5(4)] in *A v UK* (2009) 49 EHRR 29.

[151]Schedule 3 para 4(1)(e); Rule 88.28(6)(b) and Rule 88.28(8).

court in TEO proceedings to seek to balance the public interest in disclosure against the national security interest in non-disclosure, indicating that *AF* has been recognised but not fully addressed in Schedule 3. The rules provide that where the Secretary of State is required to provide a party to the proceedings with a summary of closed material she can elect not to provide the summary.[152] But if that occurs, the court can direct the Secretary of State not to rely on the material that was required to be summarised.[153]

Clearly, the intention is to ensure that the subject cannot become aware of most or all of the closed material, but that means that he or she is hampered in instructing the SA as to the most effective way, if there is one, of challenging that material, within which much or all of grounds for suspicion against him or her may lie. In some instances, the grounds may be in the open material and so could be communicated to the TEO subject and potentially challenged by the SA, but not in all. If the subject has been involved in TRA abroad, then clearly he or she will know or guess the gist of the case or much of it, but to act on the assumption that that is the case ignores the need to ensure that due process standards should be observed in formal terms (*AB v Slovakia*).[154] If in the result even the essence or gist of the case is not disclosed,[155] the court could seek to reinterpret the rules under Section 3 HRA so as to allow for the minimum disclosure required by *AF* or quash the order, *unless*, in relation to the initial review, it is found that the ECHR does not directly apply due to lack of jurisdiction. It would appear, however, clear that if the summary is not disclosed, the TEO could not be sustained in s11 proceedings, following the interpretation of Article 6(1) in *AF*. The Court of Appeal confirmed that the position was not discretionary recently in *Mohamed v Secretary of State for the Home Department; CF v Secretary of State for the Home Department*[156] in finding that the Secretary of State had to 'elect between a modicum of disclosure and withdrawing from reliance on wholly undisclosed material in such circumstances'.[157]

The question of the *degree* of disclosure required to the suspect has not been fully resolved, and the rules made under Schedule 3 do not resolve it. In *AT v Secretary of State for the Home Department,*[158] the Court of Appeal found that

---

[152]Schedule 3 para 4(2)(a) and (b); Rule 88.28(7)(a).

[153]Schedule 3 para 4(3), now reflected in Rule 88.27(7) CAP.

[154]*AB v Slovakia* (App. No. 41784/98), judgment of 4 March 2003.

[155]This is covered by s8 Justice and Security Act 2013: if the court gives permission not to disclose material, it must consider requiring the relevant person to provide a summary of the material to every other party to the proceedings; but the court must ensure that such a summary does not contain material the disclosure of which would be damaging to the interests of national security. Section 8 does not affect the essential principle deriving from *Secretary of State for the Home Department v AF (No.3)* [2009] UKHL 28; it regulates its application in CMP.

[156][2014] EWCA Civ 559; [2014] 1 W.L.R. 4240; [2014] 3 All E.R. 760.

[157]In so finding the court followed *Secretary of State for the Home Department v F* [2009] UKHL 28, [2010] 2 AC 269.

[158][2012] EWCA Civ 42.

insufficient disclosure had occurred to satisfy Article 6. If some disclosure has occurred, the TEO subject will be disadvantaged if he or she does not respond to the allegations: in *Secretary of State for the Home Department v BM,*[159] it was found that once some disclosure has occurred, the failure of the TPIM suspect to deal with the allegations to the extent that was possible having regard to the disclosure given could be taken into account as part of the case against him or her.[160]

The material available that forms the case against the TEO subject only needs to support grounds for reasonable suspicion; therefore, the burden on the state is a minimal one. But even that burden is only doubtfully discharged since the material on which that suspicion is based is not open to normal challenge, meaning that the possibility of targeting persons for subjection to a TEO on the basis of misinterpretation of their actions or of security information appears to be quite high.

12.6 Right to a Hearing Which Is Also in the Presence of the Applicant?

The right under Article 6(1) is that of access to a court, which is not absolute,[161] and to 'a fair hearing', although since the review processes relate to the determination of civil rights, not a criminal charge, the right to a hearing in the presence of the applicant or his/her representative is less well established.[162] The principle of equality of arms—one of the elements of the general fairness principle—requires that each party should be afforded a reasonable opportunity to present his or her case under conditions that do not place him or her at a substantial disadvantage *vis-à-vis* the opponent.[163] It has further been found that 'The seriousness of what is at stake for the applicant will be of relevance to assessing the adequacy and fairness of the procedures'.[164]

The Court reiterated in *Yevdokimov and others v Russia*[165] that Article 6(1) does not guarantee the right to a personal presence before a civil court 'but enshrines a

[159] [2012] EWHC 714 (Admin).

[160] At para 22. The same approach was taken in *Secretary of State for the Home Department v CC, CF* [2012] EWHC 2837 (Admin) in which CF and CC declined to give evidence once they were made aware of the allegations against them.

[161] *Golder v UK* A 18 (1975); 1 EHRR 524, para 38.

[162] It was upheld in a civil action in *Khuzhin and others v Russia* (2008) App. nos. 13470/02, 23 October 2008, para 108.

[163] See *Dombo Beheer BV v the Netherlands* A/274 (1994) 18 EHRR 213, para 33; *Ankerl v Switzerland* (App. No. 17748/91) (1994) 18 EHRR CD56, para 38. See also *AB v Slovakia* (App. no. 41784/98), judgment of 4 March 2003, para 55; *Siwiec v Poland*, App. no. 28095/08 3 July 2012, para 47; *Larin v Russia*, App. no. 15034/02, 20 May 2010, at paras 35–36.

[164] See *P, C and S v the United Kingdom* (App. no. 56547/00), 16 July 2002, para 91.

[165] (2016) App. nos. 27236/05, 44223/05, 53304/07, 40232/11, 60052/11, 76438/11, 14919/12, 19929/12, 42389/12, 57043/12 and 67481/12, judgment of 16 February 2016.

more general right to present one's case effectively before the court and to enjoy equality of arms with the opposing side'; thus, it confirmed that the state has a free choice as to the means to be used in guaranteeing litigants these rights.[166] Also, the Court has found that an oral hearing is not essential.[167] But where factual matters, or the conduct of the applicant, are in question, the personal participation of the litigant has been held to be necessary,[168] as it was in *Yevdokimov*. It has also been found that the hearing should be adversarial[169] in the sense that both parties should be given an opportunity to comment on all the evidence that is adduced.[170] Given the quasi-criminal character of TEO proceedings, and the fact that the conduct of the applicant is in issue, the possibility of a complete lack of a hearing at the initial review could be found to breach Article 6. The reliance on the SA would have some influence in creating greater fairness, but the SA's efficacy would be diminished if he or she could not communicate with the applicant after being served with the closed material, and in any event if there is no hearing the role of the SA would appear to be too minimal to create fairness. Thus, the initial review procedure may not be Article 6-compliant, so the courts' response would depend on the matter of jurisdictional competence. The rules governing the subsequent review accept that a hearing will occur, but that the TEO subject and his representative need not be present.[171] The inevitable exclusion of the TEO subject from the initial review and possibly from the subsequent review as well is very hard to reconcile with the equality of arms principle. In so far as jurisdictional competence relates to the relevance of the rights in question to the situation of the applicant, as found in *Al-Skeini*, it may be argued as regards the initial review that debarring the TEO subject from the UK does relate to Article 6 since it inevitably interferes with creating equality of arms, given that the subject cannot be present at the hearing and may face other difficulties in communicating with the SA from abroad.

13 Conclusions

The control orders/TPIMs saga is likely to differ from the TEO one, given that the method used to reconcile TEOs with international human rights norms does not lend itself very readily to a gradual court-based tempering of the scheme under the HRA. Either the UK has jurisdictional competence in relation to TEO subjects

---

[166]At para 22. The Court referred to *Steel and Morris v UK* (2005) App. no. 68416/01, at paras 59–60.

[167]*Koottummel v Austria*, App. no. 49616/06, 10 December 2009, para 19.

[168]*Insanov v. Azerbaijan*, App. no. 16133/0, judgment of 14 March 2013, para 145; *Skorobogatykh v. Russia*, App. no. 4871/03, judgment of 22 December 2009, para 64.

[169]See *Barbera* et al. *v Spain* A/146 (1989) 11 EHRR 360, para 78; *Ruiz-Mateos v Spain* A/262 (1993) 16 EHRR 505.

[170]*Mantovanelli v France* (1997) 24 EHRR 370.

[171]Schedule 3 para 2(2)(e), recognised in Rule 88.23(a).

abroad, or it does not. If TEOs are deployed and it is found eventually that it does, the scheme would probably require rapid Parliamentary modification in order to rely on it in practice without facing successful ECHR challenges. Unaccompanied by a derogation, it might also, therefore, undergo a process of human rights-based tempering in future, but the steady case-by-case infusion of human rights norms into it, as was seen in relation to control orders/TPIMs, would probably be missing. Apprehensions as to the courts' reactions to the scheme, and the potential need for such modification, may partly explain its lack of deployment, despite the likelihood that the threat from FTFs who have fought or trained with ISIS is only likely to increase from 2017 onwards.

As discussed, the TEO scheme was presented to Parliament as ECHR-compatible and as acceptable in terms of international human rights law generally, creating an appearance of constitutionality. On that basis, TEOs give an impression of legality which, as Dyzenhaus has argued, may be more dangerous than declaring a complete lack of legality.[172] They represent an experiment in testing the limits of international human rights law in relation to excluding citizens, which will be of interest to the various democracies currently confronted with nationals who owe loyalty to groups seeking to attack them. In effect, persons seeking to leave a democracy to fight with a group such as ISIS have sought to accord themselves the status of outsiders to a legal order. The International Human Rights Law framework was designed in the wake of grossly inhumane treatment by the German state of its own German citizens and so is inapt to cover the current phenomenon linked to home-grown terrorism—whereby non-state actors engage in conspiracies to murder their fellow citizens. It is possible that, therefore, reconceptualization of that framework may be needed, but this attempt of the UK to render TEOs acceptable *within* the current framework is wholly misguided.

References

Beutel AJ (2007) Radicalization and home-grown terrorism in western muslim communities. Minaret of Freedom Institute, Maryland

Chamberlain M (2009) Special advocates and procedural fairness in closed proceedings. Civ Justice Quat 28:314

Drumbi MA (2007) The expressive value of prosecuting and punishing terrorists. George Wash Law Rev 7:1165

Duffy H (2015) The 'War on Terror' and the framework of international law, 2rd edn. pp. 469–472

Dyzenhaus D (2009) The constitution of law. Legality in a time of emergency. Cambridge University Press, UK

Dzehtsiarou K (2015) European consensus and the legitimacy of the european court of human rights. Cambridge University Press

[172] Dyzenhaus (2009), 2–3. Dyzenhaus was referring to in particular to the rule of law, but the point is readily applicable to the ECHR rights.

Fenwick H (2011) Recalibrating ECHR rights, and the role of the human Rights act post-9/11: reasserting international human rights norms in the 'war on terror'. Curr Leg Probl 63:153
Fenwick H (2013) Designing ETPIMS around ECHR review or normalisation of "preventive" non-trial-based executive measures? Mod Law Rev 76:877
Fenwick H, Philipson G (2011) Covert derogations and judicial deference: redefining liberty and due process rights in counterterrorism law and beyond. McGill Law Rev 1 56:863–918
Gibney M (2014) 'Statelessness and citizenship' in Alice. In: Edwards A, Van Wass L (eds) Nationality and statelessness under international law. Cambridge University Press, UK
Milanovic M (2012) Al-Skeini and Al-Jedda in Strasbourg. Eur J Int Law 23(1):121–139
Mirna A, Harrington J (2008) The scope and content of Article 15 UDHR. Refug Surv Q 27 (3):93–109
Nanopoulos E (2015) European human rights law and the normalisation of the "closed material procedure": limit or source? Mod Law Rev 78:913
Walker C (2010) Keeping control of terrorists without losing control of constitutionalism. Stanf Law Rev 59:1395
Watt N (2014) Cameron and Clegg Seek agreement in anti-terror talks. The guardian. http://www.theguardian.com/uk-news/2014/sep/01/cameron-clegg-anti-terror-talks-british-born-jihadis-syria-iraq

Polish Martial Law on the Docket—Judging the Past and the Clash of Judicial Narratives

Jerzy Zajadło and Tomasz Tadeusz Koncewicz

Abstract The totalitarian regimes leave sometimes to the next generation a challenge of dealing with legal problems that lawyers will find later difficult to solve within the confines of democratic state governed by the rule of law. The authors analyse this process of coming to terms with the past through the prism of the Polish decree of 13 December 1981 on the Martial law. Two case studies chosen for their analysis show how two supreme Polish courts—The Polish Constitutional Tribunal and the Supreme Court—dealt with this very issue and each came up with its own understanding of how to look back on the martial law. The latter attempted to justify and uphold the judicial decisions made during the application of martial law in Poland, yet doing so, it violated basic tenets of legal axiology. The former, on the other hand, was determined to make good the damage wrought by the Supreme Court but while doing so it overstepped its own competences and in the process became a court of facts, rather than laws. The analysis shows how martial law continues to pose important conceptual and axiological questions and is everything but a matter of the past.

1 Setting the Scene

> A philosophy of life and a philosophy of law help the judge in understanding his role and in executing that role. It is important that the judge have an understanding of the philosophical discourse. Through it, he can participate in the search for truth, while understanding the

J. Zajadło (✉)
Department of Theory and Philosophy of State and Law,
Faculty of Law and Administration, University of Gdańsk, Gdańsk, Poland
e-mail: jzajadlo@prawo.ug.edu.pl

T. T. Koncewicz
Department of European and Comparative Law, Faculty of Law and Administration,
University of Gdańsk, Gdańsk, Poland
e-mail: tomasz.koncewicz@provider.pl; tomaszk@princeton.edu

T. T. Koncewicz
LAPA Crane Fellow, Program in Law and Public Affairs,
Princeton University, Princeton, USA

P. Auriel et al. (eds.), *The Rule of Crisis*, Ius Gentium: Comparative Perspectives on Law and Justice 64, https://doi.org/10.1007/978-3-319-74473-5_8

> limitations of the human mind and the complexity of human kind. With the help of a good philosophy, he will better understand the role of the law in a society and the task of the judge within it. One cannot accomplish much with a good philosophy alone, yet one cannot accomplish anything without it.[1]

In accordance with Article 28(2) of 22 July 1952 Constitution of the People's Republic[2] "Council of State may introduce the state of emergency (in Polish "*stan nadzwyczajny*") on the part or the entirety of the territory of the state, in order to safeguard the defence or the security of the state. For the same reasons, the Council of State may proclaim partial or complete mobilisation". When the Constitution was amended on 10 February 1976, Article 28(2) was renumbered and became Article 33(4).[3] The content and the wording remained untouched, though. Thus, on literal reading Polish Constitution knew only the state of emergency aimed at safeguarding the defence of the state, e.g. martial law.[4]

What follows is not a recount, or appraisal of, historical events. We leave this to the historians.[5] Our aim is rather to look at Polish martial law of 1981 from the legal perspective, and, to be more exact, from the perspectives of two Polish highest jurisdictions: Supreme Court and Constitutional Tribunal. Such comparative approach will highlight important cleavages and differences of opinion, but more importantly, show the shortcomings of the positivistic line of thinking so predominant in Polish courts when faced with question of principle that called for judicial imagination, courage and constitutional fidelity to more than just a legal text. Shortcomings of the Supreme Court pushed the Constitutional Tribunal into "identity crisis" as the latter was faced with the difficult question of judicial propriety. The Constitutional Tribunal took on the case even though, it was clear that the case was about making a judgment on the facts, whereas the constitutional review in Poland is premised on the distinction between establishing facts (province of regular judges) and judging the law (province of the Constitutional Tribunal). In the process of correcting the Supreme Court and putting things right, the constitutional court was guided by the imperative of bringing back sense of basic justice and historical closure. It did so at the expense of its own jurisdictional limits.

However, before taking on the "courts v martial law controversy", we must at least summarise the basic facts that will inform and frame the analysis that follows.[6]

---

[1]Barak (2006) 116.

[2]Journal of Laws no 33, item 232.

[3]Journal of laws no 5, item 29.

[4]Some have argued that "martial law" could be only resorted to in order to safeguard the defence of the state, whereas safeguarding state security must be left to another (unnamed) instance of an emergency state, namely "state of emergency" in the narrow (limited to security) sense (in Polish "*stan wyjatkowy*"). See more detailed discussion in Mażewski (2012).

[5]See Paczkowski and Byrne (2008) with further references.

[6]See also detailed analysis in Paczkowski and Werbian (2007). For historical background and ramifications, see also Sandford (1986) and Ash (2002a, b).

During the night on 12/13 December 1981, acting pursuant to Article 33(2) of the Constitution of People's Republic of Poland, the Council of State[7] introduced martial law in Poland. The Decree on Martial Law of 12 December 1981 was a framework legislation and contained 61 articles.[8] It was announced in Dziennik Ustaw (Journal of Laws) no. 29, item 154, whereas the publication body was dated 14 December 1981. Decree was accompanied by the Resolution of 12 December 1980 on the introduction of the martial law[9] refers explicitly to the "defence". Importantly Decree was published in the Journal of Laws first and Resolution came second which later prompted allegations of illegality of the martial law (see the analysis *infra*).[10]

With the benefit of hindsight, we now know that the printing of the said Journal of Laws only began on 17 December 1981 and finished on 18 December 1981, so it can be assumed that the content of legal regulations could have reached the addressees not earlier than 19 December 1981. Article 61 of the Decree on Martial Law provided as follows: "The Decree shall come into force on the day of its announcement, effective from the day of adoption". On 3 March 1977, the People's Republic of Poland ratified the International Covenant on Civil and Political Rights of 16 December 1966,[11] whose Article 15.1 provides: "No one shall be held guilty

[7]The Council of State was a constitutional body regulated by art. 25-27 of the 1952 Constitution. In the system of government established by the Constitution and in the daily practice of government, the Council of State's influence was predominant and overshadowed the Sejm (Parliament) defined "as the highest organ of the State authority" (art. 15 (2)) of the Constitution. On the system of government in the communist Poland see Brzezinski (2000) in particular Chapter Three "From Constitutionalism to Totalitarianism: Communist Constitutional Practice and Its Polish Application (1944–1989), pp. 58–81; Sanford (2002) in particular Chapter Two The Communist Experience and Legacy, pp. 24–49. For our analysis, the legislative competence of the Council of State to issue decrees having the force of laws and issued in the intervals between the sessions of Sejm is of paramount significance (art. 25 (1)(iv) read in conjunction with art. 26 (1) of the Constitution).

[8]Chapter One "General provisions" contained art. 1-7. The martial law might be declared on the whole of the territory for defence grounds (art. 1 (2)) and on the part of the territory to ensure the security of the state (art. 1 (3)), the legal instrument (resolution of the Council of State—art. 2 and the announcement by the President of the Council of State—art. 3); restriction of constitutional rights and imposition of obligations; extraordinary legislative powers of the Council of Ministers (art. 6) and the militarisation of parts of the territory (art. 7). Chapter II (art. 8-22) dealt with the "Rights and Obligations of the citizens during the martial law"; Chapter III "Procedure in case of extraordinary urgency related to the defence and security" (art. 23-28); Chapter IV "Functioning of the state administration and economy during the martial law" (art. 29-41); Chapter V "Preventive Measures" (art. 42-45); Chapter VI "Penal provisions" (art. 46-52); Chapter VII "Temporary and final provisions" (art. 53-61). Of all the provisions, it was art. 61 and its wording that never stopped puzzling the generations of Polish lawyers. It provided: "The decree enters into force on the day of its publication with effects from its adoption".

[9]As opposed to the Decree, the Resolution was "case—specific" and contained three short paragraphs declaring that on 13 December 1981 martial law is introduced on the whole of the territory of Poland to safeguard the security of the state and that it enters on the day of its adoption.

[10]See also Mażewski (2012) 40. L. Mażewski, *supra*, note 4, at p. 40.

[11]Journal of Laws of 1977, no. 38, item 167—Appendix.

of any criminal offence on account of any act or omission which did not constitute a criminal offence, under national or international law, at the time when it was committed. Nor shall a heavier penalty be imposed than the one that was applicable at the time when the criminal offence was committed. If, subsequent to the commission of the offence, provision is made by law for the imposition of a lighter penalty, the offender shall benefit thereby".[12]

2 Polish Supreme Court on the Martial Law—Five Minutes of Anti-philosophy of Anti-law

In the resolution of 20 December 2007, Polish Supreme Court (hereinafter referred to as "the Court")[13] ruled as follows:

> Because the Constitution of People's Republic of Poland (PRL) of 1952 did not prohibit the creation of criminal laws with a retroactive effect (the lex retro non agit principle) or a legal mechanism to initiate control of legislative provisions' conformity to the Constitution or international law, and because the position of international agreements in the domestic legal framework was not regulated, courts adjudicating in criminal cases concerning crimes under the Decree of the Council of State of 12 December 1981 on Martial Law (Journal of Laws no. 29, item 154) were not exempt from the obligation to apply retroactive criminal legislative provisions.[14]

Importantly, the Court decided to enter the resolution into the register of the principles of law. In accordance with Article 61(6) of the Law on the Supreme Court, "resolutions of the Full Court, of the joint chambers of the Court or of the Chamber become principles of law on the day of their adoption. The Court sitting in the composition of seven judges may decide that its resolution will be given a status of a principle of law". That means the resolution is binding on all other as long as it has not been revoked by the Full Chamber of the Court.[15] The resolution was adopted in the settling a legal issue mode, which resulted from instance proceedings (Article 441(2) of the Criminal Procedure Code). The problem was submitted to an extended panel of the Supreme Court (Supreme Court—Disciplinary Court) in relation to the case of Zdzisław B., in which the Prosecutor of the Institute of National Remembrance—Commission for the Prosecution of Crimes against the Polish Nation in Katowice proposed a motion for permission to make him criminally liable. Zdzisław B. is currently a retired judge of the Supreme Court, and in

[12]Officially translated into Polish and published in Journal of Laws of 1977, no. 38, item 167—Appendix.

[13]The Court functions in accordance with the Law on the Supreme Court of 23 November 2002 (Journal of Laws no 240, item 2052).

[14]Case I KZP 37/07. The resolution met with great interest from the Polish doctrine. Most commentators were critical of the Supreme Court. See Królikowski (2008), Sakowicz (2009), Zajadło (2008) and Zalewski (2008). For a rare approval see Przyjemski (2008).

[15]Art. 62. § 1 of the Law on the Supreme Court.

1982 he adjudicated in criminal cases concerning crimes under the Decree of the Council of State of 12 December 1981 on Martial Law. Because the panels of which Zdzisław B. was a member, adjudicated, among others, in cases concerning pre-trial detention of persons committing crimes between 12 (13?) and 16 (17? 18?) December 1981, the problem of the legality of those decisions, already widely discussed in judicature and doctrine,[16] naturally resurfaced. Did the adjudicating without a legal basis constitute a crime of abuse of power by judges, including the retired Supreme Court judge, Zdzisław B?

In its resolution, the Supreme Court should have addressed several fundamental legal problems: first, determining the actual moment of validity of the Decree on Martial Law, given the different dates of issuing (12 December), publication (14 December) and real availability (18 (19?) December) of that legal act; second, the problem of violating the *lex retro non agit* (or rather *lex severior criminalis retro non agit*) principle and as a result, also the *nullum crimen, nulla poena sine lege poenali anteriori* principle in the context of the wording of the cited Article 61 of the Decree on Martial Law; third, the issue of the nature of the validity of the cited Article 15.1 of the International Covenant on Civil and Political Rights in the Polish legal framework. In the opinion of the Supreme Court, the way of settling these legal issues will also affect the issue of criminal liability of judges for pronouncing sentences under the Decree on Martial Law concerning crimes committed between 12 (13?) and 16 (17?, 18?) December 1981. And the Supreme Court did indeed address the issues, but the way it did so, leave criminal lawyers bewildered, to say the least. On first reading, the resolution did not stand out from the crowd. Indeed not much was made of it, and comments were limited to brief headlines "*The Institute of National Remembrance will no longer be allowed to prosecute judges of the martial law period*".[17] It is only on closer reading of the motives that most fundamental problems and doubts resurface that make this resolution highly controversial.

What merits criticism is not only the technical aspects of the reasoning, i.e. argumentative deficiency. What is missing from the decision Anno Domini 2017 is even more appalling. From the point of view of legal philosophy, the resolution is devoid of any substantive considerations. Only here and there the Court relies on pseudo-positivism trying to prove by force after 25 years of transition that black is white and white is black. It is especially surprising given the fact that after 1989, some members of the judiciary were the first to notice the need to discuss the essence of law and the limits of its application, i.e. the role of legal philosophy in the process of creating and applying law.[18]

---

[16]The literature on the subject is extensive. Consult, for example Oniszczuk (2004) and Wróbel (2003), with further more detailed references to the case law and the literature.

[17]Rzeczpospolita of 21 December 2007, p. C1.

[18]Czech (1992)—as far as we know, only Volume I of the materials was published and some of the papers presented during the conference were never published.

Although the resolution was adopted in a relatively insignificant incidental proceeding, due to the conclusion content and the arguments mentioned in the statement of reasons it may be of capital importance to further apply criminal law instruments in the process of assessing and judging a criminal past. There is no universal model in this regard around the world.[19] A few years ago, comprehensive research was completed at the Max Planck Institute in Freiburg within the framework of the programme "Criminal Law in Reaction to State Crime" (Strafrecht in Reaktion auf Systemunrecht). It was found that there are four possible types of criminal law applied to perpetrators in response to state crime: the adopted typology is based on identifying two extreme solutions and intermediate solutions between these two extremes. So first of all, the attitude of criminal law to the past may involve renouncing prosecution, which may be referred to as a "thick line" policy. Interestingly, this solution has been adopted by very different (in terms of historical experiences) countries: on the one hand, Spain or Chile, for example, on the other hand, Russia or Belarus. The other extreme is a model of universal criminal prosecution of crimes committed in a former system. Actually, the authors of the project mention only one example of this: Germany after 1990. Intermediate solutions involve either conditional resignation from criminal prosecution (e.g. South Africa) or limited prosecution (on the one hand, countries such as Bulgaria, Poland or Hungary, and on the other hand, Argentina, Greece or Portugal).[20]

From the point of view of the Polish Supreme Court resolution, the judicature of German courts of the 1990s and the first decade of the twenty-first century provides especially interesting materials for evaluation. In our country, we are most knowledgeable about the judgments in the Berlin Wall shooters trials (so-called Mauerschuetzen). Although it is a specifically German problem, some aspects of this judicature may apply to the evaluation of the Polish legal framework, because in the last instance the case was submitted to the European Court of Human Rights in 2001.[21] One of the basic issues the Court addressed was the question of determining the standards of evaluating retroactive criminal law. However, it must be stressed that in the model adopted in Germany, the judges and prosecutors of the former GDR accused of bending the law (*Rechtsbeugung*—§ 339 of the German Criminal Code) were also brought to court. Although the Polish Criminal Code does not specify an analogical crime, it does include the provision of the above-mentioned Article 231 of the Criminal Code (formerly Article 246 of the Criminal Code of 1969), which in some circumstances may serve a very similar role, since the crime of "bending the law" may also involve applying which lead to the violation of the *nullum crimen, nulla poena sine lege poenali anteriori* principle.

[19]For comprehensive comparative account of post-communist countries Ash (2002a, b).

[20]Eser and Arnold (2002).

[21]More information can be found in Zajadło (2003) and the translations of the decisions of the European Court of Human Rights included there.

Obviously, it is not our intention to thoughtlessly copy German experiences to Polish circumstances. But on the other hand, some elements adopted by German judicature might be resorted to as universal. German courts, *mutatis mutandis* similar to Polish judicial authorities in the cases of communist crimes, faced the following choice in the cases of the "Berlin Wall shooters":

1. Deciding that the acts in question should be assessed on the basis of literal wording of laws and the actual practice of judicial authorities of former GDR and in the light of the concept of the state and law applicable then (so-called socialist rule of law)—at the time, not only the lowest rank border guards but also (or first of all) members of the highest party and state authorities were never brought to court for their crimes—in the light of this special positivism, the border regime of the GDR was legitimised both *de iure* and *de facto*, and as a result it was necessary either to refrain from prosecution at all or to acquit the accused.
2. Deciding that although the law and policy of the contemporary authorities legitimised a certain border regime, the legitimisation was contrary to:
   (a) universal, human, common moral standards undermining or questioning its legal character: as a result, law provisions excluding the illegality of certain acts should be ex ante or ex post made invalid (so-called Radbruch's formula; see analysis *infra*),
   (b) standards determined in the regulations of international human rights protection, especially the Universal Declaration of Human Rights of 1948 (despite its formally non-committal character) and the International Covenant on Civil and Political Rights of 1966 (despite a lack of formal implementation in the legal framework of the GDR)—as a result, legal provisions of the GDR excluding the illegality of acts were either ineffective due to being contrary to international law or at least had to be interpreted in a spirit favourable to human rights, which would allow for liability in line with the general principles of the Criminal Code of the GDR or FRG.
3. Deciding that the provisions of the Constitution, Criminal Code, acts regulating the border and police regime or even non-statutory regulations of real authorities (resolutions, instructions, orders, decisions, etc.) applicable in the GDR should be interpreted literally, not in the spirit of so-called social rule of law but in the spirit of a universally understood democratic legal state.

When the Mauerschuetzen proceedings occurred in Germany in the early 1990s, the most popular stance in the literature, especially literature concerning criminal law, was that described above in point 1, while the judicature included decisions from a spectrum of the stance described in point 2a supported with the argumentation described in point 2b, and an interpretation in the spirit of Rechtsstaat characterised in point 3. As time passed, both in the literature and judicature, the so-called Radbruch formula (item 2a) became dominant, concretised in the regulations of international human rights protection (item 2b). The concepts that received the most critical opinions were the ones that tried to reinterpret the GDR border regime in the spirit of democratic legal state (item 3), although this was the stance of the European Court of Human Rights.

Can we evaluate the resolution of the Supreme Court from the point of view of these three possible approaches? In our opinion, definitely yes, even if not in the light of specific dogmas of criminal law, then at least from the perspective of general legal theory and philosophy. If the substantiation proposed by the Supreme Court followed the above-mentioned specific positivism, or rather specific legal realism, and was limited to an attempt to assess the Decree on Martial Law from the point of view of legal and non-legal reality of the People's Republic of Poland (item 1), then I could at least understand it. But, unfortunately, it is not so. The reasoning in the glossed resolution exceeds this standard, because actually it is a combination of arguments that cannot be combined. The Supreme Court tried to defend the legal and non-legal reality of the People's Republic of Poland (item 1) by means of seriously using arguments that should only be applied to a democratic legal state (item 3). Disregarding the problem of the controversial "Radbruch formula", it must be emphasised that the Supreme Court also rejected the possibility of applying the above-mentioned interpretation that was favourable to human rights (item 2), and we have problems understanding the Court's motives here. This resulted in a legislative and legal hybrid, which shows that the Decree on Martial Law was alright, not only in accordance with the legal framework of the PRL but also with contemporary standards. The Court seems to be on the defensive against this charge by emphasising that the People's Republic was obviously not a democratic legal state within the meaning of Article 2 of the Constitution of the Republic of Poland of 1997. Yet this has been done to justify the lack of clear prohibition against retroactive criminal legislation, also from the point of view of Article 15 of the International Covenant on Civil and Political Rights. In fact, the Court treats the legislative and non-legislative framework of the PRL with all seriousness of legal positivism as an ideology of a democratic legal state. The reasoning falls into following steps:

1. The Constitution of the People's Republic of Poland of 1952 did not explicitly prohibit the creation of criminal laws with a retroactive effect.
2. The Constitution of the People's Republic of Poland of 1952 did not provide for a legal mechanism to initiate control of legislative provisions' conformity to the Constitution or international law.
3. The Constitution of the People's Republic of Poland of 1952 did not specify the position of international agreements in the domestic legal framework, and hence retroactive criminal legislation did not violate that framework despite different regulation under Article 15 of the Covenant on Civil and Political Rights.
4. The Constitution of the People's Republic of Poland of 1952 provided that closely observing the law is the basic responsibility of each state authority and each citizen; all public authority and public administration bodies only operate on the basis of legal regulations; judges are independent and only subject to legal acts.

5. The Law of 30 December 1950 on issuing the Journal of Laws provided that the date included in the journal as the day of issuance was also the day of announcing the legal acts included in this journal.
6. Retroactive provisions concerning martial law were issued by the State Council, a body that was constitutionally obliged to ensure the compliance of legal acts with the Constitution.

This brought the Court to the following conclusion:

7. "Neither Article 3 of the Act on issuing the Journal of Laws nor Article 61 of the Decree on Martial Law were contrary to the Constitution of the People's Republic of Poland, thus the Constitution could not be the legal basis for exempting courts from the obligation to apply legislative provisions, even if it violated the *lex retro non agit principle*"; "lack of such a regulation and not applying the requirements resulting from the *lex retro non agit* principle, or even creating retroactive provisions, indirectly meant that the legislator [...] found retroactive criminal provisions not to violate the legal framework applicable in the PRL"; "due to the lack of legal mechanism allowing the initiation of controlling conformity with the Constitution of the PRL or international law, courts adjudicating in criminal cases concerning crimes under the Decree on Martial Law were not exempt from the obligation to apply legislative provisions (including retroactive ones)", etc.
8. All this can lead to two paradoxical conclusions. On the one hand, this risky reasoning would be completely unnecessary if the authors of the martial law had been circumspect enough to print the relevant publication body early enough, i.e. during the night of 12/13 December 1981. On the other hand, on the basis of arguments included in the glossed resolution, PRL judges would have been equally obliged to apply the Decree on Martial Law even if the relevant Journal of Laws had been published much later, e.g. in June 1982, because the provisions of Article 25 and Article 31 of the Constitution of the People's Republic of Poland obliged the Chairman of the State Council to announce acts and decrees but did not specify any dates. Hence, in one of the judgments from the martial law period, we can read that: "One may not excuse themselves with the unawareness of the illegality of a certain act if the prohibitions, orders or limitations set out in the act (or decree) were announced through mass media before announcing the legal act in the Journal of Laws and if the perpetrator was aware or could become aware of the existence of such prohibitions, orders or limitations through these media (Article 24(2) of the Criminal Code)".[22]

The problem is that presenting the reasoning included in the resolution more than twenty-five years after the announcement of martial law is just a waste of time. If the glossed resolution of the Supreme Court had been adopted in the 1980s, I could understand its rhetoric and I would even be inclined to recognise its positivist character. But in 2007, in the conditions of a democratic legal state, the

[22]Judgment of the Supreme Court of 01.03.1982, V KRN 50/82—OSNKW 1982/6/39.

Supreme Court arguing this way must be aware that it is even contrary to the canons of contemporary legal positivism. Contrary to appearances, the essence of the problem does not depend on statutory provisions. In the Polish legal framework, the validity of a ban on retroactive criminal law was possible not only because on 29 December 1989 the principle of democratic legal state was introduced to the Constitution of 1952, from which the Constitutional Tribunal derived *the lex retro non agit* principle by way of judicature. It was possible first of all because the change of political system was accompanied by a change of legal culture in terms of understanding the nature of law and the limits of its application—in other words, the philosophy of law. Paradoxically, this was the stance of the chairman and reporting judge of the first adjudication panel that issued the resolution—then first President of the Supreme Court, Lech Gardocki. In 1991, in the case note on the decision of the Supreme Court of 28 September 1990, V KRN 109/90, he wrote:

> Today, on the basis of the existing judicature of the Constitutional Tribunal, we can decide that the stance of PRL courts concerning the retroactive application of the Decree on Martial Law was not only an erroneous interpretation of the Criminal Code but also a violation of the Constitution. There is nothing to prevent courts from applying the Constitution as a natural foundation for control of individual acts, including court judgments.[23]

This was also the position taken by the Supreme Court at the time. In the judgment of 24 October 1991 we read:

> The Decree on Martial Law could and did come into force after the completion of printing and distributing the whole issue, i.e. on 19 December 1981 at the earliest, and the criminality of acts included in the decree should have been counted from then, because it was then that the Decree became available and the obligation to learn its content arose, excluding unawareness of illegality of the acts.[24]

If we compare these opinions with the argumentation of the glossed resolution, we can undoubtedly see a gigantic regression in legal philosophy and glaring lack of the culture of justification.[25] Regrettably, the Court spoke *ratione imperii*, rather than *imperio rationis*.

One of the authors of contemporary refined legal positivism, H. L. A. Hart, once wrote concerning the judicature of American courts that it oscillated between two extremes—the Nightmare and the Noble Dream.[26] According to Hart, the Nightmare was a situation in which the parties to the dispute expect the court to apply the binding law but it proves impossible due to the obscurity of the law. As a result, the court has to "create" the law to a certain extent. The Noble Dream, in

[23]Published in (1991) 3 Państwo i Prawo (State and Law) 113.

[24]Case II KRN 273/91 published in LEX no. 22068.

[25]We borrow the term from influential work of Mureinik (1994), 31. For more modern restatement and application of his theory, see excellent analysis by Cohen-Eliya and Porat (2011, pp. 463–490).

[26]HLA Hart, "American Jurisprudence through English Eyes: The Nightmare and the Noble Dream" 11 Georgia Law Journal 969; Lacey (2006).

turn, means a situation in which positive law is so precise and perfect that the judge has a ready solution to use without the need to assume the role of a "lawgiver". But this situation occurs relatively rarely, or actually never. What does it have to do with the glossed judgment? I cannot help but get the impression that the statement of reasons provided by the Supreme Court kind of reverses these two extremes. The Nightmare becomes the Noble Dream, and the Noble Dream, the Nightmare. Recognising the applicability of the Decree on Martial Law in the period between 13 and 17(18) December 1981, courts only appeared to apply the law, but in fact they created it (the Nightmare). The Noble Dream would have only come true if in known circumstances the judicial authorities had thrown doubt on its legal character. This is the source of the title of this section, being a paraphrasing of a well-known speech by Gustav Radbruch. In September 1945, Radbruch gave a talk on the radio, which he later published in Rhein-Neckar-Zeitung as an essay "Five minutes of the philosophy of law". In the last, fifth minute, he wrote:

> There are principles of law, therefore, that are weightier than any legal enactment, so that a law in conflict with them is devoid of validity. These principles are known as natural law or the law of reason. To be sure, their details remain open to question, but the work of centuries has in fact established a solid core of them, and they have come to enjoy such far-reaching consensus in the so-called declarations of human and civil rights that only a dogmatic skeptic could still entertain doubts about some of them.[27]

Translating this into a more legal language, not only explicit rules but also implicit ones are binding in the legal framework. If a lawyer forgets this obvious truth, he sooner or later falls into the trap of anti-legal philosophy.

We are not going to elaborate here on the problem of motivations for the conclusion of the commented resolution, especially the arguments in its statement of reasons. If the motivation was to ultimately finish the discussion on the legal character of the Decree on the Martial Law (which might be inferred from the decision to enter it into the rules of law register), we can say that from the point of view of legal dogma it is possible, but from that of legal philosophy, it is out of the question. If the decision was motivated just by the problem of judges' criminal responsibility for the application of the Decree on the Martial Law in the period from 13 to 17 (18?) December 1981, all this pseudo-positivist argumentation is unnecessary indeed. The Supreme Court also perceives this, writing that "the criminal responsibility of a judge in this situation, just like the criminal responsibility of any other person, does not only occur when the definition of a crime under threat of penalty is met and there are grounds to render the action illegal, but it must be based on the principle of guilt". But apparently the first of these elements was decisive, for the last sentence of the statement of reasons in the resolution reads: "By the way, in the statement of reasons for the resolution, because of its content, it was unnecessary to deal with the problem of the knowledge of the judges

[27]Radbruch (1945) and Polish translation by J. Zajadło *Pięć minut filozofii prawa*, Colloquia Communia 1988–1989, 6(41)–1(42), p. 62.

adjudicating in cases concerning crimes under the Decree on Martial Law on the antedating of the Journal of Laws in which the decree was published".

The Supreme Court, both in the conclusion of, and the statement of, reasons for its resolution strangely rejected two fundamental principles embodied in the Latin legal maxims: on the one hand, the problem of the retroactive effect of criminal law (directly *lex criminalis retro non agit* and indirectly *nullum crimen sine lege*) and the effects of a lack and/or erroneous announcement of a legal act (*lex non obligat nisi promulgata*). One would be tempted to go even further and try to evaluate the resolution from the perspective of a conflict between two other contrary Latin maxims: on the one hand, *durum est, sed ita lex scripta est* (Ulpian, Digesta 40, 9, 12, 1, colloquially known as *dura lex sed lex*), and on the other hand, *lex iniusta* (or rather—*iniustissima*) *non est lex*. But this would exceed the subject of this gloss and would not fully fit the argumentation of the Supreme Court in the discussed resolution. Although the problem of judicial disobedience is still interesting for contemporary legal philosophers, especially in the field of Anglo-Saxon jurisprudence,[28] but it also predominantly refers to solving the blatant conflict between the law and morality, especially in the version promoted in the "Radbruch formula". The case that was the subject of the Supreme Court resolution is much simpler than the dilemma raised by Radbruch. The issue was not to assess whether the Decree on Martial Law was a grossly unjust law, but only whether it could/should have been applied in a certain time frame taking into consideration its defects resulting from the retroactive character and the lack of proper promulgation, i.e. whether at a specific moment and with reference to specific actions it was a valid law at all. As much and as little as that. From the legal philosophy perspective, it would be more fitting to quote not Radbruch,[29] but rather the concept of the internal morality of law by Fuller. That is because the problem involves rather the ethos of the legal profession and his (constitutional) fidelity to law rather than the issue of his criminal liability. Constitutional fidelity stands for more than a duty to observe the text. Our understanding of fidelity is more than a duty and an obligation to observe the text. As argued by J. Balkin:

> Fidelity is not simply a matter of correspondence between an idea and a text, or a set of correct procedures for interpretation. It is not simply a matter of proper translation or proper synthesis or even proper political philosophy. Fidelity is not a relationship between a thing and an interpretation of that thing. Fidelity is not about texts; it is about selves. Fidelity is an orientation of a self towards something else, a relation- ship which is mediated through and often disguised by talk of texts, translations, correspondences and political philosophy. Fidelity is an attitude that we have towards something we attempt to understand; it is a discipline of self that is related to the discipline of a larger set of selves in a society. Fidelity

---

[28]From the more recent literature, Brand-Ballard (2010), Edlin (2010), Wendel (2010) and most recent monograph by Graver (2015).

[29]In her dissenting opinion on the Radbruch formula, judge E. Łętowska emphasised that we do not only need to take into account what Radbruch wrote about state crime but also what he thought about judges' guilt and responsibility for applying such regulations. I completely agree with this view, as essentially it is consistent with the intentions of the German legal philosopher—more on this topic can be read in Zajadło (2001).

is ontological and existential; it shapes us, affects us, has power over us, ennobles us, enslaves us. Fidelity is a form of power exercised over the self by the self and by the social forces that help make the self what it is. As such, fidelity is an equivocal concept, full of both good and bad, mixed inextricably together. Fidelity is the home of commitment, sacrifice, self-identification and patriotism, as well as the home of legitimation, servitude, self-deception and idolatry.[30]

Such fidelity was sorely missing in the reasoning of the Court, and in the end it doomed the resolution[31].

3 Polish Constitutional Tribunal—Politics of Law or Politics Over Law?

Polish Constitutional Tribunal (hereinafter referred to as the "Tribunal")[32] entered the fray with its judgment of 27 October 2010. The operative part of the judgment reads:

Article 80 § 2b sentence one of the Act of 27 July 2001 Law on Ordinary Courts understood in the way that "the obvious groundlessness of a motion for making a judge criminally liable" includes the issue that requires basic interpretation of the act:

(a) is contrary to Article 2 of the Constitution of the Republic of Poland,
(b) is not contrary to Article 7, Article 10, and Article 42.1 of the Constitution, and Article 7 of the Convention for the Protection of Human Rights and Fundamental Freedoms drafted in Rome on 4 November 1950, later amended with Protocols 3, 5 and 8 and supplemented with Protocol 2 (Journal of Laws of 1993 no. 61, item 284, as amended) and Article 15 of the International Covenant on Civil and Political Rights, open for signing on 19 December 1966 (Journal of Laws of 1977, no. 38, item 167).[33]

For a legal theoretician and philosopher, the sentence of the Constitutional Tribunal of 27 October 2010 in the case K 10/08 is particularly provoking to comment on, and for several reasons: firstly, because it refers to the very essence of the phenomenon of law, in all its aspects: creation, application, interpretation, effect and observance; secondly, because on the grounds of the dispute concerning the cognition of the Constitutional Tribunal, a number of specific questions arise connected with the general theory of law application and interpretation; thirdly, because it is an interesting example to assess the rationality of legal argumentation,

[30]Balkin (1997).

[31]From the perspective of argumentative deficiency, the resolution of the Supreme Court is not an exception. The lack of constitutional fidelity among Polish judges is a systemic problem and calls for deep overhaul of adjudicatory ethos of an average judge. On this, see Koncewicz (2017b). See also the analysis *infra Epilogue*.

[32]On the Tribunal and judicial review in Poland see in-depth analysis by Garlicki (2002).

[33]Case K 10/08 published in the Journal of Laws 2010, no. 205, item 1364.

especially that something more than a casual difference in opinions occurs in the case, for nearly half of the judges of the adjudication panel presented their dissenting opinions (i.e. judges S. Biernat, A. Jamróz, E. Łętowska, M. Mazurkiewicz, M. Wyrzykowski, B. Zdziennicki).

Let's start our considerations with the following old juristic adage: *politia legibus, non leges politiae adaptandae* (politics should adapt to law, not law to politics). The reference to this Latin legal maxim requires some explanation. In our opinion, Latin adages include some wisdom accumulated through the ages, which from the point of view of professional legal methods are sometimes of rudimentary and sometimes fundamental importance. We do not know exactly the origin of the maxim used in the title of this gloss,[34] but its role in the conditions of a modern legal state is extremely important. Actually, it has a special significance from the point of view of the glossed judgment, because it is the Constitutional Tribunal that should be the basic guarantor protecting from non-legal (including political) instrumentalisation of law, regardless of motivations.[35] Taking this context into account, it is hard not to notice that something strange happened in the discussed case. It seems to be the proof of, not the primacy of law over politics demanded in the conclusion quoted in the title but to the contrary, the victory of broadly understood and differently motivated non-legal arguments over legal ones. If we consider the glossed judgment as the final result of a sequence of events, from the resolution of the Supreme Court of 20 December 2007[36] through the motion of the Ombudsman of 6 May 2008 and his pleadings of 17 April 2009 and 8 March 2010, we can see a cascade of successive instrumentalisations, each of which only resulted from the previous one. This domino effect must occur if the response to instrumentalisation is yet another instrumentalisation, triggering another one, etc.

Our aim is not to analyse in detail the legal dogmatic problems resulting from the judgment of the Constitutional Tribunal, and that is the reason for its atypical style. Rather we want to look at all the elements of the above-mentioned triad of events (the resolution of the Supreme Court → the opinion of the Ombudsman → the judgment of the Constitutional Tribunal) from the standpoint of legal theory and philosophy as manifested in the Latin legal maxims. The instrumentalisation character of the Supreme Court resolution was mainly manifested in the controlled[37] process of creating the necessity to make a decision in a form that could be entered into the rules of law register so as to conclude—once and forever, but actually only ostensibly—the subject of liability of judges for the application of the Decree on the Martial Law despite its proper publication and its retroactive nature.

---

[34]Anthologies of Latin adages and sayings do not specify its source of origin—cf., e.g. Burczak et al. (2007) 146.

[35]Zajadło (2009) 50.

[36]Case I KZP 37/07, OSNKW 2007/12/86.

[37]Judge E. Łętowska seems to express a similar view in her dissenting opinion: "referring (...) the legal issue so as to produce a resolution".

The Ombudsman's motion and pleadings, in turn, were formulated so as to enforce indirect control of the constitutional character of the Supreme Court resolution,[38] although as an act of law application it is not subject to such control within the framework of the Constitutional Tribunal cognition. Finally, the statement of reasons for the judgment of the Constitutional Tribunal is formulated so as to justify at all costs the need to issue an interpretation judgment[39] and thus confirm the existence of its cognition in the said case.

At first it might seem that the judgment is the end of the chain, because, as the Ombudsman probably intended, *Roma locuta, causa finita*. This was not to be, though. Indeed, the judgment of the Constitutional Tribunal ("*Roma locuta*") in this case is only symbolic and in practice will not be binding in any way for the Supreme Court adjudication panels. Rather it t will probably only cause another process of instrumentalisation, so the *causa* may prove not to be *finita* at all, and it will only deepen the already existing discrepancies between the Supreme Court and the Constitutional Tribunal.[40] Essentially, the glossed judgment of the Tribunal is just a formulation of prohibition of a certain interpretation and a certain scope of application of the provision of Article 80 § 2b sentence one of the Law on Common Courts Organisation for courts to observe. In this specific competition (not the proposed dialogue[41]) between the highest judicial authorities of the state, the truths expressed *mutatis mutandis* in the maxims *iniuria non excusat iniuriam*, or even *ex iniuria ius non oritur*, somehow got lost. If unauthorised extension of the authority's competence is improper, the following maxim can be used: *iniuria ex eo dicta est, quod non iure fiat; omne enim quod non iure fit, iniuria fieri dicitur* (lawlessness is called lawlessness because something occurs contrary to the law; it is said that anything that occurs contrary to the law becomes lawlessness—Ulpian, Digesta 47, 10, 1). Judge E. Łętowska expressed the same thought a little more mildly in her dissenting opinion:

[38]In their dissenting opinions, e.g. judges: S. Biernat ("the motion of the Ombudsman—J.Z. T.T. K.) was oriented against the resolution adopted by a panel of seven judges of the Supreme Court"; Judge A. Jamróz was of the opinion that "the object of complaint in the Ombudsman's motion is the Supreme Court resolution, not the provisions of Article 80 § 2b of the Act".

[39]In their dissenting opinions, e.g. judges S. Biernat ("The judgment was formulated as a so-called interpretative judgment, ruling the inconsistency of Article 80 § 2b sentence one of the Law on the Ordinary Courts construed in a certain way. I consider interpretative judgments to be acceptable and useful, but not in this case") and M. Mazurkiewicz ("The Ombudsman demands the Tribunal to establish the appropriate (…) interpretation as part of control of constitutionality of law. Due to the constitutionally specified cognition of the Constitutional Tribunal, it is unacceptable").

[40]In his dissenting opinion, judge B. Zdziennicki says: "For this system [Constitutional Tribunal, Supreme Court and ordinary courts—J.Z. T.T.K] to act efficiently, it is necessary for all its members to constantly collaborate, not to cause conflicts by completely arbitrary extension of their competences".

[41]In her dissenting opinion, judge E. Łętowska says: "[the judgment of the Constitutional Tribunal —J. Z. T.T.K.] is not conducive to dialogue and collaboration between courts".

> However, even an obvious defect [a procedural defect of the Supreme Court resolution – J. Z. T.T.K.] of the content of the resolution is no justification for "making up" for the defect caused by the Supreme Court by the activity of the Constitutional Tribunal, the latter being dubious from the competence point of view. An error must not be corrected with an activity that is erroneous in itself.

Evaluating the motion of the Ombudsman and his subsequent pleadings, we can point to Ulpian's maxim *apices iuris non sunt iura* (extreme solutions are not laws —Digesta 17, 1, 29, 4). It can be understood in two ways. In the pejorative sense, it means that even in the practice of Roman law, there was a phenomenon of instrumentalisation and bending of law by lawyers for their short-term goals, e.g. through use of ambiguities of law or loopholes. However, it must be emphasised that the phrase *apices iuris* does not have to be pejorative. In some translations it is used as a synonym of legal subtleties, i.e. refined legal reasoning.[42] It seems that both meanings are present in Ombudsman's arguments. The Ombudsman's critical attitude to the Supreme Court resolution was well known, because it was often expressed in the media.[43] But moral and legal disapproval of the Supreme Court's arguments presented in the resolution is one thing, and the possibility of initiating procedures aimed either to overturn it or to control its constitutionality by the Constitutional Tribunal in the mode provided for in the law, is another. The Ombudsman did not choose the first option resulting from Article 16(4) of the Act of 15 July 1987 on the Human Rights Defender in relation to the provisions of the Act of 23 November 2002 on the Supreme Court, because he would have had to indicate in the motion that he meant to adopt a resolution aimed at explaining legal provisions that arouse some doubts in practice or whose application causes some discrepancies in judicature".[44] Because it was difficult to indicate practical doubts and discrepancies in judicature, he used the other option, even though *prima facie* it might have seemed equally to be hazardous.

If we perceive the Ombudsman's motion and his later pleadings from the perspective of the conclusion of the judgment of the Constitutional Tribunal, a certain paradox becomes evident. In the 27-page-long statement of reasons of the Ombudsman's motion, a larger part is a crushing criticism (we agree with many of the points raised by the Ombudsman) of the arguments of the statement of reasons for the Supreme Court resolution concerning the retroactive character of the Decree on Martial Law, its improper publication and the application of international agreements in the Polish legal framework under the Constitution of 1952. The Ombudsman knew perfectly well that control of the constitutionality of the Supreme Court resolution did not come within the jurisdiction of the Constitutional Tribunal, as the resolution did not belong to the category of a „normative act". Rather, the resolution was an instance of the application process and as such fell

[42] Michalunio (2008) 35.

[43] Cf. J. Kochanowski, *Sędziowie po ciemnej stronie mocy*, Rzeczpospolita of 15 February 2008, p. A15.

[44] This is also emphasised by judges S. Biernat and M. Mazurkiewicz in their dissenting opinions.

within the exclusive competence of the Supreme Court. That is why he decided to choose more refined argumentation (*apices iuris*): because the said resolution of the Supreme Court was adopted in the mode of a legal question posed in a complaint proceeding taking place because of the application of Article 80 § 2b, he decided to complain against the method of interpreting the provision resulting from the very resolution. According to the Ombudsman, "with the resolution of 20 December 2007 (Case I KZP 37/07), the Supreme Court provided the interpretation of the first sentence of Article 80 § 2b". The Ombudsman referred to the Tribunal judicature pointing out that "when examining the constitutionality of a provision [...] it is necessary to start with its interpretation developed in court judicature". As a result, *applicatio est vita regulae* (the application [of law] is the life of a legal norm) should have been used. So if the Supreme Court resolution provided a certain interpretation of Article 80 § 2b sentence one, affecting court judicature (and this is the case according to the Ombudsman), control of the constitutionality of the normative content of the provision resulting from this interpretation is subject to the cognition of the Constitutional Tribunal. In the conclusion of the motion, the Ombudsman states that the "the disputed provision—within the meaning imposed by the discussed resolution of the Supreme Court—is contrary to Article 7 and Article 42(1) of the Constitution of the Republic of Poland, Article 7 of the European Convention for the Protection of Human Rights and Fundamental Freedoms, and Article 15 of the International Covenant on Civil and Political Rights".

The paradox is that, as item b of the conclusion of the judgment shows, the Tribunal did not agree with this argumentation. It rejected—and in our opinion rightly so—the charges of violating Article 7 and Article 42(1) of the Constitution of the Republic of Poland, Article 7 of the European Convention for the Protection of Human Rights and Fundamental Freedoms and Article 15 of the International Covenant on Civil and Political Rights, because it did not regard them to be relevant control patterns in the discussed case. The same was done, also rightly, with the additional charge raised by the Ombudsman in his pleading of 8 March 2010: the introduction of "tripartite separation of powers resulting from Article 10(1) and (2) of the Constitution of the Republic of Poland as an additional control pattern". But as a result, the Constitutional Tribunal had to focus on procedural aspects and exclude from the statement of reasons for the judgment what the Ombudsman really had in mind: critical evaluation of the content of the Supreme Court resolution concerning the Decree on the Martial Law in terms of its retroactive effect and improper publication. Here is another paradox: this substantive evaluation of the Supreme Court resolution is not included in the statement of reasons for the judgment of the Constitutional Tribunal but in the dissenting opinions of some judges (sic!). For example, judge S. Biernat writes:

> The statement of reasons for the Tribunal's judgment includes criticism of the role the Supreme Court's resolution of 20 December 2007 played in the procedure of waiving the judges' immunity, not the content of the resolution. This is understandable because of the adopted argumentation of the Tribunal. As an author of a dissenting opinion, I enjoy slightly greater freedom and consider it possible to express my view on the very content of

> the resolution of 7 Supreme Court judges. For me, the resolution is erroneous. I do not share the view of the Supreme Court that the principle *lex retro non agit* did not apply in the legal framework on the day of issuing the Decree on Martial Law.

Judge E. Łętowska expresses a similar view:

> I do not want my dissenting opinion in this case to be regarded as an expression of approval for the resolution of the Supreme Court of 20 December 2007, case I KZP 37/07, with which I disagree as a lawyer. I agree with [...] the criticism of the argument used in the resolution, concerning the lack of obligation to apply the non-retroactive effect principle if it was not expressed in the Constitution of 1952 and the lack of constitutional judiciary as a factor justifying the illegality of behaviours violating international law. What has been said exhausts the subject - *mirabile dictu* (wonderful to relate – Virgil, Georgica, 2, 30). Thus, the Constitutional Tribunal did not share, at least partially, the argumentation included in the basic motion and pleading of 8 March 2010, but it shared the additional charges extended and specified with the pleading of 17 April 2009. The Ombudsman moved there for stating the incompatibility of Article 80 § 2b sentence one of the Act of 27 July 2001 Law on Ordinary Courts[45] understood in the way that the obvious groundlessness of the motion for permission to make a judge criminally liable includes issues that require the basic interpretation of the act in conformity with the principle of certainty resulting from Article 2 of the Constitution of the Republic of Poland.

This was a reference to the above-mentioned arguments of the motion aimed to legitimate the cognition of the Tribunal in the said case in terms of examining the constitutionality of the normative content of the discussed provision assigned with the interpretation resulting from the resolution of seven Supreme Court judges. And this is basically the essence of the glossed judgment in the part in which the Constitutional Tribunal decided that "Article 80 § 2b sentence one of the Act of 27 July 2001 Law on Common Courts Organisation understood in the way that 'the obvious groundlessness of a motion for making a judge criminally liable' includes the issue that requires basic interpretation of the act is in conformity with Article 2 of the Constitution of the Republic of Poland". The dividing line between judges voting for the judgment and judges who expressed their dissenting opinions is exactly along the answer to the question of whether the Constitutional Tribunal did or did not have cognition in the discussed case. A greater part of the reasoning of the Constitutional Tribunal in the statement of reasons for the glossed judgment is devoted to this problem. The reasoning of the Constitutional Tribunal includes in a way two phases: first, the phase of deciding that there is a connection between the resolution of the Supreme Court and the provision of Article 80 § 2b sentence one of the Law on Common Courts Organisation (item III, 2 of the statement of reasons); second, the phase of deciding that the resolution of the Supreme Court determined by way of interpreting the new normative content of the provision which has and/or will have an effect on future judicature and as a result recognition of the Constitutional Tribunal's cognition in the said case (item III, 3 of the statement of reasons). In the conclusion, the Tribunal presented the following view: "As a result, we must decide that the normative content included in the legal

[45]Journal of Laws no. 98, item 1070, as amended.

provision of the Supreme Court's resolution with the character of a legal principle may also be the object of constitutional control. Furthermore, in the case of abstract control and control in the mode of legal questioning, it is not required that the interpretation of the Supreme Court entered into the rules of law register be binding and require uniform practice from a formal point of view from all law-applying authorities".[46] And further (item III, 5 in fine of the statement of reasons): "Taking this into consideration, the Constitutional Tribunal decided that Article 80 § 2b sentence one of the Law on Common Courts Organisation in the questioned scope is contrary to the principle of certainty of legal provisions resulting from Article 2 of the Constitution". In my opinion, this reasoning is burdened with logical fallacy. It is true that the Constitutional Tribunal in its statement of reasons for the judgment demonstrated convincingly a connection between the Supreme Court's resolution and Article 80 § 2b sentence one of the Law on Ordinary Courts. But it does not result in any way from the Supreme Court's resolution that each case concerning a judge applying the provisions of the Decree on Martial law in a specific time and with regard to specific acts must meet the premise of "obvious groundlessness". It shows only that this may occur. Hence, the resolution of the Supreme Court did not create new normative content of the provision of Article 80 § 2b sentence one of the Law on Ordinary Courts by way of interpretation but it only determined the scope and possibilities of its application with regard to a certain group of cases. As a result, in my opinion, the Tribunal drew a false conclusion (cognition of the Constitutional Tribunal in the discussed case) from a true premise (the connection between the Supreme Court's resolution and the provision of Article 80 § 2b sentence one of the Law on Common Courts Organisation).

The problem only seems to concern competences, because in fact it also has a deep legal and theoretical dimension. In our opinion, the expression "normative content assigned by way of interpretation" is an euphemism. Indeed, each interpretation (i.e. also the process of application of law) is assigning a provision a certain normative content. If so, there is a question about the boundary between situations in which "normative content assigned by way of interpretation" is subject to control by the Constitutional Tribunal and situations in which such content does not apply. It is hard to find such precision in the previous Constitutional Tribunal judgments quoted in the statement of reasons for the glossed judgment, which may suggest that it is the object of its arbitrary assessment. At an absurd level, it could mean that any precedential decision of a common court as an act of law application (i.e. its interpretation) which determined the direction of subsequent judicature may be subject to Constitutional Tribunal control. In my opinion, in the discussed case, it is unimportant that the interpretation had the form of a Supreme Court resolution

[46] The Constitutional Tribunal differentiated here (incomprehensibly, at least for us) formal requirements in cases of constitutional review by way of constitutional complaint and abstract review and legal questions posed by ordinary judges. Convincing criticism of such differentiation is presented in the dissenting opinion of judge M. Wyrzykowski.

entered into the register of legal principles.[47] The data of the Institute of National Remembrance which is quoted in the statement of reasons for the judgment and which was to be proof of practice of proceedings in the subject of waiving judge immunities after the adoption of the resolution of seven Supreme Court judges on 20 December 2007 refer to already existing and potentially anticipated facts, not law. We may not rule out that the practice would have been similar if instead of the Supreme Court's resolution entered into the rules of law register there had been more than ten judgments determining the so-called consolidated jurisdiction approach. Actually, theoretically the same effect might have been achieved by one "convincing" Supreme Court judgment. To conclude, I think—similarly to all the judges presenting their dissenting opinions—that the Constitutional Tribunal does not have cognition in this particular case.[48] In the final instance in this case, however, its control of the normative content assigned by way of interpretation means interference in the process of law application and thus does not meet the concept of hierarchical control of normative acts within the meaning of the Act on the Constitutional Tribunal. We may not rule out that, first, the whole previous jurisdiction approach of the Tribunal had been erroneous, second, that the judgments of the Tribunal concerning its "new" competence were determined *ad casum* by actual situations and cannot be generalised. So with some terminological reservation, we agree with the view of judge E. Łętowska expressed in her dissenting opinion that this case does not involve interpretation subject to Constitutional Tribunal control, but rather is an example of subsumption. Because we understand subsumption as assigning a specific actual situation to a specific legal norm, we would rather call it the determination of the scope of applying a norm *in abstracto*, which is not subject to the cognition of the Constitutional Tribunal, but forms part of law application.

4 Epilogue—Judging Martial Law: On the Constitutional Fidelity and the Weight of the Past

To conclude, two points are in order.

First, from the perspective of legal philosophy, there is a close connection between the resolution of the Supreme Court and the Ombudsman's motion and pleadings, but there is also a fundamental difference between them. The basic defect

[47]An opposite view of the Constitutional Tribunal in the statement of reasons: "Assigning a resolution the effect of legal principle means that the resolution is not an act of specific application of law but an interpretative act, separate from the application of law *in concreto*". Therefore, pertinent question arises: Does this mean that each Supreme Court resolution entered into the register of legal principles is subject to the review exercised by the Constitutional Tribunal (*argumentum a simili*)?

[48]Particularly detailed argumentation is included in the dissenting opinion of judge M. Wyrzykowski.

of the Supreme Court resolution is that it exists in the first place. Even more problematic is the content of the resolution. As for the Ombudsman's motion and pleadings and the judgment of the Constitutional Tribunal, it is the opposite as it their very existence that is problematic. This brings to mind Ockham's razor *entia non sunt multiplicanda prater necessitatem* (plurality should not be posited without necessity. Indeed, it seems that the discussed cases involved a process of creating unnecessary entities, caused by the aforementioned cascade of non-legal instrumentalisation: the resolution of the Supreme Court, the Ombudsman's motion in the present form and the judgment of the Constitutional Tribunal were unnecessary. Many refined arguments (*apices iuris* in the approbative meaning) in fact serve non-legal instrumentalisation purposes (*apices iuris* in the pejorative sense). The effect is that the argumentation in many points loses its precision and subtlety of a razor, becoming heavy and crude like a baseball bat. It would have been much better if—as suggested by all the judges presenting their dissenting opinions—the Constitutional Tribunal had dismissed the case under Article 39 section 1 item 1 of the Constitutional Tribunal Act due to the impermissibility of issuing a judgment and at the same time referred in the statement of reasons for the decision to all the doubts arising from the Supreme Court's resolution, especially those concerning the retroactive effect, defective promulgation of the Decree on Martial Law and the validity of international law.

Last but not least, martial law on the docket of Polish courts invites us to ask burning question about the judicial ethos of Polish judges when faced with unjust laws. It brings to the fore the challenge of judging the past.[49] As such it raises more general questions about the readiness and intellectual capability of Polish judges to stand up to the challenge of just and fair adjudication, one that would embrace the constitutional fidelity and do indeed justice, rather than merely technocratically apply written law (*lex*). This is a long-lasting legacy of communism and positivistic vision of legal system. Times have changed, but judicial approaches to interpretation and legal reasoning and the judicial ethos, all lag behind. Culture of justification with the *power of arguments*, not mere *arguments of power* is needed.[50] Judicial legitimacy is derived from transparency and from weight of arguments and not only from "*who* says", (dominant approach "I, Supreme Court rule hereby …") but also "*how it is said*". Constructive interpretation must take place of the reigning infatuation with the literal interpretation. The latter overpowers and incapacitates Polish judges which was evident in the approach adopted by the Supreme Court. Mere attempts to consider the text in the light of the general scheme or the law's *ratio legis* are treated as inadmissible judicial activism.

The interpretation is good when it is constructive and holistic that builds discursive legitimacy of the courts today. Literal interpretation might end up to be an instance of judicial evil, even though strictly speaking it will be performed according to the law (understood as *lex*). While the Supreme Court resolution is a

[49]We borrow the term from McAdams (2001).

[50]See powerful plea in this vein by Łętowska (2010, 39).

classic example of judges failing dramatically on the axiological front, the Tribunal was caught in between the limits of its jurisdiction, on the one hand, and the bringing the necessary equilibrium between dominant *lex* and missing *ius*.[51] There was only so much that the Tribunal could have done cleaning up after the Court. This raises important questions for our understanding of the fidelity to Polish Constitution. Fidelity must not be simply a matter of text and following the letter of the law. Being faithful to the document and the institutions it creates is more a state of mind, not mere practice. As such constitutional fidelity has a lot in common with constitutionalism which is not only about the document, but rather about the state of mind, limited government and culture of restraint. Fidelity can refer to the original meaning of the constitutional document or to its fundamental core or to the text as such, speak to the principles and concepts that are embedded in the Polish constitutional structure and tradition, principles that make up our constitutional identity. Fidelity and its object thus have the potential of explicating who we were, where we came from and where we are headed and finally, strives to grasp in the possible way, who we are today. Each constitutional document has its past, present and future, and these three temporal dimensions are linked by the rationale of the underlying principles of values. Principles and values that make up the constitutional identity must be interpreted so as to ensure both the continuity of the messages contained therein and their durability. What is needed is the compromise and equilibrium between necessary change that embraces *The New* and the stability that caters to *The Tradition*. The latter enables us to move forward and set our gaze on the future while not forgetting about the past and about the places we come from. In other words, constitutional interpretation must be conservative (preserving the values) and reformative (reading these in the light of ever-changing circumstances). Future emerges at the intersection of both dimensions: looking back and staying in the present. Again as argued by Balkin:

> Fidelity is a sort of servitude, a servitude that we gladly enter into in order to under- stand the Constitution. To become the faithful servants of the Constitution we must talk and think in terms of it; we must think constitutional thoughts, we must speak a constitutional language. The Constitution becomes the focus of our attention, the prism of our perspective. Our efforts are directed to understanding it-and many other things in society as well-in terms of its clauses, its concepts, its traditions. Through this discipline, this focus, we achieve a sort of tunnel vision: a closing off to other possibilities that would speak in a different language and think in a different way, a closing off to worlds in which the Constitution is only one document among many, worlds in which the Constitution is no great thing, but only a first draft of something much greater and more noble. And to think and talk, and focus our attention on the Constitution, to be faithful to it, and not to some

[51]On the gap between *ius* and *lex* in Polish courts see series of papers by T. T. Koncewicz, *Prawo i niesprawiedliwość, (Law and Injustice)* Gazeta Wyborcza 11 September 2012, *Sądzie sądź, (Judges, do justice)*, POLITYKA no 50, 12 December 2012, *Jaka interpretacja w polskim sądzie (What kind of interpretation in the Polish court?)*, Rzeczpospolita 8 November 2013, *Sędziów polskich trzeba uczyć, (Polish judges must be taught)*, IN GREMIO 3/2013 and *Nie(ludzki) polski sąd ((In)human Polish Court)*, IN GREMIO 4/2013.

> other thing, we must bolt the doors, shut out the lights, block the entrances. Fidelity is servitude indeed. But this servitude is not so much something the Constitution does to us as something we do to ourselves in order to be faithful to it.

Such understanding of fidelity underscores aspirational function of the constitutional document. It aspires to reflect "us" in the best, and not perfect, way. It aspires to capture this reflection, and yet it will never achieve this goal in a definite and final way, since "*we*" change and evolve along with the document. Preamble to the Polish Constitution shows the commitment to which Polish nation aspires, commitments that are anchored in the past, developed and refined in the present and carried over into the future. It means that the Constitution's commitments have not been yet met. This never-ending meandering between the past and the backward-looking and the future with its forward-looking is a matter of constitutional reflection and politics. Such pacting must be undertaken by each generation which has its own distinctive role to play in spelling out what the constitutional pact mandates today. Constitutional fidelity underpins this process and arises at the interstices of practice, text, interpretation and culture. The fact that the promise of the Constitution was not fully realised (argument often repeated by the new Polish majority in favour of rejecting the Constitution) must not detract from our fidelity. Quite to the contrary, it should fuel it and make us try even harder to make these commitments a reality. It is in this sense that the constitutional fidelity is about generational reading of the document. It is not about uncritical iconoclasm. It is about pragmatic recognition that our constitutional allegiances are shaped, reshaped, re-examined as we move forward and as the world around the Constitution changes and fluctuates. There is no place for fear of failure, because failure is the part of the fidelity as no Constitution is perfect. Fidelity is about the journey and the process, rather than a boat and final destination. Past must be the key to the future, but not only. After all, constitutions that are meant to last must be understood as documents made for people of fundamentally different views, as Justice Oliver Wendell Holmes rightfully said. Again American constitutional tradition of looking to the past in a constructive way might be used here:

> We turn to the past not because the past contains within it all of the answers to our questions, but because it is the repository of our common struggles and common commitments; it offers us invaluable resources as we debate the most important questions of political life, which cannot fully and finally be settled.[52]

Each generation should build on the best of the past and move forward with this baggage. After all, this is exactly what the Preamble to the Polish Constitution mandates. This is the kind of fidelity we have in mind, and the one that should inform the understanding of the constitutional commitments the judges should owe to the Constitution of 1997.

At this point, the fidelity of an average judge to the Constitution, as painfully reminded by the resolution of the Supreme Court on the martial law, remains

---

[52]Balkin and Siegel (2009) 4.

simply unknown. It also shows that much work remains to be done. *Firstly*, the legal world of an average Polish judge continues to be dominated by Montesquieu, formalism and unflinching faith in the rationality of the lawmaker.[53] Polish judge is a true believer in what Lord Reid ridiculed 40 years ago as a fairy tale that bad decisions are given, when a judge muddles the password. As a rule, the fairy tale goes, simply uttering "Sesame open up" should do the trick.[54] As a result when a case breaks the mould and calls for more than just textual reconstruction, Polish judge is awe-stricken and defenceless and turns his/her eyes towards legislator pleading for [...] more text. The legislator acquiesces and enacts new text which is only good, though, until new controversy arises and a judge come knocking on the door yet again [...]. What results is a vicious circle.

Secondly, given the historic baggage of Polish judges and their limited understanding of judicial function, the positive reception of the resolutions at the "bottom" of the judicial ladder must not be taken for granted. The weight of the past and old habits might obviate the embrace by the ordinary judges of the resolutions of the supreme courts. The minds of Polish judges continue to be hostage to the belief that the Constitution is a purely declaratory document with no normative content and no role to play in the judicial resolution of disputes.[55] As a result, constitutional document is often relegated to the margins of the judicial practice. The ideology of bound judicial decision making as developed by the leading Eastern legal theoretician and philosopher of law Jerzy Wróblewski has been keeping Polish judges captive for decades now.[56] This ideology rests on the textual positivism and formalism and stands for the limited law and limited sources of law, with the role of the judges reduced to the mechanical application of the legal text. The judges acted exclusively on the plain meaning of a statutory text and framed their decisions as the inevitable and the only correct deduction from the text in any case. As a result, Polish judges have been rightly described as perfect examples of "textual judges" and impervious to the context in which the legal text operates. Their interpretation was and still is invariably code-bound which means that a judge's role consists in simply reconstructing the pre-existing standards enacted and changed, when necessary, by the legislator. The so-called presumption of "rationality of the legislator" assumed that the legislator can do no wrong and provides *ex ante* for all possible circumstances in which law in the only form known to judges inscribed in codes, will be applied in the future. Should the existing law prove to be insufficient, it is not the business of the judge to override the clear textual meaning of the text, but for the legislator to amend accordingly.

We would argue that 25 years after transformation, the approach marked by the mechanical approach to law and by textual positivism continues to be one of the most long-lasting legacies of the communism. The fear of being creative and critical

[53]See also illuminating analysis by Claus (2005).

[54]The quip comes from his celebrated essay Reid (1972).

[55]More on this Koncewicz (2017a).

[56]See English version of his most famous treatise Wróblewski (1991).

is omnipresent, and every attempt by a judge to interpret the statute beyond the text is seen as an example of judicial overreaching and dismissed with scorn as inadmissible judicial imperialism. What follows is the self-imposed image of a judge, who, in the words of one commentator, resembles "an anonymous grey mouse, hidden behind piles of files and papers, unknown to the outside world …", who is not used to "stand by his opinion and defend them in the public" which then results in the structural judicial independence, but no mentally independent judges.[57] As one leading textbook on the subject succinctly put it: "*the courts* (of Eastern Europe) *try to follow the letter of the law, however problematic and absurd the results may be which this course produces*".[58]

All the above clouds our plea for constitutional fidelity with lingering doubts as to its feasibility in practice. After all, "constitutional fidelity" is based on the rejection of the unwavering belief among Polish judges that any case can be decided by relying on textual statutory arguments. It takes ordinary judges out of their comfort zone in a dramatic fashion as it makes the Constitution part and parcel of the judicial decision-making process. It calls on the judges to evaluate critically the statutes, and it empowers them to fully embrace their forgotten role of being judges over the "Constitution *and* statutes", not only judges applying and interpreting statutes, judges who are ready to, and know how to, critically look at the statutes and discover the element of *ius* to guide them in their daily interpretation.

Stakes could not be higher: embracing the philosophy of law *or* plunging into the abyss of legal anti-philosophy and formalism that leads nowhere and strikes at the very heart of judicial legitimacy.

References

Ash TG (2002a) Memory and power in post-war Europe: studies in the presence of the past. In: JW Muller (ed). Cambridge University Press

Ash TG (2002b) The Polish Revolution: Solidarity, 3rd edn. Yale University Press

Balkin J (1997) Agreements with hell and other objects of our faith. 65 Fordham Law Review 1703

Balkin JM, Siegel RB (2009) Introduction. In: JM Balkin, RB Siegel (eds) The constitution in 2020. Oxford University Press

Barak A (2006) The judge in a democracy. Princeton University Press, p 116

Bobek M (2008) The fortress of judicial independence and the mental transitions of the Central European Judiciaries. 14 European Public Law 99

Brand-Ballard J (2010) Limits of legality: the ethics of lawless judging. Oxford University Press

Brzezinski M (2000) The struggle for constitutionalism in Poland. Palgrave Macmillan

Burczak K, Dębiński A, Jońca M (2007) Łacińskie Sentencje I Powiedzenia Prawnicze. C H Beck

Claus L (2005) Montesquieu's mistakes and the true meaning of separation. 25 Oxford Journal of Legal Studies 419

---

[57]Bobek (2008) 14 European public law 99.

[58]Kühn (2011) at 201 (our emphasis).

Cohen-Eliya M, Porat I (2011) Proportionality and the culture of justification. 59 The American Journal of Comparative Law 463
Czech B (1992) Filozofia prawa a tworzenie i stosowanie prawa: materiały Ogólnopolskiej Konferencji Naukowej zorganizowanej w dniach 11 i 12 czerwca 1991 roku w Katowicach. Ośrodek Terenowy przy Sądzie Wojewódzkim 1992
Edlin DE (2010) Judges and unjust laws: common law constitutionalism and the foundations of judicial review. University of Michigan Press
Eser A, Arnold J (eds) (2002) Strafrecht in Reaktion Auf Systemunrecht, Volume 5, Polen. Ungarn. Max Planck Institute
Garlicki LL (2002) The experience of the polish constitutional court. In: W Sadurski (ed) Constitutional justice, East and West: democratic legitimacy and constitutional courts in post-communist Europe in a comparative perspective. Kluwer Law International
Graver HP (2015) Judges against justice—on judges when the rule of law. Springer
Hart HLA, American jurisprudence through english eyes: the nightmare and the noble dream. 11 Georgia Law Journal 969
Koncewicz TT (2017a) Mechanical Jurisprudence under Strain? Eastern Europe Judiciary under the European Influence. In: M. Zubik (ed) Human rights in contemporary world. Essays in honour of Professor Leszek Garlicki, 2017
Koncewicz TT (2017b) Polish judiciary and constitutional fidelity: beyond the institutional "great yes"? http://verfassungsblog.de/polish-judiciary-and-constitutional-fidelity-beyond-the-institutional-great-yes/
Królikowski M (2008) Glosa Do Uchwaly Sądu Najwyższego Z Dnia 20 Grudnia 2007r. (Ref. No. I KZP 37/07). Przegląd Sejmowy 243
Kühn Z (2011) The judiciary in Central and Eastern Europe: mechanical jurisprudence in transformation? Martinus Nijhoff Publishers
Lacey N (2006) A life of H.L.A. Hart: the nightmare and the noble dream. Oxford University Press
Łętowska E (2010) Transformations in law interpretation: towards a universal approach—the phenomenon, causes and symptoms. In: J Jemielniak, P Miklaszewicz (eds) Interpretation of law in the global world: from particularism to a universal approach, Springer
Mażewski L (2012) Problem legalności stanu wojennego z 12–13 grudnia 1981 r. Studium z historii prawa polskiego, Von Borowiecky
McAdams AJ (2001) Judging the past in unified Germany. Cambridge University Press
Michalunio SJC (2008) Dicta. Zbiór Łacińskich Sentencji, Przysłów I Powiedzeń. Editio Maior, Wydawnictwo WAM
Mureinik E (1994) A bridge to where? Introducing the interim bill of rights. 10 South African Journal on Human Rights 31
Oniszczuk J (2004) Konstytucja Rzeczypospolitej Polskiej w orzecznictwie Trybunalu Konstytucyjnego na poczatku XXI w., 1st edn. Kantor Wydawniczy Zakamycze
Paczkowski A, Byrne M (2008) From solidarity to martial law: the polish crisis of 1980–1981 : a documentary history. Central European University Press
Paczkowski A, Werbian A (2007) On the decision to introduce martial law in Poland In 1981. Two Historians Report to the Commission on Constitutional Oversight of the Sejm of the Republic of Poland. Working Paper of the Woodrow Wilson International Centre for Scholars. https://www.wilsoncenter.org/publication/the-decision-to-introduce-martial-law-poland-1981-two-historians-report-to-the
Przyjemski SM (2008) Glosa Do Uchwały SN Z Dnia 20 Grudnia 2007 R., I KZP 37/07. PiP 127
Radbruch G (1945) Fünf Minuten Rechtsphilosophie. Rhein-Neckar-Zeitung, 12 Sept 1945
Reid L (1972) The judge as law-maker. 12 Journal of the Society of Public Teachers of Law (New Series) 22
Sakowicz A (2009) Problematyka Odpowiedzialności Karnej Sędziów Stosujących Przepisy Dekretu O Stanie Wojennym Z Mocą Wsteczną (Glosa Do Uchwały SN Z Dnia 20 Grudnia 2007 R., I KZP 37/2007. VII Miscellanea Historico-Iuridica 209
Sandford G (1986) Military Rule in Poland: The Rebuilding of Communist Power, 1981–1983, 1st edn. Palgrave Macmillan

Sanford G (2002) Democratic Government in Poland: Constitutional Politics Since 1989, 2002 edn. Palgrave Macmillan
Wendel WB (2010) Lawyers and fidelity to law. Princeton University Press
Wróbel W (2003) Zmiana Normatywna I Zasady Intertemporalne W Prawie Karnym. Kantor Wydawniczy Zakamycze
Wróblewski J (1991) The judicial application of law (Bańkowski Z, MacCormick N). Springer
Zajadło J (2001) Formuła Radbrucha: filozofia prawa na granicy pozytywizmu prawniczego i prawa natury. Wydawnictwo Arche
Zajadło J (2003) Odpowiedzialność za Mur: procesy strzelców przy Murze Berlińskim. Wydawnictwo Arche
Zajadło J (2008) Pieć Minut Antyfilozofii Antyprawa. Glosa Do Uchwały SN Z Dnia 20 Grudnia 2007 R., I KZP 37/07. Gdańskie Studia Prawnicze—Przegląd Orzecznictwa 161
Zajadło J (ed) (2009) Łacińska Terminologia Prawnicza. Wolters Kluwer
Zalewski W (2008) Iuspozytywizm Kontra Sprawiedliwość. Glosa Do Uchwały SN Z Dnia 20 Grudnia 2007 R., I KZP 37/07. Gdańskie Studia Prawnicze—Przegląd Orzecznictwa 127

Emergency as a State of Mind—The Case of Israel

Suzie Navot

Abstract Since its establishment in 1948, Israel has been in a state of war and in extended periods of emergency. The Declaration of Independence founded Israel as a 'Jewish and democratic' state, but since the very beginning a 'state of emergency' was declared, which is permanent ever since. Furthermore, one-fifth of Israel's citizens are Arab nationals (Palestinian Israelis) who wish to preserve their culture, religion and language, while sympathizing with the Palestinian nation and the Arab world, with which the state of Israel is in a state of ongoing belligerency. In the 1967 war, Israel occupied populated territories, which created serious debates about the civil status and general fate of the Palestinian population of the West Bank and the Gaza Strip. The Supreme court of Israel allowed Palestinians to appeal against decisions made by the military commanders of the occupied regions, sharply defending the need to protect human rights even in times of emergency. War and terror acts have resulted in an almost daily examination of restrictions of human rights, pressing the need to find the right balance between defending those rights and protecting national security. This paper will present, first, the Israeli model of a state of emergency, the different types of power granted to the executive, its normative framework, and its uses in the past and present as well as parliamentary and judiciary control. Second, it will disclose the difficulties a permanent state of emergency poses: how the ongoing executive power may lead to the misuse of emergency rules by politicians, applying unusual methods and procedures in circumstances that have nothing to do with emergency; how parliamentary control tends to weaken, how power shifts from Parliament to the executive and how emergency legislative tools seem to 'migrate' even to constitutional amendments. The article will discuss the unique role of the Supreme court of Israel (sitting as the High court of Justice) as a powerful controller of emergency regulations, measures and decisions. The court's activist rulings on military and security cases, coupled with its criticism of government powers, have played a most significant role in shaping Israel's state of emergency. Last, it will analyse the new anti-terrorism law

S. Navot (✉)
The Striks School of Law, College of Management Academic Studies, Rishon Lezion, Israel
e-mail: suzie@netvision.net.il

P. Auriel et al. (eds.), *The Rule of Crisis*, Ius Gentium: Comparative Perspectives on Law and Justice 64, https://doi.org/10.1007/978-3-319-74473-5_9

approved on 15 June 2016—a further step within the global war on terror—a law which creates new offences, significantly expands both the state's counterterrorism powers and its definitions of terrorist organizations and terrorist acts.

1 Introduction

Many countries suffer from terror threats. Terrorism defies democracy and challenges democratic states, while naturally some of the means available to fight terrorism are illegal and unjustifiable according to democratic standards. Clearly, traditional, time-consuming legislative steps fail when states require urgent legislative tools. The war on terrorism might require the reaching of decisions that are inconsistent with democratic values. In this war, the end might be confused with the means. Democracies must make difficult and delicate decisions on ways to balance national security and human rights, while employing emergency mechanisms to counter the threats. The question of whether the rule of law and emergency powers may coexist is not uniquely Israeli in nature,[1] and nations worldwide have discovered—sometimes the hard way—that ordinary legal instruments that suit ordinary times may be lacking when counterterrorist action is required.

In one of the Supreme court's judgments on Israel's state of emergency, Justice Elyakim Rubinstein summed up, in one paragraph, the unique case of Israel:

> Israel is a normal state that is also abnormal. It is normal in being an active democracy that protects basic rights—including free elections, freedom of speech, and the independence of the judiciary and the attorney general—fundamentally fulfilling its destiny as a Jewish and democratic state. It is abnormal because it is the only democracy under a constant threat of annihilation; because despite having peace treaties with Jordan and Egypt and certain political agreements with the Palestinians, its relations with its neighbors have not yet been properly arranged; and because the war on terrorism continues and will probably continue for the foreseeable future. We still may not rest under our vine and fig tree.[2]

2 The Constitutional Background

2.1 *The Birth of a New State (of Emergency)*

Since its establishment, Israel has been in a state of war and in extended periods of emergency. On 29 November 1947, the United Nations (UN) General Assembly endorsed the Partition Plan, which represented the basis for the establishment of a

---

[1]For a theoretical overview and a comparative study of legislation and practices see: Khakee (2009), Ackerman (2004).

[2]HCJ 3091/99 Citizens' Rights Association v The Knesset (decided on 8 May 2012).

Jewish state.[3] According to the Partition Plan, three independent entities were to be established: a Jewish state, an Arab state and another entity under a UN-governed international regime in Jerusalem. While the leadership of the Jewish settlement in Palestine accepted the UN Resolution, the Arab countries rejected[4] the legitimacy of a new Jewish state and launched a comprehensive attack against the Jewish settlement, starting what Israel has since called the 'War of Independence'.

On 14 May 1948, the leaders of the Jewish organizations, known as the National Council, declared the establishment of the state of Israel, publishing a document that was later known as the «Declaration of Independence».[5] This declaration stated that once the British mandate ended and until regular and elected government bodies started functioning, the National Council would serve as the state's Constituent Assembly. It further stated that the 'setting up of the duly elected bodies of the state'[6] would be done 'in accordance with a Constitution, to be drawn up by a Constituent Assembly no later than the first day of October 1948'.[7]

The Provisional National Council's first legislative act was the enactment of the Law and Administration Ordinance 1948,[8] which partially arranged the distribution of powers in the new state and the transition from the mandate to the new government. In this law, Israel incorporated British Mandatory law in general, along with mandatory emergency regulations.[9]

The Law and Administration Ordinance provided the first constitutional principles in the newborn state, but it only had the status of ordinary primary legislation. This Ordinance was enacted in the first days of the state and was aimed at reflecting the main principles regarding the roles and powers of the various branches of government.

Section 9 of this Ordinance acknowledged the Israeli Parliament's power to declare an 'emergency situation'. It further stated that when the government declares an 'emergency situation', it has the power to promulgate 'emergency

[3]General Assembly Resolution 181, *Resolution Adopted on the Report of the* AD HOC *Committee on the Palestinian Question*, A/Res/181 (II) (29 November 1947), www.un.org/en/ga/search/view_doc.asp?symbol=A/RES/181(II) (Last Visited 21/3/2017).

[4]The Question of Palestine & the United Nations (United Nations Department of Public Information—DPI/2276—March 2003), www.un.org/Depts/dpi/palestine/ch2.pdf (Last Visited 21/3/2017).

[5]The declaration of the Establishment of the state of Israel, Official Gazette: Number 1; Tel Aviv, 5 Iyar 5708, 14.5.1948 Page 1 www.knesset.gov.il/docs/eng/megilat_eng.htm.

[6]Ibid.

[7]Ibid.

[8]The Law and Administration Ordinance, 5708-1948.

[9]British (Mandatory) defence emergency regulations derive from British enactments between 1937 and 1945, during Britain's mandate over Palestine. These regulations have the status of primary laws, they apply notwithstanding any law, and they may amend any law with and without modification, and remain in force with no time limit.

regulations' that carry the power to abolish or amend any existing law.[10] Section 9 included the basic features of the constitutional regulation of national security in Israel: the power of the Parliament to wave its sovereignty and sole power to legislate, by declaring a state of emergency; and the power of the government to overstep the boundaries between the executive branch and the legislative branch for a limited period of time.[11] In addition to the power to promulgate emergency regulations, Israel enacted several laws that included provisions stating that they would be in force only when a declaration of a state of emergency is in force.

Five days after the Declaration of independence, the Provisional state Council declared a state of emergency. This state of emergency has prevailed until today.[12] The reasons for this ongoing emergency are varied. Since its establishment, wars were fought in Israel at least once every decade with one or more of its neighbouring Arab states. Israel has confronted terrorism almost constantly—and with greater intensity following Israel's occupation of the West Bank and the Gaza Strip in the 1967 Six-Day War. The occupation of populated territories created serious debates about the civil status and general fate of the Palestinian population of the West Bank and the Gaza Strip. The 1980s saw the eruption of the first Palestinian uprising (*Intifada*) largely targeted against the Israeli occupation. Although in the 1990s many believed the Israeli–Palestinian conflict which was drawing to an end, it actually assumed a horrific new shape in the 2000s when Palestinian suicide bombers exploded in Israeli cities, and curfews were routinely imposed on West Bank cities. This Palestinian second *Intifada* and Israel's retaliatory and preventive operation during the 2000s gave rise to several serious questions as to how a balance might be struck between defending human rights and meeting the security needs of the state during a time of war. A decrease in terrorist attacks has been experienced in recent years, but the feeling of conflict that is still unresolved is part

[10]Section 9 reads: When a state of emergency has been declared by the legislature, any member of government empowered by the government to do so may 'introduce emergency regulations for the benefit of state protection, public safety and the maintenance of vital supplies and services'. These regulations stay in force for a period of three months and can be extended only by an act of Parliament.

[11]Barak Erez (2013), p 430.

[12]Since 2001 Basic Law: the Government (clause 38) grants the authority to announce a state of emergency to the Knesset (for a year) and if the Kneesset cannot convine to the government (for a week with a possibility of extension), the Knesset has announced a state of emergency on 7/11/2016, thus prolonging the state of emergency by year another year. This practice was challenge at the HCJ 3019/99 Association for Civil Rights in Israel v Knesset (decided 8.5.2012) the petitioner claimed that the announcement was not justified and undermines the rule of law. The court criticized but did not rule the state of emergency void. 'The Israeli government, in its reply to an HCJ appeal … has admitted that the use of emergency powers is a governmental practice. Its officials stated in their reply to the appeal submitted by the Association for Civil Rights in Israel (ACRI), that ending the declaration of emergency would deny the ability of the government to administer effectively since several civil laws are conditioned by the declaration of an SOE and that the process of replacing them with formal normative laws is still ongoing, Thus, part of the logic of sustaining the state of emergency is to prevent a legal vacuum, rather than simply to ensure security' at Mehozay (2012).

of Israel's daily life. The Israeli–Palestinian conflict is rooted in a seemingly intractable dispute over land claimed both by Jews as their Biblical birthright and by the Palestinians who seek self-definition. Despite repeated attempts to end the conflict between the Israelis and the Palestinians, there is no peace settlement in sight. It is worth mentioning that within public opinion there is little or no real legislative conflict on the war on terrorism—in contrast to parliamentary and public conflict over issues to do with Israeli control of the Occupied Territories.[13]

To sum up this brief introduction, it seems that the unique history of Israel is the main reason that keeps the emergency state 'alive and kicking'. Still, until the 70s, the use of emergency regulations was relatively small and focused primarily on the needs of security. It was only after the 70s that emergency regulations expanded and were applied also in the economic field. As we shall see, not only Israel's unique history but also its fragile constitutional framework had a direct effect on the powers of the executive branch.

2.2 A Constitution 'in Stages'

Upon the establishment of the state, in 1948, Israel's Declaration of Independence determined that 'the establishment of the elected, regular authorities of the state' would be 'in accordance with the Constitution which shall be adopted by the Constituent Assembly'. The Constituent Assembly was thus elected in January 1949 as both a constituent and a legislative body. The Constituent Assembly—later renamed 'The First Knesset'—conducted extensive debates on the future constitution. But in the absence of consensus on the need for a constitution, its content and form, constitutional deliberations reached a deadlock. Before it dispersed, the First Knesset endorsed a 'compromise' that became known as the 'The Harrari Resolution'.[14] According to this compromise, Israel would introduce a constitution 'in stages': the constitution would be composed of chapters, each comprising a single basic law unto itself.

Following this Resolution, the First Knesset eventually dispersed, transferring its powers to the next and all subsequent Knessets' meaning that Israel started out without a constitution or a bill of human rights, based on the British tradition of parliamentary sovereignty. In the early years, the prevailing concept was that the Knesset was legislatively sovereign and 'omnipotent' and that the Supreme court was not competent to review its legislative acts.

[13]Friedberg and Hazan (2010).

[14]The Harrari Resolution reads: 'The First Knesset charges the Constitution, Law, and Justice Committee with preparing a draft of the State Constitution. The Constitution will consist of separate chapters, each chapter constituting a basic law in its own. The chapters will be presented to the Knesset … and all of the chapters shall be consolidated into the State Constitution'. www.knesset.gov.il/description/eng/eng_mimshal_hoka.htm#4 (last visited 21/3/2017). For a historical overview and discussion see Navot (2014), pp 8–12.

The upshot of the Harrari Resolution was that the initial decision to adopt a complete constitution for the state of Israel was deferred and replaced by the process of enacting a constitution chapter by chapter—a process that leads to the enactment of fourteen basic laws[15] but was never completed and has yet to produce a full constitution.

By 1992, almost all of the basic laws that deal with government institutions in Israel had been adopted, but the proposal to pass a basic law dealing with human rights provoked great controversy in the Knesset. Therefore, another political compromise split the Basic Law: human rights into a number of separate basic laws. This process made it possible for the Knesset to agree and support the constitutional entrenchment of particular, consensual human rights, while leaving pending the discussion of 'problematic' rights, such as freedom of religion, speech, and conscience; equality.

Following this new 'compromise', two basic laws dealing with human rights were enacted in 1992: Basic Law: Human Dignity and Liberty and Basic Law: Freedom of Occupation. Both basic laws include a 'limitation' clause, similar to the one found in the Canadian Charter of Rights and Freedoms. The basic laws on human rights of 1992 changed Israel's constitutional structure and were followed by a crucially important ruling handed down in 1995, the *Mizrahi Bank* decision.[16] In this monumental decision, the Supreme court (sitting as the court of final resort for appeals, in a civil proceeding) declared that basic laws in Israel had a 'supra-legal' constitutional status, and that the court is empowered to enforce the limitations they entail by judicial review of Knesset legislation, even if that power is not specifically mentioned in the basic laws. The basic laws on human rights and this Supreme court decision were later known as the 'constitutional revolution'.[17]

This constitutional revolution started a new era in Israel's constitutional law—a textual period, in which there allegedly exists a constitutional text and the Supreme court has the power of judicial review. As the Supreme court stated, the basic laws form the Israeli constitution. It is not a complete constitution, but rather a lame and restricted one. The Supreme court has nullified some fourteen laws (mainly specific sections) over the past two decades, all following judicial rulings stating that these

---

[15]Bascic Law: The Knesset (1958); Basic Law: Israel Lands (1960); Basic Law: The President of the state (1964); Basic Law: The Government (1968—amended 1992: mixed election system, amended 2001: return to system of proportional elections); Basic Law: The State Economy (1975); Basic Law: The Military; Basic Law: Jerusalem Capital of Israel (1980); Basic Law: The Judiciary (1984); Basic Law: The State Controller (1988); Basic Law: Freedom of Occupation (1992); Basic Law: Human Dignity and Liberty (1992); Basic Law: Referendum (2014); Two temporary provisions Basic Law: State Budget (Special Provisions) (Temporary Provision) enacted in 2009 and extended since till 2016 and an additional Temporary Provision for the years 2017–2018 all in order to determine that the state budget would become a biannual judgment. The first amendment let to a petition to the Supreme court at the case of HCJ 4908/10 Bar-On MK v The Knesset (2011) that challenged the constitutionality of the amendment. The petition was rejected. A new petition questioning the amendment of 2017 is awaiting the courts rulling.

[16]CA 6821/93 United Mizrahi Bank Ltd. v. Migdal Cooperative Village, 49(4) P.D. 221 (1995).

[17]For an opposite view see Gavison (2005–2006).

laws disproportionally impaired human rights. The fact that much of the constitutional revolution is based on case law instead of on legislation may be perceived as another layer of instability in Israel's legal–political structure. [18]

3 The Legal Framework for Governmental Emergency Powers

The declaration of a state of emergency enables emergency legislation; in other words, the executive authority is empowered to enact regulations that deviate from regular parliamentary legislative procedures.[19] As such, they may be enacted expeditiously and may also be changed or amended with flexibility in order to adjust them to a dynamic, changing reality. Given that these governmental powers are exercised during times of emergency, they are characterized not only by granting power to impose far-reaching restrictions on individual freedoms, but also by their deviation from, and even the violation of, fundamental principles of law.

Israel's system of emergency legislation comprises several mechanisms:

1. British Defence (Emergency) Regulations, 1945;
2. The power to enact emergency regulations according to Sections 38 and 39 of Basic Law: The Government;
3. The power granted to the Minister of Defence to detain a person by way of administrative detention, under the Emergency Powers (Detention) Law, 1979;
4. Existing restrictions on freedom of association and freedom of expression by force of the government's power to declare a group of a people as a 'terrorist organization' under the Prevention of Terror Ordinance, 1948, recently abolished and replaced by a new anti-terrorism law.[20]

3.1 British Defence (Emergency) Regulations, 1945

The Defence (Emergency) Regulations, 1945, originated in the British mandate period and were promulgated by the High Commissioner pursuant to the King's Order in Council. They have the status of primary legislation, despite their name—'regulations'. Therefore, they are valid regardless of whether a state of emergency has been formally declared. Over the years, the Knesset has revoked some of the British (defence) regulations but to date has rejected all proposals to repeal the regulations in their entirety.

---

[18]Mehozay (2016), p 41.

[19]Section 39 of Basic Law: The Government.

[20]The anti-terrorism law, 2016. See also Hofnung (1991), Dershowitz (1971).

Today the British (defence) regulations include, for example, the power to close an area for security purposes. They have special importance in the Occupied Territories of the West Bank, where they are regularly used. British (defence) regulations provide the legal basis for powers of deterrence and even of punishment, including powers of seizure and confiscation, entry and searching of premises, censorship, curfew and demolition of houses.

As we shall on Part III, the Supreme court of Israel (sitting as the High court of Justice) practises judicial review of the exercise of all emergency powers. Although the court does not have the power to declare the British (defence) regulations void, since the enactment of Basic Law: Human Dignity and Liberty in 1992,[21] the court stated that these regulations are part of the legislation of a democratic state and therefore must be interpreted according to the basic principles of Israeli law.[22] In a series of judgments, the court ruled that by force of the British (defence) regulations, the power to demolish houses could be exercised exclusively for military operational purposes or as a deterrent measure, for the prevention of future acts of violence. Specifically, the court ruled that the military commander is not permitted to order the demolition of the houses of suicide terrorists and their senders as a punitive measure. The exercise of this specific power involved punishing the innocent and therefore bore traces of collective punishment. However, despite this ruling, the court rejected almost all of the petitions filed on this matter, while accepting the declarations of the security authorities that this was a preventative measure aimed at deterring potential terrorists.[23] The court also rejected the claim that exercising the power to demolish houses contradicted the provision of Basic Law: Human Freedom and Dignity. In actual fact, this method is rarely used by the security forces; however in 2015–2016, several houses of terrorists in the Occupied Territories have been demolished, following HCJ decisions that rejected petitions against this power.[24]

---

[21]Section 10 of Basic Law: Human Dignity and Freedom, all laws enacted prior to 25.3.1992 are immuned from judicial review according to this basic law.

[22]HCJ 2161/96 Sharif v. Home Guard Commander IsrSC 50(4) 485, Section 7 [1996]; HCJ 5290/14 Qawasmeh v. Military Commander of the West Bank, Section 22 (11.8.2014); HCJ 4597/14, Awawdeh v. Military Commander of the West Bank, Section 17–18 (1.7.2014).

[23]*See* the case of *Abu Fareh*, HCJ 2006/97Abu Fareh Ganimat v GOC Central Command 51(2) PD 651 [1997]. For elaboration on this subject see Kretzmer (2002), p 69.

[24]In 2014, several human rights organizations submitted a petition to the HCJ requesting the court to declare the use of regulation 119 unlawful. The court rejected the petition while reciting its previous decisions according to which the regulation is to serve as a deterrence tool and not as a punishment one that the use of the regulation should be done with caution and subjected to the principle of proportionality. See HCJ 8091/14 Hamoked: Centre for the Defence of the Individual v The Defence Minister (31.12.2014). See summary of the case in English at the Motion for further hearing in the judgment handed down by the Supreme court in HCJ 8091/14, HCJFH 360/15 HaMoked—Centre for the Defence of the Individual, founded by Dr. Lotte Salzberger v Minister of Defence (12 November 2015) www.hamoked.org/files/2015/1159125_eng.pdf.

3.2 Emergency Regulations

Before discussing emergency regulations, it should be emphasized that the Israeli government is the executive authority, which follows the laws as outlined by the legislative authority and therefore is involved in secondary legislation. In Israel, secondary legislation is more detailed and has a greater impacts on everyday life than primary legislation.

Ideally, secondary legislation only implements policies that were enacted as primary legislation. One of the basic principles of the democratic rule of law is that core regulations should be enacted as primary legislation since this process safeguards the principles of participation, publicity and majority rule.[25]

The emergency regulations are the only legislative acts that may alter, temporarily nullify or set terms for existing laws and may also be employed to impose or raise taxes or other mandatory payments.[26] The normal rule is that only a Knesset law may alter another law, but an emergency regulation is not a Knesset law. Emergency orders are dubbed 'regulations' and not laws since they contain the main characteristics of secondary legislation and may be legally sanctioned by bodies so empowered by law and for purposes stipulated by law. They carry legislative power, enabling ministers to issue emergency decrees that can override primary law.

The constitutional framework for emergency regulations is Basic Law: The Government,[27] which defines the powers of the executive branch. Section 1 states that the government is the executive authority of the state. Sections 38 and 39 refer to emergency situations.

According to Section 38, the power to declare an emergency situation is a parliamentary power given to the Knesset. Section 38(a) states:

> Should the Knesset ascertain that the state is in a state of emergency, it may, of its own initiative or, pursuant to a government proposal, declare that a state of emergency exists. When such a declaration is in force, the government is empowered to promulgate emergency regulations that may change current laws, for a period not exceeding three months.

It is the Knesset that may declare a state of emergency, which may remain in force for one year,[28] after which the Knesset can renew its declaration if it sees fit. Since 1992, the Knesset has renewed the state of emergency declaration annually.

Section 39(a) states that during a state of emergency the government may make emergency regulations 'for the defence of the state, public security and the maintenance of supplies and essential services'.

---

[25]Mehozay (n 19) 43.

[26]Section 39 of Basic Law: The Government.

[27]As amended in 1992.

[28]Section 38(b) to Basic Law: the Knesset states: The declaration will remain in force for the period prescribed therein, but may not exceed one year; the Knesset may make a renewed declaration of a state of emergency as stated.

As above mentioned, emergency regulations may alter any law, temporarily suspend its effect or introduce conditions, meaning that the government 'legislative' powers in these regulations are equivalent to primary legislation.

Emergency regulations are limited to three months, and only the Knesset is entitled to extend their validity, by law. This restriction has existed since the establishment of the state and is intended to ensure that any long-term arrangement is effected exclusively by way of Knesset legislation, in independent, self-sustaining legislation. As such, even if the law was only adopted after three months, this does not impair its validity.[29]

As we shall see further on, case law has tended to interpret the requirements and consitions for emergency regulations (the defence of the state, public security and the maintenance of supplies and essential services) particularly broadly, and the ambit of 'legitimate goals' is interpreted as covering not only the need to confront threats to the existence of the state but also as including crisis situations compelling the adoption of special measures for the maintenance of essential services.[30]

3.3 Administrative Detention

Administrative detention or detention without trial—the aim of which is not to punish a person for past misdeeds but rather to prevent any danger posed by his future actions to national and public security—is possible since the British mandate under the British Defence (Emergency) Regulations, 1945.

In 1979, Israel revoked the specific sections dealing with administrative detention and enacted the Emergency Powers Law, which allows administrative detention only during a state of emergency under the Basic Law: The Government. Because of the continuous nature of the declaration of emergency, the validity of this law has not expired. Resort to the extraordinary method of administrative detention within Israel has been quite sporadic, but it is used more frequently in relation to the activists of terrorist organizations in the West Bank.

A person can only be placed in administrative detention when there is no less grave method of preventing the danger posed by his actions. Section 2 of the Emergency Powers (Detention) Law, 1979, empowers the Minister of Defence to

---

[29]HCJ 243/52 Bialer v. Minister of Finance, 7 PD 429, where it stated that 'Where the Knesset, by its own legislation, extends the 'validity' of national emergency regulations enacted by a particular minister, it effectively expresses its affirmative view of the regulations, and furthermore that for the duration of the extended period it vests them with a stamp of approval in the form of primary legislation. What this means is that at least from the date of the extension, the regulations are legal in every sense'.

[30]In HCJ 2994/90 Poraz v The Government of Israel 44(3) PD 317 [1990], the court stated that providing for new immigrants ('Alya') is an essential service; in HCJ 6971/98 Paritzky v Minister of the Interior 53(1) PD 763 [1998], the court ruled that the preservation of the right to vote is an essential service.

detain a person for a period of six months and to periodically extend his detention for additional periods of six months, without limitation, if he believes that reasons of national and public security still compel his detention. The detention must be confirmed by the President of the District court within 48 h of the arrest, and the decision can be appealed before a justice of the Supreme court. The courts have emphasized the extreme nature of administrative detention, and that it must therefore be limited to extraordinary cases and circumstances. 'The power granted to the Minister of Defence is far-reaching and exceptional, because it enables him to deny a person's freedom without regular legal process, and as such must be exercised with tremendous caution and only in cases where the danger to national and public security is grave, and there is no other way of avoiding the danger'.[31]

3.4 *The New Anti-terrorism Law*

On 15 June 2016, the Knesset approved a new counterterrorism law, which significantly expands both the state's counterterrorism powers and its definitions of terrorist organizations and terrorist acts. This new law combines most provisions of existing anti-terrorism law, replacing numerous defence regulations enacted by the British mandate more than 70 years ago, and mainly, replacing the Prevention of Terror Ordinance,[32] that has been used since the establishment of the state. This law will be discussed in Part IV.

3.5 *Governmental Residual Powers and Declaration of War*

Two further basic features of the regulation of security matters in Israel should be mentioned. The first refers to governmental powers during a national emergency. According to the Basic Law: The Government, the government is the executive and 'is authorized to perform in the name of the state and subject to any law, all actions

[31]AAD 1/82 Kawassma v. Minister of Defence PD 36(1) 666, 669 [1982].

[32]The Prevention of Terror Ordinance prevented the creation, and activities, of terrorist organizations, and its application was restricted to states of emergency. A group of people was considered to be a terrorist organization if 'it resorts in its activities to acts of violence calculated to cause death or injury to a person or to threats of such acts of violence'. The Ordinance established a prohibition on the activities of a terrorist organization, including membership thereof, and delivering propaganda speeches at a public meeting or over the radio on behalf of the organization. The goal of the Prevention of Terror Ordinance was to prevent all activity of terrorist organizations, the same aim as the new anti-terrorism Law. Over the years, a number of organizations have been declared, by the government, to be terrorist organizations (according to the Defence Ministry web site—eighteen declarations under the Prevention of Terror Ordinance and one under the new anti-terrorism law). See www.mod.gov.il/Defence-and-Security/Fighting_terrorism/Pages/default.aspx.

which are not legally incumbent on another authority',[33] but this power has been interpreted as inapplicable to actions which infringe human rights or to new initiatives aimed at the regulation of new areas of law (where power lies only with the legislature).[34]

The second refers to the declaration of war. This is regulated by Section 40 of Basic Law: The Government, which provides:

> 40. (a) The state may only begin a war pursuant to a government decision.
>
> (b) Nothing in the provisions of this section will prevent the adoption of military actions necessary for the defence of the state and public security.
>
> (c) Notification of a government decision to begin a war under the provision of subsection (a) will be submitted to the Knesset Foreign Affairs and Security Committee as soon as possible; the Prime Minister also will give notice to the Knesset plenum as soon as possible; notification regarding military actions as stated in subsection (b) will be given to the Knesset Foreign Affairs and Security Committee as soon as possible.

The power to commence a war is thus vested in the government. Notably, the law distinguishes between a declaration of 'war', according to Section 40, and a declaration of an emergency situation (state of emergency) declared upon the establishment of the state, meaning that Israel has de facto various possible 'states of emergency'. The fact of Israel being at war is not normatively identical to a 'regular' state of emergency. In terms of constitutional law, Israel does not recognize a special category of constitutional powers known as 'wartime powers', as distinct from powers conferred by virtue of the state of emergency. It should be noted that in Israeli law there is also no binding connection between the existence of a state of war, which has legal ramifications, and an official declaration of the government to start a war.

The provisions in basic law the government were 'intended to ensure that the state of Israel would not begin a war without a decision of the government, which has collective responsibility [...]. These provisions are a tangible expression of the responsibility of the government to the Knesset'.[35]

Section 40(a) of the basic law did not define what constitutes 'starting a war' within the meaning of the section. According to the Supreme court, this is a complex question that is multifaceted. The definition of the concept of 'war' cannot be separated from the foreign affairs of the state and the functioning of the government in the sphere of international relations. It is actually the government which is entitled to determine that a military operation that it decided to carry out does not

[33] Section 32.

[34] See HCJ 11163/03 Supreme Monitoring Committee for Arab Affairs in Israel v Prime Minister 61(1) PD 1 [2006] (in Hebrew). See Barak Erez (n 12) 429–432.

[35] HCJ 6204/06 Beilin v. Prime Minister [1.8.2006] versa.cardozo.yu.edu/sites/default/files/upload/opinions/Beilin%20v.%20Prime%20Minister.pdf.

constitute 'starting a war' but merely military operations. The government has broad discretion in all matters of foreign and defence policy.[36]

4 Emergency and Judicial Review

It is impossible to describe the development of the Israeli emergency constitutional and legal framework, without considering the role of the Supreme court sitting as the High court of Justice. The HCJ's impact on emergency issues is crucial, as is its influence on Israeli society. The Supreme court is the highest court in Israel, and it plays two different roles: it is the court of final resort for appeals against verdicts handed down by district courts, and thus rules on civil, administrative and criminal matters. In addition, it sits as the High court of Justice and hears petitions against state authorities and other tribunals.

The HCJ resulted from a historical, accidental and unplanned process that created an unusual situation, in which certain complaints (administrative grievances of individuals harmed by government authorities) are filed directly with the Supreme court. During the British mandate, the lower courts (magistrates' and district courts) were presided over by local judges, Jews or Arabs, while the Supreme court was exclusively composed of British judges. The policy was that local judges should handle ordinary civil and criminal issues, but disputes that pertain to the mandate authorities should be heard, from beginning to end, by judges from the British establishment. Thus, it was determined that the Supreme court should address administrative disputes.

After Israel had been established, this structure was no longer needed, but the judicial situation did not change as the newly founded state decided to keep the mandate's administrative and legal structures in place. Accordingly, the HCJ kept operating as it had done previously, only presided over by Israeli judges. Soon it became central to the development of justice and the basic principles of democracy —mainly the rule of law. Over the years, the HCJ has proven its willingness to confront the government, including on security-related issues.

Until the 1980s, the HCJ set a threshold requirement of standing as a precondition for hearing petitions, and many issues were treated as unjusticiable. Following various political and social changes in the 1980s, the HCJ dropped these justiciability barriers, thereby becoming an influential—even dominant—force in shaping the Israeli constitutional system. The court's activist adjudication on political, military and security issues, coupled with its criticism of government powers, is famous worldwide. Presently, it plays the most significant role in shaping Israel as a democratic society.

After the 1967 Six-Day War, the HCJ became accessible to Palestinian residents of the Occupied Territories who believe they were harmed by the military

[36]Ibid.

government's actions. Many Palestinians have filed appeals against allegedly illegitimate actions undertaken by Israeli forces as part of their military operations. Petitions were filed[37] during combat, including by suspected terrorists, which meant that decisions had to be made in real time.

Supreme court President Barak wrote:

> Is it proper for judges to review the legality of the war on terrorism? Many, on both extremes of the political spectrum, argue that courts should not become involved in these matters. Critics argue that judicial review undermines security, while others claim that judicial review unjustifiably legitimizes governments' actions against terrorism. Both arguments are unacceptable. Judicial review of the legality of the war on terrorism may make this war harder in the short run, but also fortifies and strengthens the people in the long run. The rule of law is a central element of national security.[38]

The court has generally dismissed claims concerning the non-justiciability of the choice of military means, even where petitions are filed during the course of battle. Nonetheless, the judicial examination itself takes into account the relatively broad range of reasonable decisions that may be adopted by the security authorities and relies almost absolute on military assessments regarding the effectiveness of the measures adopted, their necessity and their proportionality.

The nature of the war against terror and the different tools granted to the Israeli executive have generated increasing readiness on the court's part to conduct an in-depth, substantive examination of the methods utilized by the army. But, both on the public and parliamentary levels, judicial intervention in security military-related matters has been criticized.

It should be reminded that until the 1990s, the scope of judicial review was limited to the invalidation of executive decisions. Legislation was immune from the power of judicial review, following the British tradition of sovereignty of parliament.

One of the most important cases of the last decade deals with the fact that the state of emergency has not been withdrawn for more than 60 years since Israel was founded. In 1999, a petition was filed with the HCJ by the Association for Civil Rights (ACRI), requesting that the court order that the state of emergency is terminated, arguing that this ongoing situation is both unjustifiable and damaging to the rule of the law, the separation of powers and basic laws. In an unanimous ruling delivered more than ten years later,[39] the court held that the petition had 'run its course' because since ACRI filed its petition, the state had slowly abolished several emergency laws. Justice Rubinstein said that while 'much work remains to be done' on the issue, the government should be allowed to complete the legislative process. The threats to Israel's existence still remain, Justice Rubinstein added. Still, it was only to be expected that emergency legislation should match the 69-year-old democratic state, and this goal is achievable.

---

[37]For an overview see Barak (2014).

[38]Barak (2002).

[39]HCJ 3091/99 Association for Civil Rights v the Knesset (decided 8.5.2012).

4.1 Judicial Limitations on Emergency Regulations

According to Basic Law: The Government, there are several restrictions on emergency regulations. The first states that they can be issued only during a state of emergency, which is a theoretical limitation, because Israel has been under a continuous state of emergency since its establishment. The second limitation sets the objectives of emergency regulations, *i.e.* they must be in accordance with 'the defence of the state, public security and the maintenance of supplies and essential services'. The third restriction limits their validity to three-month duration.[40] The contents of emergency regulations are similarly demarcated, both in legislature and in case law. Furthermore, Basic Law: The Government subjects the contents of the emergency regulations to specific restrictions: 'emergency regulations may not prevent recourse to legal action or prescribe retroactive punishment or allow infringement of human dignity'. Similarly, a restriction appears in a number of laws, and especially in basic laws, according to which emergency regulations cannot alter the arrangements specified in them, temporarily suspend them, or make them subject to conditions. These restrictions are supplemented by other restrictions grounded in case law, which are intended to secure the inviolability of individual rights or of the fundamental principles of the system, except to the extent necessitated by the state of emergency. The Supreme court may exercise judicial review over regulations, and for that purpose, their status is equivalent to that of secondary legislation. As such, judicial review is not limited to cases in which there is a contradiction of provisions in other basic laws and also includes the grounds of unreasonableness and proportionaity.[41]

Another important limitation on the use of emergency regulations derives from Basic law: Human Dignity and Liberty, which includes the main constitutional provisions on the protection of human rights in Israel. According to Section 12 of this basic law, it cannot be suspended or amended by emergency regulations. In addition, emergency regulations may limit the application of the rights guaranteed by the basic law, only subject to the condition that the denial or restriction shall be for a proper purpose and for a period and extent no greater than is required. Whether such emergency regulations meet this standard is a question subject to judicial review.[42]

Still, the HCJ did not intervene in emergency regulations until the 1990s. In the Poraz case,[43] the HCJ struck down emergency regulations from 1990, which established an expedited procedure for the approval of building plans—by suspending the provisions of the Planning and Construction Laws. During the very period in which the regulations were enacted, the Knesset was discussing similar

---

[40]Section 39(5) of Basic Law: The Government.

[41]Section 39(6) of Basic Law: The Government, HCJ 6971/98 Paritzky v Minister of the Interior 53(1) PD 763 [1998].

[42]Barak Erez (n 12) 434.

[43]HCJ 2994/90 Poraz v The Government of Israel 44(3) PD 317 [1990].

legislative bills. The court ruled that in view of the fact that the Knesset was conducting an expedited legislative process, it was appropriate to wait until the completion of the legislative process, and there were no grounds for exercising the power of emergency regulations.

The outcome of the case is actually a new rule according to which if the possibility for prompt legislation by the Knesset exists, then the power of the executive to enact emergency regulations must be subordinated to it.

In the *Paritzky* case, the court explicitly ruled that: 'Emergency regulations cannot be enacted unless the emergency situation prevents the legislation of a law [...] the requirement is that the impossibility of legislating the law be caused by the state of emergency prevailing in the state, in other words, emergency legislation may only be enacted if the Knesset is unable to conduct regular legislative proceedings as a result of the state of emergency'.[44]

4.2 *Judicial Review of Administrative Detentions*

The exercise of the power of administrative detention seriously infringes basic principles such as the rule of law and the notion according to which it is forbidden to negate a person's freedom other than by a legal process in which his guilt is proved. The granting of this power is grounded in the perception that certain circumstances compel the adoption of deterrent measures against a person liable to commit actions that may prejudice public security, where the person considered to be dangerous is not indictable under the conventional criminal law. The rule is that the power to order administrative detention cannot be used as a penal measure. In keeping with this rule, the Supreme court ruled that 'Since the administrative detention order is intended to prevent an anticipated danger, the reasonability test must be used. In other words, there must be an evaluation of the actions and words of the detainee as evidenced by the material—which usually includes confidential material—in order to determine the degree of danger than can be expected from him in the future [...] another factor to be considered as part of the evaluation is the nature of the activity [...] [it must pertain to particularly heinous offences that may damage national or public security]'.[45] The test accepted in the case law is that of 'near certainty'. The court may only approve administrative detention if persuaded that 'it is almost certain that the detainee will commit grave crimes unless his freedom is limited by way of detention'.[46]

In fact, the power of administrative detention should only be used if proved that there is no possibility of conducting regular criminal proceedings: 'Where it is possible to adequately ensure national and state security, where necessary, by an

[44]HCJ 6971/98 Paritzky v Minister of the Interior PD 53(1) 763 [1998].
[45]AAD 8788/03 Federman v Minister of Defence PD 58(1) 176 [2003].
[46]AAD 4/94 Ben Horin v The state of Israel PD 48(5) 329, Section 9 [1994].

arrest detention order anchored in the regular criminal proceedings, there is no justification for resorting to special emergency powers, intended for exceptional circumstances, in which national or public security necessitate a person's detention without there being any other legal possibility of achieving that result'.

One of the most difficult subjects discussed to date in Israel, before a nine-justice bench, was the issue of whether administrative detention can be ordered when the detainee does not pose any immediate danger to state security, but rather, serves as a 'bargaining chip' for the purposes of negotiations for the release of, or information regarding, Israeli prisoners and soldiers missing in action.

The petitioners, 10 Lebanese citizens, were brought to Israel between 1986 and 1987 by the security forces. There were prosecuted for being members of hostile terrorist groups, found guilty and imprisoned. Despite serving their full sentence, they were not released. Legally, they were held in 'administrative detention', ordered by the Minister of Defence under Article 2 of the Emergency Powers (Detentions) Act. The objective of this imprisonment, however, had nothing to do with their conduct or acts. They were held in an Israeli prison for the sole purpose of being used as 'bargaining chips' for negotiations with Islamic groups. Israel believed that Islamic groups (mainly Hezballah) held one or more Israeli soldiers missing in action.[47]

The Lebanese hostages appealed to the Supreme court on a number of occasions. In November 1997, the Supreme court determined (by a majority vote of 2:1) that the Lebanese hostages' administrative detention for the sole purpose of being used as 'bargaining chips' was valid. In 1998, the court decided to hold a further hearing on the case. The decision following this additional deliberation was handed down in April 2000, reversing (by a majority of 6:3) the decision of 1997. Therefore, the Lebanese hostages were released and returned to Lebanon. The judgment of the majority was based on an analysis of the detention powers and whether the motive for holding the hostages—the possibility of exchanging prisoners—was legally justified.

The court stated that in a democratic state, a person posing danger to state security can be placed under administrative detention, yet this power cannot be extended to a person who himself does not pose such a danger and is held only as a 'bargaining chip'. Such detention infringes the principles of human dignity and liberty in such a deep and profound way that it cannot be tolerated in a state that aspires to the values of liberty and dignity, even for reasons of state security. The court determined that the goal of administrative detention is the prevention of danger to state or public security as posed by the detainee himself and may be used provided that there are no other means of attaining that goal by having resort to the criminal law.

This ruling led to the enactment of the Imprisonment of Illegal Fighters Law, 2002, which authorized the Chief of the General Staff to order the imprisonment of person who participated in hostile activities, but who were not entitled to the status

---

[47]AAD 7048/97 Anonymous v Minister of Defence, 53(1) PD 721 [2000].

of 'prisoner-of-war' in accordance with international law (instead, falling into the category of 'illegal combatants'), in the event that the Chief of Staff had reasonable grounds to believe that [...] [the prisoner] was an illegal fighter, and that his release would prejudice state security'.[48]

4.3 The Supreme Court and the War on Terror

The Supreme court's significant contribution to the protection of human rights, even in times of emergency, is perhaps a unique feature of Israel's constitution. Since the very early stages of the state of Israel, the Supreme court has defended human rights and created what was to be known as the Bill of Judicial Rights. This comprises customary rights developed in case law which, by virtue of the principle of *stare decisis*, have transformed into binding legal norms in Israel.

The war on terror and the ongoing conflict with the Palestinians have posed and still pose many difficult constitutional questions because the special tools which are employed in times of emergency might threaten the liberties of the population; they are meant to defend, violate human rights and conflict with other democratic values. It has been argued that the courts should avoid intervening when decisions or laws are made to fight terror in times of emergency. Prof. Barak, former President of the Supreme court of Israel, cited Cicero[49] to make his point:

> They say that when cannons roar, muses are silent. Cicero expressed a similar idea when he said *inter arma silent leges* (in times of war, the law is silent). These are regrettable statements. I hope they do not reflect democracies today. I know they do not reflect the way things should be. Every battle a country wages, against terrorists or any other enemy, follows rules and laws. There is always law, domestic or international, according to which the state must act. And the Law needs Muses most urgently then when cannons roar. We need laws most in times of war.[50]

Israel has conducted a tight and effective judicial review and control on national security topics, mainly since the 90s. One of the clearest examples occurred on the eve of the First Gulf War of 1991. Concerned that Iraq might use non-conventional weapons against Israel, the Israeli Ministry of Defence decided to hand out protective kits in the Occupied Territories, but only to the Jewish settlers and not to the Palestinians. A Palestinian resident filed an urgent petition with the HCJ, arguing that this decision was discriminatory. The HCJ accepted the petition and ordered the IDF commander to issue protective kits to the Palestinians as well. Justice Barak wrote in his verdict that, even in times of war, 'the military commander must uphold the law. The power of a society to stand up against its enemies is based on

---

[48]Section (b)(1) of the Imprisonment of Illegal Fighters Law (2002).

[49]Marcus Tullius Cicero. His actual wording was 'Silent enim leges inter arma'.

[50]Barak (n 39) 151.

its recognition that it is fighting for values that deserve protection. The rule of law is one of those values'.[51]

This verdict indicates that the HCJ would be willing to hear and sometimes even support petitions against military activities, even if they are filed during an actual war or in times of terror attacks. Clearly, Israeli adjudication in this field is characterized by HCJ judicial control. Neither arguments of standing nor claims that issues are non-justiciable prevented the court from passing judgment on the IDF officers' decisions. Time and again, the HCJ has rejected claims that issues it has addressed were non-justiciable or should not be measured by legal criteria. Each and every case was reviewed on its merits, as the court has insisted for many years that a balance must be struck between often-conflicting values, such as the need to protect the state and the security of its residents on the one hand, and the need to uphold human dignity and liberty on the other. In practice, the court restricted the Executive's choice of means and tools in its response to terrorism. Justice Barak put it plainly in several cases, stating: 'A democracy must actually fight terror 'with one hand tied behind its back'[52] because the means that terrorists use cannot be employed by democracies.'

Following this approach, the HCJ delivered a long and impressive series of verdicts on the war on terror.[53] For example, in the targeted assassinations case,[54] the HCJ dealt with the military tactic of 'eliminating' leading Palestinian militants, field commanders and infrastructure coordinators. Applied mainly in the context of the *Intifada*, this method was the Israeli reaction to 'escalating Palestinian violence', but often triggered further escalation and retaliatory Palestinian operations. The HCJ set several mandatory rules: assassinations must not be carried out if less harmful means can be employed and harm to innocent civilians must be avoided as much as possible. Such harm is only lawful if it meets the proportionality requirement, which means that Israel may not target terrorists if the expected collateral damage is too great. Here, as in other cases, Justice Barak reiterated that democracies may not use every tool and certainly may not match the terrorists' methods.

In another landmark decision, the Supreme court addressed *the General Security Services (GSS)* interrogation and investigation handed down a verdict in September 1999 on which the nine-judge panel was unanimous: the GSS may conduct interrogations, but its physical interrogation techniques were declared illegal.[55]

---

[51]HCJ 168/91 Morcos v Minister of Defence 45(1) PD, 467, 470–71 [1991].

[52]HCJ 769/02 The Public Committee Against Torture in Israel v The Government of Israel 62(1) PD, 507, Section 39 [2006].

[53]Most of these verdicts were published in English on the Supreme court's official web site, under 'Fighting Terrorism within the Law'. See elyon1.Court.gov.il/VerdictsSearch/EnglishStaticVerdicts.html.

[54]HCJ 769/02 The Public Committee Against Torture in Israel v The Government of Israel (1)62 PD, 507 [2006]. elyon1.court.gov.il/Files_ENG/02/690/007/a34/02007690.a34.HTM.

[55]HCJ 5100/94 Public Committee against Torture v The Government of Israel 56(4) PD, 817 (1999). See also Amand (1999).

The petitioners argued that the physical means employed by GSS investigators not only infringed the human dignity of suspects but also constituted criminal offences. The HCJ ruled that a balancing test is necessary for dealing with interrogation rules. The balancing process resulted in a set of rules of reasonable interrogation. These rules are based on preserving the suspects' humanity while observing the classic IDF concept of 'purity of arms' during the interrogation. They reflect reasonableness, common sense and fairness. Democratic states need such rules because illegal investigations harm not only the suspects' dignity but also that of society. Thus, a reasonable interrogation is necessarily free from torture and other cruel, inhuman and degrading treatment of suspects—all of which are prohibited. There are no exceptions, and there is no room for balancing. The court stated that investigators who employ violent means might be held criminally liable.

Nevertheless, the court assumed that if a GSS investigator is criminally indicted after applying physical interrogation methods while seeking life-saving information, the 'necessity' defence may be available in the right circumstances. The 'necessity' exception is likely to arise in cases known as 'ticking bombs',[56] when there is an immediate need to preserve human lives. However, this exception does not offer a priori approval to employ such wrongful means. The court's judgment led to the introduction of the *Shin Bet* Law of 2002, which outlines the legal framework for the GSS, but does not deal with interrogations.

Essentially, these cases are part of Israel's dialogue with the international community that closely monitors Israel's activities in the Occupied Territories. These 'security' verdicts explore the impossible situation faced by Israel when combatting terrorists who attack it and then find refuge among innocent civilians[57] and present a sensitive statement of defence for Israel's constant war on terror. In the vast majority of security-related cases presented before the HCJ, the judges promoted the proportionality principle as a way of striking a balance between security needs and harm to human rights, stressed the need to avoid sweeping and generalizing solutions that deny human rights, urging the authorities to examine each case by its unique criteria and merits and established the principle that security considerations do not always take precedence. At the same time, these verdicts are mainly declaratory and do not intervene in the military commanders' considerations.

The court's judicial review of IDF activities in the Occupied Territories often reveals gaps between judicial rhetoric and the actual result. Arguably, this is an active approach *de jure*, but an abstention from de facto intervention. Although the HCJ was willing to discuss almost every petition filed against IDF operations in the territories, even in real time, and examined the security forces' authority to use various means and whether those means were proportionally employed, it approved of almost every method that the IDF employed in its war on terror and rejected most of the petitions. It must be stressed that the Supreme court never endorsed the

---

[56]This term refers to a situation in which a suspect, arrested by the GSS, has information about an imminent and even evolving terrorist event that cannot be prevented without that information.

[57]For additional reading; see Rubinstein and Roznai (2011).

argument of 'security above all', nor did it accept charges that the violation of human rights is an Israeli policy.

5 The Migration of Emergency Mechanisms

Emergency in Israel appears to be a 'state of mind' within the political branches. Emergency powers are part of the legal and political system, a perpetual aspect of normal political life.[58] The meaning of this state of affairs, for the political regime, is that emergency mechanisms are always at hand and may be used also for issues that have nothing to do with national security.

Since the early days of the state, the declaration of a state of emergency allowed for legislation that goes beyond security needs, such as the Emergency Land Requisition (Regulation) Law of 1949; and the Commodities and Services (Control) Law, of 1958, by virtue of which dozens of decrees governing supervision of the various sectors of the economy were set, overseeing, for example, the manufacture and marketing of fuels as well as the supervision of the prices of chocolate.[59]

The obvious characteristics of a state of emergency are the need for urgency and temporary: there is an urgent need to take actions beyond the usual order of things, and therefore government may deviate from the law. Still, when the government is used to having emergency tools at hand, the distinction between everyday life and exceptional ways of decision-making, blurs.

Friedberg and Hazan argue that the balance of power between Israeli governments and the *Knesset*—in emergency legislation and the war on terror—has shifted, slightly, in favour of the legislature, and that the involvement and influence of the *Knesset*, particularly in its oversight capacity, undoubtedly increased. Until the 1980s, the *Knesset*'s influence in these policy areas was minimal, and the government had almost unlimited powers to combat terrorism. After 1979, the legislature became more visible and more assertive. This shift towards incorporating policy and procedures into legislation as the method of choice—as opposed to accepting unfettered executive emergency powers—is a significant enhancement in Israel's democratic development.[60]

---

[58]Mehozay (n 19) 105.

[59]By November 2016, there were 23 decrees which regulate the following: pesticide, cosmetics, radiation machinery for medicinal use, dangerous toys, import and export of diamonds, activating of a cable car, manufacturing and selling of honey, manufacturing and trading of animal feed, manufacturing of milk, treatment of fish, installation of elevators are just some of the examples. There are still seven laws linked to the emergency state declaration dealing, among others, with supervision over seacraft, arrests, seizing of land and over time; see The Joint Committee regarding declaration of state of emergency—an overview regarding legislation which validity conditional of a state of emergency declaration (November, 2016) main.knesset.gov.il/Activity/committees/ForeignAffairs/LegislationDocs/Emergency_5.pdf (Hebrew).

[60]Friedberg and Hazan (n 14) 184–185.

Perhaps a different explanation to the rise of Knesset emergency legislation—as opposed to governmental use of emergency regulation—may be found in Israel's political framework. In practice, the Israeli Parliament is quite weak. The government rules the legislative process, minimizing the possibility of passing laws that it does not support. The tools at the disposal of the Knesset for scrutinizing the government are not terribly effective. A real opposition to the government within the Knesset rarely exists due to the many parties that comprise the opposition, which ideologically has almost nothing in common between them. In recent years, the executive has been gaining power while the legislature has become weaker and often seems willing to condone the transfer of powers to the executive branch.[61] This appears to be a global phenomenon that does not depend on the type of constitutional system, be it republican or parliamentary. Furthermore, Israel's government is able to operate outside the Knesset's control, by using emergency powers even for administrating routine economic policies. With these emergency legal mechanisms available, Israel's governing authorities can choose the best legal tool to serve their desired ends. Legislation can be passed quickly and almost at the government's will. As Mehozay puts it: If one legal mechanism might be challenged or meet the limits of its authority, another is available instead. As a result, this flexibility enables the state to extend its sovereign power and achieve political ends that would otherwise be impossible. All the while, the state maintains a degree of legitimacy by operating behind a veil of legality.[62]

Several examples may be seen to enhance this migration of unusual methods and procedures to circumstances that have nothing to do with emergency.

5.1 *Economic and Financial Ends*

Emergency tools have been used not only for the protection of the state and its people during a time of imminent threat. Emergency powers have migrated and have been used to achieve desired economic ends, such as implementing fiscal or monetary policies and settling labour disputes.

During the 70s period, there was a sharp increase in the use of administrative emergency orders applied for socioeconomic ends. In 1985, an emergency regulation called the Economic Regularization Emergency Law of 1985 (known as 'the Omnibus Law' or 'the Arrangements Law') was passed as a supplement to the economic program for stabilizing the economy to halt raging hyperinflation and to stop workers' wages from eroding further. The Omnibus Law was first enacted following the difficult situation of the Israeli economy at that time, a situation which resulted in a governmental emergency program that contradicted in part existing laws and agreements in central sectors such as labour relations, wages and taxes.

[61]Martinez (2006).

[62]Mehozay (n 13) 84.

In order to validate the legality of the economic program, the government grouped a combination of laws and legislative adjustments in a number of different areas under one roof and brought them to the Knesset for approval en bloc. The Omnibus Law, which originated as an emergency law, has since that time become customary and is annually brought before the Knesset in tandem with the Budget Law.[63,64]

The first petition against legislative procedures that resemble the Arrangements Laws was filed in 2003, seeking a unique remedy—that the law be nullified not because it unlawfully impaired rights anchored in basic laws, but also because its enactment process was flawed. This petition,[65] was rejected and the law was not quashed, but the court's verdict sharply chastised the Arrangements Law proceedings. Justice Beinisch stated that this type of law is problematic in terms of due democratic process. It is characterized by a hasty legislative procedure that makes it practically impossible for MKs to seriously debate the law, impairing the decision makers' ability to reach educated conclusions and to form opinions. Not only is the bill insufficiently discussed, it also detracts from the Knesset's ability to effectively supervise the legislative process itself.

[63]Nahmias and Klein (1999); The Arrangements Law: Issues and International Comparisons (Written in Hebrew and translated into English by Dr. Susan Hattis Rolef Head of the International Desk The Knesset Research and Information Centre, 2006) www.knesset.gov.il/mmm/data/pdf/me01237.pdf.

[64]The Omnibus Law of Arrangements is presented to the Knesset as a government-sponsored law. The law is considered supplementary to the Budget Law and combines an assortment of laws and legislative adjustments that the government deems it necessary for the Knesset to adopt and approve in order to enable it to carry out its policy and economic plan. The Omnibus Law of Arrangements differs from the majority of laws enacted by the Knesset in its structure and its legislative process. While regular laws deal with one specific, well-defined topic, the Omnibus Law of Arrangements serves as a 'platform' for laws and legislative adjustments in various areas. Moreover, while other proposed legislation is turned over to particular Knesset committees for deliberation as per the legislative norm in parliamentary systems, the Omnibus Law of Arrangements is passed to one committee (usually the Finance Committee) as a single unit and that committee deliberates on all sections of the law within a short, predetermined period of time at the end of which it returns the legislation to the Knesset plenary for final approval. In the current situation, the Omnibus Law of Arrangements serves as a unique governmental instrument that aids the government, through reliance on the coalition majority, in speeding up legislation, overcoming parliamentary obstacles and proposing legislative activities and bringing them to completion without systematic deliberation, appropriate oversight and critiquing. The special structure of the Omnibus Law of Arrangements and its speedy and peculiar legislative process arouse strenuous criticism both within and outside of the Knesset. The criticism is focused on the political-civic and legal aspects; deviation from the norm of democratic governance that demands accountability, transparency and an effective system of checks and balances in public policy formation in general and in legislation in particular. Despite repeated criticism, to date no significant steps have been taken to rescind the law or to introduce qualitative changes in its makeup.

[65]HCJ 4885/03 The Poultry Growers Organization v The Government of Israel 59(2) PD, 14 [25] [2005].

These legal mechanisms utilized by governments to execute economic regulations are still available today in Israel despite the fact that they have been used significantly less in recent years.

5.2 Temporary Legislation

In recent years, the Knesset has increasingly[66] used 'temporary provisions' in times that are perceived as 'special' due to national security threats. It seems that in doing so, it attempts to show the HCJ that though this particular law infringes human rights, the fact that it is temporary makes it 'proportional' and thus the court should avoid nullifying it if petitioned to do so. The Knesset has been naming new laws 'temporary provisions'—particularly when the laws in question deal with security issues and had been argued to violate human rights. Such ad hoc, temporary legislation is the Knesset's way of signalling that it is aware of the harm that this legislation may cause to human rights, but since the law is provisional, that harm should be viewed by the court as proportional and therefore refrain from declaring it unconstitutional. Referring to this phenomenon, the court stated that: 'The fact that basic rights are harmed by a temporary provision due to ad hoc needs can indeed indicate the proportionality of that harm. The fact that the harm is temporary, since 765 the legislation is a temporary provision, reflects on our appreciation of the might, 766 depth, and extend of the harm caused to a basic right.'[67]

Time-restricted laws that impose certain limitations for a given period may survive the constitutionality test and judicial review, but history has shown that the validity of most of these laws is extended time and again. For example, an amendment to the Criminal Proceedings Law was introduced in 2006 by way of a temporary provision, stating that a judge may rule on the extension of detention of persons held on suspicion of security offences, even if they are not presented before a judge. The validity of this amendment was extended as soon as it expired. In 2011, a nine-judge HCJ bench ruled that this amendment was unconstitutional because it conflicted with Basic Law: Human Dignity and Liberty.[68] The 2003 amendment of the Citizenship Law that bans family reunions between Israeli Arabs

[66]Ittai Bar-Siman-Tov, Temporary Legislation, Better Regulation and Experimentalist Governance: An Empirical Study (July 10, 2016). Forthcoming, Regulation and Governance. Available at SSRN: https://ssrn.com/abstract=2807564: the study showed that even though only 8/7% of Israeli legislation is of the temporary kind there is a rising trend in the use of such legislation in the last fifteen years, during which, the temporary legislation comprises 15.41%. See page 14.

[67]HCJ 7052/03 Adalah v The Interior Minister 71(2) PD, 202 [2006].

[68]Deputy HCJ President Eliezer Rivlin stated that the legal proceeding does not address absentees but only present individuals. One of the most basic foundations of criminal law is that a person should not be tried in absentia. Justice Rivlin stressed that the defendant's right to be present at his own trial is part of the right to honest proceedings, which is a basic premise of the law and a protected constitutional right. He deducted the importance of this principle from the habeas corpus doctrine; see CC 8823/07 John Doe v The State of Israel, at [20] (decided on 11.2.2010).

and Palestinians who reside in the Occupied Territories was also introduced as a temporary provision, but its validity was extended on numerous occasions. In early 2012, the HCJ rejected yet another petition against this law by a majority of six of the 11 judges.

Temporary legislation is part of the discourse between the Israeli Parliament and the Supreme court. The Knesset often needs specific measures to fulfil political and security needs. Provisional laws have become a 'tool' used by the Knesset to attempt to avoid judicial review, arguing that the problematic law is 'temporary' and therefore 'proportional'. Still, the tolerant approach by the Israeli Supreme court towards temporary laws is gradually changing into a regular judicial review approach when laws defined as 'temporary' are prolonged more than once.[69] It would seem that at least some of the Supreme court judges view such frequent extensions with suspicion, feeling that the Knesset might be trying to institutionalize complicated and sensitive issues, while simultaneously skipping over the need to conduct an orderly public debate and attempting to ignore the meaning of problematic legislation as part of Israeli law.

5.3 Temporary Constitutional Amendments

The temporary provisions—which have been increasingly employed by the Knesset in recent years—have been used also for an amendment in one of Israel basic laws. Emergency legislative tools seem to 'migrate' even to constitutional amendments.

Each year, as in many other states, Israel regularly introduces an Annual State Budget Act,[70] but in 2009, the Knesset decided to irregularly introduce a two-year budget, which it then decided to anchor in a provisional order of a basic law. A year after this provisional basic law was enacted, the government decided that the biennial budget was preferable and decided to extend the Act by another two years to cover 2011 and 2012. This amendment was unique because it was an extension of a provisional measure that was meant to be 'temporary' in nature.

Addressing a petition against this 'provisional constitutional amendment', a seven-judge panel unanimously rejected a petition that challenged the constitutionality of amending a basic law. Their ruling, however, contained harsh remarks about the procedure chosen by the Knesset for this move. Nevertheless, the court was not convinced that this was the case in which the Supreme court should intervene in the Knesset's basic law-making as a constituent authority. However, the fact that the possibility was discussed indicated that the court acknowledged its

---

[69]HCJ 6298/07 Ressler v The Knesset (21.2.2012). versa.cardozo.yu.edu/sites/default/files/upload/opinions/Ressler%20v.%20Knesset.pdf.

[70]By the power of the instruction contained in Section 3(a) of Basic Law: The State's Economy, s 3(a)(1) states that 'the state budget shall be anchored in a law' and s 3(a)(2) reads: 'The budget will be marked for one year and present expected and planned government expenditures.'

power to do so and did not deny its prerogative to judicially review even amendments of basic laws by the constituent power.

5.4 The New Anti-terrorism Law

On 15 June 2016, the Knesset approved a new counterterrorism law, which significantly expands both the state's counterterrorism powers and its definitions of terrorist organizations and terrorist acts. The new law combines most provisions of existing anti-terrorism law, replacing numerous defence regulations enacted by the British mandate more than 70 years ago.

The new law it aims to establish provisions both in criminal and administrative law, including special enforcement powers in order to combat terrorism, to prevent the establishment, existence and activities of terrorist organizations and of terrorist crimes committed by terrorist organizations or individuals.

The law includes a long definition's chapter, which includes, among other things, a broad definition of a 'terrorist organization' and 'terrorist act'. The definition of 'terrorist organization' includes, for example, not only the 'first circle' (the terrorist organization itself) but also the 'second circle', meaning an organization that works, sustains or helps a terrorist organization. Before this new law, the definition was narrower (within the law prohibiting the financing of terrorism) and did not include this second circle.

The law deals with the procedures for the declaration of a terrorist organization, and a special chapter deals with penalties and punishment, which includes a list of 16 offences related to terrorism and includes also a new offence: the heading of a terrorist organization:

> the head of the terrorist organization or he who manages it, or who takes part in directing the terrorist organization as a whole, directly or indirectly, shall be liable of imprisonment for 25 years; if the terrorist organization's activities also include murder—shall be liable of life imprisonment and this punishment only.

Among other offences: being a member of a terrorist organization, enrolment of membersand the offence of solidarity with a terrorist organization and incitement to terrorism. The law prescribes punishment for this offence in the case of the publication of praise, support or sympathy, flag, etc. In any case, for the specific indictment under the offence of solidarity, the approval of the Attorney General is required.

As for evidence and procedure, the law stipulates stricter punishment for an offence which is an act of terrorism and states that the court must note in its judgment that the conviction was of an act of terrorism. The law establishes that he who commits the offence of an 'act of mass terror' shall bear life imprisonment.

The law establishes special provisions allowing for the deviation from the Penal Code, the Evidence Ordinance and the Criminal Procedure Law. For example, the prescription of offences: The Criminal Procedure Law [Consolidated Version], 1982—states that unless otherwise specified, the prescription of a crime punishable by death or life imprisonment—is 20 years. Meaning that 20 years after the commitment of such a crime, a person cannot be tried. The new law allows for prosecuting after 20 years provided that the reason for not filing an indictment (nor directed an investigation or proceedings) is that the suspect was abroad and could not be brought in for questioning or trial in Israel.

The law allows for the extension of detention periods in order to allow effective interrogation of terror suspects. The extensions would be granted following hearing conducted in the absence of the detainee, and the law sets the specific periods of time for these extensions. It also allows seizure and forfeiture, both administrative and in criminal cases. It allows, for example, forfeiting the property of the head of a terrorist organization and in certain circumstances, to foreclose on the property discovered even after sentencing.

It is worth mentioning that the law requires the Minister of Justice to report to the Knesset every year, on the first of June, including the number of indictments filed during the year, for example under Section 24 (identification with a terrorist organization and incitement to terrorism).

This law has recently been passed, and it has not been yet discussed or interpreted by the HCJ. Interestingly, in its decision on the continuity of the declaration of emergency, the Supreme court has pointed to the new Law as one of the steps taken by the government in order to get prepared for the non-renewal of the declaration of emergency situation.

6 Conclusion

Israel has struggled for its existence since its establishment, constantly living in a state of emergency. It is a Jewish and democratic state that consistently faces security threats. But emergency powers in Israel have played a much bigger role than their principal function of protecting the state and its people in times of imminent threat. What may have emerged as a pragmatic temporary solution in 1948 became a systemic and permanent mechanism used for various political and economic ends. Emergency powers go far beyond what is commonly understood as security measures and are one of the constitution characteristics of the Israeli regime.

The unique nature of the Israeli condition derives from the constant prolonging of the declaration of the emergency situation. Still, an end to the formal emergency situation is difficult to foresee, taking into consideration the continuous threats Israel faces. As Justice Rubinstein pointed out: '*We may not ignore the fact that Israel has not yet found comfort and peace. Indeed, it experienced relatively long periods of relative calm, but regrettably the winds of war never stopped blowing ... Israel's situation was and still is sensitive and complicated, and in such a situation, the state authorities must not be left without the powers they need in emergency times.*'[71]

Acknowledgements I wish to thank Rosa Feldman for her valuable assistance.

References

Ackerman B (2004) The emergency constitution. Yale Law J 113:1029

Amand MGS (1999) Public Committee against Torture in Israel v. The State of Israel et Al: landmark human rights decision by the Israeli High Court of Justice or Status Quo maintained. N C J Int Law Commercial Regul 25:655

Barak A (2002) A judge on judging: the role of a supreme court in a democracy. Harvard Law Rev 116:19

Barak A (2014) International humanitarian law and the Israeli Supreme Court. Israel Law Rev 47:181

Barak Erez D (2013) The National Security Constitution and the Israeli condition. In: Sapir G, Barak Erez D, Barak A (eds) Israeli constitutional law in the making. Hart Publishing, UK

Dershowitz AM (1971) Preventative detention of citizens during a national emergency—a comparison between Israel and the United States. Israel yearbook on human rights, vol 1, p 295

Friedberg C, Hazan RY (2010) Israel's prolonged war against terror: from executive domination to executive–legislative dialogue. In: Owens JE, Pelizzo R (eds), The war on terror and the growth of executive power?: a comparative analysis. Routledge (July 30)

Gavison R (2005) Legislatures and the quest for a constitution: the case of Israel. Rev Const Stud 11:345

Hofnung M (1991) Israel–state security versus the rule of law. Nevo, Jerusalem

Khakee A (2009) Securing democracy? A comparative analysis of emergency powers in Europe. Centre for the Democratic Control of Armed Forces (DCAF) Policy Paper. https://www.files.ethz.ch/isn/99550/PP30_Anna_Khakee_Emergency_Powers.pdf

Kretzmer D (2002) The occupation of justice: The Supreme Court of Israel and the occupied territories. SUNY Press, USA

Martinez JS (2006) Inherent executive power: a comparative perspective. Yale Law J 115:2480

Mehozay Y (2012) The fluid jurisprudence of Israel's emergency powers: legal patchwork as a governing norm. Law Soc Rev 46:137

Mehozay Y (2016) Between the rule of law and states of emergency: the fluid jurisprudence of the Israeli regime. SUNY Press, USA

Nahmias D, Klein E (1999) Hok Hahesderim: Bein Kalakala Lepolitika (The arrangements law: between economics and politics). Position paper no. 17. The Israel Democracy Institute, Jerusalem (Hebrew)

Navot S (2014) The constitution of Israel: a contextual analysis. Hart Publishing, UK

Rubinstein A, Roznai Y (2011) Human shields modern armed conflicts: the need for a proportionate proportionality. Stanford Law Policy Rev 22:93

[71]HCJ 3019/99 Association for Civil Rights in Israel v Knesset (decided 8.5.2012) Justice Rubinstein's verdict at [11].

The French Case or the Hidden Dangers of a Long-Term State of Emergency

Cécile Guérin-Bargues

Abstract Since January 2015, French politics are regularly shaped by the scourge of terrorist operations carried out on its territory. State of emergency was declared in November 2015 and had several time been renewed until October 31st 2017. Its legal regime has been modified and strengthened in both November 2015 and July 2016. The aim of this article is twofold. First, it underscores the tremendous extent of the executive power under state of emergency. Second, it aims at showing how state of emergency leads to paradigm shifts that affect the functioning of the French political powers. This change is not limited to security prevailing over liberty, but it is also apparent in many other fields. For instance, politicians tend to view state of emergency as the means needed to fight against a recurring terrorist danger. State of emergency that has been conceived as a legal answer to a temporary threat tends in France to become permanent. Its very nature is thus modified. Another paradigm shift can be seen in the fate of the balance of power doctrine. The classical doctrine according to which Parliament is expected to defend liberty and to impose limits on executive power tends to be forgotten. Not only every steps have been taken in order to avoid primary judicial review of the 20 November 2015 law. But Parliamentary debates also illustrate how much members of Parliament, under the pressure of a traumatised public opinion, are ready to give the executive power even more prerogatives than what is asked for. State of emergency thus appears as a perilous status: not only for everyday liberties but also because of a hidden danger: it may alter in the long run the normal functioning of public institutions.

C. Guérin-Bargues (✉)
Institut Michel Villey pour la culture juridique et la philosophie du droit,
University Paris Nanterre, Paris, France
e-mail: cecbargues@aol.com

P. Auriel et al. (eds.), *The Rule of Crisis*, Ius Gentium: Comparative Perspectives on Law and Justice 64, https://doi.org/10.1007/978-3-319-74473-5_10

1 Introduction

The state of emergency has been at the heart of French political and legal life ever since its declaration on the night of 14 November 2015, following the attacks on the Bataclan concert hall and until October 31st 2017 the day of its termination. The institution was established *ex nihilo* by the law of 3 April 1955. At the time, it was intended to provide a means of dealing with the attacks by Algerian rebels on a territory that still belonged to France. Over the years, and with use, its legal status has undergone various changes. The most extensive such change resulted from the law of 20 November 2015 which extended the state of emergency declared on 14 November by three months and, under the guise of modernisation, further increased the powers of the administration. It has since been extended on five further occasions.[1]

The scope of the powers conferred upon the administration (the Prime Minister, the Minister of the Interior and Prefects[2]) has varied from one extension to the next. For instance, the possibility of conducting house searches by day as well as by night, which is one of the measures that infringe most heavily upon Constitutional liberties, was authorised from 14 November to 26 May 2016. The law of 20 May 2016 extended the state of emergency once again. However, by making no mention of such searches, it put an end to them.[3] This possibility was nonetheless reactivated and extended by the law of 21 July 2016, following the attack in Nice and was maintained by the law of 19 December 2016.

The other powers conferred upon the administration, however, derive simply from the implementation of the state of emergency itself and thus do not require any specific mention in the prorogation bill. These powers are nonetheless extended to a remarkable degree, with the possibility of: placing anyone suspected of posing a threat to security and public order under house arrest, in a place determined by the prefect[4]; regulating the right to stay and freedom of movement of people and vehicles[5]; and disbanding associations that could compromise public order.[6] The administration also has the power to: 'order the temporary closure of entertainment

[1]In addition to Law No. 2015-1501 of 20 November 2015, which extends the state of emergency by three months, mention should also be made here of Law No. 2016-162 dated 19 February 2016 (for another three-months extension); Law No. 2016-629 of 20 May 2016 (two-months extension); Law No. 2016-987 dated 21 July 2016 (six-months extension); Law No. 2016-1767 dated 19 December 2016 (seven-months extension) and Law No. 2017-1154 dated 11 July 2017 (three-months extension).

[2]Prefects are representing the Minister of the Interior within the French territory.

[3]Specific mention should in fact be made of Article 11, subparagraph 1, of the law of 3 April 1955, in the decree declaring the state of emergency, or in the law that extends its enforcement, to authorise the carrying out of searches by day as well as by night.

[4]Law of 3 April 1955, Article 6.

[5]Article 5.

[6]Article 6-1.

venues, drinking establishments and meeting places'[7]; forbid processions and shows[8]; search bags and vehicles[9]; and order the handing over of weapons.[10] Since the Algerian War (1954–1962), never has such a broadly conceived emergency regime been applied in metropolitan France, and over such an extended period of time. If the state of emergency remains in force until the date specified by the law of 19 December 2016, France will have been under this regime, which infringes upon public liberties to a particularly marked degree, for over twenty months, from 14 November 2015 to 15 July 2017.

The efficacy and legitimacy of such a long-term application of this legal system are certainly questionable.

Its efficacy in practical terms is difficult to measure. A parliamentary report has in fact examined around ten attacks that were thwarted thanks to the actions of the intelligence and security services.[11] Nonetheless, it is impossible to ascertain the specific role played by the state of emergency provisions in this regard, as compared to the rules of ordinary law.[12] Any such role was no doubt minor; the report notes that specialists in the fight against terrorism, despite having been interviewed during the state of emergency, make barely any mention of the measures taken within its framework.[13] In fact, the efficacy of the state of emergency appears to rapidly decrease the further one gets from the date on which it was declared. As such, a statement issued on 13 January 2016 by the Committee of the National Assembly, which is responsible for overseeing the state of emergency, indicates that, by that point in time, the mechanism had already exhausted most of its effects. The figures relating to the two most widely employed measures speak for themselves. On 12 January 2016, 3021 police searches and 381 administrative summonses had already been issued. As the public authorities wanted to benefit from the element of surprise associated with the declaration of a state of emergency, almost a third of these searches were ordered during the seven days following the Bataclan attacks.[14] The efficacy of the mechanism, which derives from its

[7]Article 8.

[8]Article 8.

[9]Article 8-1.

[10]Article 9.

[11]National Assembly, Pietrasanta Report, drawn up on behalf of the commission of enquiry on the steps taken by the State in the fight against terrorism, 5 July 2016, 262.

[12]One of the projects, at least, was thwarted following an administrative search carried out under the state of emergency. Ibid. p. 143.

[13]Ibid. p. 262.

[14]The updated figures, as at 11 July 2016, confirm such a concentration of measures in the first weeks of the state of emergency, when there were no fewer than 3594 searches, and 400 summonses.

destabilising effect, is thus closely linked to the element of surprise, which is quick to dissipate.[15] In short, as one senator stressed during the debate on 20 July 2016 on the extension of the state of emergency: 'renewing [...] the state of emergency will have very little practical effect'.[16]

Moreover, recourse to the state of emergency, as an emergency form of legislation, seems in some senses superfluous, given that identical measures can be adopted under ordinary legislation. This is the case, for instance, with the procedure for blocking access to sites that incite terrorism. Pursuant to Article 11 of the Law of 1955, as amended, this procedure merely 'duplicates' an identical legislative framework introduced in 2014.[17] Furthermore, several ordinary laws were adopted in the last few months to reinforce the fight against organised crime, terrorism and their financing.[18]

The specific contribution of the state of emergency to the fight against terrorism is thus minimal. When an offence is discovered, administrative searches can nonetheless result in criminal proceedings. In December 2016, out of a total of over 4000 administrative searches, almost 670 led to such proceedings. However, only a few of these were linked to terrorism, with the vast majority concerning incitement to terrorism.[19] Ultimately, only twenty proceedings that resulted, at least in part, from an administrative search actually led to the anti-terrorist section of the Paris Public Prosecutor being called upon.[20]

Such an observation naturally leads one to call into question the link between such measures and the terrorist threat, which was used to justify the implementation of the state of emergency and its extensions. State of emergency legislation should not be placed on the same level as ordinary legislation. Like any exceptional regime, its use should be limited to the strictly necessary. This is evidently not the case, though, since this emergency legislation, the implementation of which was justified on the basis of exceptional circumstances, is essentially being used in the manner of ordinary law. Such a process ultimately results in the transformation of a legal system that is reactive in nature (the state of emergency as a reaction to an attack) into a preventive mechanism. Yet, conferring a preventive function upon emergency legislation implies that it is regarded, at all times, as a possible

---

[15]In this context, the Pietrasanta Report mentions a noteworthy anecdote recounted by Mr. Partick Mairesse, Director of Public Safety for the Department of Isère: '*As soon as the second day after the declaration of the state of emergency, we were greeted with the outburst: 'At last! I'd been waiting'. For some, this is a question of standing! What's more, we found a computer at the home of a radicalised individual with its contents entirely wiped, except for one result in the search history relating to the state of emergency! And that was only Sunday evening*'! ibid. p. 262.

[16]Jacques Mézard, Official Journal, debates 20 July 2016.

[17]Article 12 of Law No. 2014-1353 dated 13 November 2014, which strengthened the provisions concerning the fight against terrorism and amended the law of 21 June 2014 to support confidence in the digital economy.

[18]See, for instance, the French Criminal Code, Articles 421-2-1, -2, -3, -4, -5, etc.

[19]Discovery of video messages or flags, for example.

[20]Pietrasanta Report, as above, p. 262.

alternative to the well-calibrated procedures and measured solutions that make up the legal system in times of peace.

The state of emergency thus appears to have only a very relative effect in the fight against terrorism. However, as soon as it is necessary to call into question the foundations of the normal operations of French public institutions, it becomes remarkably effective. Article 16 of the Declaration of the Rights of Man and of the Citizen, which forms part of the Constitutional norms in force in France, specifies that: 'Any society in which rights are not guaranteed, or in which there is no determined separation of powers, has no Constitution'. One could nonetheless justifiably worry that the perpetuation of a state of emergency in France might result in the calling into question of both (1) the balance of powers and (2) the guarantee of rights.

2 Calling into Question the Balance of Power

The state of emergency disrupts the separation of power by emphasising the primacy of the executive branch (2.1) with the support of legislative powers (2.2) and without any prior control by the Constitutional Council (2.3).

2.1 The Primacy of the Executive

The appropriation of power by the executive in connection with the state of emergency is by no means a new development. Indeed, a dual appropriation, of both a formal and material nature, can be seen as early as 1960. It was through an Order issued on 25 April 1960[21] that the Parliament conferred the power to declare a state of emergency upon the President of the Republic. However, this administrative act, which amended the law of 3 April 1955 on an essential point, was passed through a parliamentary enabling act.[22] This act authorised the government at the time to undertake a certain number of legislative measures, 'under the signature of General de Gaulle', President of the Republic at the time. The Head of State thus assigned himself the authority to declare a state of emergency. Since then, in accordance with the primacy of the executive under the Fifth Republic,

[21]Order No. 60-372 of 15 April 1960, which amends certain provisions of Law No. 55-385 of 3 April 1955, establishing a state of emergency.

[22]Law No. 60-101 of 4 February 1960, which, under Article 38 of the Constitution, authorises the government to take certain measures in order to maintain law and order, safeguard the State and improve peace-making and administration in Algeria. This mechanism is provided for under Article 38 of the Constitution. Pursuant to Article 13 of the Constitution, the President of the Republic is responsible for signing orders and decrees deliberated upon in the Council of Ministers.

'a state of emergency is declared by a decree from the Council of Ministers',[23] that is, through a text signed by the Head of State. As such, the President of the Republic enjoys extended discretionary power when it comes to declaring a state of emergency and establishing its scope of application at the territorial level. Indeed, this dimension was very clearly conveyed during the televised appearance of the President of the Republic, François Hollande, on the evening of 13 November 2015, while the attacks in Paris were still underway. Before the Council of Ministers had even had time to meet, he specified that 'they would make two decisions': in addition to calling for the 'closure of the borders', 'a state of emergency would be declared [...] across the territory'.

The power to declare a state of emergency is a highly important presidential prerogative. Followed by implementing decrees, it immediately leads to a considerable strengthening of the powers conferred upon the administrative police authorities, as has already been suggested. However, in practice, the implementation of a state of emergency illustrates that these prerogatives are often quickly employed for reasons other than those initially used to justify the declaration of the state of emergency. For example, not long after the attacks on November 2015, Paris was set to host COP 21, the United Nations conference on climate change. Twenty-seven house arrests and 130 measures prohibiting demonstrations were ordered against environmental campaigners who clearly had no links with Salafist elements. These house arrests testify to the freedom of interpretation that the state of emergency grants the executive branch since it assumes the right to act for reasons beyond those that served to validate the declaration of the state of emergency in the first place. It is true that, after twelve days, the state of emergency can only be extended by law. The significance of such an intervention by the Parliament cannot, however, be overestimated, where circumstances favour a consensus between the executive and legislative branches and the freedom of the former to act.

2.2 Parliamentary One-Upmanship

First of all, we will examine the procedure for the adoption of the law of 20 November 2015. This law not only extended the state of emergency by three months but also substantially amended the law of 3 April 1955. Despite this dual effect, however, it was adopted extremely quickly thanks to a particularly strong consensus between the two chambers: it was passed less than a week after the state of emergency was declared. Clearly, the priority for parliamentarians was to provide the government with the means to protect public order, rather than to set themselves up as guardians of liberties.

The classic doctrine, according to which the purpose of legislative power is to restrict the repressive inclination of the executive branch, appears to lose most of its

[23]Order No. 60-372 dated 15 April 1960, as mentioned above, Art. 2. Para. 1.

force during a state of emergency. Far from acting as an opposing power, Parliament allowed itself to be swayed by majority logic and, faced with traumatised public opinion, did not hesitate to overstep the government's wishes. For example, it was on the basis of a proposal made by parliament that house arrests for individuals were extended to twelve hours,[24] rather than eight as proposed in the draft law. Furthermore, certain parliamentarians took very little heed of Constitutional constraints by proposing round-the-clock standby duty at home, for instance, at the risk of transforming house arrests into an administrative detention which, under Article 66 of the French Constitution, requires the intervention of a judicial judge.[25] Equally, the new Article 11(2) of the amended Law of 1955, concerning online services, the redundancy of which has already been stressed, also resulted from a parliamentary initiative.[26] It was originally intended to limit the procedural safeguards established by the law of 2014. Numerous other examples could be proposed. Suffice it to say that, as a rule, amendments proposed by parliamentarians that were geared at achieving that difficult balance between the need for effectiveness and respect for laws and liberties were almost systematically rejected. The options retained offered the advantage of allowing for 'greater policy manoeuvreability'.[27]

The parliamentary debates that presided over the adoption of the fourth extension of the state of emergency, by the law of 21 July 2016 (following the attack in Nice on the evening of 14 July), generated much more heated exchanges than the previous ones. These were nonetheless brief; once again, the law was adopted in under 48 h even though the public authorities had declared, up to the morning of 14 July, that it would be possible to put an end to the state of emergency and that ordinary legislation would from then on suffice in the fight against terrorism. The debates thus testified to a clear calling into question of the government's capacity to guarantee the safety of the French people. This parliamentary one-upmanship affected, first of all, the length of the extension; the extension was for six months, even though the government had proposed that it be for three. The parliamentary amendments also led to a further strengthening of the provisions of the law of 3 April 1955. The Senate adopted a particularly ambiguous provision, facilitating the closure of places of worship that are the site of statements inciting hatred and

[24]Amendment 40, defended by Mr Ciotti during the debate in the National Assembly on 19 November 2015.

[25]Amendment No. 4 by Mr. Larrivé in the Commission. In its decision QPC 2015-527, dated 22 December 2015, the Constitutional Council stressed that house arrests cannot last longer than twelve hours. However, this did not stop certain senators, during the debates on the extension of 21 July, following the attacks in Nice, from proposing an amendment to increase the duration of house arrests that can be ordered by the Minister of the Interior from twelve hours to twenty-four hours. Rachline Amendment, senatorial debates of 20 July 2016.

[26]Initiative of the radical group in the National Assembly.

[27]This expression is taken from an address by the Madame Secretary, during a debate in the Commission concerning the laws of the National Assembly, which took place on 19 November 2015.

violence.[28] This 'media-oriented' amendment thus led to 'the addition of texts rather than the application of existing ones'.[29] The law of 21 July also authorised a wide-scale prohibition of gatherings and marches, not for the classic reasons associated with public order, but simply in light of the administrative authorities' incapacity to guarantee participants' safety.[30] Another amendment led to the introduction of a system of preventive identity checks, including baggage and vehicle searches, without the authorisation of the public prosecutor, contrary to the stipulations of ordinary law.[31] Lastly, the law circumvents the effects of the Constitutional Council's decision of 19 February 2016, which judged the seizing of material and computer data during administrative searches to be unconstitutional due to the lack of authorisation by a judge. The solution adopted is unconvincing given the requirements of the Constitutional Council. For, pursuant to Article 5 of the law of 21 July 2016, seizures can be conducted freely, and only the utilisation of data requires the authorisation of an administrative judge hearing applications for interim measures.

However, strengthening the more freedom-curbing provisions of the law of 3 April 1955—with the agreement, or even on the initiative of, parliamentarians—is not the only effect that the laws of 20 November 2015, 19 February 2016, 20 May 2016, 21 July 2016 and 19 December 2016 have in common. For in addition, neither one is subject to any form of a priori control by the Constitutional Council.

2.3 *The Absence of Any a Priori Referral to the Constitutional Council*

Two types of Constitutionality controls exist in France. A priori controls are carried out prior to the enactment of a law. This process is not obligatory and involves a referral to the Council, either by a political authority (the President of the Republic, the Prime Minister, the President of the National Assembly or of the Senate) or by a minority of parliamentarians (at least 60 deputies or 60 senators). It applies to all Constitutional norms, whether substantive (rights and freedoms) or procedural in nature. A posteriori control was introduced more recently. Since 1 March 2010, this procedure has enabled the Constitutional Council to control legislative provisions already in effect. It is applied in the case of pending lawsuits and exclusively in relation to the rights and freedoms guaranteed by the Constitution. It presupposes

[28]Article 3 of the law of 21 July 2016, amending Article 8 of the law of 3 April 1955.

[29]These were the words of Senator Jacques Mézard, on 20 July 2016, during the examination by the Commission of the future law of 21 July 2016.

[30]Idem.

[31]Article 4 of the law of 21 July 2016, which inserted Article 8-1 into the law of 3 April 1955. This was authorised by the prefect; the prosecutor merely needed to be informed.

that a litigious provision has not been subject to any a priori control, except in the event of a change in circumstances, in law or in fact.

Every effort appears to have been made, each time state of emergency has been renewed and strengthened by law, to avoid an a priori referral to the Constitutional Council. Yet a priori referral could have made it possible to render a posteriori control inadmissible. During the parliamentary debates in November 2015, however, the Prime Minister repeatedly declared that he was 'extremely hesitant about a referral to the Constitutional Council', inasmuch as 'it is always risky to call upon the Constitutional Council'.[32] This public admission, on the part of a Prime Minister, of personal distrust in an institution intended to offset majority rule is clearly shocking. Above all, it is a glaring contradiction of an address apparently geared at bringing the state of emergency under the rule of law. How can the executive branch so implicitly proclaim its desire to have free rein, while at the same time referring to the notion of the rule of law, which necessarily implies subjecting executive power to a system of surveillance and increased monitoring?[33]

The fact remains, however, that no referral to the Constitutional Council was made before the promulgation either of those laws. Yet a posteriori control of Constitutionality can only partially compensate for the absence of a priori control. Thus, the bill of extension of 21 July 2016 includes several provisions that relate not to the extension of the state of emergency, but to the escalation of the fight against terrorism.[34] These form Title II, which underscores the heterogeneous nature of the law and testifies to the incorporation of the state of emergency in the fight against terrorism. Essentially, this is a series of measures added by the more radical parliamentarians, and which had hitherto been rejected by the government. These concern: the withdrawal of automatic reduced sentences and of the possibility of placing people convicted of terrorist offences under a restricted-release regime[35]; harsher sentences[36]; and the adoption of a mandatory ban on entering the French territory.[37] These provisions do not amend the law of 3 April 1955, then, which is the legislative basis of the state of emergency, but rather the Penal Code and the Code of Criminal Procedure. Yet Article 45 of the French Constitution prohibits 'rider legislations', that is, provisions introduced by an amendment that bears little connection with the original text.[38] However, this calling into question of an enacted law constitutes a violation of Constitutional rights and freedoms,

[32]Senate, session on 20 November 2015.

[33]On this subject, see Rosanvallon (2015).

[34]Cf. Circular dated 22 July 2015 concerning the state of emergency. Presentation of the provisions of Law No. 2016-987 dated 21 July 2016 to extend the application of Law No. 55-385 dated 3 April 1955 regarding the state of emergency and introduce measures to step up the fight against terrorism. *Bulletin officiel du Ministère de la Justice* (Official Bulletin of the Ministry of Justice), JUSD1620976C.

[35]Article 8 of the law of 21 July 2016.

[36]Article 13.

[37]Article 14.

[38]Avril (2014), 240.

rather than simply failing to comply with parliamentary procedure. As such, these provisions could have been censured by the Constitutional Council, as part of an a priori control process, but not within the framework of a posterior control.[39]

The long-term state of emergency, the efficacy and legitimacy of which is indeed questionable, thus appears to be fraught with risks. Not only does it increase the prerogatives of the administrative powers; it also encourages the public authorities to emancipate themselves from the balance of power, involving the prevalence of the executive branch, which is quick to misuse the powers conferred upon it; a parliamentary one-upmanship geared at overstepping the prerogatives required by the government to maintain public order; and abandoning the task of protecting rights and freedoms to those due to be tried, through a referral to the Constitutional Council under a system of a posteriori control. The classic republican doctrine, which established Parliament as the main guarantor of freedoms, now seems a thing of the past. Yet if the balance of power is called into question, the same can also be said for guaranteed rights.

3 The Lack of Guaranteed Rights

The laws of 20 November 2015 and 21 July 2016 strengthen the powers of the administration, without any real prior judicial control. Despite being intended to act as a guarantor of freedom, the ordinary judge is removed from the control process for all measures adopted under a state of emergency, in favour of the administrative judge (3.1). As far as the legal basis for this state of exception is concerned, it is in fact subject only to a posteriori control, which has only marginally improved upon the safeguarding of liberties (3.2).

3.1 Removal of the Ordinary Judge in Favour of the Administrative Judge

Since November 2015, the French Government has continually stressed that the state of emergency was being strengthened to better defend the rule of law. To avoid contradiction, it therefore had no choice but to provide safeguards. However, in France, the actions of the administration are traditionally brought before a specific judge and subject to a specific law. This explains the provision of the law of 20 November 2015, which adds Article 14(1) to the law of 3 April 1955. Pursuant to this article, 'measures taken on the basis of this law are subject to the control of the administrative judge'. Although the administrative judge has indeed often strived to safeguard freedoms, the provision does not in fact add anything to

[39]On this subject, see Cassia (2016a), 148.

ordinary law. In French law, as a matter of principle, administrative acts fall under the control of the administrative judge.

Acts adopted under a state of emergency are thus subject to the control of the administrative judge. However, Article 66 of the Constitution establishes the judicial authorities, rather than the administrative judge, as the guarantor of individual freedom. The role of the ordinary judge is nonetheless restricted here to the dimension established by the combined effect of state of emergency legislation and the jurisprudence of the Constitutional Council.[40] This is set forth principally in Article 11 of the law of 3 April 1955, as amended by the laws of 20 November 2015 and 21 July 2016. This article stipulates that the public prosecutor must be notified without delay, by being provided with a report on the search and the referral procedure.

However, the mechanism actually restricts rather than protects freedoms.[41] Having been duly informed of the procedure, without delay, the judicial authority can neither request further information, nor interrupt the process. This allows a judicial investigation to be launched immediately if evidence to suggest an offence has been committed is discovered. Only in such a case can a judge be called upon, pursuant to Article III-5 of the Penal Code, to assess the legality of the acts of the administration. For example, a criminal court can examine whether a search complies with the provisions of the Emergency Act if the related proceedings are based on evidence obtained during the search. However, one cannot overemphasise the frequency with which such an assessment of administrative acts is conducted by the judicial authorities. Administrative searches followed by judicial investigations are in fact rare. According to the figures released by the Ministry of the Interior in June 2016, only 6% of administrative searches resulted in a criminal prosecution.[42]

Thus, as a rule, under the current system, the implementation of a state of emergency is subject only to the control of administrative judges. What are the concrete effects of this?

French administrative law allows for several types of proceedings, drawing a schematic distinction between interlocutory and substantive proceedings. Interlocutory proceedings offer anyone due to be tried the possibility of obtaining an interim decision, on very short notice, to protect themselves against an unlawful administrative decision. To increase the efficacy and promptness of this type of plea, the admissibility criteria for requests and the procedural requirements are less stringent.[43] With respect to the state of emergency, interlocutory orders are generally requested by a claimant who believes there to be an urgent need to stay an administrative decision affecting their rights and freedoms, without awaiting a judgement on the merits of the case.

---

[40]Cf. infra.

[41]Here, we are reiterating part of N. Roret's analysis (Roret 2016, 13).

[42]Cassia (2016b).

[43]The administrative law concerning emergency procedures was significantly modernised and improved upon by the law of 30 June 2000.

With regard to the large number of individual decisions based on laws relating to the state of emergency, there are still very few administrative proceedings and they mainly concern house arrests. On the basis of a rigorous analysis of the statistics provided by the Council of State on 25 February 2016, Paul Cassia proposes that the proportion of challenged resolutions, in 400 or so house arrests, was scarcely higher than 18%.[44] Of these, only 11 house arrests were suspended, giving a success rate of less than 3%. Moreover, the rate of administrative proceedings seems to decrease the longer the state of emergency lasts.[45] To explain these figures, the authors mentions several factors: a lack of knowledge of the possible appeals procedures by the parties concerned; a lack of confidence in administrative jurisdiction; or simply the constraints linked to the limitation of movement associated with house arrests.[46]

Administrative searches, which are by far the most widely used measures, are thus one of the measures that form a blind spot in the control process. By their very nature, they are unlikely to be obstructed, even by means of an interlocutory proceeding. And, in a best-case scenario, they can be subject only to a liability action against the State, to obtain financial compensation. The intervention of an administrative judge is thus of limited use since it occurs a posteriori, after the violation of rights and freedoms. The 3594 house searches conducted between 14 November 2015 and 25 May 2016 only gave rise to a very limited number of litigations: just 22 pleas, concerning compensation litigations.[47] Yet administrative house searches can infringe upon a considerable number of fundamental rights, from the individual's right to privacy, to the law of presumed innocence, the right to lead a normal family life and the right to the protection of personal data.[48] That is, if the control of the administrative judge does not provide a sufficient guarantee. What guarantee, then, is offered by the Constitutional judicial authority acting on an a posteriori basis?

3.2 *The Failure of a Posteriori Controls*

As there was no a priori referral to the Constitutional Council on the matter of the amendments to the law of 3 April 1955, reference must be made to the a posteriori control decisions made since the promulgation of the law of 20 November 2015. An analysis of such decisions, however, merely supports the impression that this state of emergency is only subject to a low level of control.

---

[44]Cassia, *Contre l'état d'urgence* (n 43) 156.

[45]ibid 157.

[46]ibid.

[47]Figures taken from the summary table, updated as at 11 July 2016 and drawn up by the National Assembly using data provided by the Ministry of the Interior.

[48]See, for example, Cassia (2015).

The first a posteriori control occurred in 22 December 2015. It followed a plea made by an environmentalist known for his radical activism against the house arrest he was placed under during the 15 days of COP 21.[49] He criticised Article 6 of the law of 3 April 1955, as amended by the law of 20 November 2015, for failing to observe the rights guaranteed under Article 66 of the Constitution, and for unjustifiably infringing upon freedom from restraint. Article 6 authorises the Minister of the Interior to 'place under house arrest [...] any person [...] in respect of whom there are serious grounds for believing that their behaviour is a threat to public order and safety'. Article 66 of the Constitution establishes the judiciary as the guarantor of freedom.

The question asked to the Constitutional Council was smart inasmuch as it does not contest the terms of Article 6 so much as its application in the present case, that is, the lack of any link between the reasons for the declaration of a state of emergency, on the one hand, and for a house arrest on the other.[50] Yet the Council was content to rely once again upon the above-mentioned formulation from Article 6, making no reference to the reasons for the declaration of the state of emergency. By dint of such an omission, it approves of the administrative authorities using their powers in a manner that bears no relation to the reasons for which the state of emergency was declared in the first place.

Moreover, the regime of house arrest is found to conform with Constitutional freedoms and rights. In fact, the Council underscores the administrative nature of a house arrest ruling. It is found to be sufficiently well-defined and limited as to not constitute a deprivation of individual liberty which, pursuant to Article 66 of the Constitution, could fall within the jurisdiction of an ordinary judge.[51] In concrete terms, such a decision means that the administration is not subject to any control by a judge, on a matter that is nonetheless highly sensitive. Little attention is paid, therefore, to 'the constituent's desire to establish the judicial authorities, including (and perhaps above all) in times of crisis, as the guarantor of individual liberty'.[52]

The argument relating to freedom from restraint was also rejected. The Constitutional Council refused to see administrative house arrest as 'a disproportionate violation of' this liberty, to the advantage of two considerations. The first is both legal and contextual: a house arrest can only be delivered once a state of emergency has been declared and comes to an end when the latter expires.[53] The second is more 'respectful of liberties': house arrests are subject to the control of an administrative judge, who is responsible for ensuring that this measure is necessary, appropriate and proportional to its intended purpose.[54] However, the Constitutional Council in no way inhibits the logic behind the state of emergency, which greatly

[49]On this decision, see Roblot-Troizier (2016).

[50]See, for example ibid.

[51]Recital 5, *in fine*.

[52]Baranger (2016a).

[53]Recitals 11 and 13.

[54]Recital 12.

increases the room for manoeuver of the administration, which falls under the sole control of its judge—the administrative judge.[55]

The two a posteriori decisions made on 19 February 2016 follow the same rather unprotective pattern.

In the first of these decisions, Article 8 of the law of 1955, which allows for the prohibition of meetings and the administrative closure of certain places, is found to be in conformity with the Constitution. In response to the League of Human Rights, which denounced the lack of framework for the prerogatives conferred upon the administration, the Constitutional Council again stressed the temporary and conditioned nature of the state of emergency,[56] and the guarantee provided by the control of proportionality conducted by the administrative judge.[57]

The second a posteriori control, dated 19 February 2016, which relates to Article 11 of the law of 1955, as amended by the law of 20 November 2015, concerning administrative searches,[58] is slightly more protective. On the one hand, the Constitutional Council limited the possibility of carrying out searches at night, ruling that they must be justified 'by a situation of emergency or by the impossibility of carrying them out during the day'.[59] On the other hand, it declared the provision of Article 11, which authorises the forces of order to 'copy all computer data to which access could have been gained during the search'[60] to be unconstitutional. This measure is in fact 'comparable to a seizure', and, as such, should be subject to prior authorisation by a judge.

This relative liberalism on the part of the Constitutional Council did not last long, however. Indeed, when questioned, at the time, about the Constitutionality of Article 11 (subparagraph 1, concerning searches) of the law of 3 April 1955, prior to its amendment by the law of 20 November 2015,[61] the Constitutional Council, by the a posteriori control decision of 23 September 2016, judged this provision to be unconstitutional. It found that 'by failing to subject the use of searches to any conditions and to provide any guarantee in relation to their implementation', the legislator had not ensured 'a balance between the Constitutional goal of safeguarding public order and the individual's right to privacy'.[62] Nonetheless, the Council immediately limited the scope of its decision through the power conferred upon it by Article 62, subparagraph 2, of the Constitution. To prevent the declaration of unconstitutionality of legislative provisions already in application from

---

[55]On this point, see Le Bot (2016).

[56]Recitals 7 and 9.

[57]Recital 8.

[58]Decision 2016-536 QPC dated 19 February 2016.

[59]Recital 10.

[60]Recital 14.

[61]This concerns the first paragraph of Article 11 which, in the version prior to the law of 20 November 2015, stated that a law or decree to declare a state of emergency, or a law to extend it 'can, by way of an express provision: (1) confer upon the administrative authorities referred to in Article 8 the power to order house searches by day and by night'.

[62]Decision no. 2016-567/568 QPC dated 23 September 2016, Recital 8.

generating too much legal uncertainty, it maintains the power to 'determine the conditions and limits under which the effects brought about by the provision can be questioned'. Here, the Council did not hesitate to render its ruling of unconstitutionality ineffective by specifying, at the end of the decision that 'measures taken on the basis of provisions declared to be unconstitutional cannot be disputed on the basis of such unconstitutionality in any consecutive criminal proceedings'.

The analysis of the decision of 2 December 2016[63] also supports the impression that state of emergency is only subject to a low level of control. The plea relates to the solution set out by the legislator to get around the above-mentioned decision made on 19 February 2016. In this decision, the Constitutional Council declared the provision of Article 11, which authorises the forces of order to 'copy all computer data to which access could have been gained during the search' to be unconstitutional for want of prior authorisation by a judge. In reaction, the legislator limited the authorisation required by a referral administrative judge to the exploitation of data only but not to its mere copy. This minimal legislative guarantee was considered sufficient by the Constitutional Council.

In the light of its characteristic weakness, this a priori control could be said to correspond to the character of the state of emergency control process as a whole. However, the weakness of this control system should almost certainly be associated with the nature of the state of emergency itself, as conceived under French law. By authorising the administration to adopt security measures that heavily infringe upon freedoms and rights, it inevitably 'blurs, to a certain extent, the separation between the political, administrative and judicial authorities'.[64] In so doing, it necessarily weakens any attempt to control, or rather, to limit the administration. Such an inflexion of the normal functioning of public institutions could arguably be seen as the primary risk of its perpetuation.

References

Avril P, Gicquel JE, Gicquel E (2014) Droit Parlementaire, 5th edn. LGDJ

Baranger D (2016) Quel «État de Droit»? Quels Contrôles? Le juge des référés et le maintien en vigueur de l'état d'urgence. Note sous Conseil d'État, 27 Janvier 2016, Juge des référés, Ligue des droits de l'Homme et autres, N° 396220. Revue Française de Droit Administratif 355, 2016

Baranger D art.cit, 355

Cassia P (2015) Perquisitions administratives et état d'urgence: les droits fondamentaux entre parenthèses. Mediapart (16 Dec 2015). https://blogs.mediapart.fr/paul-cassia/blog/161215/perquisitions-administratives-et-etat-d-urgence-les-droits-fondamentaux-entre-parentheses. Accessed 18 April 2017

Cassia P (2016a) Etat d'urgence: le pot «pourri» de la loi du 21 Juillet 2016. Mediapart (29 July 2016). https://blogs.mediapart.fr/paul-cassia/blog/290716/etat-d-urgence-le-pot-pourri-de-la-loi-du-21-juillet-2016. Accessed 18 April 2017

[63]Decision no. 2016-600 QPC.

[64]Baranger (2016b).

Cassia P (2016b) Contre l'état d'urgence. Paris, Dalloz

Le Bot O (2016) État d'urgence et compétences juridictionnelles. Revue Française de Droit Administratif 436

Roblot-Troizier A (2016) Assignations à résidence en état d'urgence. Note under Council of State, Section, 11 Dec 2015, M C. Domenjoud, and under Constitutional Council, 22 Dec 2015, M. Cédric. D., No. 2015-527 QPC. Revue Française de Droit Administratif 123

Roret N (2016) Etat d'urgence: Quel rôle pour le juge pénal? Gazette du Palais

Rosanvallon P (2015) Constitutionnaliser L'état d'urgence. Le Monde (12 May 2015)

“Anything Goes”: How Does French Law Deal with the State of Emergency?

Olivier Beaud

Abstract The “Etat d’urgence”—the state of emergency in reaction to the terrorist attacks in November 2015—comes from a circumstantial law, adopted on 3 April 1955. This precarious origin has not prevented it from continuing to be the positive law. Although this law limits citizens’ rights and liberties tremendously, the Conseil d’Etat and the Conseil constitutionnel have tolerated state clerk to consolidate this derogation of French common law. This anything goes legal attitude reinforced this situation. The introduction of an a priori (1958) and a posteriori (2008) control of the constitutionality of law has not changed this situation.

1 Introduction

Unlike what happened in the wake of the January 2015 attack (known as the “Charlie Hebdo” attack), the executive power in France decided to call a state of emergency on the very same day as the attacks of 13 November 2015. Speaking on television, the head of State solemnly announced the state of emergency, authorising extended police powers at the expense of public liberties. Shortly afterwards, on 20 November 2015, the Parliament voted a law prolonging the state of emergency for three months and also making the content of the law dated 3 April 1955,

This text is the same as the speech which was delivered at the Maison française d’Oxford on 29 April 2016. It does not take into account the whole literature which was, since then, published on this topic. For all the details on the French “état d’urgence”, see in this book the previous article of Professor Cecile Guérin Bargues: “The French Case or the Hidden Dangers of a Long Term State of Emergency” and the special issue of *Revue française de droit administratif* (RFDA), May-June 2016, especially Baranger (2016) and Roblot-Troizier (2016).

O. Beaud (✉)
Institut Michel Villey pour la culture juridique et la philosophie du droit, University Paris-II Panthéon-Assas, Paris, France
e-mail: o-beaud@orange.fr

P. Auriel et al. (eds.), *The Rule of Crisis*, Ius Gentium: Comparative Perspectives on Law and Justice 64, https://doi.org/10.1007/978-3-319-74473-5_11

stricter. On 20 February 2016, the Parliament again prolonged the state of emergency for a further period of three months.[1] It is because of the two attacks that France rediscovered the existence of the state of emergency law which dates from 1955 and was used three times previously during the Fifth Republic (1961 in metropolitan France, 1985 in New Caledonia and 2005 in suburban areas).

Initially, we were tempted to give a detailed account of the state of emergency. But since Cécile Guérin-Bargues, and I have already extensively discussed the issue, in an article published in *Jus Politicum*,[2] and this colloquium is about the relationship between crisis legislation and the rule of law, we would like to try and examine the question from the broader viewpoint of the state of exception. This supposes that we examine two further states of exception, provided for in the Constitution: Article 16 and the state of siege (Article 36), while the state of emergency is governed by the law dated 3 April 1955. Thus, crisis legislation[3] does actually challenge the rule of law in France, as indeed elsewhere. However, in France, the opposition is easy to overcome because reason of state is a tradition that still controls the State's operations beneath the surface appearance of constitutionalism (2).

Any state of exception—by any name—threatens freedom and compromises the effectiveness of the Constitution as such. This is because, by definition, it supposes a derogation from, or partial or total suspension of constitutional order.[4] So that is the dilemma that arises in this case: on the one hand, the Constitution is considered the supreme and inviolable law of the Nation. As such, it must be respected not only by all citizens but also by the public authorities. On the other hand, when a state of exception is declared, the supreme law is no longer inviolable since it must be derogated from.

Derogations from the liberal order such as daytime and night-time searches and house arrests decided by the authorities are security measures allowed under the state of emergency that are breaches of constitutionally guaranteed rights and obligations that are perhaps made necessary by circumstances but cannot be justified by the idea of law and order. Therefore, an extraordinary legality must be

---

[1]The state of emergency is no more in force. It was renewed for two months by the Act of Parliament of 20 May 2016. The French President intended to let cease the state of emergency in the day before the dramatic attack of Nice (14 July 2016) which changed everything. The «état d'urgence» was then renewed by the Act of Parliament of 21 July 2016 (renewal for six months) and, recently by the Act of Parliament of 19 December 2016, and more recently by the Act of Parliament of 11 July 2017. For the end (of the state of emergency) see footnote 16.

[2]Beaud and Guérin-Bargues (2016a). This rather «long» article, updated and shortened, became a book which was published in September 2016 under the following title, Beaud and Guérin-Bargues (2016a, b). This book may be completed by the book written by Cassia (2016) which is more focused on the courts and on the administrative law, especially on the decisions of the Conseil d'Etat, the French administrative court (and the leading court, so to say).

[3]For a convenient summary of the three French states of exception (Article 16, state of emergency and state of siege), see the volume, «Les pouvoirs de crise» in the Journal *Pouvoirs* n°10, 1976 (PUF).

[4]The standard work on this topic is Schmitt (2015). The whole literature is driven by Carl Schmitt's challenge to the rule of law model. In the English literature, the reference book is Dyzenhaus (2009). See also his article, Dyzenhaus (2012).

invoked, since it alone can suspend ordinary legality. Is this opposition between constitutionalism and the state of exception irreducible? We will examine the issue in the second part of our paper, contrasting the theoretical question with a French practical case (3).

2 Two French Versions of the State of Exception: The State of Emergency and Article 16

2.1 The State of Emergency: A State of Exception That Is Stricter Than What Is Believed

The state of emergency provided for in the law dated 3 April 1955, modernised by the law dated 20 November 2015, is a state of exception that allows police powers to be extended to the detriment of public liberties. In 1955, it was the Parliament that declared the state of emergency, but since the government order dated 15 April 1960, signed by De Gaulle, it has been the responsibility of the President of the Republic to proclaim it.[5]

The two main measures enabling this legal situation to be imposed are first, day and night-time administrative searches and house arrests ordered by the Ministry of the Interior that deprive private persons of their freedom. Not only must they remain at home but they must also report to the police station several times a day. Other restrictive measures are refusal of entry or stay, curfews in the evening, or administrative dissolution of associations. In Algeria in 1955, the law on the state of emergency enabled the government to replace judicial courts by military ones. This radical measure was repealed in 2015. This type of legal regime undermines several fundamental liberties: that to come and go freely, the right to privacy and the freedom of assembly. However, what it does not allow is detention in custody. In theory, no internment camp is possible. In practice, there were camps in Algeria and France in 1961.

This brief summary of the provisions of a state of emergency would not be complete without adding that the guarantees for individuals are minimal. In 1955, the law provided a restricted right of appeal to an administrative commission against measures taken under the state of emergency. In 2015, the provisions merely reiterated common law by providing the right to contest the legality of a measure before the administrative court, first asking for its suspension (freedom referral). Some people did this with more or less success. Thus, only one house arrest was suspended before being declared illegal due to poor appreciation of the facts by the police.

The real point at issue is whether to declare a state of emergency or not. The law dated 3 April 1955 provides for two cases: first, "imminent danger due to serious

[5]See details, Beaud and Guérin-Bargues (2016b) 74–81.

infringements of law and order" and, second, "events which, by their nature and gravity, represent a public disaster". The French Council of State had two occasions, in November 2005[6] and in December 2015, to declare that the head of State, the authority of the Fifth Republic entitled to decide a state of emergency, has the discretionary right to assess the situation. The Constitutional Council was similarly cautious. On 25 January 1985, it reviewed the constitutionality of the state of emergency for the first time. And it held, in a very constructive interpretation, that Article 34 of the Constitution allowed the legislator to declare a state of exception.[7] It upheld its 1985 precedent twice, in December 2015 and February 2016, upon being seized by a request for judicial review *à la française,* confirming that most of the litigious provisions of the law dated 20 November 2015, amending the 1955 law conformed to the Constitution.[8]

The last striking feature of the legal regime of the state of emergency is the total absence of any role for the courts of law. Yet the judiciary is "guardian of individual freedoms" and "enforces this principle in the conditions provided for by law" (Article 66 C). Despite this, it has absolutely no part in monitoring implementation of the state of emergency. It is the police force and the administrative courts that deal with it, to the detriment of the judiciary. In December 2015, unusually, the President of the French *Cour de cassation* (Supreme Court) protested against the lack of recourse to the law courts. It was understandable that the Council of State have sole jurisdiction, but more difficult to understand that the Constitutional Council's precedent should lead to such a restrictive interpretation of Article 66 that it has virtually turned it into a dead letter. In effect, the courts of law have been replaced by the administrative courts, and the Cour de cassation by the Council of State, as sole protectors of our freedoms.[9]

One last word: the state of emergency can be distinguished from the state of siege[10] for one reason: unlike the latter, it does not require transfer of power from the civil to the military authorities. However, contrary to what might be thought, the state of emergency is more stringent than the state of siege provided for by the law of 1849 amended in 1879, because it allows more measures outside common law.

[6]C.E. Ord 14 November 2015, *Rolin*, req. N° 286835, published in Recueil Lebon.

[7]See Beaud and Guérin-Bargues (2016a) 92–102, and Wachsmann (1985). For a synthesis before the new state of emergency of 2015, see Rolin (2008).

[8]See the articles already quoted by Baranger (2016) and Roblot-Troizier (2016).

[9]For a review, see Le Bot (2016).

[10]It is noteworthy to add that the state of siege (*Belagerungzustand*, in German), which was created by the French Second Republic (1849), was taken as a model by Carl Schmitt when he began to study the state of exception, during the World War I. See his analysis of the statute law of 1849 in Schmitt (1978), 198–199.

2.2 *Article 16 of the Constitution: "A Reserve Constitution"?*

During the first forty years of the 1958 Constitution, at least until 2005, when a state of emergency was mentioned, all thoughts went to Article 16 of the Constitution.[11] General De Gaulle was absolutely set on this, having been traumatised by the defeat of France in 1940.

Let us analyse the content of this Article 16. For all its provisions to enter into force, the following two conditions must both be met:

- "The institutions of the Republic, the independence of the Nation, the integrity of its territory or the execution of its international undertakings" must be "seriously and immediately threatened",
- The second condition is more objective: "regular running of the public institutions" must be "interrupted".

The conditions under which it is implemented are left to the judgement of the head of State, who is merely required officially, and thus publicly, to consult the Prime Minister, the presidents of the two parliamentary assemblies and the Constitutional Council, whose opinion does not, however, bind the head of State. In the initial version of Article 16, there was no provision as to its term. Under the constitutional revision of 2008, the Constitutional Council is charged with verifying every two months whether the circumstances are still exceptional. It can be seized within one month by the appropriate authorities. Furthermore, the President of the Republic is entitled to take "*the measures required by circumstances*". He may only act with a view to giving back the means to carry out their duties to the constitutional public authorities.

A state of exception like this could be called a "reserve constitution", insofar as it provides for concentration of power in the hands of the President of the Republic. The President thus holds both legislative and executive power, and can legislate as if he were the Parliament. One precedent will give an idea of his powers, that of 1961, following the putsch of Algiers, called by generals opposing Algerian independence, on 21 April 1961. Although the putsch failed after four days, the regime provided for by Article 16 remained in force until 29 September 1961. In his speech broadcast on radio and television on 23 April 1961, De Gaulle immediately outlawed the opponents and ordered that no one obeys their orders. Under these exceptional powers, General De Gaulle was able to extend the state of emergency twice, thus replacing the Parliament for this decision.

The important point should be emphasised: in this case of the state of exception, the head of State has absolute discretion to declare the Article 16 regime applicable. In the leading case of CE *Rubin de Servens*, 2 March 1962, the Council of State

[11]The literature on the Article 16 is both huge and a little outdated. There is a PhD thesis on this subject: Voisset (1969) and a leading article Lamarque (1961) Revue de droit public 558. Also, a convenient textbook: Hamon (1994).

held that this decision was an "act of government", i.e. an act that could not be appealed against in the courts.[12] Furthermore, once the state of exception has been proclaimed by the head of State, the latter is still under no other authority since only regulatory measures taken by him can be appealed against. Where he takes legislative decisions, they become law and thus do not fall under the jurisdiction of the administrative courts (CE *Rubin de Servens*, 2 March 1962). It is difficult to find in such a legal regime any guarantees in terms of the rule of law: there are no real checks and balances, and no true judicial review is possible. The only guarantee is the virtue of the members of government—that is, the hope that the head of State will act pursuant to the finalities provided for in Article 16 and take exceptional measures to ensure the return to normal conditions. But since when has recourse to the virtue of the governors been a recipe for constitutionalism?

3 State of Exception and Constitutionalism: Re-examination of the Case of France

3.1 The Constitutionalist Model and the State of Exception

The question of the state of exception fascinates jurists for a reason that is perfectly explained by François Saint-Bonnet in his thesis on it.[13] Carl Schmitt theorised on the subject and justified it by this paradoxical formula at the start of his work on political theology: "He who decides the exceptional situation [*Ausnhmezustand*] is sovereign" (*Political theology*, 1922). In opposition to Kelsen and positivism that sees the hierarchy of laws as a series of subsumptions of the inferior norms to the superior onessz, Schmitt objects that "where necessary it is impossible to act within the framework of the superior law. Consequently the 'decision' (*Entscheidung*) is a-normal and its existence reveals the weakness of the norm, especially the constitutional norm". Schmitt does not merely claim that positive law cannot provide for everything. He argues, and it is not much different, that the state of exception reveals the truth about a State and its constitutional law, by allowing sovereignty to emerge in all its majesty. Yet it is this essential point that constitutes Schmitt's exaggerated views, a transposition of a miracle—a theological concept—into law, the "supernatural" emerging to overturn the natural character of things. Just as Article 48 of the Weimar Constitution was a moment of truth, resulting in the suspension of most of the fundamental laws by unilateral decision of the President of the Reich, so Article 16 of the 1958 French Constitution and, to a lesser degree, the state of emergency—a smaller version of the state of exception—were the moments of truth for the Constitution of the Fifth Republic.

[12]See the standard commentary in Long et al. (2015) 529.

[13]Saint-Bonnet (2001).

It is true that Benjamin Constant, the thinker of constitutionalism *par excellence*, saw a failure of the Constitution in any state of exception. However, it is possible to think the state of exception in a constitutionalist way, by trying to work out a limitation to the emergency powers. The jurist Albert Dicey demonstrated that, theoretically, it was possible to envisage a state of exception in a more liberal way. He, for instance, claimed that ascertaining whether a state of exception should be declared was a question of fact, not politics, thus ruining in advance Schmitt's thesis. Similarly, Bruce Ackerman tried to reiterate this constitutionalist gamble in his article on "The emergency Constitution". However, we will base our reasoning mainly on Bernard Manin's study[14] on "the paradigm of the state of exception", to demonstrate that a liberal or constitutionalist conception of the state of exception can be envisaged, and that it does not characterise the state of emergency *à la française.*

Using a historical analysis of the three major cases of states of emergency—the Roman dictatorship in ancient times, suspension of Habeas Corpus and martial law for common law countries, and the political siege in France—Bernard Manin points out the three characteristics of the state of exception as a constitutional institution, what he calls the three components of the paradigm of exception: "*(1) authorisation to depart from superior norms, such as those often laid down in the Constitution*; *(2) submission to special conditions ensuring that the circumstances so require (1); (3) temporal limitation of (1)*".

These are the three elements of the structure found in these three great historical experiences. Above all, they lead to the analytical definition of the state of exception that can be interpreted in a constitutionalist or a liberal way, thus conforming to the idea of the rule of law—that would limit the potentially devastating effects of such a legal regime. This constitutionalist limitation of the state of exception is needed because there is an inherent risk in the first part of this analytical definition: total or partial suspension of the constitution. As seen earlier, in concrete terms, any state of exception is a kind of "bomb" or "landmine" placed in the middle of the Constitution, which is why they have such a bad reputation. Actually, the "landmine" does not need to be placed in the Constitution, since it can also be placed in an ordinary law, as witnessed by the French experience of the state of siege (first law dated 9 August 1849) and the state of emergency (law dated 3 April 1955).

Let us note first that even in the first component of the state of exception, there is a limiting aspect in the expression "authorisation to depart from superior norms". In other words, a state of exception is not just declared arbitrarily; the leaders who do so have been authorised thereto. Now, this sort of habilitation does contain a seed of limitation of powers since traditionally, it is a third party that designates the authority of the executive body vested with the absolute power. For instance, in Rome, the dictator was mostly chosen by the consuls and sometimes by the people (and the result is that dictators do not appoint themselves). Similarly, the suspension

[14]Manin (2015). This article was first published in English: Manin (2008).

of Habeas Corpus was ordered by the Crown, but that power was vested in it by the Parliament which, thus, habilitated the executive to detain suspects without trial. Here again, the Crown did not concentrate all the powers. Finally, as regards the state of siege, the French Parliament had the power to declare it and it was imposed on the executive, part of the power being transferred to the army, even though the latter remained under parliamentary control. In all these cases, the state of exception interpreted in constitutionalist manner included a liberal aspect since there was no concentration of power in the hands of a single body.

The second element of this analytical definition of the state of exception can also be interpreted liberally. It is up to the law to provide for the cases in which a state of exception may be declared. Now, depending on whether an extensive or restrictive interpretation is made of the "circumstances" triggering the state of exception, that interpretation can be an authoritative, or liberal, or constitutionalist one. It is constitutionalists when we try to circumscribe as accurately as possible the cases in which it is possible and licit to declare a state of exception. This is the case more particularly for the state of siege. In 1849, the state of siege could be decreed in the event of a "threat to the Nation's (or State's) exterior or interior security". In 1879, the Republican members of Parliament, suspicious after the use that Mac Mahon almost made of it after the coup of 16 May 1877, demanded that the conditions for its use be clarified. That is why they replaced the broad provision of the 1849 law, which said that it could be declared in the event of "imminent peril due to a foreign war or an armed revolt" (Article 1). Bernard Manin explains this change by quoting the commission that had drafted the 1878 bill and had acknowledged that they had wished to "protect ordinary law against the *impulses or even the errors* of the legislative branch". Thus, in 1879, French politicians were wary of the potentially excessive authoritarianism of the parliamentary assemblies, be they democratically elected or not.

3.2 The Authoritarian Aspect of the French Example Is Revealed by Its Comparison with the Constitutionalist Model

This study of the paradigm of exception seems decisive for our argument, because it casts a backlight on the regimes of Article 16 and the state of emergency that are not thought in "constitutionalist" terms. It is such a well-known aspect of Article 16 that we do not need to go into it here. We will merely recall that in the latter case, the head of State concentrates two immense powers. It is he, and he alone, who decides to implement the Article 16 regime (the "inaugural" decision), and it is he, also, who takes the "measures" required by the circumstances, under this extraordinary regime. We would like to demonstrate here that, even in the case of the state of emergency under the law of 3 April 1955, the three components identified by Bernard Manin in his paradigm of the state of exception are thought in an "authoritative" way and not a constitutionalist one. This authoritarian feature of the state of emergency can be observed in three different ways.

First, there is no counter-power provided in this regime of the state of emergency, but, on the contrary, a worrying concentration of powers since the executive branch decides the implementation of the state of exception and takes the decisions (measures) for its application. Bruce Ackerman calls this "French unilateralism",[15] and he is right to highlight its authoritarian nature. He also uses a French expression to describe the scope of the powers vested in the executive branch, noting that they have "*carte blanche*" to do what they deem necessary with total disregard for constitutionalist principles.

But, the retort comes, there is a theoretical counter-power since the time lapse between the declaration and the continuation of the measure would give the Parliament the time to exercise control over the executive when it decides to extend. But in fact, during that first, extremely brief, time lapse it has been shown that Parliament always follows the executive. If the state of emergency continues, the extension seems to be automatic too. So upon close examination of this first aspect of the state of emergency, it is clear that applied in France, it follows an authoritative interpretation that is miles away from constitutionalism, which exists in both theory and practice as vouchsafed by comparative constitutional history.

However, it is above all the second element of the state of exception that gives more cause for concern in the law dated 3 April 1955. The circumstances leading to a state of exception are "imminent peril arising from serious disruptions of law and order" and the case of "public disaster" that, as we saw earlier, were added merely to distract attention in 1955. More vague, woolly criteria would be hard to find: "imminent peril", "serious disruptions" and "law and order". Was it not this condition that allowed Jacques Chirac to declare a state of exception in November 2005 after the urban uprisings, despite the fact that there were serious reasons for doubting the usefulness of its implementation in the circumstances of the time?

It should be noted in this regard that in his aforementioned article, Ackerman considered that the mere threat of a terrorist attack does not justify declaring a state of emergency. For it to be justified, there must not just be a "*clear and present danger*", but truly an "*actual attack*". The state of emergency is reactive and not preventive. If we admit that a mere threat, an imminent danger, is enough to justify a state of exception, then anything becomes possible for the executive branch. The risk of "political manipulation" by the security services who, under the blanket of defence secrecy, can invoke terrorist threats to incite the government to take preventive measures is too great for such criteria to be envisaged. On the other hand, a past fact such as a terrorist attack is sufficient justification for declaring a state of exception. This strict separation between the terrorist threat and terrorist acts, according to Ackerman, allows the substantial risk of "normalising extraordinary powers" that is inherent to any state of exception, to be avoided. It is striking to note that few people in France, or at least among the government, are conscious of the

[15]Ackerman (2004).

considerable risk entailed by Article 1 of the law dated 3 April 1955. Its description of the conditions under which the state of emergency should be declared is too vague and woolly.

Finally, the last condition is the most important. It is the "temporal limitation". The law dated 3 April 1955 contained temporal provisions. The first was that the Parliament must extend the state of exception not later than twelve days following the proclamation by the head of State. The government order dated 15 April 1960 merely provides that the law "shall fix a definitive time limit" but it is difficult to draw legal conclusions from this. It has not prevented a double extension of the state of emergency in 2015–2016. The Council of State has on several occasions stated that a state of emergency is necessarily a short-lived one, based on its interpretation of the provisions of the law dated 3 April 1955. However, no provision has been made to control the term of the state of emergency.

What is the greatest matter for concern is elsewhere: the current French government intends to combat terrorism by means of the state of emergency. This is clearly what emerges from the grounds invoked for the new constitutional bill. It is also what appears to be the case judging from an interview of Prime Minister Manuel Valls on the BBC in January 2016 during the Davos economic forum, where he said, in answer to the journalist's question, "War is using every means in our democracy to protect the French people. So in fact we are in a state of emergency. We shall see if we can extend it". "Until when?" asked the journalist. "Until whenever necessary". "Does that mean forever?" questioned the journalist. "*Well, obviously, until we can sort out Isis*", replied the Prime Minister. Yet to the same journalist he had also said that "we can't live in a state of emergency all the time". Although the French government later vigorously denied his statements following the dissemination of this interview by the AFP, it did not prevent the French press from headlining the risk of a "permanent" or "perpetual" state of emergency.

We should above all say that French governments have sought to use the state of emergency against terrorism. Yet there is a clear contradiction here that we should underline: the state of exception is provided to address a temporary, conjunctural threat. Its structure is based on the idea that the threat triggering it is itself temporary; "If the circumstances do not disappear after a short time, one of the fundamental conditions for using such institutions is missing" (B. Manin). Now, the new terrorism afflicting the world for over fifteen years, even more in France's case, since it was unfortunate enough to be the target of terrorist acts as early as 1986, is not a temporary phenomenon, but an enduring situation. How can we not agree with Ackerman when he says we have entered into a global terrorist era that is both episodic and enduring? It is episodic since the attacks occur from time to time, and also enduring, because they will continue to occur inevitably, because they are made possible by new circumstances. There is therefore theoretical inadequacy between the state of exception and the combat against terrorism (the main idea in the aforementioned article by Bernard Manin). Whereas the combat against terrorism is necessarily ongoing, any state of emergency is designed to be temporary. The paradigm of the state of exception is therefore not the right one for the combat against terrorism.[16]

Yet the French State has decided to use it, with nobody to take offence at their methods. "*Anything goes*": we used this expression to show you that in a culture that does not have a check and balances system, such misuses of power are possible. In this regard, the authorities concerned, and first and foremost the Council of State, but also—not at all surprisingly—the Constitutional Council [*Conseil constitutionnel*], have failed in their duties when addressing the intellectual and practical challenges of this new terrorist wave.

References

Ackerman B (2004) The Emergency Constitution 113. Yale Law J 102

Baranger D (2016) 'L'état d'urgence dans la durée' Revue Française de Droit Administratif

Beaud O, Guérin-Bargues C (2016a) "L'état d'urgence de Novembre 2015 : Une Mise En Perspective Historique et Critique" Jus Politicum

Beaud O, Guérin-Bargues C (2016b), *L'état d'urgence. Étude constitutionnelle, historique et critique* (1ère édition, LGDJ)

Cassia P (2016) *Contre l'état d'urgence*. Dalloz

Dyzenhaus D (ed) (2009) Civil Rights and Security. Ashgate

Dyzenhaus D (2012) The state of emergency. In: Rosenfeld M, Sajó A (eds) The Oxford Handbook of Constitutional Comparative Law. Oxford University Press

Hamon F (ed) (1994) *L'article 16 de La Constitution de 1958*. La Documentation française

Lamarque J (1961) 'L'état de Necessité et l'article 16 de La Constitution de 1958'. Revue de droit public 558

Le Bot O (2016) 'État d'urgence et Compétences Juridictionnelles, State of Emergency and Judicial Competence Revue Française de Droit Administratif 436

Long M et al (eds) (2015) *Les grands arrêts de la jurisprudence administrative*, 20th edn. Dalloz

Manin B (2008) The Emergency Paradigm and the New Terrorism. In: Baume S, Biancamaria L (eds) Les Usages de la Séparation des Pouvoirs—The Uses of the Separation of Powers. Michel Houdiard

Manin B (2015) Le Paradigme de l'exception. L'État face au nouveau Terrorisme'. *La Vie des Idées* http://www.laviedesidees.fr/Le-paradigme-de-l-exception.html

Roblot-Troizier A (2016) 'Etat d'urgence et protection des Libertés'. Revue Française de Droit Administratif 424

Rolin F (2008) 'L'état D'urgence', *1958–2008. Cinquantième anniversaire de la Constitution française*. Dalloz

Saint-Bonnet F (2001) L'Etat d'exception. Presses Universitaires de France—PUF

[16]While proofreading this article, we learn that the Act of Parliament of 30 October 2017 had integrated the content of the state of emergency in a permanent anti-terrorist law. This meddling of normal criminal law (against terrorism) and of public exceptional law (state of emergency) is probably the worst solution, and it was the solution which was feared by the tenants of civil rights. It will be interesting to see how « our » courts will react if this bill of law will be adopted by the Parliament. There is little hope that they repeal this institutionalisation of the state of emergency. The state of emergency ceased at the 1st November 2017 (by caudicty).

Schmitt C (1978) Die Diktatur: Von den Anfängen des modernen souveränitätsgedankens Bis zum proletarischen Klassenkampf, 4th edn. Duncker & Humblot, Gmbh
Schmitt C (2015) Politische Theologie: Vier Kapitel zur Lehre von der Souveränität. Duncker & Humblot, Gmbh
Voisset M (1969) *L'article 16 de La Constitution de 1958*. LGDJ
Wachsmann P (1985) 'Cons. Const., 25 Janvier 1985, Décis. n° 85–185 DC, *Loi Relative À L'état D'urgence En Nouvelle-Calédonie*' Actualités juridiques—Droit administratif 362

The German Reticence Vis-à-Vis the State of Emergency

Matthias Jestaedt

Abstract The German Basic Law can, in many respects, be read as an answer to the "conditions of the Weimar Republic" that were considered to have contributed to the National Socialist's course towards totalitarianism. This is also the case as regards the eschewal or repression of the state of emergency during which the regular mechanisms guaranteeing the rule of law no longer fully function. The German 1949 Constitution that established an "actively defensive democracy" on the one hand consciously refrained from providing a state of emergency on the other hand. The 1968 constitutional amendment introducing provisions on the state of tension and the state of defence (Article 80a and Articles 115a–115 l) also consciously avoids taking recourse to the state of emergency. Lastly, neither did the Federal Constitutional Court (BVerfG) integrate the state of emergency into its jurisprudence. Whether in connection with the terrorism of the "Rote Armee Fraktion" ("RAF") in the 1970s or in connection with the "war on terrorism" after 11 September 2001: The Federal Constitutional Court never developed a special doctrine—deficient with regard to the rule of law—for the review of public, particularly legislative, measures aimed at combating terrorist acts. On the contrary, it defended the rule of law in the light of these new threats from the state and civil society without compromise.

1 Introduction

Maybe we can add a new dimension to our reflections by taking a glance at France's largest neighbour. Regarding the terrorist threat, Germany and France are in a broadly similar position, even though Germany has not so far been subjected to a terrorist attack comparable to the one on Charlie Hebdo or the Bataclan. Being a member state of the European Union and a contracting state of the ECHR, Germany

M. Jestaedt (✉)
University of Freiburg, Institut für Staatswissenschaft und Rechtsphilosophie, Freiburg im Breisgau, Germany
e-mail: Matthias.Jestaedt@jura.uni-freiburg.de

P. Auriel et al. (eds.), *The Rule of Crisis*, Ius Gentium: Comparative Perspectives on Law and Justice 64, https://doi.org/10.1007/978-3-319-74473-5_12

is furthermore bound by the same legal framework in terms of international and supranational obligations. And yet, for the neighbour on the other side of the Rhine, the legal concept of the state of emergency does not play a significant role in facing the post-9/11 terrorist threat. Germany does not resort to this highly contested legal regime, but takes recourse to other means. In what follows, I will examine these means as well as their background.

2 The Long Shadow of Weimar and the "Third Reich"

Let me start with the latter and explain shortly, why the legal concept of the "state of emergency" is held in such disrepute in Germany.

The Basic Law of 23 May 1949[1] is to be understood as a reaction to the "Weimar circumstances" on the one hand and to the political, moral, legal, cultural and social catastrophe of National Socialism on the other. This concerns both, the Basic Law in general and the dispositions aiming at the protection of the state order against external threats in particular. The Weimar Constitution of 1919[2] provided notably two means for facing an extraordinary crisis: The so-called suppressions of the Constitution ("*Verfassungsdurchbrechungen*") and the "emergency decrees" ("*Notverordnungen*") having force of law. The "suppressions of the Constitution" were statutes adopted by the qualified majority otherwise required for a constitutional amendment. These statutes could suppress constitutional provisions in specific situations and can thus be described as constitutional amendments motivated by and limited to those specific situations that were not, however, reflected in the constitutional wording itself. Rather more important were the "emergency decrees" according to the infamous Article 48 sec. 2 of the Weimar Constitution. This provision authorised the President of the Reich to take the measures necessary to re-establish law and order in the case that public safety and order were seriously threatened or disturbed, and, if necessary, to resort to the armed force. To this end, he could suspend the exercise of several civil rights, namely individual liberty, the inviolability of the home, the privacy of correspondence, the freedom of opinion, the freedom of assembly and association and the right of property through legislative decrees. From 1930 onwards, the President of the Reich Paul von Hindenburg exercised this right increasingly. With the so-called Enabling Act ("*Ermächtigungsgesetz*") of 24 March 1933, officially entitled "Act for relieving the distress of the people and the Reich" ("*Gesetz zur Behebung der Not von Volk und Reich*")[3], the suspension of civil rights was carried to the extreme. This law

---

[1] "Grundgesetz für die Bundesrepublik Deutschland" of 23 May 1949, Bundesgesetzblatt (BGBl. = federal official journal) 1949, p. 1.

[2] "Verfassung des Deutschen Reichs" of 11 August 1919, Reichsgesetzblatt (RGBl. = official journal of the Reich) 1919, p. 1383.

[3] RGBl. 1933 I, p. 141.

conferred major legislative powers to the government of the Reich under Adolf Hitler and thus marginalised the original legislative organs Reichstag and Reichsrat. With this, the transition to a lawless state became unavoidable.

With the help of the Western Allies, the founding fathers (in German one would rather say: the mothers and fathers of the Basic Law) reacted to this in several ways: Firstly, "suppressions of the Constitution" were no longer admitted; henceforth, the constitution could not be amended but by a law modifying the text explicitly (Article 79 sec. 1 sentence 1).[4] Secondly, the legal regime of "emergency decrees" having force of law was omitted without replacement. Thirdly, the general clause on the legal regime governing a national crisis was dropped. In contrast, the 1949 original version of the Basic Law did not contain any kind of special regime adapted to emergency situations—except for the legislative emergency (Article 81)[5] that concerns but a special case of the loss of parliamentary confidence in the federal chancellor, and the so-called internal emergency (Article 91)[6] containing federal provisions on police operations crossing the boundaries of the federal states. Fourthly, the rule of law ("*Rechtsstaat*") is intimately linked with judicial review: On the one hand, the guarantee of judicial protection against any act of public

---

[4]Article 79 sec. 1 sentence. 1 BL: "This Basic Law may be amended only by a law expressly amending or supplementing its text." (All translations of articles of the Basic Law are from *Christian Tomuschat/David P. Currie* in: Deutscher Bundestag (ed.), Basic Law for the Federal Republic of Germany, 2012.).

[5]Article 81 BL: "(1) If, in the circumstances described in Article 68, the Bundestag is not dissolved, the Federal President, at the request of the Federal Government and with the consent of the Bundesrat, may declare a state of legislative emergency with respect to a bill, if the Bundestag rejects the bill although the Federal Government has declared it to be urgent. The same shall apply if a bill has been rejected although the Federal Chancellor had combined it with a motion under Article 68. (2) If, after a state of legislative emergency has been declared, the Bundestag again rejects the bill or adopts it in a version the Federal Government declares unacceptable, the bill shall be deemed to have become law to the extent that it receives the consent of the Bundesrat. The same shall apply if the Bundestag does not pass the bill within four weeks after it is reintroduced. (3) During the term of office of a Federal Chancellor, any other bill rejected by the Bundestag may become law in accordance with paragraphs (1) and (2) of this Article within a period of six months after the first declaration of a state of legislative emergency. After the expiration of this period, no further declaration of a state of legislative emergency may be made during the term of office of the same Federal Chancellor. (4) This Basic Law may neither be amended nor abrogated nor suspended in whole or in part by a law enacted pursuant to paragraph (2) of this Article."

[6]Article 91 BL: "(1) In order to avert an imminent danger to the existence or free democratic basic order of the Federation or of a *Land*, a *Land* may call upon police forces of other *Länder*, or upon personnel and facilities of other administrative authorities and of the Federal Border Police. (2) If the *Land* where such danger is imminent is not itself willing or able to combat the danger, the Federal Government may place the police in that *Land* and the police forces of other *Länder* under its own orders and deploy units of the Federal Border Police. Any such order shall be rescinded once the danger is removed, or at any time on the demand of the Bundesrat. If the danger extends beyond the territory of a single *Land*, the Federal Government, insofar as is necessary to combat such danger, may issue instructions to the *Land* governments; the first and second sentences of this paragraph shall not be affected by this provision."

authority was introduced (Article 19 sec. 4);[7] on the other hand, the Federal Constitutional Court was created and equipped with unprecedentedly far-reaching competences. And fifthly, the Basic Law founds an "actively defensive democracy" ("*wehrhafte Demokratie*"), that is a regime for the protection of the liberal and democratic order. As a consequence, the two most important restrictions of political rights, that is the forfeiture of basic rights (Article 18) and the prohibition of a political party (Article 21 sec. 2),[8] can be pronounced but by the Federal Constitutional Court itself.

With this, the framework for the German constitutional state after the Second World War is drafted: The liberal and democratic constitutional order is actively defended against its enemies—but without transferring legislative competences to the executive and on the condition that the highest standards of legal protection be preserved.

3 The Later Constitutional Amendments Concerning the Rearmament and the State of Defence ("Wehrverfassung" and "Notstandsverfassung")

The Basic Law in its original version could, to a certain extent, afford to forego the regulation of an emergency regime by excluding the state of emergency, for Germany was still subjected to the Western Allies' guardianship. More precisely, until 5 May 1955, Germany was subject to the occupation regime. To the degree that it regained its sovereignty, the question of how to approach internal and external threats to sovereignty arose. Thus, two important constitutional amendments were adopted in 1956 and 1968 concerning, on the one hand, the rearmament and, on the other, the state of defence ("*Wehrnovelle*" und "*Notstandsnovelle*").

The 1956[9] amendment of the Basic Law permitted Germany's rearmament after its accession to the Western European Union and the NATO in 1955. The 1968 amendment did not come about but through the Grand Coalition of Christian and Social Democrats. As a modification of or an amendment to almost 30 dispositions of the Basic Law, it represents one of the most comprehensive of the 60 constitutional amendments the Basic Law has so far undergone. Three normative complexes lie at its core: Firstly, the state of defence, requiring the determination that

---

[7]Article 19 sec. 4 sentence. 1 BL: "Should any person's rights be violated by public authority, he may have recourse to the courts."

[8]Article 21 sec. 2 BL: Parties that, by reason of their aims or the behaviour of their adherents, seek to undermine or abolish the free democratic basic order or to endanger the existence of the Federal Republic of Germany shall be unconstitutional. The Federal Constitutional Court shall rule on the question of unconstitutionality."

[9]Cf. "Gesetz zur Änderung des Grundgesetzes" of 19 March 1956, BGBl. 1956 I, p. 111.

the federal territory is under attack by armed forces (Article 115a[10] et seq.—11 provisions in total), secondly, the state of tension (Article 80a),[11] a sort of preliminary stage preceding the state of defence that requires an aggravated situation of interstate conflict running the risk of escalation, and thirdly, the disposition that "the Armed Forces may be employed only to the extent expressly permitted by this Basic Law" (Article 87a sec. 2)[12,13].

In the event of an external armed aggression against the federal territory, Article 115c sec. 2 authorises the legislator to restrict two fundamental rights more easily and more extensively than under regular circumstances; this concerns namely the temporary facilitation of confiscations and the extension of the period of detentions. Even this provision, that has not so far been enacted, does not, however, allow for a restriction of judicial guarantees. Such is the general conception of the Basic Law: The rule of law ("*Rechtsstaat*") that is also and in particular a rule of judicial review ("*Rechtswegestaat*"), remains intact even in the event of an external armed aggression.

The proverb "Necessity knows no laws" has no basis in the German constitutional order. Put differently: The country of Carl Schmitt, the theorist of the state of emergency and the state of exception par excellence, encountered its road to Damascus after the intense and dissuasive experience with the state of emergency during the 1930s, that is during the final period of the Weimar Republic and the transition to the Nazi regime. With its constitutional order, the Federal Republic makes every effort to capture and defuse emergency situations through the application of the regular constitutional standards. This should not be misunderstood to

[10]Article 115a sec. 1 BL: "Any determination that the federal territory is under attack by armed force or imminently threatened with such an attack (state of defence) shall be made by the Bundestag with the consent of the Bundesrat. Such determination shall be made on application of the Federal Government and shall require a two-thirds majority of the votes cast, which shall include at least a majority of the Members of the Bundestag."

[11]Article 80a BL: "(1) If this Basic Law or a federal law regarding defence, including protection of the civilian population, provides that legal provisions may be applied only in accordance with this Article, their application, except when a state of defence has been declared, shall be permissible only after the Bundestag has determined that a state of tension exists or has specifically approved such application. The determination of a state of tension and specific approval in the cases mentioned in the first sentence of paragraph (5) and the second sentence of paragraph (6) of Article 12a shall require a two-thirds majority of the votes cast. (2) Any measures taken pursuant to legal provisions by virtue of paragraph (1) of this Article shall be rescinded whenever the Bundestag so demands. (3) Notwithstanding paragraph (1) of this Article, the application of such legal provisions shall also be permissible on the basis of and in accordance with a decision made by an international body within the framework of a treaty of alliance with the approval of the Federal Government. Any measures taken pursuant to this paragraph shall be rescinded whenever the Bundestag, by the vote of a majority of its Members, so demands."

[12]Article 87a sec. 2 BL: "Apart from defence, the Armed Forces may be employed only to the extent expressly permitted by this Basic Law."

[13]The famous right of resistance constituted by Article 20 s. 4 BL ("All Germans shall have the right to resist any person seeking to abolish this constitutional order, if no other remedy is available.") has no practical relevance.

mean that it is embarking upon a path of some self-sufficient, naive normativism. On the other hand, it clearly opposes the glorification of the exception and the overrating of the state of exception that can be found in Carl Schmitt's "Political Theology": Whereas Schmitt conceptualised normality and normativity from the perspective of the exception and in reference to it,[14] the German post-war constitution makes every effort to maintain the liberal democratic order by way of the law, namely by means of a staggered system of guarantees and institutions. It does this in full knowledge of the fragility of normality as well as normativity arguing with legality—an argument that is always efficacious in Germany.

4 The Terrorism of the Red Army Faction and the Acoustic Surveillance of Private Homes ("Großer Lauschangriff")

During the time between 1970 and 2000, two aspects are or of outstanding importance here: the struggle with left-wing terrorism emanating from the extremist group the Red Army Faction (RAF) and its successor organisations and the implementation of the acoustic surveillance of private homes in 1998. In view of the time allotted to me and the fact that we shall turn to the time after 9/11 later, I will remain brief:

In the 1970s, the Red Army Faction has put the Federal Republic to a serious test on the domestic front by committing attacks on and kidnapping members of the political, judicial and economic elite. The Federal Republic responded by adopting several security laws—notably the total ban of direct contact with detainees[15]—but without modifying the Basic Law and its guarantees. In the late 1990s, the situation was different: The challenges that organised crime posed to security eventually led to the constitutionalisation of the acoustic surveillance of enclosed spaces in which alleged offenders are present: In 1998, the basic right to the inviolability of the

[14]Cf. Schmitt (2015), 21: "Die Ausnahme ist interessanter als der Normalfall. Das Normale beweist nichts, die Ausnahme beweist alles; sie bestätigt nicht nur die Regel, die Regel lebt überhaupt nur von der Ausnahme. In der Ausnahme durchbricht die Kraft des wirklichen Lebens die Kruste einer in der Wiederholung erstarrten Mechanik." (ibid. 15: "The exception is more interesting than the rule. The rule proves nothing; the exception proves everything: It confirms not only its rule but also its existence, which derives only from the exception. In the exception, the power of real life breaks through the crust of a mechanism that has become torpid by repetition".)

[15]"Gesetz zur Änderung des Einführungsgesetzes zum Gerichtsverfassungsgesetz" of 30 September 1977, BGBl. 1977 I, p. 1877.

home was amended so as to permit the acoustic surveillance of people outside the home ("*Kleiner Lauschangriff*") as well as in their homes ("*Großer Lauschangriff*") to combat serious crime.[16]

What links both developments is the major role played by the judiciary, notably by the Federal Constitutional Court. This role paves the way for the following period, namely the changes in the security legislation occurring after 11 September 2001. Since the 1950s, the Federal Constitutional Court grew to become a powerful guardian of the Constitution who has proclaimed itself a constitutional organ. With its vast competences, notably vis-à-vis the legislator and the specialised judiciary, the Court has assumed its mandate of the protection of the constitution—and above all of the protection of fundamental rights—forcefully and offensively.[17] It gave effect to the reticence of the Basic Law vis-à-vis the state of emergency within the whole legal order. And it reinforced this effect by denying the existence of an unwritten emergency reserve that could have permitted the limitation of fundamental rights in an imminent crisis. It thus highlighted the intangibility of the constitutional order, for which criminals are offenders to be sanctioned for their offences in a procedure that is itself in conformity with the rule of law, but not enemies devoid of rights who are to be eliminated by any means. The constitutional state showed its strength by not having the perspective of those fighting against the liberal democratic order imposed upon itself.

The Federal Constitutional Court even insisted upon the constraints of the constitutional state vis-à-vis the constitution-amending legislature. The Court has thus reinterpreted the constitutional provision introducing the acoustic surveillance at home into the Basic Law in the light of the inviolability of human dignity as stated in Article 1 of the Basic Law, arguing that acoustic surveillance of the core

[16]Article 13 sec. 3–6 BL: "(3) If particular facts justify the suspicion that any person has committed an especially serious crime specifically defined by a law, technical means of acoustical surveillance of any home in which the suspect is supposedly staying may be employed pursuant to judicial order for the purpose of prosecuting the offence, provided that alternative methods of investigating the matter would be disproportionately difficult or unproductive. The authorisation shall be for a limited time. The order shall be issued by a panel composed of three judges. When time is of the essence, it may also be issued by a single judge. (4) To avert acute dangers to public safety, especially dangers to life or to the public, technical means of surveillance of the home may be employed only pursuant to judicial order. When time is of the essence, such measures may also be ordered by other authorities designated by a law; a judicial decision shall subsequently be obtained without delay. (5) If technical means are contemplated solely for the protection of persons officially deployed in a home, the measure may be ordered by an authority designated by a law. The information thereby obtained may be otherwise used only for purposes of criminal prosecution or to avert danger and only if the legality of the measure has been previously determined by a judge; when time is of the essence, a judicial decision shall subsequently be obtained without delay. (6) The Federal Government shall report to the Bundestag annually as to the employment of technical means pursuant to paragraph (3) and, within the jurisdiction of the Federation, pursuant to paragraph (4) and, insofar as judicial approval is required, pursuant to paragraph (5) of this Article. A panel elected by the Bundestag shall exercise parliamentary oversight on the basis of this report. A comparable parliamentary oversight shall be afforded by the *Länder*."

[17]See Jestaedt et al. (2011).

area of private life is not admissible—even if this leads to restrictions on the prosecution of organised crime.[18] This legal opinion was, nevertheless, criticised in legal practice and legal scholarship for lack of legitimacy and practicality.

5 The Security Legislation After 11 September 2001 and the Federal Constitutional Court

With this decision of the Constitutional Court, we are already entering the most recent phase starting with the terrorist attacks on the Twin Towers in New York and the Pentagon in Washington on 11 September 2001. At the national level, the German strategy in the "war on terror" is characterised by a significant quantitative as well as qualitative extension of the security services' power to intervene without, however, amending the Basic Law. Hence, proceedings were brought before the Court for practically all newly adopted security laws. In its jurisprudence, the Court has applied its regular, that is strict, scrutiny concerning the conformity with fundamental rights. Even more so: In 2008, the Federal Constitutional Court has deduced a new so-called computer right ("*Computergrundrecht*") from the general right to privacy, that serves as a safeguard of privacy against online searches and external manipulations, under the cumbersome name "right to the confidentiality and integrity of IT systems" ("*Recht auf Gewährleistung der Vertraulichkeit und Integrität informationstechnischer Systeme*").[19]

Since 2003, not a year has passed without at least one important decision concerning new security measures; until now, the number amounts to approximately 20 decisions[20]—thus exceeding the number of decisions the Court has issued on questions of European integration since 2000. The decisions, that are predominantly taken by the First Senate, concern numerous and manifold powers to intervene newly introduced after 11 September 2001, namely (and in chronological order) the access to mobile phone communication data,[21] the telecommunications

[18]Cf. BVerfGE (= Collected decisions of the Federal Constitutional Court) 109 (= volume), 279 (310–325, notably 318–324) (= pages) [2004].

[19]Cf. BVerfGE 120, 274 (274 [Leitsatz 1], 302 et passim) [2008].

[20]2003: BVerfGE 107, 299–339. –(2004): BVerfGE 109, 279–391; 110, 33–76. –(2005): BVerfGE 112, 304–321; 113, 348–392. –(2006): BVerfGE 115, 118–166; 115, 320–381. –(2007): BVerfGE 118, 168–211. –(2008): BVerfGE 120, 274–350; 120, 378–433. –(2010): BVerfGE 125, 260–385. –(2011): BVerfGE 129, 208–268; 130, 1–51. –(2012): BVerfGE 130, 151–212; 132, 1–39. –(2013): BVerfGE 133, 241–272; 133, 277–377. –(2015): BVerfGE 139, 245–285; 140, 160–211. –(2016): BVerfG, judgment of 20 April 2016, 1 BvR 966/09 et 1 BvR 1140/09 (= file reference), available at http://www.bverfg.de/e/rs20160420_1bvr096609.html.

[21]Cf. BVerfGE 107, 299–339 [2003].

surveillance,[22] the GPS tracking,[23] the dragnet surveillance,[24] the Aviation Security Act (including the power to shoot down a high-jacked passenger airplane that is being used as a weapon),[25] the bank account enquiries by fiscal and prosecution authorities,[26] the online searches,[27] the automatic number plate recognition,[28] the data retention,[29] the creation of an anti-terror database[30] as well as the increased powers of the Federal Criminal Police Office ("Bundeskriminalamt").[31] Concerning some legal provisions such as the Aviation Security Act and data retention, the Court has even been seized several times.

Without analysing these decisions in detail (approximately 15 of them cover 40 or more printed pages of opinion, four even over 100!), four general observations can be made—despite all the differences in detail—that can be understood as a clear signal regarding the state of emergency:

- Firstly: A special constitutional regime linked with the existence of the terrorist challenge for state and society, a "discount" on the rule of law in answer to the terrorist threat so to say, is rejected categorically. The "war on terror" does not suspend the regular fundamental rights and the legal protection connected with them, including access to the Constitutional Court.
- Secondly: The principle of proportionality constitutes the key criterion for assessing the infringements of fundamental rights committed by the security authorities—down to the last detail of the dispositions in question. In this regard, the most recent decision of the First Senate concerning the Act on the Federal Criminal Police Office (the "BKA" Act) from 20 April 2016 is particularly impressive: More than 250 paragraphs of the decision are dedicated to the principle of proportionality with its (four) elements "legitimate aim of the intervention", "suitability of the measure to achieve the aim", "necessity of the measure to achieve the aim" and "proportionality in the narrow sense".[32] The orientation towards the principle of proportionality is reflected in the opinions, most of which follow a "yes, but"-pattern: In principle, a legislative decision—and thus the measure chosen and the aim pursued—is endorsed, but in detail, the use of the measures is reprimanded arguing that a milder measure,

[22]Cf. BVerfGE 110, 33–76 [2004].

[23]Cf. BVerfGE 112, 304–321 [2005].

[24]Cf. BVerfGE 115, 320–381 [2006].

[25]Cf. BVerfGE 115, 118–166 [2006].

[26]Cf. BVerfGE 118, 168–211 [2007].

[27]Cf. BVerfGE 120, 274–350 [2008].

[28]Cf. BVerfGE 120, 378–433 [2008].

[29]Cf. BVerfGE 125, 260–385 [2010]; 130, 151–212 [2012].

[30]Cf. BVerfGE 133, 277–377 [2013].

[31]Cf. BVerfG, judgment of 20 April 2016, 1 BvR 966/09 et 1 BvR 1140/09, http://www.bverfg.de/e/rs20160420_1bvr096609.html.

[32]Cf. BVerfG, judgment of 20 April 2016, 1 BvR 966/09 et 1 BvR 1140/09, available http://www.bverfg.de/e/rs20160420_1bvr096609.html, §§ 93–97, 98–102, 103–144, 145–354.

that is an equally efficient but less intrusive measure, exists or that the intervention leads to legal disadvantages disproportionate with the aim pursued.[33] Thereby, the Court recognises that the constitutional state can defend itself and its citizens against terrorist threats, but may not use every means to this purpose.
- Thirdly: That the Constitutional Court has by now continuously dealt with the post-9/11 security laws for more than a decade has not lead to a less stringent control of fundamental rights, that is to a reduced standard regarding the density of control and the rigour of the criteria. If anything, a development to the contrary can be observed. For instance, the fact that the Constitutional Court has dealt with legislative attempts to establish a legal framework for data retention in conformity with the constitution three times[34] proves that the Court does not go easy on the legislator, but rather insists on the compliance with the fundamental rights standards it has defined.
- And fourthly: A curtailment of legal protection, that is a reduction of the judicial control of executive security measures, is not accepted as a matter of principle. The (not very numerous) legislative attempts in this direction are unexceptionally being branded as fundamental rights violations. In Germany, the rule of law proves itself also and especially as a rule of judicial review.

To sum this up in one sentence: Germany meets the new threats emanating from international terrorism with a significant expansion of the legal powers to intervene for the benefit of the security authorities—quantitatively as well as qualitatively; this development is, however, accompanied by a narrow and strict constitutional jurisprudence that takes corrective action time and again and upholds fundamental rights protection even under the conditions of unknown threats.

6 Conclusion

On a final note, I will return to the title of my reflections, that is "The German Reticence Vis-à-Vis the State of Emergency". Under the Basic Law, that has now been in force for more than 65 years, Germany has always demonstrated a clear reserve towards the recognition of the state of emergency as a legal regime in considering it an inferior type of the rule of law. The manner, in which this reticence manifests itself, has evolved over the different phases of German history, one could also say: It has developed and was differentiated along with the different challenges. The Germans remain confident in and committed to the conviction that

[33]Paradigmatically: BVerfG, judgment 20 April 2016, 1 BvR 966/09 et 1 BvR 1140/09, available at http://www.bverfg.de/e/rs20160420_1bvr096609.html, §§ 90 et seq.

[34]Cf. BVerfGE 125, 260–385 [2010]; 130, 151–212 [2012]; BVerfG (Third Chamber of the First Senate), judgment of 8 June 2016, 1 BvQ 42/15, available at http://www.bverfg.de/e/qk20160608_1bvq004215.html; judgment of 8 June 2016, 1 BvR 229/16, available at http://www.bverfg.de/e/rk20160608_1bvr022916.html.

the rule of law can and must only prove itself through legal means. So far, this attitude has proven itself by and large. Hopefully, it will stay this way.

References

Jestaedt M et al (2011) Das entgrenzte Gericht—Eine kritische Bilanz nach sechzig Jahren Bundesverfassungsgericht. Suhrkamp

Schmitt C (2015) Politische Theologie: Vier Kapitel zur Lehre von der Souveränität. Duncker & Humblot

FSC
www.fsc.org
MIX
Papier | Fördert gute Waldnutzung
FSC® C083411

Kolibri 360 GmbH
Ferdinand-Jühlke-Straße 7
99095 Erfurt, Deutschland
produktsicherheit@kolibri360.de